FAMILY TRANSFORMED

FAMILY TRANSFORMED

Religion, Values, and Society in American Life

Steven M. Tipton and
John Witte Jr.
Editors

Georgetown University Press
Washington, D.C.

Georgetown University Press, Washington, D.C.
© 2005 by Georgetown University Press. All rights reserved.
Printed in the United States of America

10 9 8 7 6 5 4 3 2 1   2005

This book is printed on acid-free paper meeting
the requirements of the American National Standard
for Permanence in Paper for Printed Library Materials.

As of January 1, 2007, 13-digit ISBN numbers will replace
the current 10-digit system.
Paperback: 978-1-58901-066-6

Library of Congress Cataloging-in-Publication Data

Family transformed : religion, values, and society in American life / Steven M. Tipton,
John Witte, Jr., editors
    p.   cm.
    Includes bibliographical references and index.
    ISBN 1-58901-066-3 (pbk. : alk. paper)
    I. Tipton, Steven M. II. Witte, John, 1959–
    BL2525.F37 2005
    306.85'0973—dc22   2005008374

Excerpts from Mary Douglas's *Natural Symbols: Explorations in Cosmology* (New York:
Pantheon Books, 1982) appear in chapter 1 by permission.

Contents

Tables and Figures

Tables

Acknowledgments

This volume is one of a series of new volumes to emerge from the Project on Sex, Marriage, and Family and the Religions of the Book, undertaken by the Center for the Study of Law and Religion at Emory University. The project seeks to take stock of the dramatic transformation of marriage and family life in the world today and to craft enduring solutions to the many new problems it has occasioned. The project is interdisciplinary in methodology: It seeks to bring the ancient wisdom of religious traditions and the modern sciences of law, health, public policy, the social sciences, and the humanities into greater conversation and common purpose. The project is interreligious in inspiration: It seeks to understand the lore, law, and life of marriage and family within Judaism, Christianity, and Islam both in their genesis and in their exodus, in their origins and in their diasporas. The project is international in orientation: It seeks to place current American debates over sex, marriage, and the family within an emerging global conversation. This combination of interdisciplinary, interreligious, and international inquiry featured in the project as a whole is at the heart of the methodology of this volume.

The editors of this volume wish to express our deep gratitude to our friends at the Pew Charitable Trusts in Philadelphia for their generous support of the Center for the Study of Law and Religion at Emory University (and its predecessors, the Center for the Interdisciplinary Study of Religion and the Law and Religion Program). We are particularly grateful to the president of the Pew Charitable Trusts, Rebecca Rimel, and to its program officers Susan Billington Harper, Luis Lugo, Julie Sula, and Diane Winston for masterminding the creation of the center, along with its sister centers at ten other American research universities—a bold and visionary act of philanthropy that is helping to transform the study of religion in the American academy.

We also wish to express our deep gratitude to our Emory Center colleagues, April Bogle, Eliza Ellison, Anita Mann, Amy Wheeler, and Janice Wiggins, for their extraordinary work on our project titled "Sex, Marriage, and Family and the Religions of the Book." During the past four years, these five colleagues have helped to create a dozen major public forums; an international conference with 80 speakers and 750 participants; and scores of new journal, electronic, and video publications. They are now overseeing the production of thirty new books to come from the Sex, Marriage, and Family Project, along with administering a new center project, commenced in the autumn of 2003, titled "The Child in Law, Religion, and Society." For their editorial and production work on this volume in particular, we thank the center's project director Eliza Ellison, and associate editor Amy Wheeler.

We owe a special word of appreciation and admiration to Don S. Browning—the Robert W. Woodruff Visiting Professor of Interdisciplinary Religious Studies at Emory University and the Alexander Campbell Professor of Ethics and the Social Sciences Emeritus at the University of Chicago—who joined us in the leadership of this project. Don Browning is the dean of interdisciplinary family studies in this country, and he was uncommonly generous in lending his time and talent in leading this project with us. He was equally generous in allowing us to draw on the strengths and resources of his decade-long Religion, Culture, and Family Project at the University of Chicago supported by the Lilly Endowment, Inc. His coauthored volume, *From Culture Wars to Common Ground* (1997), and his new monograph, *Marriage and Modernization* (2003), will long endure as classics in the field of interdisciplinary family studies.

Introduction: No Place Like Home

Steven M. Tipton and John Witte Jr.

As cradle of conscience, matrix of membership, and first school of love and justice, how does the family shape moral meaning and practice in American society today? What do families ask of us in turn to grasp their growing diversity, sustain their coherence, and protect their fragility for our own sake and for the common good of society?

To engage these questions, this volume brings together scholars from the standpoints of anthropology, demography, ethics, history, law, philosophy, primatology, psychology, sociology, and theology. One line of inquiry reveals the ritual codes, iconic symbols, and moral dramas of modern families, along with the family rules, rights, and interests elaborated in our civic, legal, and economic institutions. This inquiry documents how modern American families have, paradoxically, grown both more regulated and deregulated, marketized and therapeutized, and secularized and sacralized anew.

A second line of inquiry charts the biology of family values, the demography of nuclear marriage, and the economic struggles of U.S. families across class and racial/ethnic differences. This inquiry notes both the progress and problems of modern families and clarifies who bears the burdens and gains the benefits of marital and family restructuring. A third line of inquiry maps the enduring rites and changing sites of courtship, marriage, and family life in America, especially among members of the middle class and communities of faith. It also weighs the mounting social science evidence supporting the continuing utility and validity of the intact nuclear family.

A fourth and final line of inquiry draws on history, law, and comparative cultural criticism to interpret both the enduring and elastic forms and norms of sex, marriage, and family life in the West. It assesses the challenges posed today by new advocacy for same-sex marriage, and deinstitutionalized and delegalized coupling. This inquiry pays particular attention to the role that religious ideas, institutions, and practices have played in the drama of the modern family, and it judges their potential to shape its future direction.

Part of the promise of such a wide-ranging interdisciplinary inquiry lies in its recognition of the family both as a distinctive institution in its own right and as an institution that is deeply interwoven with other institutions. Modern schooling, work, leisure, consumption, legal regulation, public administration, and social security in retirement all shape and color the ways we court and marry, bear and raise children, and make and break family bonds.

At the same time, most Americans see marriage and family life as the loving, playful, caring heart of what makes life worth living, and a society worth living in and working for. Marriage and family life not only realize romance but also inspire hard work and justify key aims of public policy and provision. In this sense, it does take a society to raise a family, as Robert Bellah argues in his epilogue to this volume, even as it takes the actuality and ideals of a family to grasp the moral order of our society as a whole, to justify it, and to judge it.

This essential intersection of the family with manifold other institutions and sectors of society can be seen clearly in the development of children and of parent-child interactions. Developmentalists from Rousseau to Erikson and Gilligan have shown, in various ways, how family life sits at the center of modern society.[1] By Erik Erikson's account, for example, children develop through sequential stages of social practices and relationships in nurturance, play, learning, work, and public engagement, which are set in concentric circles of institutional arrangement marked by virtues that are at once personal, parental, and social. Ethics of authority and self-expression are both relatively strong for any individual as child, parent, and lover within the modern family. The ethics of cost-benefit consequences and the play of interests, at once cooperative and competitive, hold sway in business and bureaucratic life, circumscribed by contract and regulation, appeals to rights, shared responsibilities, and minimal obligations not to injure. Among friends and lovers, expressive feelings are the norm, whereas reciprocal responsibilities, duties, and householding calculations arise between spouses.[2]

This institutionalized interplay of different modes of moral meaning within marriage and the family in themselves—and in their interactive relations to schooling, work, romance, government, and public life, interpenetrated by religion and law in particular—underlies the interdisciplinary study of the family embodied in this volume.

Modern Families in Trouble

Although it is clear that the family lies at the heart of modern Western society, it is equally clear that traditional norms and forms of the family are in trouble today. All too familiar statistics tell a striking story. From 1975 to 2000, roughly one-quarter of all pregnancies ended in abortion in the United States. One-third of all children were born to single mothers. One-half of all marriages ended in divorce. Three-quarters of all African American children were raised without fathers regularly present. Children from broken homes proved two to three times more likely to have behavioral and learning problems as teenagers than children from two-parent homes. More than two-thirds of juveniles and young adults convicted of major felonies from 1970 to 1995 came from single- or no-parent homes.[3]

Less familiar but no less striking is the dramatically expanding time middle-class Americans spend on the job at the expense of the time they spend at home, at prayer, at play, or in community activities with their spouse and children. This holds true not only for "bright-collar" professionals privileged with well-paid callings but also for others, especially women. During the past three decades, many Americans have been working ever-longer hours at stagnant wages in white-collar and service jobs, just to pay the bills and keep their families afloat as public provision shrinks, unionized manufacturing jobs vanish along with their family wages, and the costs of middle-class life continue to spiral.

In particular, the cost of having children has risen much more sharply than the cost of going childless for middle-class Americans during the past generation. Between 1983 and 1998, the price of housing for married couples with children rose 79 percent in real terms, almost triple its increase for childless persons, according to the Federal Reserve Board, as parents waged bidding wars for homes in safe neighborhoods with good public schools. As decent jobs with family wages for unskilled and semiskilled labor dwindled in number, the premium rose on higher education, along with its costs and competitive pressures. Married couples with children are now twice as likely as childless couples to file for bankruptcy, three times more likely to be late in paying their bills, and far more likely to face foreclosure on their homes.

Conversely, the sharply rising cost of having children has led many Americans, especially in the middle class, to have fewer children or none at all during the past few decades. Between 1980 and 2000, the percentage of childless women between the ages of forty and forty-four years doubled, and so did the percentage of women who had only one child. Birthrates and economic cycles have long been correlated, as, for example, during the depths of the Great Depression and the peaks of the postwar business-and-baby boom. But the longer-term prospect of economically prudent middle-class Americans forgoing children should give every citizen pause to consider children as a common good and shared social responsibility in an era of controversy over Social Security, private pensions, and public spending on education and child welfare. That is true if for no other reason than the fact that all of us, even the childless, expect future generations to take on the current U.S. debt of $6.7 trillion and the $40 trillion in potential obligations to those now elderly or aging, in order to care for us.[4]

The American middle class doubled in size and real household income between 1946 and 1968. Since then, it has become more pressured and pinched, in contrast to the fortunate few in the nation's wealthiest households, where the great economic gains of the past twenty years have been concentrated. In the broad middle class, rates of social hardship have risen as median income has fallen further behind the cost of living. Nearly one in three working families with children under the age of twelve years in 2000—many with two parents working in low-wage jobs and earning incomes well over the official poverty line—faced at least one critical hardship over the course of a year, such as going without food, being evicted, or failing to receive needed medical care. In 2002, Americans without health insurance increased by 2.4 million to a total of 43.6 million—15.2 percent of the population, according to the Census Bureau. This included 11.6 percent of all children under eighteen, some 8.5 million. It also included 20.2 percent of all African Americans, 32.4 percent of Hispanics, and 49 percent of those living in poverty and working full-time—in comparison with 10.7 percent of all non-Hispanic whites.[5]

The income gap between rich and poor Americans more than doubled from 1979 to 2000, according to the Congressional Budget Office.[6] The poor, meanwhile, are more often with us. Nearly one in eight Americans now lives in poverty, according to Census Bureau figures in 2002 and 2003, a proportion comparable to a generation ago, after poverty rates dropped from almost one in six Americans to one in nine between 1993 and 2000. The poor include more than one in five U.S. Hispanics and nearly one in four African Americans. They also include one in six children under the age of eighteen, according to Census Bureau figures in 2000, and more than one in three Hispanic children and African American children. Whites nonetheless account for two of three poor Americans, children and adults alike, with many of them living in rural areas and small towns, not in the inner city. The number of American families living below the poverty line went up by more than 300,000 in 2002, to 7 million, from 6.6 million in 2001, according to the Census Bureau's American Community Survey, based on $17,960 in 2001 income and $18,392 in 2002. The number of children in poverty rose by more than 600,000 during the same period, to 12.2 million, an increase of half a percentage point. The proportion of children under age five living in poverty jumped a full percentage point to 19.8 percent from 18.8 percent a year earlier. During 2002, the number of Americans living in poverty increased by 1.7 million and median household income declined by 1.1 percent, dropping $500 to $42,400 overall, with declines of 3 percent for blacks and 2.9 percent for Hispanics.[7]

American families have grown much more diverse in comparison with the postwar paradigm of husband and wife with two-plus children living together in a house of their own, like Ozzie and Harriet or Cosby and Harriet. Such cases make up a small fraction of American households today. Blended and mixed families, childless couples, remarried or rematched couples, cohabiting couples: They all ask for our attention in enabling them, including couples of the same sex, to practice the virtues of mutual care and consolation that the institution of marriage and family aims to nurture. They also ask us to open our hearts and minds to work out conceptions of callings generous enough to embrace the actual diversity of the ways we live, including the vocation of living unmarried and uncoupled. For in our time, it is single-individual households that have increased most of all. Americans are living longer, and longer on their own. They marry and bear fewer children later in life, they divorce more often, and they spend more time living alone before and between marriages, after the kids have gone, and after their spouse has died.

Families and Traditions

These sobering statistics on the crisis of the modern American family make it doubly imperative that our interdisciplinary inquiry include an ample dose of history, religion, and comparative study. Western and other cultural traditions have faced family crises on this scale before. Their carriers and critics have found in them the resources to heal and reinvent the institutions of marriage and family life. We can work to rebalance orthodoxy and innovation, and justice and liberty, with respect to our enduring and evolving sexual mores, marital norms, and householding practices in coherent relationship to the political and economic arrangement of the distinctive ways of life embodied by particular societies in given historical moments. The prospect of such healing and reinvention is no less likely today, so long as thinkers, advocates, and activists, along with political, religious, and civic leaders, ponder these problems in good faith and join with their fellow citizens to direct their deliberations to good works in behalf of the society as a whole.

This is not to say that history and religion provide a ready-made panacea for our modern family crises. For the family teachings of Judaism, Christianity, Islam, and other traditions, when viewed in their historical genesis, exodus, and leviticus, hold a bewildering variety of laws, lores, and liturgies on sex, marriage, and family life. There are ample continuity, convergence, and confluence within and across these religious traditions. But there are also conflict, confusion, and contradiction in the inner dialogues and interrelations of biblical traditions with one another and with the not-so-secular traditions of the modern world—with liberal, contractarian, and communitarian traditions in the usage of philosophy or law, for example, or with republican, utilitarian, or expressive traditions in the usage of sociology or American studies.

Different genres, logics, metaphors, and stories span these religious traditions, and also mark them off. Compare the pointillism of Jewish law and its practical primacy of Leviticus to Genesis, for example, with the tack of early Protestant biblicism back to Genesis as the Ur-narrative to revise the religious law and magisterial teaching of the medieval Catholic Church. In asking who governs and by what authority when it comes to legal and moral matters of marriage and the family—for example, divorce, abortion, spousal abuse, child neglect, or sodomy—compare the relatively sustained collaboration between Islamic jurists and caliphs with religious law and courts in diasporic Judaism serving as forms of stateless government in defining the moral order and boundaries of ghetto communities denied full political participation in host societies that threatened their self-understanding as well as their survival. Consider relationships between political and religious institutions—and between majority and minority religions—in the predominantly Christian West before and after the Protestant Reformation. If the United States remains "a nation with the soul of a church" in any institutional or cultural sense, we may well ask whether that bears problematically on issues of sex, marriage, and family life, insofar as this nation in its religious roots is predominantly Anglo-Protestant, not only Christian; and likewise predominantly Christian, not only biblical; and biblical, not Asian.

When it comes to democratic self-government in the United States, it is "we the people" who decide—not kings and priests, not prophets and religious judges. In principle, we govern ourselves as citizens of a democratic republic and believers who voluntarily belong to given communities of faith within a denominational society, in which "church and state" are seen as distinct institutions each governed by its own members. But how we govern ourselves in practice is still worth weighing carefully case by case, particularly because "family values" now flag highly polarized wedge issues in American electoral politics that in turn underscore problems of unequal representation, power, and voice in the American polity.[8]

In this sense, we can ask which institutions govern sex, marriage, and family life; to what extent; and through what forms of practical authority and character formation. We can consider what sorts of citizens are nurtured in marriages and families of this or that kind; and what sorts of marriages and families are shaped in turn by laws, policies, and economic forces of this or that kind. We can compare the moral good of the married state variably generalized in the Jewish, Islamic, and Christian canons for the holiness of human beings, created and redeemed by God, with its value for modern individuals generalized as equally rights-bearing citizens, freely choosing associational actors and prudent market transactors contractually free to enter or exit whichever (non)marital states they prefer among a variety of postmodern possibilities. These include cohabitation and serial monogamy, "open marriage" and effectively closed "dating" for long periods between adult partners with separate households, and of course de facto temporary marriage in contrast to officially fixed-duration marriage. Many of these options are marked by psychological openness, interpersonal fluidity, and civil liberty in a highly disciplined world of gender-dedifferentiated but class-bound technical, professional, and managerial work performed by educated elites.

Jewish, Christian, and Islamic canons define human beings as creatures of a biblical Creator God, with certain virtues, duties, norms, and practices marking this constitutive relationship and making them both truly good and godly. Yet these traditions also define persons—female and male, spouses and parents, guardians and dependents—as distinctive sorts of members and nonmembers of specific kinds of religious communities and societies. If we periodize and distinguish these societies as more or less modernized and globalized, we can link the cardinal moral virtues these societies prize in both persons and institutions, and the virtuous social practices they require. Then we may be better able to discern when it is apt or inapt to apply particular forms of traditional religious wisdom regarding contraception, abortion, divorce, or sodomy to questions on such matters that American citizens and lawmakers face today.

Then we may also be better able to understand canonical praise of procreation, or natural-law reasoning against artificial contraception, in a modern society that has undergone the demographic transition to lower fertility rates coinciding with shifts from labor-intensive agriculture to industry to a more knowledge-intensive and capital-intensive kind of postindustrial economy. We may also be better able to grasp tradition itself as a continuity of conflicts over what is real and how we should live together in accord with reality. Then traditions appear less like moral blueprints or monoliths and more like "is/ought" cultural conversations and multivocal, multilocal moral arguments—carried on by both reasoned persuasion and faithful affirmation, to be sure, but also by exemplary enactment through inspiring ritual, myth, and morally fruitful living.

Conversely, modern common sense can be questioned more deeply in the light of religious traditions. In its origins, Jewish law, for example, underscores how profoundly we can be misled by projecting clear-cut contemporary distinctions among discrete religious, political, and familial forms of cultural meaning situated in separate institutional spheres onto the encompassing accounts by axial-period religions of what is really real and how human beings ought to live in accord with reality, including the reality of a biblical God who creates the whole of existence and all human beings, created male or female. Make that both male and/or female, in truth, just as Genesis tells us by telling the story twice. And just as Leviticus tells us that by performing this or that act just so, and so sustaining this or that prescribed sexual, marital, and familial practice, we are not only following the law but also becoming it, that is, seeking to be one and holy as our God is one and holy.[9]

Biblical traditions are grounded in the axial-period social world whose conflation of religious, political-military, and kinship institutions frames moral logics of act-specific norms, rules, and principles within the symbolic narratives of virtue ethics as moral dramas. These unfold as stories of good persons engaged in good practices and social relationships within specific social situations structured by good social institutions in accord with the true order of a universe divinely created, redeemed, and sustained. Interlocking virtues define persons, practices, and institutions alike within these "thick" layered narratives.

At first glance, such narratives of virtue seem most at home in the modern social world within the separate sphere of the family and private life—including romance, courtship, and marriage—popularly stylized in family-situation comedies, boy-meets-girl films, and romantic novels, for example. At second glance, however, implicit narratives of personhood, relationship, and social ontology underlie and inform the apparently "thin" logics of the play of interests and market exchange in modern economies, and the logics of civil rights and liberties in modern associational polities, bound by legal duties, rules, and entitlements legislated by more or less representative governments, and elaborated in the regulations and procedures of modern administrative states.

If we own our bodies, for example, we should be free to use them as we choose to serve our own interests or follow our own feelings. If our bodies are gifts of God or temples of the Holy Spirit, we should be inspired and obliged to treat them accordingly with reverence to glorify God or serve the Spirit. In pursuit of happiness or salvation, we are likewise bound or free if we are members of the body politic or the church as the Pauline body of Christ, in contrast to fluid voluntary associations of citizens voting their own interests or spiritual seekers following their own inner lights. Through such moral metaphors we order and enact the institutions we inhabit, and through us these institutions rethink and remake themselves in practice.[10]

This leads us back to questions of text and context, of elites and masses, of canonical and noncanonical scriptures, and more or less authoritative traditions. Who speaks to whom, and for whom? What do eons-old canonical texts and traditions, surrounded by contextual silence and opacity, have to say to our own historical moment and social situation? In the course of any such communication, does historical retrieval or reconstruction necessarily give way to constructive and practical kinds of cultural reformation in terms of law, ethics, and religious doctrine? How is it possible, in sum, to be true to tradition and speak truly to today's hard questions of marriage, sex, and family life? Facing such questions, we sustain the social world we inhabit as mean-ing-making animals faithfully created in the cultural image of a biblical God, and we wonder at the world we have made.

The Flow of This Volume

This, then, is something of the interdisciplinary premise and promise of this volume. Families are highly complex institutions constituted through practices with variable norms, habits, forms, and functions. Families are constantly shaped and reshaped by shifting texts and contexts, traditions and liturgies, laws and customs, within the societies and cultures of which they are parts and products. No one discipline can monopolize the study of the family. No one logic can master its full complexity.

In chapter 1 in part I of this volume, on the interplay of nature and tradi-tion in conceiving the family, Robert Bellah depicts the family in "habit and history" by distinguishing between the ritually condensed code and mythic moral drama of family life; and the rules, rights, and interests elaborated in the civic, legal, and economic institutions that frame families in modern society. Bellah probes how modern American families in the course of their social differentiation and specialization have become emotionally more inti-mate yet structurally looser. They have grown more egalitarian and individu-alistic yet more regulated by an administrative state and more disciplined by middle-class schooling and work. The family today can be both critically af-firmed and reformed, he judges, for example, in seeking ways to extend the mutual care and consolation of marriage to same-sex couples.

Complementing Bellah's approach, the primatologist Frans de Waal re-veals the biology of "good-natured" family values in chapter 2. Human fam-ilies evolved in a larger context universal to primates, to check male–male competition over mates, avoid inbreeding, and counter male infanticide in an environment demanding cooperation to provide food and protection against danger. Human pair-bonding is part and parcel of a larger social whole, within which it is fully integrated. Because we derive from chimpanzee- and bono-bo-like ancestors, in evolutionary terms societies come first instead of be-ing formed from the merging of families, whereas romantic love comes much later in shaping the way we pick partners and make marital commitments.

Natural law ethics today should read evolutionary biology closely, argues the theologian Stephen J. Pope in chapter 3, to appropriate selectively and critically its views of sex, marriage, and the family. Nature in evolutionary theory is neither purposive nor normative. It is a competitive if also coopera-tive process of mutation and selection, not a smoothly integrated "order of

creation" in Thomistic terms. Yet distinguishing scientific and moral modes
of discourse provides a basis for bringing biology and natural law ethics into
dialogue, for example, to clarify how and why lasting and stable marriages
must empower women and enable men to be good providers. Marriage and
the family are "natural" in the sense that they are institutions that build upon
and enable the satisfaction of biological desires and drives in forms that contribute to human well-being in a comprehensive sense, embracing individuals, communities, and society.

In part II, our inquiry turns to exploring the American family today as
"contested terrain," as the sociologist Robert Wuthnow puts it in chapter 4,
crowded by problems ranging from divorced, abusive, or absent parents to de-
ficient wages, health care, and schooling. Yet the family holds happiness and
embraces mutual care for most Americans, who rank its importance above that
of friends, religion, work, play, and politics. Religious ideals suffuse family
debates, and interpretations of family decline or transformation are deeply
normative. The family fails to live up to new cultural expectations as a "haven in a heartless world," for example, or to sustain an intimately emotional,
sexual, and spiritual "SuperRelationship" between romantic soul mates.

More structural interpretations stress how economic shifts from heavy
agricultural and industrial labor to lighter clerical and service work not only
multiply women in the labor force but also empower them in the home, even
if women and children still bear the brunt of the hardships inflicted by divorce, and overall trends in reported marital happiness have remained un-
changed over the past generation. Other structural views stress how postindustrial, globalized economic changes have combined with regressive cuts in
taxes and public provision during the past few decades to concentrate greater
instability in marriage and trouble in the family among the undereducated
and underemployed, who are far likelier to be black or brown than white.

These social problems require responsive changes in economic policy
and social welfare spending to address their causes instead of obscuring them
by blaming the victims. Religion is a powerful, promising force to strengthen
families, proposes Wuthnow, through its formative teaching and practice in
congregations and small groups; its specific programs for family counseling,
teen pregnancy, day care, and the like; and its larger-scale denominational
and parachurch efforts to influence family policy and legislation on issues
such as family leave, day care, and welfare reform.

Although it is statistically accurate to say that since 1975 roughly a quarter
of pregnancies in the United States have been aborted or that half of all marriages have ended in divorce, the economist Robert Michael makes clear in
chapter 5 that this is not the whole story. For the past twenty years or so, about
4 million babies have been born annually, and today forty-nine of every fifty

U.S. couples choose to stay married each year. Roughly the same propensity to form a dyadic heterosexual partnership marks the cohort of women who came of age in the days of Ozzie and Harriet as those who have done so since Cosby and Harriet with much higher levels of education. The social institutions of formal marriage and family life continue to serve important functions such as spousal collaboration, specialization, and complementarity in the division of domestic labor, and reciprocity between generations in caring for young and elderly dependents.

At the same time, argues Michael, changes in the economy, government, technology, and the rules of sexual activity have made for real generational differences in these institutions. So have shifting public policies, whose mixed consequences we should weigh with care and whose shape we should seek to change only with close attention to its complex interconnections with the diverse ways we actually live, think, and govern ourselves.

Thus governments have taken over some functions in caring for the poor and elderly from families and marital partnerships. Growing job markets for more educated and skilled labor have attracted more second partners from marriages, depreciated the gains from specialization and economies of scale in marriage, and made both divorce and staying single longer more feasible options, especially for those with higher incomes who can afford to live separately yet enjoy sexual activity without the pre-pill risk of pregnancy. Although Americans initially marry much later now than in 1950, they eventually marry nonetheless, and they pair off at the same rate by age twenty-five once we count cohabitation as well as marriage. They now divorce at historically high rates, but two of three divorced women remarry, and married partners report more sexual activity and sexual satisfaction than do singles. Economic analysis shows how public policy can make divorce less frequent by making it more costly, for example, but it cannot justify doing so in terms of the public good in contrast to the aggregated interests of individuals as client-citizens.

Conversely, economic analysis cannot only point out rising income inequality in the United States during the past quarter century, its correlation with poverty concentrated among black and Hispanic families, and the extraordinary plight and bleak prospects of children in these families. It can also raise if not answer the question of whether recent welfare-to-workfare reforms have cut the cost of welfare transfers for middle-class taxpayers at the expense of increasing the numbers of poor children and their misery.

If the family is indeed in trouble, ask the sociologists Claude Fischer and Michael Hout in chapter 6, since when and for whom is that the case? They integrate the evidence of increasing divorce, remarriage, and single-individual households into a striking story of Americans living longer, and longer on their own, amid more pervasive age grading and economic inequality along class-bound, color-coded lines of education and occupation. We marry later, have fewer children, and finish parenting earlier in life. We still yearn for lifelong love yet seek to exercise more autonomous choices in smaller, less stable families more tightly and unequally pinched in ways that hinder such choices, make life harder, and make society less fair. The proportion of children living with fewer than two parents in the United States jumped after 1970 and peaked in the mid-1990s at one in three children overall and two in three black children. Yet the best-educated white and black women are not much more likely to be single parents today than a generation ago, and only one in ten white children with a college-educated parent heading the household now lives in a single-parent home.

Americans still prefer the household of a married couple with children, and more Americans now spend more of their lives in marriage than several generations ago, given longer life spans and better health, pregnancy planning, and infertility treatment. But in recent decades, the second choice after living married with children has shifted from living with other relatives or in institutional settings such as poorhouses to living alone, cohabiting, or parenting on one's own. Standards for a good marriage have risen and exits from bad marriages have widened in light of growing values of self-attainment and independence, especially for women, with marriage now more often delayed or broken by choice than blocked by poverty or dissolved by death or illness. Such personal autonomy carries costs, Fischer and Hout conclude. We need to bear them through responsible public policy and personal commitments in the case of children raised by single parents and families fragmented by divorce, for example, even as we recognize that many but not all Americans now spend more years visiting their aging parents, watching their children grow up, and enjoying the company of their spouses.

In part III, reasons and rites for and against marriage and the family are counted and evaluated. In recent decades, older ideals of marriage in America as a permanent social institution and a legally binding contract have been challenged by views that marriage is more of a personal lifestyle to be entered and exited freely, for example, via unilateral or no-fault divorce. In chapter 7, the demographer Linda J. Waite and the psychologist William J. Doherty weigh the social-scientific evidence for the costs and benefits of marriage. They probe its social role in responsible fathering, and they reflect on this connection in moral and theological terms. Married persons tend to have better physical and emotional health than single persons, enjoy more sexual activity, and produce and accumulate more economic assets. They raise children who experience better outcomes, on average, than those raised in other situations. At least in part, these differences arise because of the greater social support, intimacy, trust, and economic advantages of marriage, and they vary with the character of a given marriage. Psychological health, for example, comes only from good-enough marriages, ranked happy or very happy by the partners, whereas unhappy marriages actually make things worse by generating more psychological distress than does single life.

Similarly, the evidence from relatively weak, poor, or absent relationships between children and their unmarried or divorced fathers confirms that though a woman may be a mother all her life, a man is likely to be present as a father only if he has a wife and, moreover, to be a good father only if he gets along with his wife. Active and attentive fathering contributes measurably to children's well-being, after controlling for more or less effective mothering, judge Waite and Doherty. It also accords with moral recognition of human interdependence in a philosophical ethics of responsibility, and with biblical traditions of a voluntarily entered but then binding covenant between father and child.

Dating and mating behavior has changed significantly in recent decades, reports the American family expert Barbara Dafoe Whitehead in chapter 8, and so have the institutions that once mapped the pathway to marriage. Traditional aims and attitudes about marriage have diversified, especially among middle-class young adults who postpone the search for a life partner until they have left the campus for the world of work and a more commercialized, computerized "partner market" that now includes more single parents and divorcees as well as never-married singles. During the past generation, the age of first marriage for the college-educated has jumped some five years and lengthened single life into "twentyhood," more widely separating the timing of first sex and first marriage, and loosening the normative ties between the two. Cohabitation has increased tenfold and attained mainstream moral acceptance, even as it has grown more varied into nonnuptial, prenuptial, opportunistic, and courtship forms, which may lead more or less directly to marriage or define a more or less critical alternative to it.

Young adults today still prize marriage as a personal life goal and as the ultimate expression of commitment, Whitehead observes. But they have intensified their desire to marry an emotionally intimate soul mate and best friend. They have downplayed the institutional aspects of marriage, including having children, gaining economic independence from parents, and embodying civic or religious ends. Marriage now comes later in the life course of young adults, who believe they should invest first in their own education and career advancement to stabilize marriage and survive divorce in a social world of risky relationships. This yields a new sequence of moral maxims to be followed before going on to marry and have children: Finish school; live on your own; get out of debt; get a job and get ahead at work; and gain personal life experience, including intimacy with more than one romantic partner.

Marrying later does increase marital stability, especially for women who finish college, but delayed marriage favors men's timetable for married parenthood over that of women. The likelihood of multiple sex partners and cohabitation increases with a longer period of sexually active single life, moreover, and these behaviors increase the odds of divorce. Marital delay among sexually active singles also increases the risk of unwed parenthood, which sharply reduces chances of ever marrying, especially for women. During the past generation, a relatively deregulated partner market has arisen in place of a comprehensive system of romantic courtship supported by middle-class families, colleges, and communities of faith. This market—dramatized by the entertainment media and wired through the Internet—leaves a serious yet cloudy gap between good matchmaking for marriage and parenthood and hooking up for casual sex or long-term relationships. Scholars need to chart this gap more closely, Whitehead concludes, to aid parents, teachers, counselors, and the clergy in better educating and enabling young adults to choose a life partner.

In America today, there is no place like home, or so it seems, and nobody at home, more often than not, except the cat and the answering machine. In chapter 9, the anthropologist Bradd Shore tests such popular impressions in a cultural analysis that explores thicker descriptions of the intricate web of family life. It probes for deeper insights into the ritual rhythm and dynamics of the family's making and remaking, its undoing and renewing, across generations in the image of redemptive rites of passage and community, all-American revivalism, and the deep play of recreation, romance, and the re-creation of our social selves. This dramaturgy commingles our innermost aspirations and fears with the paradoxical challenges that we have to leave home to make a home of our own, we have to move on to move up, and we have to work harder and longer to make our domestic dreams come true, even if this leaves us less time at home to enjoy them.

In comparison with traditional forms of family life, Shore observes, middle-class American families today reveal the atomized isolation of lineal from collateral kin, and the modularity, mobility, and individualism of related social institutions. Families are loosened by coordination with a panoply of age-graded, segmented leisure activities. They are framed by the bureaucratic grid of schooling, middle-class employment, and public administration in our society. Yet the rites of modern family life enact the family as a social whole greater than the sum of its individual parts. They span its generations, as the children leave home and begin to share with their parents fewer pragmatic interests and more of the storied memories and practices of a mythic and moral order.

Part IV samples the multiple sources and resources at hand to sustain and reform modern marriage and family life, including ethics, history, law, religion, and comparative cultural critiques. The family embodies the heart of the matter, argues the political ethicist Jean Elshtain in chapter 10, when it comes to our hopes and fears about human destiny and possibility in a society dedicated to equality and freedom, and challenged by responsibility for the vulnerable and dependent. Through the lens of family life, Americans and others can better see the larger cultural forces of public and private as refracted in our liberal society, and they can make out how neither one can be reduced to the other or rendered morally unaccountable to it. Within the family, we can best recognize how our bodies both enable and limit our freedom as individuals, however expanded by technological control, and we can best answer the call for the nurturing care and love we need from infancy to aging unto death.

We can likewise judge the abstracted and strategic disembodiment of much contemporary communication, from pop culture entertainment and advertising to the Internet, in contrast to the concretely embodied, interactive nature of practical relations in the family, and so among friends, fellow citizens, teachers, and students. Real communities make real demands on us, argues Elshtain, and they include weak and vulnerable members. They generate conflicts where human wills clash, which must be mediated and bounded in ways we learn first in families. Only in the family can we engage conflicts between the worlds of work and love, including the time-starved stress of dual-earner families. The craft of familial love and moral formation is itself hard work that takes shared time, effort, and attention. Both modern administrative states and capitalist economies serve to loosen family bonds to allocate labor more efficiently and extend the sway of free-market exchange. These are crucial conflicts an ethical polity must face.

Are the challenges of familial love, freedom, and moral formation peculiar to today's world? The conventional caricature of the early modern family depicted a loveless, tyrannical domain where a man ruled his wife, children, and servants as paterfamilias. The wife labored as a domestic servant and sexual slave of her husband. Children toiled in the kitchen, shop, and fields until they were old enough to fetch a good price for a marriage to a mate of their father's choosing. The alternative life of a celibate cleric or a cloistered nun was not much better, but even that bleak option was taken away by the zealous Protestant reformers. This left Protestant women and children to chafe under perpetual patriarchal tyranny until the liberating reforms of the modern Enlightenment finally gave them real choices.

This conventional story finds little support in the archives, the historian Steven Ozment demonstrates in chapter 11. The early modern family was just as complex and variable an institution as our modern family. To be sure, there were families that lived up to this bleak caricature, but the more typical early modern family was much kinder and gentler. In both late medieval and early modern Protestant Europe, marriage depended in its essence on the mutual consent of both the man and the woman, and the right to marry was jealously protected by both Protestants and Catholics alike. To be sure, women lacked many of the civic freedoms that men enjoyed, but both married and unmarried women played a key role in the preindustrial economy and society, and married women shared much power with their husbands within the home and beyond. Both law and custom provided women and children with recourses and resources to combat husbands and fathers who were abusive, not least ample claims on marital property and alimony and other support from their husbands in the event of separation or divorce. To be sure, children sometimes chafed under mercenary parents who reduced them to servants in the domestic economy and commodities in the marriage market. But the archives hold a massive farrago of documents testifying to the tender love of parents and children, and to the enduring presence of and preference for the loving nuclear family.

Echoing Ozment, the legal historian John Witte demonstrates in chapter 12 that, in the Western Christian tradition, marriage and the family have long been viewed as a multifaceted institution. Marriage is a contract, formed by the mutual consent of the marital couple and subject to their wills and preferences. Marriage is a spiritual association, subject to the creed, code, cult, and canons of the religious community. Marriage is a social estate, subject to special state laws of property, inheritance, and evidence and to the expectations and exactions of the local community. And marriage is a natural institution, subject to the natural laws taught by reason and conscience, nature and custom. These four dimensions, Witte shows, are in a sense complementary, for each emphasizes one aspect of the institution—its voluntary formation, religious sanction, social legitimation, and natural origin, respectively. These four perspectives have also come to stand in considerable tension, however, for they are linked to competing claims of ultimate authority over the form and function of marriage—claims by the couple, the church, the state, and nature and nature's God.

The story of the Western tradition of marriage and the family is, in part, the story of how these four perspectives and authorities shifted in priority. Catholics gave priority to the spiritual perspective of marriage, giving the church final authority over marriage and family life. Protestants emphasized the social perspective, shifting final authority to the state. Enlightenment exponents emphasized the contractual perspective, shifting final authority to the private couple themselves. In broad outline, the Catholic model dominated Western family law until the sixteenth century. From the mid-sixteenth to the mid-nineteenth centuries, Catholic and Protestant models, in distinct and hybrid forms, dominated Western family law. In the past century, the Enlightenment model has emerged, in many instances eclipsing the theology and law of Christian models. Though these Enlightenment reforms have helped to bring greater liberty and equality within the modern household, they have also tended to tear marriage and the family from their essential public and social connections, reducing them to a simple and terminal private contract. Witte thus argues for a return to a more public, nuanced, and plastic understanding of forms and norms of marriage and the family.

Heated debates over the forms, functions, and forums of the family today are not peculiarly American. They are parts and products of the massive movements of globalization and modernization of the past century, argues the theologian and social scientist Don Browning in chapter 13. These twin forces of modernization and globalization have brought ample improvements to many families—higher incomes, better education and health care, more equality for women, greater protections and opportunities for children, improved mobility for workers, new protections of human rights, and more. But these positive consequences are unevenly distributed, and they are frequently accompanied by negative consequences, such as the collapse of communal controls; the impoverishment of mothers and their children due to abandonment, divorce, and nonmarital births; the increased violence of youth; aggressive new forms of coerced prostitution and illegitimacy; sharp increases in transient nonmarital cohabitation; and the growing absence of fathers from their children.

Modernization and globalization should not and cannot be stopped, Browning argues, but their corrosive effects on marriages and families must be and can be slowed. What it will take, however, is a new international practical-religious dialogue between the major world religions designed to place the state of marriages and families before the world community. Modern religious communities have been too silent and acquiescent in debates about marriage and the family. Modern marriages and families have proved too important and essential to the health of individuals and communities to be left to corrode and collapse in the wake of global economic and technological advances. Religious communities of all sorts must thus retrieve and reconstruct their formidable intellectual and institutional traditions to revive and reform the modern family.

In his epilogue, Robert Bellah explains both the need for and the value of an interdisciplinary understanding of the modern family as a multidimensionan institution inseparable from the structural arrangement and moral ordering of society as a whole. In this light, in contrast to the early-modern myths that families come before society in a state of nature and become the building blocks of its free association by contract, it takes a society to raise a family no less than it takes families to embody the mutual care and shared responsibility at the heart of every society. Only by reintegrating families into the just moral order of the larger community and society can we truly strengthen them, for example, by providing the steady employment, attentive health care, and decent education family members need. Only thus can we ask families in turn to take a stronger part in animating our religious and civic life.

Notes

1. Jean-Jacques Rousseau, *Émile* [1762], trans. Allan Bloom (New York: Basic Books, 1979); Erik Erikson, "Life Cycle," in *International Encyclopedia of the Social Sciences*, ed. David Sills (New York: Macmillan / Free Press, 1968), 286–92; Carol Gilligan, *In a Different Voice* (Cambridge, Mass.: Harvard University Press, 1986).

2. Steven M. Tipton, "Social Differentiation and Moral Pluralism," in *Meaning and Modernity*, ed. Richard Madsen, William M. Sullivan, Ann Swidler, and Steven M. Tipton (Berkeley: University of California Press, 2002), 15–40.

3. John Witte Jr., *From Sacrament to Contract: Marriage, Religion, and Law in the Western Tradition* (Louisville: Westminster John Knox Press, 1997). Also see the chapter by Witte in the present volume.

4. Elizabeth Warren and Amelia Warren Tyagi, *The Two-Income Trap: Why Middle-Class Mothers and Fathers Are Going Broke* (New York: Basic Books, 2003); James Sarowiecki, "Leave No Parent Behind," *New Yorker*, August 25, 2003, 48.

5. Heather Boushey, Chauna Brocht, Bethney Gundersen, and Jared Bernstein, *Hardships in America* (Washington, D.C.: Economic Policy Institute, 2001); Robert Pear, "Big Increases Seen in People Lacking Health Insurance," *New York Times*, September 30, 2003, A1, A19.

6. Lynnley Browning, "U.S. Income Gap Widening, Study Says," *New York Times*, September 25, 2003, C2, summarizing the 2003 analysis by the Congressional Budget Office of government income and tax data for the year 2000, and related studies by the National Bureau of Economic Research and the Center for Budget and Policy Priorities.

7. Lynnette Clemetson, "Census Shows Ranks of Poor Rose by 1.3 Million," *New York Times*, September 3, 2003, A8; and Clemetson, "More Americans in Poverty in 2002, Census Study Shows," *New York Times*, September 27, 2003, A1, A10.

8. Sidney Verba, Kay Lehman Schlozman, and Henry E. Brady, *Voice and Equality: Civil Voluntarism in American Politics* (Cambridge, Mass.: Harvard University Press, 1995).

9. Mary Douglas, *Leviticus as Literature* (Oxford: Oxford University Press, 1999).

10. Mary Douglas, *How Institutions Think* (Syracuse, N.Y.: Syracuse University Press, 1986), esp. chaps. 4, 8.

Part I
All in the Family: Levels of Analysis, Angles of Vision

Chapter 1
Marriage in the Matrix of Habit and History

Robert N. Bellah

In the debate over the family in recent years, the question has been raised as to whether the family is a sacred institution or an obsolete tyranny. Even those of us who are not prepared to think of marriage as tyranny are probably not entirely happy to think of it as an institution either. As my coauthors and I pointed out in *The Good Society*, Americans do not really much like the idea of institutions and this, for two reasons.[1] First, institutions come down from the past, are based on largely unexamined traditions and habits, and therefore probably do not really fit our current needs. Second, institutions are oppressive—at the extreme, one thinks of prisons and mental asylums—and they limit our free individual choice.

Actually, this way of thinking about institutions is modern, though it has been around for a while; it is, if I may put it this way, part of the tradition of modernity. One of the earliest thinkers to express the modern criticism of inherited institutions was René Descartes in the seventeenth century. At the beginning of the second part of one of the founding documents of modernity, *Discourse on Method*, Descartes describes the typical European town of his day.[2] Such a town is simply a hodgepodge, a jumble of buildings from different eras, in different styles, of different forms and shapes, and the streets on which they are situated are often crooked, narrow, and inconvenient. How much better, says Descartes, if we could just tear the whole thing down and start over, putting up orderly buildings on straight streets with proper right angles. In other words, Descartes's idea of an ideal town is not one inherited from the past but one designed anew from a rational blueprint. For Descartes, the town was a metaphor for our inherited institutions and ways of thought. But in the twentieth century, the Romanian dictator Nicolae Ceausescu actually did pull down much of old Bucharest and erect "orderly" buildings in its place, with a result that was not charming at all. Then Descartes makes an even more remarkable move. He regrets that during the early years of his life his mind was filled with opinions, stories, and baseless information, entirely unexamined by reason, and he wishes that he might have been born at the age of twenty with his mind uncluttered with so much useless material. I do not even want to think of what kind of monster an unsocialized infant of twenty might be!

So let me start by saying that although every imaginable criticism of institutions, including the institutions of marriage and the family, has some basis, without institutions we would not be free, we would be dead. In every aspect of our lives, we depend on the relationships that institutions make possible. This is not in the least to say that they are perfect or that they are not in need of continuous reform and improvement; only that doing away with them altogether is a monstrous idea, as attested by the actions of those in the twentieth century who have tried it, such as Ceausescu and Pol Pot—though I think some of our rational choice theorists are, in their own way, trying to do something quite similar.

Aristotle is a philosopher who can help us understand why Descartes's wish to be born at the age of twenty is not a good idea either. For Aristotle, habit is an important starting point. In his *Ethics,* virtue, his fundamental ethical term, is, he says, a habit, in Greek a hexis, that is, a "formed state of character" that is in control of our emotions.[3] We are judged, therefore, not by our emotions but by the settled dispositions, the habits, which control our emotions. Aristotle draws from this definition a conclusion that may surprise us or even offend us: He says that the young are not fit students for ethical philosophy, for they are too apt to be led by their feelings and they have not yet developed the habits that would allow them to appreciate ethical reflection. Ethics, as he says, is, after all, not an exact science, and its object is not knowledge but action.[4] So bright young people might well study modern moral philosophy—Kant's categorical imperative, for example, or Bentham's greatest good for the greatest number—for it involves purely theoretical ideas and the young can be quite good at theory. But little good it would do them ethically, Aristotle would say, if they do not already have the habits required for living an ethical life.

Of course, Aristotle is quick to add, the matter is not one of chronological age, for there are some who are forever too "young" to understand ethics, and some relatively young people might already have acquired virtuous habits. Still, it is worth considering the fact that Aristotle, who wrote voluminous critical treatises on just about everything, and was willing to discourse at great length on all manner of ethical problems, begins not with talk but with habit, and he says in effect that without habit talk about ethics is worthless. What is shocking to us about this is that Aristotle seems to be overriding individual freedom, and worse yet, the individual freedom of the young, and insisting in an utterly authoritarian manner that he will not even teach them about ethics until they have learned proper habits.

Socrates famously questioned whether it is possible to teach virtue, and Aristotle's argument here helps us understand why. Philosophical teaching is, after all, always a matter of discursive, analytical, talk. Habit is clearly something else. What is that something else? To understand the difference between these two approaches, I turn to Mary Douglas's remarkable book *Natural Symbols,* which I have reread carefully several times in my life, each time with increasing profit.[5] Douglas takes some interesting observations of Basil Bernstein's about London families in the mid–twentieth century and uses them to construct a general theory of the relation between social control and symbolic codes, a theory that I think sheds a great deal of light on our problem of habit and of the relation of habits to institutions. Bernstein noted that there were two rather different forms of family in his sample and that these two forms differed by class. Working-class families used what he called positional control systems and restricted speech codes, and middle-class families used personal control systems and elaborated speech codes. Because the word "restricted" is invidious in a way that I think neither Bernstein nor Douglas intends, I will henceforth speak of "condensed" rather than "restricted" speech codes in contrast to elaborated ones, and I will make this terminological change even when quoting them.

Douglas describes the condensed speech code that is generated in the positional family:

> The child in this family is controlled by the continual building up of a sense of social pattern: of ascribed role categories. If he asks "Why must I do this?" the answer is in terms of relative position. Because I said so (hierarchy). Because you are a boy (sex role). Because children always do (age status). Because you are the oldest (seniority). As he grows, his experience flows into a grid of role categories; right and wrong are learnt in terms of given structure; he himself is seen only in relation to that structure.[6]

Douglas notes that this pattern can be found in some aristocratic as well as working-class families. In any case, what I want to emphasize is that condensed code is based on the taken-for-grantedness of institutions: That is what it means to call it positional. There is a real social world there, and we understand each other and ourselves only in relation to it. She then describes the other form:

> By contrast, in the family system which Professor Bernstein calls personal a fixed pattern of roles is not celebrated, but rather the autonomy and unique value of the individual. When the child asks a question the mother feels bound to answer it by as full an explanation as she knows. The curiosity of the child is used to increase his verbal control, to elucidate causal relations, to teach him to assess the consequences of his acts. Above all his behaviour is made sensitive to the personal feelings of others, by inspecting his own feelings. Why can't I do it?

Because your father's feeling worried; because I have got a headache. How would you like it if you were a dog?[7]

Douglas quotes Bernstein to the effect that in the middle-class family, the child is being regulated by the feelings of the regulator: "'Daddy will be pleased, hurt, disappointed, angry, ecstatic if you go on doing this.' . . . Control is effected through either the verbal manipulation of feelings or through the establishment of reasons which link the child to his acts."[8]

But let me back up a step with an example. A friend of mine was standing waiting for an elevator in his apartment building overhearing a conversation between a mother and a small child. The child was whining about something or other most persistently, and the mother was calmly and extensively explaining why the child could not have what she wanted. The child persisted with rising whiny tones, and the mother continued to reiterate all the reasons why not. My friend was becoming increasingly uncomfortable with this apparently interminable palaver when the mother finally said quite firmly and briefly: "Because I'm the mother and you're the child, that's why." What this mother had done was to shift rather abruptly from the elaborated code to the condensed code. This example suggests that Bernstein's two codes are not mutually exclusive and that all of us use both of them at least some of the time.

Let me use this example to link back the two codes to the idea of institutions. Condensed code is always institutionally rooted. When the mother finally invokes the mother–child relation, she is invoking a whole institutional context, a set of habits if you will, that requires parents to care for children and children to grow up and flourish under that care. Elaborated code floats free from institutions and is rooted more in the ideas and feelings of individuals. It may be used to criticize institutions, but it can never float entirely free of them, for it takes them for granted as the very basis from which criticism is possible.

I would argue for the priority of institutions, and the condensed code that expresses them, in part because no one ever starts with the elaborated code. All children begin with positional control and the condensed language code because personal control and the elaborated code require skills that no newborn has. The relation between mother and child, or perhaps we should better say between parent and child, is necessarily positional, that is, institutional, because highly asymmetrical; an infant needs to be held, cared for, talked to, or sung to but cannot be addressed with elaborate appeals to feelings or reasons, at least not for quite awhile. In fact, interaction with an infant looks suspiciously like habit, or its close relation, ritual. Linguists have discovered that in all cultures parents speak to infants in something they call "motherese," a kind of simplified, highly repetitive, singsong, partly nonsense, kind of language, one that communicates feeling rather than informa-tion. Each language has its own version of motherese, to be sure, but the basic characteristics seem to be quite universal. Nonverbal communication with an infant is probably even more important. Erik Erikson suggested that the "greeting ceremonial" between mother and child, marking the beginning of the infant's day, is the root of all subsequent ritualization.[9]

Infants become human because of habitual, nondiscursive, verbal, and nonverbal interaction with adults, which is, in Basil Bernstein's terms, nec-essarily positional in control and condensed in speech code. The function of this kind of interaction is to position children, to give them an identity rela-tive to others, to provide them with a social, an institutional, location.

So far I have been trying to insist, because of the low esteem we have these days for things like habit and ritual, not to speak of institutions, that positional control and condensed code are rather basic to our humanity and cannot really be dispensed with. So why did we develop personal control and the elaborated code in the first place? In contemporary society, Douglas links them to the division of labor, which has a differential impact on working-class and middle-class families:

> It is essential to realize that the elaborated code is a product of the division of labour. The more highly differentiated the social system, the more specialised the decision-making roles—then the more the pressure for explicit channels of communication concerning a wide range of policies and their consequences. The demands of the industrial system are pressing hard now upon education to produce more and more verbally articulate people who will be promoted to en-trepreneurial roles. By inference the condensed code will be found where these pressures are weakest [that is to say, among people whose jobs are both routine and require little verbal facility].[10]

Although Douglas finds the social basis for positional control and con-densed code in some modern professions—the military, for example—most of the professions that increasingly dominate the higher echelons of our occu-pational world require people well versed in personal control and elaborated speech. The symbolic analysts, as Robert Reich characterizes our top profes-sionals, are critical by their very job description. Douglas characterizes them as follows:

> Here are the people who live by using elaborated speech to review and revise existing categories of thought. To challenge received ideas is their very bread and butter. They (or should I say we?) practise a professional detachment toward any given pattern of experience. The more boldly and comprehensively they apply

their minds to rethinking, the better their chances of professional success. Thus the value of their radical habit of thought is socially confirmed, and reinforced. For with the rise to professional eminence comes the geographical and social mobility that detaches them from their original community. With such validation, they are likely to raise their children in the habit of intellectual challenge and not to impose a positional control pattern.[11]

Indeed, she goes on to say, they are likely to prefer personal forms of control and to focus on feelings rather than rules in child rearing. As a result, "ideas about morality and the self get detached from the social structure."[12] It is not that children raised in such a milieu lack ethical ideas; sensitivity to the feelings of others can arouse strong ethical passions when others are observed to be suffering. The problem is that without some positional sense of institutional membership and without strong condensed symbols, ethical sensitivities may simply dissipate into good intentions without leading to sustained moral commitments.

Douglas is very evenhanded in her sense that we need both modes of relating. She affirms "the duty of everyone to preserve their vision from the constraints of the condensed code when judging any social situation. . . . We must recognise that the value of particular social forms can only be judged objectively by the analytic power of the elaborated code."[13] She is well aware that condensed codes in the context of institutional authority can be both authoritarian and unjust. "Do it because I said so," is an example of condensed code that carries the implication of some, perhaps quite unpleasant, nonverbal sanction that will follow if the recipient of the command rejects it. Except under conditions of extreme emergency, an elaborated request for reasons is justified. Similarly the condensed statement "Little girls don't do that" is open to challenge with respect to the whole taken-for-granted definition of gender. These are the kinds of reflection that lead "us" to presume that personal control and elaborated code are always preferable to the alternative.

Yet Douglas warns us against precisely that conclusion:

> There is no person whose life does not need to unfold in a coherent symbolic system. The less organized the way of life, the less articulated the symbolic system may be. But social responsibility is no substitute for symbolic forms and indeed depends upon them. When ritualism is openly despised the philanthropic impulse is in danger of defeating itself. For it is an illusion to suppose that there can be organisation without symbolic expression. . . . Those who despise ritual, even at its most magical, are cherishing in the name of reason a very irrational concept of communication.[14]

So where does Douglas leave "us," including her? She is not asking us, as some converts to various forms of fundamentalism are, to abandon our personal and elaborated selves and jump back into the positional box. No, she is asking us with all our critical rationality to see that we need both forms of control and both codes. She writes:

> In the long run, the argument of this book is that the elaborated code challenges its users to turn round on themselves and inspect their values, to reject some of them, and to resolve to cherish positional forms of control and communication wherever these are available. . . . No one would deliberately choose the elaborated code and the personal control system who is aware of the seeds of alienation it contains.[15]

But the question remains, in what sense can we, products of personal families and modern educational and occupational systems, "deliberately choose" aspects of positional control and condensed code? I will argue that some dialectic, some complementarity, must be sought because giving up either alternative would exact too high a price. I think we know the price of going back into the box of some kind of closed traditionalism. Can we explore further the implications of Douglas's warning about trying to live in the elaborated code alone?

If we see that trying to live in the elaborated code alone would mean that we would have to make up our lives as we go along, that we could take nothing for granted, because we would have no institutional context to tell us where we are, we can begin to see that it is not only undesirable but impossible. Douglas's dichotomy may be too stark, for even the citadel of critical reason, the modern university, is an institution, with the habits and rituals that institutions always entail. What I do in delivering a paper, giving a lecture, is a ritual, one to which we are so habituated that we hardly recognize it as a ritual, even though it is a fairly complex one.

But, we might ask, are not some institutions in modern society based entirely on elaborated codes, are not they purely rational? Economic institutions, for example? Yet, in recent years, economists have been rediscovering what was once called institutional economics. The economist Geoffrey Hodgson suggests why institutions are as essential in the economy as anywhere else in our social life:

> In a world of uncertainty, . . . institutions play a functional role in providing a basis for decision-making, expectation, and belief. Without these "rigidities," without social routine and habit to reproduce them, and without institutionally conditioned conceptual frameworks, an uncertain world would present a chaos of sense data in which it would be impossible for the agent to make sensible decisions and to act.[16]

But in economic life, institutions do more than provide a basis for decision making. One of the most fundamental institutions in the economic realm is the contract. A contract provides the trust, the faith, if you will, that the other party will not violate promises just because it is in his interest to do so, and that there is legal recourse if he does. A capitalist economy is not based on rational choice alone, but on widely accepted institutions, ultimately on trust. As Émile Durkheim said, a contract finally depends on noncontractual understandings that lie behind and guarantee it. We saw what happened in postcommunist Russia when the shock therapy of privatization recommended by American economists produced mafia-style manipulation and not rational capitalism, because the institutional basis for a modern economy did not exist.

Even though, I have argued, institutions are indispensable in every sphere of our lives, this is a truth not obvious to moderns, especially modern Americans. We have seen Douglas noting that in the modern occupational system—especially its upper echelons where professional expertise and the skills of verbal criticism are highly rewarded—institutional loyalties are not only not valued but are hardly understood. Since Douglas wrote, the trends she noted have become ever more pervasive. A good recent discussion of these trends is Robert Wuthnow's *Loose Connections*, a book whose very title expresses the problem.[17] In America, and increasingly in other developed nations, people are not plugged in very tightly to groups and associations; they may volunteer a few hours a week for a while, but they will not join an organization that will expect their loyalty and commitment for the long haul, or at least they are much more reluctant to do so than once they were. Even commitments to marriage and family, leave aside to job and vocation, are much more fragile, much more dependent on individual mood, than they used to be. "Loose connections" is a powerful metaphor by itself, but Wuthnow pairs the metaphor of loose connections with another metaphor that partly explains it: porous institutions.

Porous institutions do not hold individuals very securely; porous institutions leak. In a world of porous institutions, it is hard to have any connections that are not loose. One thinks of the family. Whereas in 1960 one in four marriages would fail, today one in two will. And a lot of consequences follow from that. The fastest growing category of households is those with one member, which now amount to 25 percent of all households. Families, as we know, do not necessarily consist of two parents and their children. Husbands and wives drift in and out, often bringing children from a former marriage with them, resulting in what are called blended families. However successful families are in coping with these conditions, there is always the uncertainty: Will this marriage last? Will my parents divorce?

Douglas has urged us to "cherish" the condensed code and the institutions that make it intelligible wherever they are available. But how can we moderns, immersed as we are in the critical elaborated code, understand such an injunction? Let me try to answer that question by turning to the contemporary philosopher Alasdair MacIntyre. In his recent book *Dependent Rational Animals,* he points out that our philosophical tradition, going all the way back to Aristotle, assumes the standpoint of an independent, autonomous, adult male. But the truth of our condition is that we come into the world dependent; end our days dependent; and are often, more often than we like to admit, dependent all during our lives.[18] But dependency is by definition positional. Without institutions, dependency would just be a disaster. We have to define ourselves in relation to others because we need them. The elaborated code requires that we see ourselves, or pretend to, as entirely apart from the world, totally free to pursue our own interests and express our own feelings. What I am trying to say is that for us to feel at home in the condensed code and appreciate the institutions on which we depend, we would have to give up the illusion of absolute autonomy and recognize that we are related to, and even dependent on, others.

Let me turn finally to marriage to show that though it can be, as with the Taliban, an obsolete tyranny, it can still, properly understood, be affirmed as a sacred institution. In the traditional view of marriage, husband and wife become one flesh. Indeed, Genesis 2:24 says: "Therefore shall a man leave his father and his mother, and shall cleave unto his wife: and they shall be one flesh." That is positional control and condensed code with a vengeance, and, not surprisingly, moderns find it very hard to take. I have been to weddings in Berkeley where husband and wife becoming one flesh has been strongly and explicitly disavowed. In one such ceremony, the man and woman were sent into two different rooms for a moment to symbolize that they are separate people and will continue to be separate after the marriage. And, of course, there is a good reason. When people said that man and wife become one flesh, whose flesh did they have in mind? In the passage in Genesis, the man cleaves to his wife, so we might imagine that it is her flesh that he becomes. But that has not been the conventional interpretation. Fair enough. If positional control and condensed code have been used to affirm gender inequality, and who could deny that they have, why not jettison the whole idea of one flesh? Because gender inequality is not all that that ancient symbolism affirms. And because we, children of criticism, can reaffirm the institution of marriage critically, disavowing the inequality while affirming the solidarity.

The price of giving up the symbolism of one flesh altogether is high. If we do that, we are tempted to believe that leaving a marriage is no different from entering one. We can speak of a "starter marriage" or a marriage with "term limits"—humorously, of course, but there is a lot of truth in humor. But, upon reflection, if we really want to get married, and the great majority of

Americans still do (even many gays who are not allowed to), then we may not really like the implications of the idea of marriage as an easily broken contract. It was Hegel who said, "Marriage is not a contractual relationship. On the contrary, though marriage begins in contract, it is precisely a contract to transcend the standpoint of contract."[19] In other words, Hegel is saying marriage is a contract to enter a noncontractual relationship. I am not saying, and neither is Hegel, that divorce is never justified, but that it is a last resort, because marriage is a solidarity so central, not only to the couple but also to their children and everyone around them, that it is not lightly to be tossed aside. As Douglas has pointed out, strong social solidarity is almost always symbolized by body images. That husband and wife become one flesh is not too strong an image for what marriage really is.

My insistence on institutions and the condensed code does not at all mean that I oppose reform. As Douglas has argued, inherited institutions need to be monitored constantly with the elaborated code, not so they can be abandoned but improved. Just because I believe so strongly in marriage, I think today it requires a major reform: It should be extended to include same-sex couples. Why stable, well-institutionalized relations between gay people should threaten marriage more than transient and unstable relations between them is something I have never been able to understand. The argument against gay marriage by the people that I respect most, such as Nicholas Boyle and Stanley Hauerwas—namely, that marriage is a productive relation because it can give rise to children, whereas a gay relationship could only be based on consumption, and that it is only a form of recreation—seems to me entirely unconvincing.[20] Gay and lesbian couples often do want children by artificial insemination or adoption. Heterosexual couples often choose not to have children at all. As in almost every sphere today, nothing can be taken for granted in marriage—straight, or if it were possible, gay. The idea that marriage entails the nurture of children, which I think is essential, is something that in our world cannot be imposed, but of which people must be persuaded.

But there is another basis for marriage that, I believe, has equal dignity with the fact that married couples can have children: the kind of love and support in a committed relationship that is hard to find anywhere else. The book of Ecclesiastes in its wonderful prose makes my case, even when the reference is not explicitly to marriage:

> It is better that you should be together than one; for they have the advantage of their society. If one fall he shall be supported by the other. Woe to him that is alone, for when he falleth he hath none to lift him up. Again, if two lie together, they are warm; but how can one be warm alone? (4:9–11)

Anyone in a long marriage, when the children have left home years ago, knows that "the advantage of society," as Ecclesiastes puts it, is at the heart of marriage, important though children (and grandchildren) are. Why should we want to deprive same-sex couples of that consolation?

When I was asked to write this chapter, I was given a very full plate. I was told that it should treat sex, marriage, and the family in the context of law and religion. Out of this mix, I have chosen to focus on marriage and to show what kind of thing marriage is by considering it as an institution. And given the bad reputation of institutions in our society, I have spent most of my time trying to explain what institutions are and how they relate to other forms of action in our society. But it is just in thinking of marriage as an institution that I hope briefly to clarify its relation to law and religion.

At first glance, one might think that law is a pure example of elaborated code and that its purpose is to enhance the efficiency of transactions, not to undergird institutions. That is the teaching of Judge Richard Posner and the very influential law and economics school.[21] But is law really like Ceausescu's Bucharest, or is it like the European towns that Descartes found so problematic? One learns a great deal of critical thinking in law school and must indeed become adept in the elaborated code. But does not one also have to learn a lot of condensed code, language that lawyers take for granted but lay people scarcely understand? And can we simply dismiss that condensed code as professional mystification, or is it an abbreviated way of referring to centuries-long experience with the reality of legal adjudication? The English law professors who most recently translated the sixth-century legal text *Justinian's Institutes* give us pause when they write in their introduction:

> One question to be considered, not of course decisive but not unimportant either, is how deeply rooted our current ways of thinking and teaching actually are. If it were true in the law schools that [and here they quote a recent author] "our basic conceptual apparatus, the fundamental characterizations and divisions which we impose on the phenomena with which we deal, do not reflect the values of our own times but *those of the last century*" we might well be disposed to view them as contingent and probably mistaken. However, when the truth is that those same categories of legal thought have been surviving critical onslaughts in different jurisdictions and under different political systems since the time of Justinian in the sixth century and Gaius in the second, we are bound to approach the issue of radical reform at least with some self-doubt.[22]

If we look at the opening of *Justinian's Institutes,* which the translators argue has been of incalculable influence on all Western legal systems, not only continental civil law but common law systems as well, we may discern something else that has largely dropped from modern consciousness, namely, that law in all traditional societies has been grounded in religion. The *Institutes* opens with the words "*In Nomine Domini Nostri Jhesu Christi*" (In the name of Our Lord Jesus Christ). And the first paragraph begins, in Birks and McLeod's translation, "Justice is an unswerving and perpetual determination to acknowledge all men's rights. Learning in the law entails knowledge of God and man, and mastery of the difference between justice and injustice."[23]

Why marriage and family as institutions, and the law in which they are grounded, should partake of the sacred, should have something religious about them, is largely unintelligible on the basis of contemporary assumptions, and requires an effort of interpretation to understand. According to the presuppositions of modern philosophy and modern common sense, a person is an autonomous entity bounded by the surface of his or her body and relates to others as one sovereign state relates to another. This implies, if we know our Hobbes, that they are in a perpetual state of war with one another, absent temporary forms of truce. I think we are beginning to see, with the help of some modern philosophers and social scientists, as well as the testimony of all the great traditions, that this conception of personhood is either completely wrong or seriously one-sided. Our selves are not atomistic but relational. We would not even have a self if it were not for our relations with other human beings, with the natural world, and with the reality that underlies the world. Law and religion are two of the most fundamental expressions of that relatedness. This does not mean that they cannot be challenged or that they are not in constant need of reform. It does mean that the idea of abandoning them altogether, or the institutions they sustain, is a recipe for disaster.

With respect to many spheres of life—the status of women is an important example—we know that uncritical and habitual affirmation of the status quo has often legitimated injustice or worse. Criticism and the elaborated code that makes it possible are absolutely necessary if we are to overcome ancient and modern evils. But criticism has to be criticism of something. Criticism alone cannot provide a basis for life. Rather, criticism, like appetite in Shakespeare, can become a universal wolf that in the end eats itself. Today it would be well to realize that our critical elaborated code and our personal freedom, good as they are in themselves, cannot survive without institutions and the beliefs and practices that undergird them. In short, if we think seriously about marriage as an institution, we will not want to abandon it but to reform and renew it as one of the foundations of a good form of life.

Notes

1. Robert N. Bellah, Richard Madsen, William M. Sullivan, Ann Swidler, and Steven M. Tipton, *The Good Society* (New York: Alfred A. Knopf, 1991), 3–18.

2. René Descartes, *Discours de la méthode* (Paris: Larousse, 1934 [1637]), 21–23.

3. Aristotle, *Nichomachean Ethics,* trans. Martin Oswald (Indianapolis: Bobbs-Merrill, 1962), 1105b–1106a.

4. Ibid., 1095a.

5. Mary Douglas, *Natural Symbols: Explorations in Cosmology* (New York: Pantheon Books, 1982 [1970]).

6. Ibid., 24.

7. Ibid., 26.

8. Ibid.

9. Erik H. Erikson, "The Development of Ritualization," in *The Religious Situation 1968,* ed. Donald R. Cutler (Boston: Beacon Press, 1968), 711–33.

10. Douglas, *Natural Symbols,* 21.

11. Ibid., 31.

12. Ibid.

13. Ibid., 166.

14. Ibid., 50.

15. Ibid., 157.

16. Geoffrey M. Hodgson, *Economics and Institutions: A Manifesto for a Modern Institutional Economics* (Cambridge: Polity Press, 1988), 204.

17. Robert Wuthnow, *Loose Connections* (Cambridge, Mass.: Harvard University Press, 1998).

18. Alasdair MacIntyre, *Dependent Rational Animals: Why Human Beings Need the Virtues* (Chicago: Open Court, 1999).

19. G. W. F. Hegel, *Philosophy of Right,* trans. T. M. Knox (Oxford: Oxford University Press, 1942), para. 163, 112.

20. Stanley Hauerwas, *A Better Hope: Resources for a Church Confronting Capitalism, Democracy, and Postmodernity* (Grand Rapids: William B. Eerdmans, 2000), 50; Nicholas Boyle, *Who Are We Now?* (Notre Dame, Ind.: University of Notre Dame Press, 1998), 59.

21. For a quick overview of Posner and his opinions, see the New Yorker profile, "The Bench Burner: A Judge's Subversive Opinions," by Larissa MacFarquhar, *New Yorker,* December 10, 2001, 78–89.

22. *Justinian's Institutes,* trans. with intr. Peter Birks and Grant McLeod (Ithaca, N.Y.: Cornell University Press, 1987), 26.

23. *Justinian's Institutes,* 35, 37.

Chapter 2
The Biology of Family Values:
Reproductive Strategies of Our Fellow Primates

Frans B. M. de Waal and Amy S. Pollick

Marriage accomplishes two goals related to human reproduction: It binds two individuals of the opposite sex together while creating morally reinforced restrictions on external sexual relations; and in doing so, it provides a context in which the male enjoys a reasonable certainty of paternity. Getting males to invest in offspring requires a confidence in paternity exceeding that of other primate males, who often live in promiscuous societies. Not that other primate males know anything about paternity—and even in humans such knowledge is not required for the evolution of a pair-bond. Whenever males invest in the rearing of young, natural selection will favor males who preferentially target their own offspring over males who are not as discriminating with their resources and efforts. How males accomplish this targeting is variable, and in animals (e.g., many birds) it occurs without any knowledge on the actors' part of genetics or paternity.

No other primate besides humans knows marriage, and very few have heterosexual pair-bonding, which we assume to be antecedent to marriage—marriage being the symbolic confirmation of the pair-bond—socially, morally, and religiously sanctioned. Even though pair-bonds do exist in a small number of other primates, such as the gibbons and marmosets, other primates differ significantly from humans in that each family defends its own territory, keeping other individuals out. The human pair-bonded unit, or nuclear family, in contrast, is part of a larger whole within which it is fully integrated. There is some isolation and privacy for the unit, but to a much lesser degree than for those territorial families in other primates. Human families are part and parcel of the society. We thus fully agree with Robert Bellah's point that the society, the polis in Aristotle's words, is prior to the family.[1] In evolutionary terms, there first must have been the larger society, within which developed the human family. The alternative path would be the merging of families, meaning that families came first and the larger society second. Because humans derive from chimpanzee- and bonobo-like ancestors, however (see figure 2.1), this scenario is unlikely.

To understand the institution of marriage and the human family from an evolutionary perspective, we shall explore basic principles of sexual behavior,

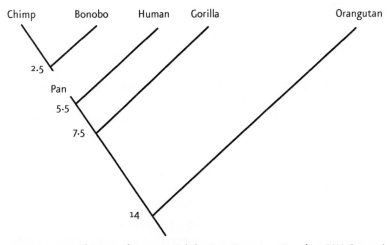

Figure 2.1. Tree of Origin of Humans and the Four Great Apes Based on DNA Comparisons Showing How Many Million Years Ago Species Diverged
Note: Chimpanzees and bonobos form a single genus: Pan. The human lineage diverged from the Pan ancestor about 5.5 million years ago. Since bonobos and chimpanzees themselves diverged after this, about 2.5 million years ago, neither one is closer to us than the other. The gorilla diverged earlier, hence is more distant from us, as is the only Asian great ape, the orangutan.

mate competition, and sexual selection in our primate relatives. This exploration will take us to issues every human community needs to deal with, and every other primate community as well, such as the avoidance of inbreeding, competition among members of the same sex, and the problem of male infanticide. After this exploration, we shall return to the issue of monogamy and marriage and place it in this evolutionary context.

Sex and Sexual Competition

The primate order is divided into several groups: prosimians, monkeys, and apes. Humans are essentially a kind of ape, even though we usually do not see ourselves as such, because we share a common ancestor with the gibbons, orangutans, gorillas, chimpanzees, and bonobos, which are the other apes. The apes are not to be confused with monkeys, which are generally smaller, have tails, and are more distant from us. Our direct lineage split off from our closest extant relatives, the chimpanzee and bonobo, about 5 million years ago, which in evolutionary time is like yesterday (see figure 2.1).

What is confusing about the primate order is that there are so many different social systems. This makes it difficult to simply compare our system with that of the other primates, and so we need to seek general principles within the variation that exists. Perhaps some of these principles apply to our societies as well. In doing so, let us start with a particularly widespread kind of monkey: the macaque. Macaque society is hierarchical, rigid, and matriarchal. A top-ranking female's daughter is guaranteed to also rank high. This is true of granddaughters, as well—females spend their entire lives within a matriline that consists of several generations of females. The converse is also true; a low-ranking female's daughter stays at the bottom of the hierarchy. It is important to point out that rank is not genetically determined; a female remains highly ranked because she has a social network of support. In captivity, one can let a high-ranking family adopt an infant from a low-ranking family. In such cases, the infant will assume the rank of its adoptive family when it grows up, which shows that rank is socially inherited.

Even though female kin band together in matrilines, there are males in the group as well. These males are immigrants, having arrived from other groups, and hence they have no or few relatives in the group. The resulting mix is a promiscuous, multimale system. Males copulate, in principle, with all females, though high-ranking males copulate more often than low-ranking ones, and there exists little or no connection or association between the male and his offspring. All adult males are "uncles" for the younger generation in their group, even though one of these "uncles" is their father. Apart from the dominance rank of males, which has an effect on their access to females, there is the important issue of female choice, which means that the females have a degree of control over which males they mate with.

For evolutionary biologists, the driving force of evolution, the main factor in natural selection, comes down to individual reproductive success: What characteristics does the individual possess that enable him or her to produce more and better offspring? Females need to assess the quality of the genes used to fertilize their ovum, and thus there exists, to a certain degree, female choice. Female primates do not consciously know anything about genetics, but natural selection favors females who choose to mate with high-quality, vigorous, and healthy males. Females need to care about mate quality, because (in the primates at least) they produce only one offspring at a time, or sometimes two, and can therefore afford to be choosy. Males, conversely, tend to go for quantity, having the capacity to fertilize many females, and they barely put any effort into rearing their offspring. Thus, male primates typically compete over access to females, and not the other way around. Female competition does occur, though, in species that form pair-bonds. If males are involved in caring for offspring, they will be choosy with which female they embark on this effort, and the females will compete over the best providers, as is the case in many birds as well as in human society. Females are also fierce competitors for food, which is needed to successfully raise offspring. For this reason, females have been dubbed the "ecological sex." Females distribute themselves according to the food resources (which can be dispersed or clumped, scarce or abundant, seasonal or year-round), whereas males, mainly interested in access to females, map onto the female distribution.

Intrasexual competition may give rise to sexual dimorphism, and because this competition is more pronounced in males than females, males often show sexually selected characteristics. Charles Darwin first proposed this idea in 1859, in *The Origin of Species*. When a physical characteristic is said to be sexually selected, this particular feature may lack any apparent survival value, except insofar as it relates to mate selection. A widely known example is the peacock's tail, which is an elaborate, ornate, and showy appendage that can seriously hinder the male's movements, such as when the male needs to escape from a hawk. It is extremely attractive to females, however, and for this reason has become a consistent feature of the bird. In essence, female preference for a good-looking tail has reinforced the selection for this uniquely male trait through generations. This is an important point to consider, as explained by Geoffrey Miller, when thinking about human evolution and why we see males showing behavior patterns that at first sight may not seem adaptive, such as bungee jumping or writing poetry.[2]

We also need to consider what keeps these sexually selected traits honest—that is, what prevents a male of inferior health from sending out false advertisements. For example, a peacock might have a showy tail but not the reproductive goods to back it up, and consequently females make a poor choice among mates. What keeps the tail "honest," or a true indicator of fitness, is the so-called "handicap principle." Originally developed by Amotz Zahavi, this principle suggests that sexually selected traits are costly or detrimental to the health of the male—only then can the female rest assured that the male's physical characteristics are truly reflective of his condition.[3] Thus, the above-mentioned peacock's tail hinders the male's movements, in effect telling the female, "Yes, I have this burdensome tail but because I'm so fit, it doesn't matter." These characteristics show up in generation after generation of males because the females rely on them to make choices about healthy males. This handicap principle is now widely accepted as an explanation for a variety of sexually selected traits.

A common sexually selected trait of primates is the size difference between males and females, which can be quite large. Certain males are twice the size of females and have enormous canine teeth, which females do not have. For example, golden monkey males are twice the size of females and theirs is a "harem" society, in which one male has a group of several females.

Orangutans are also highly sexually dimorphic, with the male sporting huge cheek flaps and an impressive coat of long red hair that is lacking in females, who look like juveniles next to the adult male. These physical differences are the direct result of competition over females, which is automatically fiercer the more a single male monopolizes females. To keep potential contenders away, he needs to look unbeatable.

An entirely different kind of male rivalry takes the form of so-called sperm competition.[4] Some of the competition over females takes place at the level of sperm production, with some males producing more sperm than others. The male who makes the most sperm has a better chance of fertilizing the female, thus enhancing his chances for reproductive success. These particular males will have large testes. If we think about the human female-to-male ratio in weight, which is about 85 percent, we come to realize that we are not very sexually dimorphic and, given our relatively small testicles, human males probably also have low sperm competition. In the gorilla, there is almost no sperm competition because the alpha male, or silverback, has an exclusive harem and thus does not need to worry about other males mating with his females on a regular basis. In chimpanzee society, conversely, many males compete together for a variety of things, so sperm competition results. Male chimpanzees and bonobos have very large testicles, much larger than human males, both in absolute terms and even more so relative to body size.

In sum, sexual competition among males is rampant in the animal world and has led to male ornamentation that attracts females and large male size to deter male rivals. It has also led to sperm competition. In all of this, the human species is relatively moderate, which probably has to do with the fact that in our societies male competition is mitigated by males' need to cooperate in hunting and warfare. Human male competition is constrained, as a result. And given the heterosexual pair-bonding in our societies, we also have female competition over mates, more so than many other primates.

Chimpanzee Politics

Chimpanzees signal their fertility through swellings on their posteriors, and their menstrual cycles are roughly as long as ours—thirty-five days—within which genital swellings last for about ten days. It is in this swollen period that males follow females and try to mate. Females also express active interest and will often solicit certain males for mating opportunities. Male chimpanzees are extremely hierarchical. They are very political animals in that they form not only hierarchies but also coalitions to achieve higher positions.[5] In that sense, they very much resemble a human political system. To rank high, you need to be popular, and so favors must be given and deals need to be made. Within this system, one can become the alpha male with the support of a few other males, but the alpha must do the others favors down the line when he achieves that higher position. If the new alpha fails to do so, the supporting males will withdraw their support and undermine the new alpha's position. This makes for a delicate, transactional system, one based on reciprocity, bribery, and other Machiavellian tactics.

The dominant male is an easily recognizable individual. He pumps himself up by making his hair stand on end (known as pilo-erection), making him look larger than he really is. He is greeted with bowing by the lower-ranking males and females. These rituals serve to confirm and maintain the hierarchy. If there is no stable hierarchy, much trouble ensues among the males. Males will confront each other and fight to a much greater extent than if they were coexisting within a clear hierarchy. Fighting is actually quite rare among adult males, but when they are competing for rank, they sometimes must literally fight it out to figure out who has top priority to all resources, females included. At the same time, all this male competition leads to male cooperation in chimpanzee society.

We tend to dichotomize these tendencies in nonhuman animals, asking whether they are either a competitive or cooperative species. The chimpanzee is an excellent illustration of how these two tendencies coexist. The males compete intensely for rank and constantly busy themselves affirming their status, but they are also extremely cooperative. In fact, hierarchies are usually a sign of cooperation in a species. That the two also go together in human society is known from a classic social psychology experiment, in which Muzafer Sherif et al., engendered competition among boys in a summer camp.[6] If you pit one group against another, each will quickly form a strong hierarchy. The hierarchy gets strengthened under pressure from an outside force. This principle also works in politics, with leaders gaining strength from dealing with outside threats, sometimes ones they create themselves. So we see how cooperation, strangely enough, underlies hierarchies and increases focus on leadership.

In the animal kingdom, if males compete intensely, coalitions tend to form. This is akin to team sports, which are highly competitive but also highly cooperative. Take a basketball team, for example; the sport cannot function without cooperation among its team members. And so male lions, male baboons, male dolphins, and male chimpanzees are all good examples of males who have strong alliances that serve to facilitate access to females. The male who is a loner and not a member of any team is not going anywhere, and he will likely never enjoy mating opportunities.

We can compare the chimpanzee to the human male because both are highly competitive, the latter male especially so in the corporate structure. Even though there is a lot of infighting within the corporation, such as about who gets the corner office, the members must stick together to defeat other corporations. Otherwise their collective interests will be damaged. Just as there is a high level of cooperation as well as a high level of internal competition in human corporate life, we see the analogs of this in chimpanzee society. Chimpanzee males conduct warfare against neighboring groups and do so in a highly consolidated fashion; if they did not, the foreign groups would invade their territories. We see how competition and cooperation are not mutually exclusive aspects of society, be it human or ape.

All this talk of competition and cooperation has focused on males. What about females? In *You Just Don't Understand,* Deborah Tannen discusses the differences in conversational style between the human genders.[7] She emphasizes how quickly men can fight and reconcile—for example, arguing in the boardroom meeting leads to fighting, but after a short break they are laughing together. Women do not do this. It is harder for them to combine rivalry and friendship; they in fact make a sharp distinction between the two. For men, however, all rivals are potential friends, and all friends are potential rivals. Accordingly, men and women handle conflict and cooperation quite differently, and this is related to intrasexual competition. Similarly, chimpanzee males are good at coalition formation, where one male helps another achieve top ranking. These two will confront a third male, whom neither can beat on his own but together they can dominate.

We see many of these kinds of coalitions in our chimpanzee colony at the Yerkes National Primate Research Center Field Station in Lawrenceville, Georgia. Currently, an older male is pushing up a younger male into a position of power; in return, he may derive some of that power from the younger male. He might enjoy privileged access to females or food as a result. These male coalition partners may be sitting and grooming one another while there is a female in estrus nearby. Normally, a swollen female would induce competition among adult males such as these. But because of the support they provide to each other, they do not compete but rather pay each other in grooming currency for the privilege to mate undisturbed. This makes the stuff of transaction in male chimpanzee society, which starkly contrasts with that of the bonobo.

In sum, chimpanzee society is one of politicking, deal making, and bargaining among the males, which in the end all relates to who gets to mate with the females in estrus. Female choice is a factor to an extent, but it is very much a male-dominated society.

A Matrifocal Close Relative

The bonobo is almost the opposite of the chimpanzee in many ways, even though the two apes are close relatives. One of the earliest primatologists, Robert Yerkes, had a bonobo but did not know it. Yerkes studied Panzee, a chimp, and Prince Chim, whom he thought was a chimp but was in actuality a bonobo (figure 2.2).

Figure 2.2. Robert Yerkes with Two Apes in His Lap, Both of Whom He Believed to Be Chimpanzees

Note: This photo was taken in 1923, well before the discovery of the bonobo as a distinct species. We know now that the ape on the right, named Prince Chim, was a bonobo. Prince Chim was described by Yerkes as an anthropoid genius, far gentler than any other ape he knew.

Source: Photograph by Lee Russell, courtesy of the Yerkes National Primate Research Center.

At the time, the bonobo had not yet been recognized as a separate species. This happened only in 1929. In his 1925 book *Almost Human,* Yerkes marveled at how Prince Chim seemed so human, calling him an anthropoid genius, and he described the bonobo's altruistic, caring behavior toward Panzee, who was terminally ill.[8] Bonobos are far more empathetic, generous, and altruistic than chimpanzees. They also build a society that is extremely different from that of chimpanzees.[9]

Chimpanzee males have substantial muscle mass, enormous strength in their arms, and a thick neck; all their weight is concentrated in their upper bodies. They possess five times the strength of the human male. Even though they are shorter than humans, they are far stronger than we are. The bonobo, conversely, has much narrower shoulders and furthermore has black ears, fine hair, light-colored lips, and reduced eyebrow ridges. Both the chimpanzee and bonobo live in multimale societies, so we do not see the nuclear family structure as we do in humans. Family life does not revolve around a male/female pair and its offspring, it is entirely a female affair.

Bonobo females could not be more different from chimpanzee females. The bonobo has extended sexual receptivity, much contact with other females, and alliances with one another, and she is generally dominant in social life. Females dominate in all known captive colonies of bonobos, and we know from the field that females claim the best food and often chase males, hence tending to have the upper hand. The males are more muscular than the females and have sharp canine teeth, like chimpanzee males, but they have the disadvantage in that they are very uncooperative with each other. Bonobo females cooperate better than males, which is the opposite of the situation for chimpanzees. Ironically, the reduced male cooperation in bonobos is due to reduced male competition; this fits our earlier explanation that male cooperation generally occurs when males are rivals. Female bonobos are sexually receptive much of the time, reducing rivalry among the males, causing them to lose the ability to form effective alliances. Bonobo females are the ones who have successful alliances, not the males, and so they have a gateway to dominating the males. They do so collectively, by chasing them as a group. And the females are far from gentle if they catch a male.

The female pattern strongly affects males. Male bonobos do engage in sexual competition, as do all primate males, but their success in this depends on the support of females, and particularly that of their mother. Bonobo males stay all their life in the same group in which their mother lives. They follow her around in the forest, and those males who have high-ranking mothers tend to reach the top of the male hierarchy. This is a system totally different from that of chimpanzees, in which dominance is decided among the males themselves with little female influence.

The female alliance in bonobo society can be viewed as a solution to an important problem known as infanticide. In many apes, and also humans, infanticide is a grave problem for the females. Infanticide is thus virtually unknown in bonobo society, and one reason for this could be that females effectively dominate males. The other reason involves obscured paternity, as explained below.

Bonobo Sex

The very first suggestion that the sexual behavior of bonobos might differ from that of chimpanzees came from observations at European zoos. Wrapping their shocking findings in Latin, two German scientists, Eduard Tratz and Heinz Heck, reported that chimpanzees mate more *canum* (like dogs) and bonobos more *hominum* (like people).[10] In those days, in the 1950s, anthropologists viewed face-to-face copulation as a human cultural innovation, thus ignoring the fact that evolution has adapted our species anatomically for such intercourse by moving the vulva into a frontal position.

It is impossible to understand the social life of the bonobo without attention to its sex life. Whereas in most other species sexual behavior is a fairly distinct category, in the bonobo it has become part and parcel of social relationships, and not just between males and females. Bonobos engage in sex in virtually every partner combination: male–male, male–female, female–female, male–juvenile, female–juvenile, and so on. Bonobos become aroused remarkably easily, and they express this in a variety of mounting positions and genital contacts. Sexual behavior is flexible; bonobos use every position and variation one can imagine. Thus, whereas chimpanzees almost never adopt face-to-face sexual positions, bonobos do so one out of three times during copulations in the wild, and even more often in captivity. Furthermore, the frontal orientation of the vulva and clitoris suggest that the female genitalia are adapted for this position. Perhaps the bonobo's most characteristic and most common sexual pattern is so-called genito-genital rubbing, or GG-rubbing, between adult females (figure 2.3).

One female clings with arms and legs to another—almost the way an infant clings to its mother—while the other female, standing on both hands and feet, lifts her off the ground. The two females then rub their genital swellings laterally together with the same rhythm as that of male thrusting during copulation. Given the rather prominent clitoris of bonobo females, there can be little doubt that their grins and squeals during GG-rubbing reflect orgasm-like experiences. Absent in the chimpanzee, this behavior has been observed in every bonobo group, captive or wild.

Figure 2.3. Genito-Genital Rubbing between Two Bonobo Females
Note: In this ape species—equally close to us as the better known chimpanzee—sex often serves nonreproductive functions relating to female alliances, which provides the "weaker" sex with its power base, as well as conflict resolution and tension reduction.
Source: Photograph by Frans de Waal.

Setting out to study the aftermath of aggression in the bonobos of the San Diego Zoo, in California—at the time, the world's largest captive colony—the first author spent his time in front of the ape enclosure with a video camera. The camera was switched on at feeding time, which turned out to be the peak time for sexual activity. As soon as an animal caretaker approached the enclosure with food, the males would develop erections. Even before the food was thrown into the enclosure, the bonobos would be inviting each other for sex; males would invite females, and females would invite males as well as each other.[11]

In almost all animals, the introduction or discovery of attractive food induces competition. There are two reasons to believe that sexual activity is the bonobo's answer to this competition. First, any object, not just food, that arouses the interest of more than one bonobo at a time tends to result in sexual contact. What such situations share with feeding time is not a high level of excitement but the possibility of conflict over possession. Whereas this leads to squabbles in most other species, bonobos are remarkably tolerant, perhaps because they use sex to divert attention and change the tone of the encounter.

Second, bonobo sex also often occurs in aggressive contexts unrelated to food. For example, one male chases another away from a female, after which the two males reunite and engage in scrotal rubbing. Or one female hits a juvenile, to which the juvenile's mother responds by lunging at the aggressor, which is immediately followed by sex between both females. Chimpanzees kiss and embrace during reconciliations yet rarely engage in sex, whereas bonobos use the same sexual repertoire then as they do at feeding time. The art of sexual reconciliation may well have reached an evolutionary peak in the bonobo.[12]

Incest Avoidance

Because incest may lead to inbreeding, and because inbreeding reduces the viability of offspring, animals generally avoid it. The chief preventive measure for both chimpanzees and bonobos is female migration (note that this is different from many monkeys, in which males tend to do the outbreeding). When adolescent females leave their mother and siblings to join a neighboring community, they go through a difficult transition that certainly would not be worth all the risk in the absence of significant benefits. The trade-off is that they get to mate with unrelated males, and hence avoid inbreeding. They do not do so knowingly; it is assumed that during evolutionary history, females who migrated produced healthier offspring than females who did not.

When Chie Hashimoto and Takeshi Furuichi studied the sexual behavior of wild bonobos, they found that, though males become more sexually active with maturation, females do not.[13] On the contrary, the investigators speak of a "sexually inactive" state in young females in the period immediately preceding their departure from the natal group. Perhaps it keeps them from developing sexual relations with brothers and possible fathers. Females generally leave at the age of seven years, when they develop their first little genital swellings. Equipped with this passport, they become "floaters," visiting neighboring communities before permanently settling down into one.

The situation is different for males, who remain in their natal group. Given that males cannot get pregnant, they do not risk much by having sex with relatives. It is the females in their group who stand the most to lose from such contact. We assume, therefore, that mothers and sisters avoid sex with sons and brothers. The way these inhibitions may come about is through early familiarity—the basic mechanism assumed to underlie incest avoidance in a wide range of species, including our own.

The second mechanism for inbreeding avoidance is known as the Westermarck Effect. Edward Westermarck was a Finnish-Swedish sociologist who incorporated Darwinian thinking into his work at the turn of the previous century.[14] He proposed a mechanism that upset both Sigmund Freud and many anthropologists, who were convinced that there would be rampant sex within the human family if it were not for the incest taboo. Freud believed that the earliest sexual excitations and fantasies of children are invariably directed at close family members, and Claude Lévi-Strauss declared the incest taboo the ultimate cultural blow against nature: The incest taboo permitted humanity to make the passage from nature to culture.

Westermarck proposed that early association (e.g., that normally found between parent and offspring and among siblings) kills sexual desire. Hence, the desire does not exist to begin with. On the contrary, individuals who grow up together from an early age develop an actual sexual aversion for each other. Westermarck proposed this as an evolved mechanism with an obvious adaptive value: It prevents the deleterious effects of inbreeding.

In the largest-scale study to date, Arthur Wolf spent a lifetime examining the marital histories of Taiwanese women in a "natural experiment" dependent on a peculiar Chinese marriage custom.[15] Families used to adopt and raise little girls as future daughters-in-law. This meant that they grew up since early childhood with the family's son, their intended husband. Wolf compared the resulting marriages with those arranged between men and women who did not meet until their wedding day. Fortunately for science, official household registers were kept during the Japanese occupation of Taiwan. These registers provide detailed information on divorce rates and number of children, which Wolf took as measures of, respectively, marital happiness and sexual activity. His data supported the Westermarck Effect: Association in the first years of life appears to compromise marital compatibility. Others before Wolf studied marriages in Israeli kibbutzim, and they found that children do not have sexual intercourse with, let alone marry, unrelated children of the opposite sex with whom they have grown up together in the same peer group.

These findings are especially damaging to Freud, because if Westermarck is right, then Oedipal theory is wrong. Freud's thinking was premised on sexual attraction between members of the same family, an attraction that needs to be suppressed and sublimated. His theory would predict that unrelated boys and girls who have grown up together marry in absolute bliss because there is no taboo standing in the way of their primal sexual desires. In reality, however, the signs are that such marriages often end in misery. A second victim is Lévi-Strauss, who built his position entirely on the assumption that animals lead disorderly lives, in which they do whatever they please, including committing incest. Monkeys and apes are subject to exactly the same inhibitory mechanism as proposed by Westermarck, however. This was first observed by Kisaburo Tokuda in a group of Japanese macaques at the Kyoto Zoo, in the 1950s.[16] A young adult male who had risen to the top rank made full use of his sexual privileges, mating frequently with all the females except for one: his mother. This was not an isolated case; mother–son matings are strongly suppressed in all primates. Even in the sexy bonobos, this is the one partner combination in which intercourse is rare or absent. Observation of thousands of matings in a host of primates, both captive and wild, has demonstrated the suppression of incest.

Infanticide

A baffling phenomenon that also must be considered when discussing primate sexual reproduction is infanticide, which has become a dominant feature of theories about primate social organization and certain work on human monogamy. Infanticide was discovered in the 1960s by primatologists who saw certain species of monkeys, most famously the Hanuman langur, killing offspring in their group. If the male took over a harem of females, he would kill the infants before mating with the females. Initially, this behavior was considered pathological and abnormal, but we now have a multitude of data on birds, lions, bears, and mice providing evidence for its widespread existence.

Infanticide theory says the following: Let us say that a male takes over a group that contains females with dependent offspring, who are still nursing and taking up the female's resources. The male will then have to wait for a certain amount of time before he can fertilize the female because she is lactating and caring for her offspring. Lactation suppresses ovulation. If the male has a tenure for only four years or so and the waiting period lasts a year, he has lost 25 percent of his time with that particular female in terms of reproduction, which is the only thing that counts for evolutionary success. By killing the female's offspring, the new male gives himself an opportunity to fertilize her and produce offspring far earlier than if he had to wait. That is the crux of infanticide theory: Males kill dependent offspring of other males to increase their own reproduction. It is sexually selected behavior; that is, it is not a survival strategy but a reproductive strategy to counter competition from members of the same sex.

From the male's perspective, this may seem a good strategy, but from the female's perspective it is invariably counterproductive. Females must come up with ways to combat this destructive behavior. The anthropologist Sarah Hrdy, who developed the above theory, speculated about the different counterstrategies that females may employ, and how infanticide fits into social organization in general.[17]

One way females may prevent infanticide is through concealed ovulation. A female primate may hide the fact that she is ovulating, or she may have false ovulation so that the males perceive her as sexually attractive even though she is not fertile at the time. The idea here is that males will try to avoid killing infants that they sired themselves, not consciously (because we do not assume that male primates know about paternity), but by following a simple rule of thumb that has been selected into male behavior. The rule is: Do not attack offspring of females with whom you have mated in a particular time window before the offspring was born. Males following such a rule would avoid killing their own offspring.

Bonobo females may have taken this strategy to its extreme by having so many sexual encounters with so many males that no male can apply any simple rule to spare their own offspring, and so the males may have been selected to refrain from attacking any infants at all. The bonobo estrus cycle is longer than that of the chimpanzee. During the nonswollen days, chimpanzees will not mate; but bonobo females do, as do humans. Bonobo females have swellings when they are pregnant, when they are certainly not ovulating. Taking all this into account, the chimpanzee female has been calculated as having a swelling and being sexually receptive for only 5 percent of her adult life—only 5 percent of her entire life is the chimpanzee interested in sex and males interested in having sex with her. Comparatively speaking, that is very little time! In the bonobo, that percentage jumps to a whopping 50 percent. As mentioned, the female bonobo will engage in sex during the ovulatory phase of her cycle, and she has swellings when she is pregnant as well as when she is lactating. This can be construed as false advertising because she is saying to the males with her swelling, "I'm in estrus and fertile" when she really is not. So, female bonobos have sex for more than 50 percent of their adult life, and for humans the estimates are even higher.

Monogamy and Marriage

There are other ways of preventing infanticide, however, and humans have "chosen" exactly the opposite way of the bonobo. We have increased paternity certainty through the formation of heterosexual pair-bonds. The evolutionary scenario may have unfolded something like this: Female hominid ancestors suffered from infanticide, but some males became guards for females, meaning that as soon as he fertilized her, he traveled with her and stayed close to protect his future offspring from other males who might be infanticidal. Males who did so reproduced better in an environment in which infanticide was common than did males who moved from female to female. The guarding behavior gave way to provisioning: The male began to aid the female with the infant and take care of offspring himself, even if only to a limited degree. Such behavior would only benefit a male's reproduction if he could be reasonably sure of his paternity. From an evolutionary perspective, there is no point for males to invest energy in a female's offspring that are not his. And so paternity certainty had to increase for provisioning behavior to increase as well. These developments led to the evolution of the nuclear family, which benefited both the female's and the male's reproduction.[18]

The nuclear family can be viewed, then, as a device against infanticide but with a completely different strategy than that used by our close relative, the bonobo. The bonobo female confuses paternity to make males reluctant to kill any infants, but the human female took the opposite direction, providing paternity certainty to the male. The cost of this strategy—nothing is for free in nature—was greater control by males over female reproduction, as reflected in many practices in human society unknown in apes, the most important one being marriage. This transaction, which offers the male increased paternity certainty and the female paternal assistance, allows for shorter interbirth intervals, because, with males helping out, women can wean babies faster and speed up reproduction as a result. Chimpanzees and bonobos cannot produce offspring less than five or six years apart because lack of male care constrains the speed with which females can raise and produce offspring.

So, when our species moved in the direction of the nuclear family, when male care became a component of offspring rearing, we were able to speed up reproduction tremendously as compared to that of the great apes. Part of the success of our species thus resulted from our ability to develop a different, more efficient child-rearing system from that of our nearest relatives. The nuclear family, as we know it, is rather unique in the primate world, but it evolved in a larger context that is quite universal, relating to male–male competition over mates, the need to avoid inbreeding, and the advantage that females derive from countering male infanticide. For those skeptical about a possible role of infanticide in the shaping of human society, including the family, the deliberate killing of offspring of captured women after war is common in the anthropological record. The Bible also offers insights, such as the description of Pharaoh ordering all male children killed at birth (Exod. 1:16). Most famously, King Herod "sent forth, and slew all the children that were in Bethlehem, and in all its borders from two years old and under" (Matt. 2:16; see figure 2.4).

The human family probably was shaped by forces quite different from the romantic love emphasized today. It started out as an absolute necessity, an

Figure 2.4. "Slaughter of the Innocents"
Source: This woodcut by Addreas Osiander (1498–1552) is from *Harmoniae Euangelicae libri quator* (Antwerp: Matthaeus Crommius, 1540) and is reprinted courtesy of the Kessler Reformation Collection of the Pitts Theological Library at the Candler School of Theology at Emory University.

arrangement providing reproductive advantages in a harsh environment in which food was hard to obtain and protection against dangers priceless. Love came later, and it is related more to the way we pick partners and the need for long-term commitment.

Notes

1. See the epilogue to this volume by Robert Bellah.
2. Geoffrey F. Miller, *The Mating Mind: How Sexual Choice Shaped the Evolution of Human Nature* (New York: Doubleday, 2000).
3. Amotz Zahavi and Avishag Zahavi, *The Handicap Principle* (New York: Oxford University Press, 1997).
4. T. R. Birkhead, *Promiscuity: An Evolutionary History of Sperm Competition* (Cambridge, Mass.: Harvard University Press, 2000).
5. Frans B. M. de Waal, *Chimpanzee Politics: Power and Sex among Apes,* rev. ed. (Baltimore: Johns Hopkins University Press, 1998 [1982]).
6. Muzafer Sherif, O. J. Harvey, B. J. White, W. R. Hood, and C. W. Sherif, *Intergroup Conflict and Cooperation: The Robber's Cave Experiment* (Norman, Okla.: University Book Exchange, 1961 [1954]).

7. Deborah Tannen, *You Just Don't Understand: Women and Men in Conversation* (New York: William Morrow, 1990).

8. Robert M. Yerkes, *Almost Human* (New York: Century, 1925).

9. A. R. Parish and Frans B. M. de Waal, "The Other 'Closest Living Relative': How Bonobos (*Pan paniscus*) Challenge Traditional Assumptions about Females, Dominance, Intra- and Inter-Sexual Interactions, and Hominid Evolution," in *Evolutionary Perspectives on Human Reproductive Behavior*, ed. D. LeCroy and P. Moller (New York: Annals of the New York Academy of Sciences, 2000), vol. 907, 97–113.

10. Eduard P. Tratz and Heinz Heck, "Der afrikanische Anthropoide 'Bonobo,' eine neue Menschenaffengattung," *Säugetierkundliche Mitteilungen* 2 (1954): 97–101.

11. Frans B. M. de Waal, "Tension Regulation and Nonreproductive Functions of Sex in Captive Bonobos (*Pan paniscus*)," *National Geographic Research* 3 (1987): 318–35.

12. Frans B. M. de Waal, *Bonobo: The Forgotten Ape* (Berkeley: University of California Press, 1997).

13. Chie Hashimoto and Takeshi Furuichi, "Social Role and Development of Non-copulatory Sexual Behavior of Wild Bonobos," in *Chimpanzee Cultures*, ed. Richard W. Wrangham, W. C. McGrew, Frans B. M. de Waal, and P. Heltne (Cambridge, Mass.: Harvard University Press, 1994), 155–68.

14. Edward Westermarck, *The Origin and Development of the Moral Ideas*, vol. 1 (London: Macmillan, 1912).

15. Arthur P. Wolf, *Sexual Attraction and Childhood Association: A Chinese Brief for Edward Westermarck* (Stanford, Calif.: Stanford University Press, 1995).

16. Kisaburo Tokuda, "A Study of Sexual Behavior in the Japanese Monkey," *Primates* 3, no. 2 (1961–62): 1–40.

17. Sarah B. Hrdy, "Infanticide among Animals: A Review, Classification, and Examination of the Implications for the Reproductive Strategies of Females," *Ethology & Sociobiology* 1 (1979): 13–40.

18. C. P. van Schaik and R. I. M. Dunbar, "The Evolution of Monogamy in Large Primates: A New Hypothesis and Some Crucial Tests," *Behaviour* 115 (1990): 30–62.

Chapter 3
Sex, Marriage, and Family Life:
The Teachings of Nature

Stephen J. Pope

This chapter examines various types of scientifically based arguments about what nature teaches, and does not teach, concerning human sex, marriage, and the family. It investigates whether and how these natural teachings are captured in institutions of marriage and the family and in moral norms governing sexual behavior. The chapter has three sections: The first concerns evolutionary theory, the second takes up natural law ethics, and the third offers a natural law evaluation of evolutionary theory. My thesis is that contemporary natural law ethics ought to attempt a critical and selective appropriation of evolutionary views of sex, marriage, and the family.

It needs to be acknowledged that a treatment of this length can offer only a superficial discussion of a very complicated topic. This chapter can proceed only through some gross generalizations that ignore important differences between various schools of thought in both evolutionary theory and natural law ethics, the full analysis of which would require a more lengthy treatment for their full analysis.

Evolution and Sex, Marriage and Family

Evolutionary thinking about sex began with Darwin's *The Descent of Man and Selection in Relation to Sex* (1871).[1] Darwin proposed that some traits would be produced by sexual selection if the benefits of such traits were to outweigh their costs. He proposed two kinds of sexual selection: (1) intrasexual selection—male–male competition, seen in significant disparity between average male and female body size (the "sexual dimorphism" of elephant seals and gorillas), and in the evolution of weapons and ornamentation, for example, horns in stags; and (2) intersexual selection, in which females exercise choice of mates, a process that Darwin thought led to the evolution of male traits that females would find appealing, such as physical prowess in gorillas and the peacock's tail.

Sociobiologists investigate sexual selection in terms of differential "biological investments" made by males and females.[2] As a general rule, males in most mammal species copulate and move on without giving any more attention to the resulting offspring. Males from our own species are different, but why? A man makes 150 million sperm every day of his life and has "enough genetic information in a single ejaculation to repopulate half of the USA."[3] A woman, conversely, releases only 450 eggs in her entire reproductive lifetime. A man is theoretically capable of reproducing after every copulation, but a woman can bear one child a year and even then only until the onset of menopause. Men, of course, have been known to be fertile well after retirement age.

Evolutionists argue that this asymmetry leads to two competing sexual strategies. Men can afford to engage in casual sexual encounters because they are not forced by the facts of biology to face the consequences of impregnation. Women do not have this luxury. Because fertilization can follow a single sexual encounter and entails high costs, women must be much more selective and discriminating than men. Male sexual jealousy is universal, and the sexual "double standard" is very common.[4] Male fear of cuckoldry lies behind veils, chastity belts, female circumcision, harems, foot binding, and a host of other practices.

Pair-bonding can be a significant corrective to the male problematic. Concealed ovulation and constant sexual receptivity allow for nonreproductive sex that creates a bond between mates. The human sexual bond contrasts with the pattern among most other primates, including the highly sexual bonobos, whose sexual activity does not seem to build individualized male–female bonds. It is unclear, Malcolm Potts and Roger Scott observe, "whether any species other than humans, chimpanzees and some monkeys actually have orgasms."[5] The symmetrical balance of male–female orgasms, evolutionists suggest, may also function as a reciprocal bonding mechanism.[6] The human sexual bond is critically important in evolutionary terms because it provides a strong motivation for men to stay with their mates and to give them the kinds of aid, at least in the forms of protection and provisioning, that are critically important for the demanding task of rearing their vulnerable and dependent children. Perhaps, as Frans de Waal points out, this bonding process might have begun in evolutionary terms when males began to stay with their female mates to guard their vulnerable newborns against infanticide by other males.[7]

These conflicts led evolutionists to underscore the deeply conflicted nature of male sexuality, working from an innate proclivity for moderate polygamy toward an emotionally bonded monogamy. Yet men are not the only ones who struggle. Women are attracted to men other than their mates. Cuckoldry detracts from the man's interests much more than the woman's, but if discovered it can lead to desertion and a significant reduction of resources.[8] The ultimate male deterrent of course is the threat and use of physical violence. Most lethal is male-on-male violence; least common is female-on-female violence.[9]

Sociobiologists find competition in family life as well as mating patterns. According to the logic of Mendelian genetics, every child shares half her genes with each parent and half her genes with her siblings, but she is genetically identical with herself. Proceeding on the evolutionary assumption that degree of concern is proportionate to degree of genetic relatedness, sociobiologists argue that individuals are strongly prone to prefer their own interests to those of others. Thus in theory, and other things being equal, a child would be inclined to care for his or her own interests twice as much as for the interests of a sibling. Experience teaches that this preference can be a lot stronger. Sibling rivalry has biological roots, especially when energies are focused on eliciting resources from parents. For their part, parents can be expected, other things being equal, to treat their children equally because they share the same degree of genetic relatedness. But parents are inevitably faced with conflict between themselves and individual children, because children have genetic reasons for preferring their own interests to those of either their parents or siblings.[10]

The sociobiological approach to sex, marriage, and the family has been strongly criticized for genetic reductionism; biological determinism; "adaptationism"; and committing the naturalistic fallacy, that is, attempting to derive a moral "ought" from a natural "is."[11] The adaptationist assumption that every trait provides an advantage in the competition for reproduction led to some particularly farfetched sociobiological explanations, for example, regarding the alleged fitness benefits attending lifelong constitutional homosexuality.[12]

Evolutionary psychologists attempted to avoid these pitfalls. They are more careful and tend to be less easily convinced of "panadaptationism," or what Stephen Gould called "panglossianism,"[13] than early sociobiologists. They are more apt to take into account evolutionary by-products, evolutionary change, and neutral evolutionary drift, as well as other nonadaptive biological determinants (e.g., mutations).

Steven Pinker, who joins cognitive science to evolutionary psychology, insists: "To say that the mind is an evolutionary adaptation is not to say that all behavior is adaptive in Darwin's sense."[14] Behavior as such did not evolve—"what evolved was the mind,"[15] a complex functional system composed of "psychological faculties or mental modules" adapted to a vast array of specialized activities.[16] The mind is made up of a highly complicated network of specialized functions suited to solve countless particular kinds of challenges, to locate objects in motion, to move over difficult terrain, to locate edible food, and so on. Yet human minds operate within cultures, and they cannot be interpreted apart from them. Instead of explaining the adaptive value of certain behaviors, evolutionary psychologists theorize about the evolution of specialized mental traits that at one time at least were adaptive for members of the species. A greater acknowledgment of cultural variability made evolutionary psychologists less prone to move quickly from generalizations about nature to moral norms.

The evolutionary psychologist David Buss, however, has made the same kind of generalizations about sex that one finds in sociobiology. He maintains that men and women are characterized by inherent psychological differences regarding "mate selection." Men have evolved to be relatively more attracted to youth and physical beauty in women and women to be relatively more attracted to social status and economic success in men. Men, he holds, have a proclivity for casual sex, desire sexual variety, and are more subject to visual arousal.[17] Buss argues that his cross-cultural studies suggest that these tendencies are innate, part of the species' "biogram," and not just created by particular cultures.

The feminist anthropologist Sarah Hrdy laments the fact that so much energy has been spent on these kinds of preference studies.[18] According to Hrdy, sexual behavior is often much more complicated and reasoned than this position suggests. Thus the female preference for men with money makes a lot of sense in most contemporary societies, given the significant limits they impose on female economic opportunity.[19] Behavior traits need not be innate or rooted in biology to be pervasive across societies.

What does the evolutionary approach to sex imply for marriage? Marriage is a social contract, a prototypical case of "reciprocal altruism," a relationship based on balanced tit-for-tat exchanges that benefit both parties and provide the social basis for the development of "kin altruism." Altruism in its technical sociobiological sense is found in behavior that, intentionally or not, adds to its recipient's genetic success at some cost to the agent's fitness. "Kin selection"[20] theory accounts for the selection of biologically based affective predispositions to favor kin over nonkin in assistance giving, loyalty, self-denial, and so on. The theory of reciprocal altruism offers an evolutionary account of another important element of human conduct[21]: the widespread inclination to form alliances, partnerships, and cooperative agreements with nonrelated or distantly related kin. Various forms of direct reciprocity can be distinguished from the indirect reciprocity seen in actions directed to individuals that might be returned by third parties or larger collectivities.[22]

Marriage, evolutionists argue, functions as a form of mutually beneficial reciprocal altruism. Our culture presumes that romantic love precedes
marriage and benefits both parties. Yet reciprocity is also found in mating
practices in cultures with arranged marriages, live-in partners, or polygamy.
Mates need not be regarded as working from conscious motives to reproduce.
In fact, it is probably best if they are moved by romantic emotions, as long
as these contribute to the formation of reproductive pair-bonds rather than
leaving them fixed on nonreproductive sex. The brain and emotions are wired
to love and care for others. The metaphorical "selfish gene" works best with
fully emotionally developed adults who fall in love, bear children, and then
selflessly care for them.[23]

The term "reciprocity" should not disguise the fact that significant tension is built into the structure of the mating relation. Competing sexual strategies lead to frequent conflict among married couples over sexual accessibil-
ity, the allocation of money and other material resources, the investment of
time and effort, degrees of emotional commitment, and so forth. They can
also generate various forms of mutual deception, sexual infidelity, and abuse.
It certainly is not a pretty picture, Buss says, but knowledge of these "psychological mechanisms" and of the "crucial contexts that activate those mechanisms" brings both understanding and a basis for intervention, modification,
and perhaps even the improvement of behavior.[24]

One brief if oversimplified example suffices to illustrate this approach.
Buss argues, "A man's ability and willingness to provide a woman with resources are central to his mating value, central to her selection of him as
a marriage partner, central to the tactics that men use in general to attract
mates, and central to the tactics that men use to retain mates."[25] Marital dissolution worldwide is connected to male provisioning failure; but the converse, female provisioning failure, does not constitute legitimate grounds for
divorce in a single known culture.[26] Buss's point is that if society wants lasting
and stable marriages, it must allow men to be good providers.

What does this imply about ethics? Nature per se, Buss argues, does
not provide moral teachings but provides data to be used by various moral
perspectives. Instead of deriving the *ought* from the *is,* Buss seeks to use information about nature to clarify options for ethics, including means of em-
powering women. Identifying differences between men and women—even
differences rooted in one way or another in biological nature—need not be an
inherently sexist enterprise. Neither is it in any way definitive for morality,
unless someone thinks that what is natural is ipso facto either inevitable or
morally good. Thus even if it is natural for men to seek more partners and for
women to be more sexually discriminating, there is no need to regard these
predispositions as giving moral legitimacy to the double standard. Under-

standing the conditions that tend statistically to favor various "mating strategies" (e.g., when it "pays" a female to defect from one mate and become available for another) provides "the possibility of choosing which to activate and
which to leave dormant."[27] We are not left with absolutely no moral resources,
however. Nature may be amoral but, Buss notes, it is more compatible with
some moral perspectives than others. He regards monogamy as excessively
restrictive. The sheer plethora of sexual diversity lends support, Buss thinks,
to an ethic of toleration.

Natural Law

In some ways, one would be hard pressed to find two positions more opposed than evolutionary theory and natural law ethics. Saint Thomas Aquinas,
the classical exponent of medieval law theory, regarded bestiality, sodomy,
autoeroticism, and any interference with the natural finality of the "marriage
act" as "unnatural," but he also regarded adultery, fornication, and rape as
violations of the natural law (though according to the biological purpose of
sex, these acts were attacks on natural law as based in "right reason"). "Natural" for Thomas meant "good," not morally neutral or premoral. He valued
marriage and the family as social institutions that allow for the expression of
natural inclinations in a way that promotes the good of individuals and the
community. They are natural but not reduceable to mere biology.

Theologically, these natural inclinations are understood in terms of the
order of creation produced by God, the "Author of nature." Because we live in a
fallen state, traditional Christianity taught, we are constantly prone to deviate
from the order of nature, and so, ideally, sacraments, prayer, and ethics work
under the influence of grace to restore human behavior to its proper natural
order. And of course for Thomas the richest level of human existence is not
nature but grace, the realm of sanctity, asceticism, spirituality, eschatology,
and especially their culmination in eternal union with God. As the rational
creature's "participation" in the eternal law of God, the natural law provides
the basic and elementary—if not the most elevated or excellent—moral framework regulating sexual activity, spousal interaction, and family relations.

Natural law includes the proper moral ordering of love, an essential capacity shared by all human beings and indeed, analogically, by all creatures.
Love was above all a metaphysical reality for Thomas, a movement to a good
appropriate to the agent's nature. As the first inclination of appetite to the
good,[28] love is the principle of action.[29] Human beings, Thomas thought,
naturally love one another. The order of charity, based on the cooperation of
grace with natural love, moves us to care for "the nearest and dearest." We

are tied by matter and form to biological relations and by affection and so-cial communion to close friends, both within and outside the family circle. We love those nearest to us more than those who are more distant. Relations based upon biological connection have a general priority over all other kinds of union because they "touch our very substance" and are therefore prior to and more permanent than (prior et immobilior) all other relations, all of which can change over time. It is morally "fitting" that we love our parents more than acquaintances, even if the latter are more interesting or attractive in other ways, and it is right that we love our own children more than others'.[30] The subject of love cares for the needy object of love, both inside and outside the family, but parental care is "most necessary for the common good."[31] And, of course, by this Thomas meant not merely physical care but especially spiri-tual guidance.[32] Because one's children are "part" of oneself, parents love their children more than vice versa. This natural connection even grounds the moral legitimacy of using violence, at least as a last resort—to defend one's children from lethal harm because "one is bound to take more care of one's own life than of another's."[33]

Our usual sense of the term "love" emphasizes action, commitment, and concern, but Thomas also understood love to be rooted in "complacency."[34] He believed that the subject of love must experience a moment of acceptance, appreciation, and quiescent acceptance of what is good before it moves into its active promotion and pursuit. Mutuality is a fact of human psychology: We tend to love those who love us and to ignore or be indifferent to others, and we take pleasure in those who take pleasure in our company. Every person is created in the image of God, capable of eternal fellowship with God, and therefore a "neighbor"; no one is excluded from the "universe of moral obli-gation" on any grounds.[35]

Love for those who are needy is expressed in the virtue of mercy, but here again the natural order of love is retained in Christian ethics. Jules Toner cap-tures the sense of care for Aquinas when he says that care is "only the form love takes when the lover is attentive to the beloved's need."[36] Thomas did not understand caregiving in a narrowly parochial way, as a love of kith and kin that is essentially unconcerned about more remote people. To be sure, Thomas believed that because the goal of almsgiving is to meet the needs of others in a sufficient manner, they should not be distributed with an utter lack of discrimination.[37] Thomas, moreover, continued the tradition set by earlier canonists and theologians who claimed that almsgiving should ob-serve the order of charity, "which requires that, other things being equal, we should, in preference, help those who are more closely connected with us."[38] First priority among all connections that bind a person was given to ties of common household and especially to "natural friendships, based upon ties of blood, like those of parents for their children."[39] Thus to impoverish oneself and one's family to aid the poor was considered by Thomas to be sinful rather than heroically virtuous.[40]

Marriage and family, however, do not always take priority over other objects of love. Thomas recognized multiple schemes of priority relevant to different spheres of life, modes of connection, and shared goods—for example, the "intercourse of kinsmen is in natural matters, that of fellow citizens is in civic matters, that of the faithful is in spiritual matters, and so forth."[41] Because different spheres of social life require different priority systems, claims of kinship only precede other claims in the arena of basic well-being. Thus in cases of conflict between needs of a friend and needs of a stranger, the urgency of the latter can override the prima facie priority given to the former. Even claims of kinship can be overridden by more urgent need from other quarters; for example, one may "give some costly delicacy to a sick servant, that he does not give to his own son in sound health,"[42] and one ought to "succor a stranger, in extreme necessity, rather than one's own father, if he is not in such urgent need."[43]

Returning to the broad perspective on the created order, we can recall that Thomas presumed a normative and primarily philosophical view of nature based on Aristotelian finality: A person functioning according to his or her inbuilt inclinations is acting "according to nature"; departures from these natural inclinations amount to harmful contradictions to nature. Caring more for a business associate than for one's own children would be morally disordered. Some departures from nature are more grievous and therefore more morally grave than others. For instance, in sexual ethics, bestiality and masturbation are more direct assaults on the order of nature than, say, fornication and seduction.

Natural sex takes place between a man and a woman and in a way that does not deliberately obstruct the spontaneous outcome of sexual intercourse. Thomas held that we have an ethical obligation to conform to the natural purpose of sex for two reasons: (1) Doing so is good for the agent, as is every act "according to nature"; and (2) it adheres to the will of God, the Author of nature. Contemporary natural law ethicists continue to view God as the Author of nature, but those accepting evolutionary theory do not accept the notion of an "intelligent design" common among some evangelical Christians.[44] They presume some version of a God who creates in an improvisational way through the patterns and contingencies of the evolutionary process.[45] This is a crucially important theological point, because how one sees God in relation to nature significantly influences the kind of normative weight one is liable to expect to find in natural structures, including those involved in sex and reproduction.

Contemporary Catholic ethicists divide not over whether sex has natural purposes but over their normative status. Traditionalists argue that each and every act of intercourse ought to remain open to procreation, typically, as in the case of John Paul II, because doing so is in accord with the plan of God and the only way fully to give oneself in radical love. This position amounts to a personalist reconfiguration of the Thomistic precedent.

Revisionists, in contrast, find it difficult to know how to approach this claim, because it seems to be an attempt to describe the nature of love but is not subject to any means of empirical confirmation or even examination. Phenomenological descriptions are prone to circularity: Phenomenon X has the traits A, B, and C. Anyone who does not find these traits does not grasp the nature of X, and anyone who claims to understand phenomenon X in the absence of A, B, and C is simply mistaken about the meaning of X. True self-giving love cannot include artificial contraception, and anyone who claims that true self-giving love is compatible with the use of artificial contraception simply has misunderstood the nature of radical self-giving love. This approach suffers from circularity: It posits that a particular virtue includes certain necessary conditions and then argues that any failure to include all stipulated conditions by definition falls short of the virtue—indeed, sinfully so. Whoever controls the stipulations controls the discussion, which is not subject to review on empirical grounds.

Revisionists, in any case, are prone to rely more significantly on ordinary experience. They hold that marriages need to be open to procreation as a general good shared over the course of their life together but not in every act of intercourse. They claim that complete self-giving love—say, in a forty-year-old married couple with seven children—is not necessarily frustrated by the attempt to foreclose the possibility of further procreation. Though traditionalists hold that artificial birth control is never licit, revisionists regard it as a general "premoral disvalue" but judge its concrete moral status on a case-by-case basis.[46]

One point that divides traditionalists and revisionists concerns the existence of kinds of acts that are considered to be "intrinsically evil," that is, material acts that can never be ethically legitimate for any intentions and under any circumstances. The traditionalist, at least one of a more rigorously consistent nature, for example, would hold that a hemophiliac husband infected with HIV is not allowed ethically to use a condom to protect his wife from contracting the virus because the use of an artificial birth control device is against the natural law. His only options are to practice abstention or to have intercourse and accept the risk that his wife might contract the disease.[47] The revisionist argues that intention, relationship, circumstances, and consequences all have to be considered when making a moral decision of this degree of complexity and conflict. The former position carries the advantage of clarity and consistency, but it is attended by the disadvantage of confusing goods that in general and in the abstract contribute to human flourishing with the specific and practical needs of concrete individuals who are striving to live well in very difficult situations. The same kinds of concerns obtain in difficult cases involving divorce and remarriage, same-sex marriage, sterilization, adoption, and a host of related issues.

Natural Law and Evolutionary Theory

We can now turn to the relation between natural law and contemporary evolutionary theory. Again, their prima facie relation is one of uncompromising mutual opposition. Nature is a competitive if also cooperative evolutionary experiment, not a smoothly integrated "order of creation," as Thomas thought. According to evolutionary theory, human beings, rather than initially created in a well-ordered manner and then fallen by a perverse act of pride, have always been conflicted, manipulative, selfish, and prone to deceit and violence, though capable of derivative forms of altruism.

This image of humanity, echoing in many ways the writings of Thomas Hobbes, is almost the mirror opposite of the social and teleological anthropology that has typically been presupposed by natural law. So whereas the former builds an ethic out of natural ordering for the sake of the highest good, the latter uses ethics to control it for the sake of survival. Natural law regards marriage as the normative context of sex and procreation; evolutionism views only an array of "mating strategies" to which it is bound to be morally neutral. The former regards the whole sphere of the "moral" as a way of describing the pursuit of true happiness through virtue and right action; the latter regards the moral as, at best, a means of resolving intragroup conflict and attaining a modicum of social stability and order.

Nature in evolutionary theory is neither purposive nor normative, for two important reasons: (1) Purposes come from the minds of human agents and do not reside in physical structures, acts, or processes unless a mind puts them there (as in designing an automobile engine); and (2) even if there were natural purposes in organisms, one cannot infer, at least from a purely scientific standpoint, that such purposes are morally obligatory (biologists do not say that bats "ought" to eat bugs or that our lungs have a "moral obligation" to breathe).

In response to the first claim, an advocate of natural law might point out that evolution is replete with examples of functionality: Organs evolve because they are adaptive—the eye to see, the heart to pump blood—this is their "purpose," why they exist in the first place. Purposes, unlike intentions, do not have to be produced by minds to exist in nature. Applied to sex, natural law theory is right to hold that the natural function of sex, at least in the human species, includes reproduction and affective bonding. Yet evolutionists do not conceive of evolution in terms of Aristotelian final causes. Organisms function the way they do because of natural selection. As the evolutionist Ernst Mayr explains, "It is illegitimate to describe evolutionary processes or trends as goal-directed (teleological). Selection rewards past phenomena (mutation, recombination, etc.) but does not plan for the future, at least not in any specific way."[48] Evolution is a wasteful process of trial and error; changes in the evolutionary process are not goal-directed. Species continue to exist or evolve because they have specific traits that give them a fitness advantage under specific evolutionary circumstances. There is no fixed order of nature, no progress, no inherent natural purpose unrelated to reproduction.

"Natural" in evolutionary terms simply means predictable and occurring with some regularity under set conditions. Thus it is "natural" for people to form in-groups, to discriminate against members of out-groups, to help friends, and to be suspicious of strangers. It is "natural" to deceive, threaten, manipulate, mutilate, and kill one's enemies under certain conditions. Frans de Waal and others have argued that engaging in infanticide can be "natural."[49] As T. H. Huxley insisted some time ago, "The thief and the murderer follow nature just as much as the philanthropist."[50]

Is there any way to harmonize natural law and evolutionary theory, or at least put them within shouting distance of one another? No, at least not if they are understood to be two competing theories of science, moral perspectives, or ideologies. Yet it seems to me that differentiating scientific and moral modes of discourse provides a basis for thinking about rapprochement between the science provided by evolutionary theory and the moral insight offered by natural law ethics. One cannot help but notice how often evolutionists slip into subtle, or not so subtle, forms of inappropriate moralizing—for example, when they endorse the value of tolerance, accept not only the dominance of the "selfish gene" but also the selfish individual, encourage a sexual ethic of "consenting adults," and describe the universe as an "amoral" construction of a "Blind Watchmaker,"[51] a metaphor that is no less philosophical than the contrary theistic claim that the universe has a moral purpose. Natural lawyers, for their part, often make assumptions about empirical matters that are subject to scientific investigation, for example, when they describe human beings as "social," make judgments about the status of embryonic life, and offer generalizations about the psychological and social effects of certain kinds of sexual activity. In response to traditionalist natural law views of homosexuality, for example, one can ask: Must all forms of gay sex always be inherently morally debilitating? And how would one ever know enough to make this kind of sweeping empirical generalization? Evolutionists qua scientists can speak about purposes only in the sense of biological functions, and not in a moral sense. Conversely, advocates of natural law increase the plausibility of their positions to the extent that they show some empirical basis for them.

Applied to sex, marriage, and the family, this suggests that natural law can appropriate scientific evolutionary claims about human behavior without also accepting ideological positions that are often joined to them. Evolutionary psychology is unhelpful, and even downright destructive, as a moral ideology based on unsubstantiated speculation, metaphysical materialism, ontological reductionism, genetic determinism, and ethical egoism. Natural law challenges evolutionism when it paves over the complexities, richness, and diversity of human behavior.[52]

This said, there is no reason why natural law ethics cannot accept the findings of evolution regarding the strictly biological dimensions of human sexuality, sexual behavior, marriage, and the family. As in Thomas's day, natural law today needs to build upon available knowledge of nature rather than ignore it. "Truth cannot be against truth."[53]

Evolutionary theory offers theories about common human experiences: Siblings are rivals; young males fight, either physically or intellectually, to enhance their status and reputation with the opposite sex; mothers do not like men to threaten their babies; and so forth. There seems to be no reason why natural law cannot allow that there are some ultimate, remote evolutionary reasons for these patterns. Nor is it odd to think of the development of morality as a way of monitoring compliance and noncompliance in situations of reciprocity and cooperation and of inhibiting forms of conflict and promoting order in the midst of competing incentives.

Sexual desire presents an area of interest to both evolutionists and natural lawyers. Sexual desire is an enormously powerful motivation devised by nature for spreading genes into the next generation. We were sexy long before we could conjugate verbs; sexual desire preceded by many millions of years the exponential growth of the human brain between 600,000 and 100,000 years ago. These millions of years have "wired" us to be among the most sexually active of all species. And of course advertising agencies have become extremely clever at manipulating our evolved pleasure circuitry with artificial stimuli that lead to forms of pleasure detached from interpersonal love, let alone procreation.

Evolutionary insights into the special channeling of care can also be appropriated by natural law. It comes as no surprise to natural law theory that parents naturally give special care to their children, that married couples cooperate in systems of reciprocity, and that family ties call for greater degrees of self-denial than do many other forms of friendship.[54] Nor is it a surprise that, in general, children without healthy parents in an intact family will tend to suffer and be at a social disadvantage.

Evolutionary thinkers tend to stress the dark side of human nature. This is in part because they have followed the modern reductionistic tendency to explain higher human capacities in terms of lower drives and pressures. Natural law, conversely, reverses this direction and attempts to relate the lower impulses of our nature to our most noble aspirations. It strives to be realistic about the various causes of human discontent and disorder but also to appreciate the fact that men and women have significant natural capacities for love, care, and commitment within marriage and the family.

Natural law relates moral standards to the human good, which includes sex, companionship, reproduction, and kinship. This affirmation is significant not only for communities in which the value of marriage, sex, and procreation is called into question (as it has been with periodic revivals of Manicheanism) but also for communities like our own, in which erotic desires are overvalued, limited only by voluntary consent, and not adequately balanced with a commitment to more important human goods.

This said, natural law does not regard the human good as exhausted by sex, companionship, reproduction, and kinship, which when taken as supreme goods imply, respectively, various forms of hedonism, sentimentalism, familialism, nepotism, and tribalism. The human good embraces *all* aspects of human nature—not only the physical, chemical, and biological but also the social, cultural, psychological, emotional, intellectual, moral, and religious dimensions of human existence. This is important in societies that place so much importance on the family as a "haven in a heartless world" that they fail to appreciate both higher goods than the family and the significance of wider responsibilities to social justice within the larger community.[55]

Human flourishing incorporates the full range of human goods and assimilates amenable components of human nature. Presuming that they exist, evolved "inbuilt mechanisms" of the sort discussed by Pinker and Buss provide "matter" to be related to the larger natural movement to the good. Consider some specifics. Sexual jealousy can be virtuous if it means that one is vigilant in protecting one's beloved or intolerant of unfaithfulness (indifference to a spouse's philandering is hardly a sign of a healthy marriage). But jealousy can obviously also be a terrible vice when it leads to disordered possessiveness, an attempt unjustly to control the beloved, and even the wildly irrational suspicion and murderous rage of Othello.

Consider also what evolutionists have identified as an "inbuilt mechanism" that identifies individuals as one of "us" or one of "them." This tendency can be used for good, as when it creates strong bonds in a business or small company, or the camaraderie of Henry V's "band of brothers." But it has also been liable to manipulation by dictators, and it has played some role in the development of xenophobia, racism, mob violence, exploitation, colonialism, and genocide. Both of these evolved mechanisms can be developed in virtuous or vicious ways, and their expression depends on human choices, social context, and the moral ideals for which we strive.

The greatest human moral ideal is love, the affective affirmation of, and movement toward, what is recognized to be good. This includes not only romantic love but also benevolence, friendship, and solidarity. Natural law strives to shape every truly human act to be an expression of love, either as an affirmation of what is good or as the rejection of what is evil. One of the most powerful expressions of romantic love is sex, which has the capacity to put in bodily form the content of one's affections, will, and ideals. Human sex is complex and multifunctional. Natural law argues that sexual activity needs to be placed as much as possible at the service of love and commitment. The moral capacity to hold all three of these goods together—sex, love, and commitment—radically separates us from other primates. One of the greatest ways in which we care for one another is through sex. Conversely, one of the most painful ways in which people harm one another is through the misuse of sex, particularly when pursued without love and commitment. According to natural law, Don Juan's pursuit of sexual conquests is not just another strategy; it is cruel exploitation—even among consenting adults.

The institutionalization of love is found in marriage and the family. Marriage is a human way of ordering the sexual and reproductive inclinations we have in common with animals as well as the distinctive inbuilt mechanisms that comprise our own distinctive humanity. Animals go into heat, mate, and rear their young according to patterns set by evolution. Human beings, conversely, undertake interpersonal and social commitments, forge strong affective bonds, engage in frequent sex, and deliberately take up a way of life that promotes the ongoing growth of the human purposes of sexuality. Marriage and the family are thus "natural" in the same sense that Aristotle regarded forming friendships and living in political communities as "natural" to human beings. They are institutions that build upon and allow for the satisfaction of natural desires in a way that contributes to human well-being in a comprehensive sense—individually, interpersonally, and communally.

Natural law pushes moral development to ideals higher than the purely reproductive function of other mammals. Religiously speaking, this can be included in a larger, sacramental view of reality. Because of the incredible cognitive powers that the evolutionary process has bequeathed us, if we do not strive to make sex, marriage, and the family the scene of altruism, integrity, and even moral nobility, they will surely lead to levels of harm and self-destruction far worse than anything one would ever see in the animal kingdom.

Notes

1. Charles Darwin, *The Descent of Man and Selection in Relation to Sex,* 2nd ed. (New York: Hurst and Company, 1874).

2. See Edward Osborne Wilson, *Sociobiology: The New Synthesis* (Cambridge, Mass.: Harvard University Press, 1975); and Edward Osborne Wilson, *On Human Nature* (Cambridge, Mass.: Harvard University Press, 1978).

3. Malcolm Potts and Roger Scott, *Ever Since Eve: The Evolution of Human Sexuality* (New York: Cambridge University Press, 1999), 30.

4. Martin Daly, Margo Wilson, and Suzanne J. Weghorst, "Male Sexual Jealousy," *Ethology and Sociobiology* 3 (1982): 11–27; David M. Buss, *The Dangerous Passion: Why Jealousy Is as Necessary as Love and Sex* (New York: Free Press, 2000).

5. Potts and Scott, *Ever Since Eve,* 108. For an earlier discussion (1981) of this issue, see Sarah Blaffer Hrdy, *The Woman That Never Evolved* (Cambridge, Mass.: Harvard University Press, 1981), chap. 8.

6. Potts and Scott, *Ever Since Eve,* 102. See the arguments for and against the "sex as glue" theory by Jared Diamond in *Why Is Sex Fun? The Evolution of Human Sexuality* (New York: Basic Books, 1997), chap. 4.

7. See chapter 2 in this volume by Frans de Waal and Amy Pollick.

8. See Martin Daly and Margo Wilson, *Sex, Evolution, and Behavior* (North Scituate, Mass.: Duxbury Press, 1978).

9. Martin Daly and Margo Wilson, *Homicide* (New York: Aldine de Gruyter, 1988).

10. Robert Trivers, "Parent–Offspring Conflict," *American Zoologist* 14 (1994): 249–64.

11. For criticisms, see Philip Kitcher, *Vaulting Ambition* (Cambridge, Mass.: MIT Press, 1985); and Stephen J. Gould, "Evolution: The Pleasures of Pluralism," *New York Review of Books,* June 26, 1997, available at http://cogweb.ucla.edu/Debate/Gould.html.

12. See Richard C. Lewontin, "Sociobiology as an Adaptationist Program," *Behavioral Science* 24 (1979): 5–14; and Michael Ruse, *Homosexuality: A Philosophical Inquiry* (New York: Oxford University Press, 1988), 84–129.

13. Stephen J. Gould and Richard C. Lewontin, "The Spandrels of San Marco and the Panglossian Paradigm: A Critique of the Adaptationist Programme," *Proceedings of the Royal Society of London,* series B, vol. 205 (1979): 581–98.

14. Steven Pinker, *How the Mind Works* (New York: W. W. Norton, 1997), 41. Other key texts in evolutionary psychology include Jerome H. Barkow, Leda Cosmides, and John Tooby, eds., *The Adapted Mind: Evolutionary Psychology and the Generation of Culture* (New York: Oxford University Press, 1992); and, in popular literature, Robert Wright, *The Moral Animal: A New Science of Evolutionary Psychology* (New York: Pantheon Books, 1994).

15. Pinker, *How the Mind Works,* 42.

16. Ibid., 27.

17. David Buss, *The Evolution of Desire: Strategies of Human Mating* (New York: Basic Books, 1994), 215–16.

18. See Sarah Blaffer Hrdy, "Raising Darwin's Consciousness: Female Sexuality and the

Prehominid Origins of Patriarchy," *Human Nature* 8 (1977): 1–49. Also see Hrdy, *Mother Nature: Instincts and How They Share the Human Species* (New York: Ballantine, 1999).

19. See John Horgan, "The New Social Darwinists," *Scientific American,* October 1995, 151. A major counterposition to Buss and other evolutionary psychology has been developed by Alice Eagley. See Alice H. Eagley, Richard D. Ashmore, Mona G. Makhijani, and Laura C. Longo, "What Is Beautiful Is Good, But . . . : A Meta-Analytic Review of Research on the Physical Attractiveness Stereotype," *Psychological Bulletin* 110 (1991): 109–28; and Eagley, "The Science and Politics of Comparing Men and Women," *American Psychologist* 50 (1995): 145–58. More generally, see Ruth Bleier, ed., *Feminist Approaches to Science* (New York: Teachers College Press, 1986).

20. See William D. Hamilton, "The Genetical Evolution of Social Behaviour," *Journal of Theoretical Biology* 7 (1964): 1–52.

21. Robert L. Trivers, "The Evolution of Reciprocal Altruism," *Quarterly Review of Biology* 46 (1971): 35–57; Robert M. Axelrod, *The Evolution of Cooperation* (New York: Basic Books, 1984).

22. See Richard D. Alexander, *The Biology of Moral Systems* (New York: Aldine de Gruyter, 1987).

23. Richard Dawkins, *The Selfish Gene,* new ed. (Oxford: Oxford University Press, 1989).

24. Buss, *Evolution of Desire,* 159.

25. Ibid., 177.

26. Ibid., 178.

27. Ibid., 209.

28. Thomas Aquinas, *Summa Theologiae,* I-II, q. 17, a. 8. Latin references are to Sancti Thomae Aquinatis, *Summa Theologiae* (Madrid: Biblioteca de Autores Cristianos, 1963). The translation used is Saint Thomas Aquinas, *Summa theologiae,* trans. Fathers of the English Dominican Province, 3 vols. (New York: Benziger Brothers, 1947).

29. Aquinas, II-II, q. 23, a. 6.

30. Thomas used the notion of "right" in an objective sense rather than in the sense of moral power possessed by individual moral agents. See Odon Lottin, *Études de Morale Historie et Doctrine* (Brussels: Gembloux, 1961), 171–73; and Lottin, *Le Droit Naturel chez Saint Thomas d'Aquin et ses prédécesseurs,* 2nd ed. (Bruges: Beyaert, 1931).

31. Aquinas, II-II, q. 153, a. 3.

32. Aquinas, II-II, q. 10, a. 12.

33. Aquinas, II-II, q. 64, a. 7.

34. Frederick E. Crowe, S.J., "Complacency and Concern in the Thought of St. Thomas," *Theological Studies* 20 (1959): 1–39, 198–230, 343–95.

35. See Helen Fein, *Imperial Crime and Punishment: The Massacre at Jallianwalla Bagh and British Judgment,* 1919–1920 (Honolulu: University Press of Hawaii, 1977), chap. 1, esp. 18–19.

36. Jules Toner, *The Experience of Love* (Washington, D.C.: Corpus Books, 1968), 80.

37. Aquinas, II-II, q. 32, a. 10.

38. See Brian Tierney, *Medieval Poor Law: A Sketch of Canonical Theory and Its Application in England* (Berkeley: University of California Press, 1959), 44–67.

39. Aquinas, II-II, q. 26, a. 7.

40. Aquinas, II-II, q. 32, a. 9.

41. Aquinas, II-II, q. 31, a. 3.

42. Aquinas, I, q. 20, a. 4, ad. 2.

43. Aquinas, II-II, q. 31, a. 3.

44. On intelligent design, see Michael Behe, *Darwin's Black Box: The Biochemical Challenge to Evolution* (New York: Free Press, 1996); and William Dembski, ed., *Mere Creation: Science, Faith, and Intelligent Design* (Downers Grove, Ill.: InterVarsity Press, 1998). Phillip E. Johnson is one of the major opponents of theistic evolutionism; see his *Darwin on Trial* (Washington, D.C.: Regency Gateway, 1991).

45. Evolutionary theism has been developed in more detail by systematic theologians but not yet explicitly related to natural law ethics. See the writings of the Anglicans John Polkinghorne and Arthur Peacocke, the Roman Catholic process theologian John Haught, and the Reformed physicist Howard van Til.

46. See Louis Janssens, "Norms and Priorities in a Love Ethics," *Louvain Studies* 6 (1977): 207–38; and Janssens, "Ontic Good and Evil: Premoral Values & Disvalues," *Louvain Studies* 12 (1987): 62–82.

47. Potts and Scott, *Ever Since Eve*, 249.

48. Ernst Mayr, *Toward a New Philosophy of Biology: Observations of an Evolutionist* (Cambridge, Mass.: Harvard University Press, 1988), 60.

49. See chapter 2 in this volume by de Waal and Pollick; and see Glenn Hausfater and Sarah B. Hrdy, eds., *Infanticide: Comparative and Evolutionary Perspectives* (New York: Aldine de Gruyter, 1984).

50. Thomas H. Huxley, *Evolution and Ethics, and Other Essays* (New York: D. Appleton, 1894), 77.

51. Richard Dawkins, *The Blind Watchmaker* (New York: W. W. Norton, 1986).

52. See Steven Rose, *Lifelines* (New York: Penguin, 1998).

53. See John Paul II, *Fides et Ratio: On the Relationship between Faith and Reason* (Boston: Daughters of St. Paul, 1998); see also "Address of Pope John Paul II to the Pontifical Academy of Sciences," *L'Osservatore Romano*, English ed., October 22, 1996.

54. Thomistic views of natural love have been appropriated by Don Browning, "Biology, Ethics, and Narrative in Christian Family Theory," in *Promises to Keep: Decline and Renewal of Marriage in America*, ed. David Popenoe, Jean Bethke Elshtain, and David Blankenhorn (Lanham, Md.: Rowman & Littlefield, 1996). See also Stephen Pope, *The Evolution of Altruism and the Ordering of Love* (Washington, D.C.: Georgetown University Press, 1994).

55. See the epilogue to this volume by Robert Bellah.

Part II
Happily Ever After? Profiles in Motion of Marriage and the Family

Chapter 4
The Family as Contested Terrain

Robert Wuthnow

When one ponders the problems and perils of American families, it is difficult to know where to begin and even harder to find where to end. Should the high divorce rate and precarious foundations of marriage head the list? Is the number of single-parent families of special concern? How about births to teenage mothers, absent fathers, and the so-called fragile families that result? Should questions about parenting, day care, time spent with children, and the transmission of values from one generation to the next be included? What about dating, sexual behavior, preparation for marriage, and expectations about marriage among the nation's youth? Where do we consider domestic violence, spousal abuse, and child abuse? Or the alcohol and drug-related problems that tear families apart?

Do we include the special questions that arise in consideration of same-sex unions, of the needs for surrogate families among the millions of Americans who are not married or who live alone, and of the elderly who may be without families? Should emphasis be given to the particular problems of low-income families and to the needs of those with mental or physical disabilities? Does the list of concerns extend to the many families in which acute depression is a problem? Does it include medical and health-related concerns, grief and bereavement, and questions about emotional and physical support? How about the problems of families that have been victimized by crime or have a member in prison? Is the safety of neighborhoods, playgrounds, and schools an important aspect of family life that should be taken into consideration? Families' worries about securing a decent education for their children?

Does the list extend to the millions of new and recent immigrant families that struggle with language barriers, discrimination, and separation from the extended families they left behind? Shall we include credit card debt, overspending, and family bankruptcies in our list of family problems? What about the job-related pressures that rob families of time together? Do we consider the colonization of homes and family space by television and advertising? Where do we include questions about divorce laws, the so-called marriage penalty in the nation's tax codes, corporate policies toward family leave and child care, and whether or not wealthy families should transmit family wealth more easily to their heirs? And how shall we consider the implications of scientific developments in genomics and human genetic engineering that may profoundly alter what we mean by such words as "parent," "child," "family," or "person"?

The problems and perils of American families: How easily that phrase courses from brain to fingertips to word processor. Clearly, it is difficult to know where to draw the line. If all of us have been, are, or would like to be part of a family, then the problems and perils of American families are the problems and perils of us all. The *Journal of Marriage and Family* should be renamed the *Journal of Everyone*.

How, then, do we think about the role of religion in relation to family problems? Shall attention focus on the role of churches, synagogues, mosques, and temples in sustaining marriage? Their participation in efforts to provide day care? Services to low-income families? Food and shelter for the homeless? Support for the elderly? Their potential to lobby for certain bills deemed by certain political leaders to be favorable to families? Their preaching, youth programs, counseling centers, and self-help groups? Is any aspect of religion too remote for consideration? Should more attention be paid to basic teachings about the Fatherhood of God, the relational qualities suggested by the Christian doctrine of the Trinity, the symbolism associated with the church as Christ's bride, or with Mary as the Mother of God? Where do priorities rise and fall? Should religious leaders pay more attention to family ministries and less to preaching? Devote more time to marriage counseling and less to social justice? Or is it so easy to disentangle the problems and perils of families from these other concerns?

It is important to begin with questions like these that point to the expansiveness of topics that might be considered in relation to the American family. It is equally important to remind ourselves that families are not simply an arena of mind-boggling trouble. Millions of Americans get married, stay married, and live happily together. The vast majority of married Americans, in fact, report being very happy with their marriages. Many who divorce remarry and continue to be married. The trend in numbers of divorces is not always up; it is sometimes down. The same is true of trends in child abuse, youth-related violence, and teen births. Busy and financially challenged families find ways of providing care for their children. And Americans continue to have high expectations for their families and devote vast amounts of time and money to providing for their children. Americans want their families to be better and the social circumstances that support families to be better. It bothers them to think that the family is in disarray.

A significant effort has been mounted in recent years to better understand what is wrong with American families and to identify ways in which family life can be improved. It is this effort that has of necessity defined the problems and perils of American families in strategic ways—in ways that seek to identify some of the central concerns, the most significant negative trends, and the most serious factors contributing to those trends. It is an ongoing effort. But much has been learned about the state of families in the United States in recent years. Research has documented the rising divorce rate, the growing number of children reared in single-parent families, and increasing rates of child abuse. Ample evidence about rates of cohabitation, the timing of marriage, and numbers of children is also available. To be sure, there is much still to be understood about the causes and consequences of contemporary patterns of family life. Yet the compelling questions about American families have as much to do with interpretation as they do with evidence.

Hardly anyone disagrees that the family is not functioning as well as it should. The family has become a topic that pundits, public officials, social scientists, lawyers, clergy, and community leaders seem unable to leave alone. Diagnosing its ills has become a cultural industry. Opinions and recommendations reflect the full range of cultural, religious, political, and ethnic perspectives. Indeed, one might say that the family's malaise has become a cultural trope. We read into the family our deepest values and our darkest fears. It symbolizes our ideals and our shortfalls in realizing those ideals.

Understanding the ideals that give meaning to family debates is especially important in the context of questions about the role of religion. If congregations and religious leaders can help to strengthen the family, as many hope they can, it will not be only through setting up day care and teen-pregnancy centers or lobbying for better laws and government programs aimed at supporting marriage or protecting children. It will be through the power that religious institutions have to shape our values, to supply us with interpretations, and to provide us with narratives and traditions in which to ground those interpretations.

Let me begin by reviewing some of what we know about the American family. In the context of considering the family's problems, we need to acknowledge, first, that the family has been and remains a high priority to the American public, at least when polls assessing such matters are taken. In a national survey conducted in the United States as part of the 2000 World Values Survey, 95.7 percent of Americans said their family was very important (up from 93.0 percent in 1990), and this figure was substantially higher than the proportions who said the same about friends (64.5 percent), religion (56.5 percent), work (53.4 percent), service to others (50.9 percent), leisure time (42.1 percent), and politics (15.9 percent).[1] Young people, it appears, also continue to view marriage and family life as important aspirations. In national surveys of twelfth graders, 82.1 percent of girls and 72.9 percent of boys polled between 1996 and 2000 indicated that having a good marriage and family life is extremely important, and these figures were slightly higher than those obtained in similar surveys between 1976 and 1980.[2]

There are, however, indications that the public's satisfaction with family life may be eroding. For instance, in the General Social Surveys conducted by the National Opinion Research Center at the University of Chicago, the proportion of adults who said they derived a very great deal of satisfaction from their family life diminished from 43.0 percent in 1973 to 39.7 percent in 1994 (the most recent year the question was asked). Among married people, 62.4 percent in 2000 claimed to be very happy, compared with 67.8 percent in 1973.[3] In addition, family researchers find it troubling that a large minority of American teenagers—approximately four in ten among twelfth graders—doubt that they will stay married if they do get married, and that even larger numbers (about half) consider having a child without being married as a respectable alternative to married parenting.[4]

Second, divorce continues to be a factor in a large number of American families. The sharp rise in divorce rates that occurred between 1957 and 1979 appears to have ended; indeed, crude divorce rates, in comparison with both the U.S. population and among married women age fifteen years and older, are slightly lower now than in the early 1980s. Yet demographers point out that the flatness or decline in divorce rates during the 1980s and 1990s is largely attributable to the fact that fewer Americans were marrying, which in turn reflected rising levels of cohabitation among young people and an increase of approximately five years in the average age at which first marriages occur.[5] Some estimates, moreover, suggest that close to two-thirds of first marriages contracted in the 1980s will end in separation or divorce.[6] This compares with demographic estimates, drawn from a measure calculating the proportion of a given marriage cohort that voluntarily ends their union by a fixed time interval, in which approximately half of all marriages contracted in 1967 were expected to end in divorce. This figure was approximately one-third in 1950, about 10 percent in 1900, and only 5 percent in 1867.[7]

Third, research shows that many problems associated with the family appear to be more prevalent among single-parent families and among families in which divorce has occurred than among families characterized by intact marriages. Much of this research has focused on negative consequences for children. Compared with children of parents whose marriages are intact, children of divorced parents are less likely to perform well in school, more likely to exhibit behavioral problems, and more likely to have psychological and social difficulties.[8] Some research has tried to determine if these consequences may be the result of marital discord preceding divorce rather than divorce itself, but this research is inconclusive. Conflict between parents is at best a partial explanation for the effects observed in children of divorced parents.[9] The consequences of divorce are also evident among adults who experienced parental divorce as children. A national study among more than 2,500 adults found that adult children of divorced parents had lower levels of education, occupational status, and income; higher levels of economic hardship and of divorce; and lower rates of happiness in their relationships and higher levels of mistrust. These consequences were in turn associated with higher rates of depression.[10]

Many of the other consequences of divorce have been summarized by Linda Waite in her 1995 presidential address to the Population Association of America and her more recent book with Maggie Gallagher.[11] Waite shows that married people are better off, especially compared with divorced people, but also compared with widowed and never-married men and women, on a wide variety of characteristics: They are less likely to drink alcohol excessively or engage in other activities that put them at risk, their physical and emotional health is better, they live longer, they have more active and satisfying sex lives, they earn higher salaries, and they are better off financially. If divorce, by these indications, is costly to individuals, compared with being married, research also suggests that society benefits less when people are divorced than when they are married; for instance, married people are more likely than those who are divorced or single to do volunteer work, hold membership in voluntary associations, and exhibit high levels of social trust. To be sure, some of these differences are caused by the fact that different kinds of people may choose to marry and remain married than choose to divorce or remain single. Yet the evidence also seems to suggest that marriage itself is beneficial, giving people social, emotional, and financial support that carries them through bad times and contributes to happiness, well-being, and survival.

Fourth, the problems associated with divorce and single-parent households pose greater difficulties for low-income families than for families with more plentiful resources. Though the research is not entirely consistent, it suggests that the negative consequences of divorce on children's academic achievement, psychological adjustment, self-concept, and social relations are less significant or absent in higher-income families compared with lower-income families. The reason is that divorce often does bring economic hardship, especially for the mother. Higher income, therefore, provides a cushion against such hardship. It makes possible such services as day care and after-school programs, tutoring, and counseling. In contrast, poorer families not only have fewer services available but children may also be exposed to crime, drugs, and other negative social influences.[12]

Some of the consequences observed among low-income families also appear to be accentuated by the social context in which they occur. Specifically, as

William Julius Wilson's research has shown, poverty is increasingly concentrated in urban neighborhoods as a result of joblessness in these areas and flight from them on the part of middle-class families with jobs.[13] With the number of low-income urban neighborhoods increasing, researchers have become especially interested in so-called neighborhood effects on families. Some research suggests that living in impoverished neighborhoods does not result in heightened levels of divorce among married couples but apparently is associated with increasing rates of out-of-wedlock childbearing.[14] Research also shows that these neighborhood effects of socioeconomic disadvantage contribute to higher rates of adolescent sexual activity and delayed transitions to marriage among single parents.[15]

Fifth, studies indicate a broader range of concerns about the family than those that can be explained solely in terms of divorce and marital instability or conflict. For instance, in one national survey in which adults were asked to name the major issues facing the family, 44 percent said a lack of morals and values, 34 percent mentioned breakdown of the family, 26 percent named drugs, and 20 percent said violence.[16] Child abuse is a particularly serious concern. Observers speculate that child abuse has increased in recent decades; yet, unlike divorce, child abuse is more difficult to obtain accurate information about, is often concealed and underreported, and has not been subject to as much systematic investigation. But the evidence clearly suggests that it is a significant phenomenon and often pertains doubly to the family, not only because victims are members of families but also because perpetrators are often family members and other caretakers. According to one national study, for example, parents and other caretakers committed 26 percent of sexual assaults on juveniles and 49 percent of kidnappings of juveniles.[17]

Interpretations of Family Decline

What has gone wrong? Families have always faced serious problems, but the evidence of long-term increases in divorce and of significant problems in other aspects of family life has led observers to seek larger social developments that may be at the root of these problems. One way of understanding the difficulties facing contemporary families was suggested in the 1970s by Christopher Lasch in his widely read book *Haven in a Heartless World*.[18] Lasch argued that the family provides a retreat from an otherwise alienating world dominated by economic and political calculation. Whereas the outside world is typically experienced as harsh, brusque, and cold, the family offers warmth, security, and intimacy. In thinking about the purpose of the family, we therefore separate it from public life, viewing it as a private preserve in which our more cherished emotions will be gratified. But this understanding of the family ultimately proves untenable, Lasch argued. Spouses expect too much intimacy, regard each other too warmly, and harbor expectations about emotional gratification that cannot be fulfilled. Lacking other reasons for remaining married, they therefore divorce when they discover that marriage is failing to live up to its promise.

Lasch's argument, cast in several variants, has been widely applied to discussions of the family, and with some support from empirical studies. According to a survey of young adults age twenty to twenty-nine years conducted in 2001, 94 percent of never-married singles agreed that "when you marry you want your spouse to be your soul mate, first and foremost," and 88 percent agreed that "there is a special person, a soul mate, waiting for you somewhere out there." In addition, 80 percent of women in the study said it is more important to them to have a husband who can communicate about his deepest feelings than to have a husband who earns a good living. Commenting on the findings, Barbara Dafoe Whitehead and David Popenoe observed, "While marriage is losing much of its broad public and institutional character, it is gaining popularity as a SuperRelationship, an intensely private spiritualized union, combining sexual fidelity, romantic love, emotional intimacy and togetherness."[19] Drawing on in-depth qualitative interviews, Ann Swidler also shows that couples typically are guided by a romantic love myth as they contemplate marriage and as they think about making love, celebrating anniversaries, and purchasing Valentine's Day gifts.[20] She also finds, though, that this romantic ideal fades into the background most of the time. In routine day-to-day interaction, couples are guided by pragmatic interpretations that focus on schedules, getting tasks done, and spending time and money wisely.

The family as an emotional haven strikes a resonant and disturbing chord. Too much emphasis on emotional intimacy is reminiscent of the "triumph of the therapeutic," in Phillip Rieff's familiar phrase.[21] It recalls the concern expressed by Robert Bellah and his coauthors in *Habits of the Heart* about the pervasiveness of what they termed "expressive individualism."[22] Just when we thought it was good for people to value marriage and to seek deep emotional bonds with their spouses, we find that the tie is actually narcissistic. Yet the couples Swidler studied do not quite exemplify the central argument we find in Lasch. Though it was true that the romantic love myth proved sufficiently elusive to discourage some couples from staying married, it was more common for couples to switch into the pragmatic orientation and to live their days within that framework. From a practical standpoint, it is also difficult to know where to take the Laschian interpretation. Some research suggests that the very religious organizations that are most concerned about the family have been emphasizing expressivity and emotional bonding, apparently with beneficial results among husbands and fathers.[23] Should they abandon or redirect these messages?

A second way of understanding the family suggests that the strains experienced by contemporary families should be traced to changes in the labor force and especially to the growing numbers of women who are employed in the labor force. This argument emphasizes the shift from heavy agricultural and industrial work to lighter clerical and service work as the key economic development.[24] With this shift, labor became less physically demanding and thus could be performed as well by women as by men. Seeking new and often cheaper supplies of labor, business leaders thus looked to women and, in consequence, the number of women in the labor force multiplied dramatically. Having incomes of their own, American women thus gained a degree of financial independence from their husbands. Those who would have otherwise suffered in unsatisfactory or abusive marriages were now able to escape such situations through divorce.[25]

This argument casts divorce in a more positive light than some interpretations because it emphasizes economic conditions and points to the possible negative aspects of people remaining in bad marriages. It fits the data, so to speak, at least in associating the steep rise in divorce during the 1960s and 1970s with the equally sharp increase in women's participation in the labor force. However, it leaves one quandary and omits an important consideration. The quandary is why the trend in levels of marital happiness has not improved. If more people in unhappy marriages are no longer married, then those who remain married should, on the whole, be happier now than their counterparts a generation ago. That clearly is not the case. The missing consideration, which has been identified by economists, is that having a job not only makes people financially independent but also makes them more attractive as marriage partners.

Moreover, the economic hardship that researchers observe in connection with divorce suggests that there is still a significant cost to be paid, even if both partners are gainfully employed. The economic interpretations of family problems, therefore, are complex, and perhaps for this reason have not had as much traction in the popular press as arguments focusing on selfishness and moral laxity. It has been easier to believe that spouses were themselves to blame, because either their aspirations were too high or their expectations too low.

A third interpretation has sought to shift attention from middle-class families to lower-income families and from moral arguments to an emphasis on scarce resources and social injustice. An illustration of this interpretation is evident in the following statement by Judith Stacey:

Poverty and unemployment, not the selfish immorality of individuals, are the most effective predictors of and conveyor belts to nonmarital status. Regressive tax cuts and the weakening economy will exacerbate the destructive impact that economic inequality and social insecurity have on marital stability. Moreover, as the lifetime caps on welfare benefits kick in, the poverty of single parents and their children will deepen, further reducing their marital prospects. In such a context, additional policies favoring married couple families will have the paradoxical effect of reducing their ranks. Marriage is already one of the principal forms and symbols of class privilege, one that's entwined with racial privilege and, of course, with heterosexuality. That's why voting patterns now exhibit a marriage gap greater than the gender gap.[26]

This view corresponds with the differential rates of marital instability observed among blacks and whites and between low-income and middle-income families. It is an appeal for greater attention in policy circles to the special needs of the poor. Though it is sometimes associated in family discussions with liberal ideology, it has particular relevance for considerations about the role of religion, especially in view of religious organizations' efforts to speak on behalf of the needy.

It may also be useful to mention briefly the possibility of yet another interpretation, one that connects family problems with the broad shift during the past century from a society oriented toward economic production to a culture dominated by consumption.[27] In the earlier mode, there was an organic division of labor within the household, which bound spouses together in a way that no longer exists when households have primarily become units of individual consumption. In the consumer family, children play no useful role, other than succeeding in school and serving as a major market for consumer goods, which is probably a factor in the lack of worth that children may feel about themselves and in the ambivalence toward children that family researchers have observed among parents. Consumer culture also reinforces an emphasis on instant gratification and on shopping elsewhere if emotional needs are not met. It is unclear, however, whether this interpretation can be usefully applied to family problems, at least when economic growth, government policy, and family lifestyles are so intimately connected with the mandates of consumption.

The Role of Religion

These considerations bring us to the role that religion is playing—or might be able to play—in relation to the problems facing American families. We need to be clear that religion is by no means the only resource available for confronting these problems. Government, schools and other educational institutions, nonprofit organizations, counseling programs, researchers, and specially organized social movements all have an important role to play. Religion nevertheless is potentially a powerful force in the fight to strengthen America's families. Through the more than 300,000 local congregations of which it is composed, religion is a presence in nearly every neighborhood and community. Levels of participation are relatively high in comparison with active involvement in many other so-called membership organizations and relative to religious participation in many other advanced industrial societies. At least a quarter of the public attends religious services every week, and another quarter participates in services between one and three times a month. As many as 60 percent of the public hold membership in a local place of worship. And the vast majority claim to believe in God, to be interested in their spiritual life, and to regard religion as an important aspect of life.[28] Approximately half the nation's generous philanthropic giving goes to religious organizations, which in turn makes possible the nation's large numbers of clergy and other paid religious workers, the operation of religious programs both locally and at regional and national levels, and the maintenance of religious buildings and other facilities.

Research suggests that such resources, whether from religion or other programs, often do significantly mitigate the ill effects of family disruption. Religious resources include a growing number of programs concerned specifically with family problems. Many religious programs of a more general nature also have strong implications for family life. In addition, there are religiously led efforts to encourage and promote nonsectarian family programs and profamily government policies. The role of religion needs to include a consideration of the indirect and direct ways in which religious involvement may contribute to social relationships that are beneficial to families. Attention also needs to be given to the implications for families of religious teachings, especially their doctrinal and theological implications and the practices that follow from these teachings. An inventory of all that might fall under these various headings is clearly beyond the scope of this chapter, but some examples can be given to illustrate each of the ways in which religion may contribute.

Religious Programs Concerned Specifically with Family Problems

Under this heading, I have in mind such family-oriented ministries as family counseling and teen-pregnancy centers, prenuptial training and marriage-encounter retreats, and day care programs and nursery schools. American congregations have encouraged a language that was favorable to the family (a phenomenon that observers have associated especially with the boom in churchgoing and child rearing during the 1950s), and this emphasis has been noted in recent years especially among new churches, large churches, or churches seeking to define a niche in relation to broader concerns about the decline of the family.

In their study of new immigrant congregations, Fenggang Yang and Helen Rose Ebaugh observe that one of the traits of assimilation is to launch multipurpose programs that emphasize family ministry.[29] Impressionistic evidence drawn from interviews with pastors and observations of church leaflets may suggest that such family-oriented ministries are relatively common, but precise information about their prevalence is sparse. W. Bradford Wilcox, in an analysis of data obtained in Mark Chaves's *National Congregations Survey* (conducted in 1998 among the leaders of more than 1,200 randomly selected U.S. congregations), found that 20.4 percent of Americans attending conservative Protestant congregations and 22.1 percent of those attending mainline Protestant congregations described their congregational ministries as being concerned specifically with marriage, family, or parenting. From a national survey of church members conducted in 2000, Wilcox also concluded that 42 percent of persons attending conservative Protestant congregations said their church sponsored a day care program, as did 55 percent of persons attending mainline Protestant congregations.[30]

Another study, conducted by the Hartford Institute for Religion Research among a large number of congregations representing various faith traditions, found that approximately 50 percent claimed to sponsor marriage or parenting ministries.[31] Programs concerned with marriage or day care, however, do not adequately capture what congregations themselves define as family ministry. In the collection of congregational case studies edited by K. Brynolf Lyon and Archie Smith Jr., for instance, all the congregations studied sponsored a wide variety of activities under the rubric of family ministry. These activities ranged from family counseling to classes about family devotions and from discussions of gay and lesbian relations to family night suppers.[32]

Religious Programs That Have Strong Implications for Family Life

Only a step removed from efforts in the previous category are programs not specifically designed or conceived of as family ministries but that focus heavily on family relationships and provide special opportunities for strengthening these relationships. Examples include the many support groups, from Bible study and prayer fellowships to twelve-step and other self-help groups, in which discussions of family life often occur with considerable regularity. Examples also include women's or men's groups, age-graded Sunday school classes that bring together young single or married people or couples with children of similar ages, and ministries to the poor or elderly that have special implications for family life.

In my national study of support groups, 40 percent of U.S. adults said they were currently participating in a small group of some kind that met regularly and provided caring and support for its members. Two-thirds of these were sponsored by congregations or other religious organizations. The most common kinds of groups were Sunday school classes (that participants regarded as caring and supportive), Bible study groups, prayer fellowships, discussion groups, and twelve-step groups. Most of the participants claimed to take part in their group regularly, most were quite satisfied with their group experiences, and a majority had been involved in their group for at least five years. The emotional support and camaraderie provided by the groups could be regarded broadly as contributing to the family life of participants (relatively few mentioned family tensions arising because of their group involvement), and observations of group dynamics showed that concerns about marriage, child rearing, relationships with extended families, and family finances were routine topics of discussion.

In the survey, connections between group life and families were also evident: A total of 27 percent of the members of church-based groups (and 41 percent of other groups) indicated that being bothered by problems with their spouse or family was one of the reasons they had joined; among all group members, 26 percent said their group provided child care (which, in many cases, made it possible for them to participate), 23 percent said someone from the group had brought meals when a member of their family was ill, 12 percent said the group had helped them with babysitting; and, more generally, nearly everyone said they had received encouragement and witnessed examples of love in their groups.[33]

In a subsequent study, I examined the role of forgiveness in another national survey conducted among active members of Bible study groups and prayer fellowships. Forgiveness has attracted increasing interest among researchers concerned with the fragmentation of relationships in families and other settings. Approximately two-thirds of all group members in the study said forgiving other people had been emphasized "a lot" in their group; and among this number, large majorities of those who had experienced broken relationships within their families said they had been encouraged to work on healing this relationship. For instance, 71 percent of those who said they had experienced conflict with their spouse indicated having worked on improving this relationship. In a follow-up study, those whose groups had emphasized forgiveness also continued working to improve their family relationships more than a year and a half later. Further analysis of the data showed that group participation encouraged forgiveness and a sense of relationships having been healed, not so much because of the sheer social support provided by the group but because of the specific religious and spiritual content of group activities.[34]

Religious Efforts to Facilitate Family Programs and Policies

Although the preceding programs take place largely within the auspices of particular congregations and at the local level, religious organizations often participate in community-wide efforts that involve cooperative relationships among nonreligious organizations and government agencies, or engage in advocacy on behalf of family-relevant legislation, such as family-leave policies or welfare reform bills. Wilcox notes, for example, that mainline Protestant denominations have worked closely with Save the Children, a nonsectarian organization that raises money to assist children in poor families and in developing countries.[35] The Hartford Institute study found that approximately four congregations in ten helped support day care or after-school programs and that approximately the same proportion helped with elderly housing and senior citizen programs.[36] These, as well as other programs that were even more commonly supported (e.g., thrift stores and food assistance organizations), could be regarded as ways in which religious efforts help families in the wider community.

Relatively little research has been done to determine if religiously initiated or religiously supported programs are effective. The question of effectiveness has, however, been raised forcefully by government interest in faith-based service organizations. Some research suggests that faith-based programs are effective, perhaps even more so than programs lacking a faith component, in addressing certain kinds of family problems, such as substance abuse, teen violence, and juvenile delinquency. It has nevertheless been difficult to study the effectiveness of programs dealing with a wider variety of family needs. This is because programs often deal with emotional and other needs for which outcomes cannot easily be measured. It is also the case that low-income and other needy families typically seek assistance from a mix of agencies, meaning that effectiveness may pertain more to the whole mix than to particular service providers.

Preliminary results from a community study I have been conducting in the Lehigh Valley in Pennsylvania bear on these issues.[37] Of the twenty-five primary service agencies serving the community, nearly all have some connection with religious congregations, such as receiving referrals from pastors or deriving monetary support and volunteer help from church members. The agencies, nevertheless, divide clearly between those that are officially faith based, such as the Lutheran Social Services or Center City Ministries, and those that are nonsectarian, such as the Private Industry Council or United Way.

In a survey of more than 2,000 residents of low-income neighborhoods in the Lehigh Valley, we found that families that had sought assistance from any agency had generally sought assistance from more than one agency—in fact, from four agencies, on average. Nearly all had sought assistance from more than one type of agency. When asked to evaluate the effectiveness of the agencies from which they had sought assistance, respondents who had sought help from faith-based agencies gave higher overall effectiveness ratings than respondents who had not sought help from faith-based agencies. Perceptions of the trustworthiness of agency personnel showed the same pattern. However, there was also considerable variation in how specific agencies were perceived. This research, then, is suggestive of the kind of evidence that may prove useful in discussions about the role of religion, directly or indirectly, in meeting needs of low-income families.

Family advocacy raises somewhat different issues than service provision. Any review of the role of religion in relation to family would be remiss in failing to mention how religious groups have become involved in public debates about the family through specific movements, such as James Dobson's Focus on the Family, or through supporting political candidates deemed to be family friendly and in favor of family values. In an important study, Clem Brooks has examined the relationships in National Election Surveys between concern about family decline and the voting patterns of various religious constituencies.[38] He shows that concern about family decline rose significantly between 1980 and 1996 and that this concern was associated with a new and large cleavage in presidential elections. Churchgoing evangelical Protestants made up one of the largest constituencies on one side of this cleavage. Brooks suggests that the association of evangelicals with profamily issues has been a source of strength to the profamily movement, but that this association also limits how the profamily movement is viewed by the wider public. Whether this cleavage in politics concerning family issues has diminished since 1996 is as yet unclear.

Effects of Religious Involvement on Family Life

Apart from specific programs, religion also plays an important role in relation to the family simply by encouraging certain kinds of behavior on the part of individual members of congregations. Because many studies include measures of religious involvement and measures of various dimensions of family life, such as marital stability and styles of parenting, the literature examining relationships among these measures is relatively rich. Researchers have been particularly interested in whether religious involvement reinforces attitudes that may be conducive to marital fidelity and better parenting. Studies have also begun to emphasize the possibility that religious involvement generates social networks that play supportive roles in such contexts as family crises, illness, and bereavement.

A study by Christopher Ellison and Kristin Anderson examining the relationship between religious service attendance and domestic violence illustrates this line of research.[39] Ellison and Anderson analyzed data from the National Survey of Families and Households, which included information from approximately 2,800 couples (married, cohabiting, or living with a same-sex partner), both of whom answered questions about a number of topics, including domestic violence. The question about domestic violence asked, "During the past year how many fights with your [partner] resulted in you hitting, shoving or throwing things at him/her?" The partner answered a corresponding question about having been hit, shoved, or had things thrown at him or her.

When Ellison and Anderson compared the responses of people who attended religious services more or less often, they found significant differences. Among women, the odds of having been a victim of domestic violence among those who said they attended religious services at least once a week were only about half as great as among those who said they attended religious services once a year or less. Among men, the difference was almost the same. Self-reports of having physically abused their spouse (among both men and women) were also significantly lower among regular than among irregular religious attenders. These relationships reflected the *net* effect of religious attendance when other relevant factors were statistically held constant, including race and ethnicity, age, income, and education. The relationships remained present when Roman Catholics, conservative Protestants, moderate Protestants, and liberal Protestants were examined separately.

Ellison and Anderson's study also examined several reasons for the differences between regular and irregular religious attenders. They found that the differences in domestic violence could not be explained by the fact that regular attenders were better integrated into circles of friends, family, and neighbors or had networks they could rely on in an emergency than irregular attenders. Examining correlates of domestic violence, such as depression and substance abuse, also showed that these factors did not provide an explanation for the differences between regular and irregular religious service attenders. The possibility that regular attenders underreported domestic violence because it was socially desirable in their circles to do so could not be ruled out.

Drawing on other research, Ellison and Anderson speculated that the differences were probably attributable to congregations sanctifying marriage and encouraging partners to respect each other.

In another study, Lisa Pearce and William Axinn examined the effects of religious involvement on relationships between mothers and children in a panel survey conducted in Detroit between 1962 and 1985.[40] A representative sample of white mothers of children born in 1961 was interviewed in 1962. Reinterviews were conducted in 1963, 1966, 1977, 1980, and 1985. The children were interviewed in 1980 and 1985 (i.e., at ages eighteen and twenty-three). A total of 840 mothers and 840 children participated in the study. The quality of the mother–child relationship was measured by a scale composed of questions asking each person about the frequency with which the other has ideas and opinions that he or she respects, respects the other's ideas and opinions, understands and accepts the other, and enjoys talking together and doing things with the other.

The study showed that mothers who had attended religious services more often the year before the child's birth, when the child was fifteen, and when the child was eighteen reported closer relationships with their children at age twenty-three than mothers who attended religious services less often at any of these times. These relationships became statistically insignificant when the amount of subjective importance mothers attached to religion (measured in 1980) was taken into account, leading Pearce and Axinn to argue that religious service attendance mattered because it increased the salience of religion to the mother's personal identity. The responses from children were somewhat mixed. *Their* perceptions of the quality of their relationship with their mother were not related to how often their mother had attended religious services. They were higher, however, among children for whose mothers' religion was more subjectively important.

Pearce and Axinn's study also examined the effect of congruence between mother–child religious commitment on the perceived quality of their relationships with each other. Mothers reported closer relationships with their children when there was greater similarity between their own level of attendance and their child's and when the importance they attached to religion was similar to that of their child. In contrast, children reported closer relationships with their mothers only when levels of subjective religiosity were similar.

Pearce and Axinn concluded that on balance religious involvement has a positive impact on intergenerational relationships. They speculated that "exposure to religious themes such as tolerance, patience, and unconditional love through religious service attendance or religious social interactions provides parents and children with resources to improve their relationships. For example, religion may serve as a coping mechanism that helps parents deal with conflict or the independence asserted by adolescent children."[41]

But several caveats should be kept in mind in interpreting this study. First, the analysis (which included controls for child's gender, parents' education and income, and parents' marital status) explained a very small percentage of the overall variation in perceived quality of mother–child relationships (between 2 and 7 percent). Second, the weak relationships between children's perceptions and mothers' behavior suggest that mothers' churchgoing may be more effective at making them feel better about their children than in encouraging children to view their parents with fondness. Third, the findings about congruence suggest that minimally religious parents and minimally religious adolescents may get along better than highly religious parents and children who are less religious. And fourth, though the study examined the direct effects of child's gender and affiliation with conservative Protestant or Catholic churches, it did not examine these subgroups separately. Thus we are left with uncertainty about whether parents' religiosity has stronger effects on relationships with daughters than with sons and whether religiosity in some traditions affects children differently than religiosity in others.

Also drawing on the Detroit data, Arnold Thornton and Donald Camburn examined the effects of mothers' church attendance on mothers' attitudes toward premarital sex, their eighteen-year-old children's perceptions of their mothers' attitudes, the children's own attitudes, and whether children had engaged in premarital sex.[42] Mothers who attended church more often were significantly more likely than mothers who attended less often to disapprove of their children having premarital sex, to have children who perceived their mother as disapproving, and to have children who themselves disapproved. Mothers' church attendance had a stronger effect on these attitudes than other parental characteristics, such as education, income, and sexual history. The children of mothers who attended church regularly, however, were not significantly less likely than the children of other mothers to report having had premarital sex (although those who had premarital sex were somewhat more likely to have had fewer partners). The study also showed that the effects of church attendance were stronger among fundamentalists than among liberal Protestants or Catholics. The authors concluded that parents' churchgoing is probably a deterrent to children engaging in premarital sex insofar as it puts both parents and children in a context where there are clear norms against such activity.

Addressing the role of religion in possibly lowering the likelihood of divorce, Vaughn Call and Tim Heaton examined the relationships between religious participation and marital stability using data from 4,587 married couples included in the National Survey of Families and Households.[43] Church attendance for both spouses was measured in 1987, and marital status (still married or divorced) was measured five years later. The results showed that rates of marital dissolution were lower among couples where both the wife and the husband had attended church regularly. Among couples where neither spouse had attended church, the odds of being divorced five years later were 2.4 times greater than among couples where both spouses attended every week. However, the study also showed that incongruity between husband's and wife's level of attendance significantly increased the likelihood of divorce. For instance, the risk of divorce was 2.9 times greater if the wife attended weekly and the husband never attended church than if both spouses attended weekly. Overall, the authors noted, the risk of divorce was greater if one spouse attended regularly and the other did not attend than if neither attended.

This study offers an important caveat to the idea that religious involvement simply reinforces marital stability. Though it may be true that couples that attend church regularly are less likely to divorce because they receive input at church that discourages divorce, other interpretations need to be entertained. One possibility is that churchgoing signals agreement between spouses and provides them with an activity they can share. If one attends and the other does not, disagreements about values and time use may be accentuated to the point that divorce becomes more likely.

Researchers have also investigated the possible effects of a more pluralistic, fluid religious environment on marriage. For instance, the possibility that interreligious marriage may lead to divorce has been of considerable interest, especially in view of the fact that both have been increasing. Drawing on a large national sample of couples, Evelyn Lehrer and Carmel Chiswick were able to examine this possibility.[44] They discovered substantial variation in estimates of the likelihood of couples divorcing after five years of marriage.

Mormons married to Mormons had the lowest probability of divorce (13 percent), and nonreligious persons married to other nonreligious persons had one of the highest probabilities (36 percent)—a finding consistent with the idea that religious involvement is positively associated with marital stability. Other combinations with high probabilities of divorce included Jews married to non-Jews (42 percent), liberal Protestants married to Catholics (38 percent), and Catholics married to nonreligious persons (38 percent). Other combinations with low probabilities of divorce included conservative Protestants married to conservative Protestants (19 percent), liberal Protestants married to liberal Protestants (20 percent), and Catholics married to Catholics (20 percent). In general, interreligious marriages had higher probabilities of divorce than religiously homogeneous marriages. The study also found, however, that marriages in which one spouse converts to the other's religion have no higher probabilities of divorce than marriages in which both spouses are already from the same religion.

Yet another implication of religious involvement that has been examined is the possibility that participation in religious congregations gives people a wider network of friends on whom they can depend when faced with personal or family crises. The presence of such networks, it is assumed, provides assistance and emotional ballast that may help families successfully weather the inevitable problems associated with illness, bereavement, or financial loss.

One of the few studies to systematically examine the relationships between religious involvement and social ties was an analysis conducted by Christopher Ellison and Linda George of data collected from approximately 3,000 randomly selected persons in a five-county region in North Carolina in 1984. The data included questions about the number of persons to whom respondents felt close, frequency of contacts with other people by telephone or in person, the variety of help received from social networks, and the perceived quality of social relationships. The results generally showed that frequent churchgoing is positively associated with larger and more satisfying social networks. Several qualifications should nevertheless be kept in mind: The study does not rule out the possibility that people with larger social networks are more likely to attend church (rather than that frequent church attenders develop larger networks); it does not suggest that infrequent attenders are devoid of social support, only that frequent attenders have more; and, although other factors were statistically controlled, the study did not examine the extent to which relationships between church attendance and social support were present among particular subgroups of the population, such as the elderly, the young, single parents, or the needy.

These studies generally point to the possibility that religious involvement would, if encouraged, have positive effects as far as reducing marital instability and enhancing parental responsibility are concerned. Yet the conclusion that simply increasing religious involvement would be a good way of strengthening families needs to be considered with caution. During the 1970s, when most observers believe the family was weakened by rising divorce rates, religious involvement in the United States held steady. Perhaps family life would have weakened more if religious involvement had declined. But the fact that it did show significant change despite stability in religious involvement suggests that the continuation of such stability will not deter further change from taking place in family relationships in the future. Longitudinal research also suggests caution about viewing religion as a source of leverage for improving family relations. In an analysis of more than 1,000 married persons, increases in religious involvement only slightly decreased the probability of the couples considering divorce, and neither enhanced marital happiness nor decreased marital conflict.[45]

Family Implications of Religious Teachings and Practices

In studies of the kind just mentioned, the social norms implied by religious teachings and practices are often taken for granted or remain unmea-
sured. The centrality of specific teachings and practices in religious traditions, however, has also encouraged researchers to pay greater attention to
the form and content of these teachings and practices. Topics range from the
content of sermons, which may include narratives about family relations, to
formal teachings about marriage and family, to such related matters as gendered imagery of the divine, understandings of baptism, teachings about celibacy and sexuality, and questions of sin and redemption.

Much discussion has been initiated about the theological foundations of
church teachings about marriage, family life, child rearing, sexuality, sexual
preference, and related topics.[46] Some of these issues have been sources of
division within religious bodies. Questions about gay and lesbian unions have
been particularly divisive. Yet it is evident from some research that clergy and
congregants understand the importance of addressing these questions, even
where agreement may not be possible.[47] As public space, congregations provide opportunities for deeper reflection about the basic issues involved than
is often the case in policy settings or through the mass media.

Whether specific church teachings make much of a difference to how
people think and behave is harder to answer. The previously mentioned
research on forgiveness suggests that small-group discussions of forgiveness may actually encourage people to work at healing family relationships,
although it is unclear whether these discussions have long-term effects. In
surveys, people who recall hearing a sermon about money, social justice, or
helping the poor do respond differently to other questions about these topics;
yet these differences in cross-sectional surveys are not sufficient to establish
causality. Research on patterns of fertility and marital stability among Roman
Catholics has generally cast doubt on whether the Catholic Church's teachings
have had much of an effect on these aspects of family life.

The challenges these various roles of religion pose for scholars include
understanding the variety of ways in which American religion and American
families intersect and considering the consequences of religious behavior
for family life. Of special importance is paying attention to the unintended
consequences of various programs and proposals. For instance, research may
indicate that marriage is desirable because it reduces the cost to society of
various alternatives, but cost–benefit calculations may not be the most important grounds on which religious organizations wish to discuss the mer-
its of marriage. Beyond the scholarly challenges, religious leaders need to be
aware of the larger social and cultural contexts in which they work. Only by

maintaining a delicate balance between practical concerns and a larger vision can effective planning be ensured.

Notes

1. World Values Survey, U.S. Version, conducted among a nationally representative survey of 1,202 adults; machine-readable data file, available from the author.

2. Figures from Monitoring the Future Surveys conducted by the Survey Research Center at the University of Michigan, as reported in National Marriage Project, *The State of Our Unions 2001* (Piscataway, N.J.: National Marriage Project, Rutgers University, 2001), 30.

3. *General Social Survey: Cumulative Datafile, 1972–2000* (Chicago: National Opinion Research Center, 2000), http://csa.berkeley.edu; my analysis.

4. National Marriage Project, *State of Our Unions 2001*, 31.

5. Matthew D. Bramlett and William D. Mosher, "First Marriage Dissolution, Divorce, and Remarriage: United States," *Advance Data* (May 31, 2001): Number 323, http://www.cdc.gov.

6. Teresa Castro-Martin and Larry L. Bumpass, "Recent Trends in Marital Disruption," *Demography* 26 (February 1989): 37–51.

7. Samuel H. Preston and John McDonald, "The Incidence of Divorce within Cohorts of American Marriages Contracted since the Civil War," *Demography* 16 (February 1979): 1–26.

8. These effects are viewed in Paul R. Amato, "Children's Adjustment to Divorce: Theories, Hypotheses, and Empirical Support," *Journal of Marriage and Family* 55 (February 1993): 23–38; Andrew J. Cherlin, Frank E. Furstenberg, P. Lindsay Chase-Lansdale, Kathleen E. Kiernan, Philip K. Robins, Donna Ruane Morrison, and Julien O. Teitler, "Longitudinal Studies of Effects of Divorce on Children in Great Britain and the United States," *Science* 252 (1991): 1386–89; and Sara S. McLanahan and Gary Sandefur, *Growing Up with a Single Parent: What Hurts, What Helps?* (Cambridge, Mass.: Harvard University Press, 1994).

9. Thomas L. Hanson, "Does Parental Conflict Explain Why Divorce Is Negatively Associated with Child Welfare?" *Social Forces* 77 (June 1999): 1283–1316.

10. Catherine E. Ross and John Mirowsky, "Parental Divorce, Life-Course Disruption, and Adult Depression," *Journal of Marriage and the Family* 61 (November 1999): 1034–45.

11. Linda J. Waite, "Does Marriage Matter?" *Demography* 32 (November 1995): 483–507; Linda J. Waite and Maggie Gallagher, *The Case for Marriage: Why Married People Are Happier, Healthier, and Better Off Financially* (New York: Doubleday, 2000).

12. Amato, "Children's Adjustment to Divorce"; McLanahan and Sandefur, *Growing Up with a Single Parent*.

13. William J. Wilson, *The Truly Disadvantaged* (Chicago: University of Chicago Press, 1987); William J. Wilson, *When Work Disappears: The World of the New Urban Poor* (New York: Vintage Books, 1996).

14. Scott J. South, "The Geographic Context of Divorce: Do Neighborhoods Matter?" *Journal of Marriage and Family* 63 (August 2001): 755–66.

15. Dawn M. Upchurch, Carol S. Aneschensel, Clea A. Sucoff, and Lene A. Levy-Storms, "Neighborhood and Family Contexts of Adolescent Sexual Activity," *Journal of Marriage and the Family* 61 (November 1999): 920–33; Karin L. Brewster, John O. G. Billy,

and William R. Grady, "Social Context and Adolescent Behavior: The Impact of Community on the Transition to Sexual Activity," *Social Forces* 71 (March 1993): 713–40.

16. "Survey: Fears Have Shifted to Family Values," http://applesforhealth.com.

17. David Finkelhor and Richard Ormrod, "Child Abuse Reported to the Police," *Juvenile Justice Bulletin* (U.S. Department of Justice, Office of Juvenile Justice and Delinquency Prevention), May 2001, 3.

18. Christopher Lasch, *Haven in a Heartless World: The Family Besieged* (New York: Basic Books, 1977).

19. Barbara Dafoe Whitehead and David Popenoe, "Who Wants to Marry a Soulmate?" in *State of Our Unions 2001*, 13.

20. Ann Swidler, *Talk of Love: How Culture Matters* (Chicago: University of Chicago Press, 2001).

21. Phillip Rieff, *The Triumph of the Therapeutic* (New York: Harper & Row, 1966).

22. Robert N. Bellah, Richard Madsen, William M. Sullivan, Ann Swidler, and Steven M. Tipton, *Habits of the Heart: Individualism and Commitment in American Life,* rev. ed. (Berkeley: University of California Press, 1996).

23. W. Bradford Wilcox, "Conservative Protestant Childrearing: Authoritarian or Authoritative?" *American Sociological Review* 63 (December 1998), 796–809; John Bartkowski and W. Bradford Wilcox, "Conservative Protestant Child Discipline: The Case of Parental Yelling," *Social Forces* 79 (September 2000), 265–90.

24. Steven Ruggles, "The Rise of Divorce and Separation in the United States, 1880–1990," *Demography* 34 (November 1997): 455–66.

25. Frank Furstenberg Jr., "Divorce and the American Family," *Annual Review of Sociology* 16 (1990): 379–403.

26. Judith Stacey, "Family Values Forever," *The Nation* 273 (July 9, 2001): 26–30.

27. Jerome Segal, *What We Work For Now: Changing Household Consumption Patterns in the 20th Century* (Washington, D.C.: Common Assets Program, 2001), http://www.RedefiningProgress.org.

28. For an overview of religious statistics, see especially George Gallup Jr. and D. Michael Lindsay, *Surveying the Religious Landscape: Trends in U.S. Beliefs* (Harrisburg, Pa.: Morehouse Publishing Co., 1999).

29. Fenggang Yang and Helen Rose Ebaugh, "Transformations in New Immigrant Religions and Their Global Implications," *American Sociological Review* 66 (April 2001): 269–88.

30. W. Bradford Wilcox, "For the Sake of the Children? Family-Related Discourse and Practice in the Mainline," in *The Quiet Hand of God: Faith-Based Activism and Mainline Protestantism,* ed. Robert Wuthnow and John H. Evans (Berkeley: University of California Press, 2002), chap. 12.

31. Carl S. Dudley and David A. Roozen, *Faith Communities Today: A Report on Religion in the United States Today* (Hartford: Hartford Institute for Religion Research, 2001), 45; available at http://fact.hartsem.edu.

32. K. Brynolf Lyon and Archie Smith Jr., eds., *Tending the Flock: Congregations and Family Ministry* (Louisville: Westminster John Knox Press, 1998).

33. Robert Wuthnow, *Sharing the Journey: Support Groups and America's New Quest for Community* (New York: Free Press, 1994).

34. Robert Wuthnow, "How Religious Groups Promote Forgiving: A National Study," *Journal for the Scientific Study of Religion* 36 (June 2000): 124–37.

35. Wilcox, "For the Sake of Children?"

36. Dudley and Roozen, *Faith Communities Today,* 48.

37. Unpublished research based on a survey of 2,077 individuals living in the fifteen lowest-income census tracts in the Allentown–Bethlehem metropolitan area, conducted in 2002.

38. Clem Brooks, "Religious Influence and the Politics of Family Decline Concern: Trends, Sources, and U.S. Political Behavior," *American Sociological Review* 67 (April 2002): 191–211.

39. Christopher G. Ellison and Kristin L. Anderson, "Religious Involvement and Domestic Violence among U.S. Couples," *Journal for the Scientific Study of Religion* 40 (June 2001): 269–86.

40. Lisa D. Pearce and William G. Axinn, "The Impact of Family Religious Life on the Quality of Mother–Child Relations," *American Sociological Review* 63 (1998): 810–28.

41. Ibid., 824–27.

42. Arland Thornton and Donald Camburn, "The Influence of Family on Premarital Sexual Attitudes and Behavior," *Demography* 24 (August 1987): 323–40.

43. Vaughn R. A. Call and Tim B. Heaton, "Religious Influence on Marital Stability," *Journal for the Scientific Study of Religion* 36 (June 1997): 382–92.

44. Evelyn L. Lehrer and Carmel U. Chiswick, "Religion as a Determinant of Marital Stability," *Demography* 30 (August 1993): 385–404.

45. Alan Booth, David R. Johnson, Ann Branaman, and Alan Sica, "Belief and Behavior: Does Religion Matter in Today's Marriage?" *Journal of Marriage and the Family* 57 (August 1995): 661–71.

46. See esp. Don S. Browning, K. Brynolf Lyon, and Bonnie J. Miller-McLemore, *From Culture Wars to Common Ground* (Louisville: Westminster John Knox Press, 2000); and Phyllis D. Airhart and Margaret Lamberts Bendroth, eds., *Faith Traditions and the Family* (Louisville: Westminster John Knox Press, 1996).

47. Wendy Cadge, "Vital Conflicts: The Mainline Denominations Debate Homosexuality," in *Quiet Hand of God,* ed. Wuthnow and Evans, chap. 11.

Chapter 5
An Economic Perspective on Sex, Marriage, and the Family in the Contemporary United States

Robert T. Michael

A popular activity among public intellectuals is speaking about the demise of the family and the decline in marriage as a social institution. No knowledgeable observer would argue that no major social ills are associated with the American family. Consider children: Many are being reared in suboptimal settings, without proper nurturance or even nourishment; too many are harmed physically and psychologically; and many more are not given support to develop their potential. Or consider adults: Many are living in poverty, even by today's inadequate statistics, and, disquietingly, many do not have the skills to earn a living in our technologically advanced economy.

But for most of the dire statistics about the decline in marriage or the family, a different interpretation is just as valid. Take, for example, the fact that at today's rate of marital instability, half of all marriages will end in divorce. Now, all marriages end, either in dissolution or death. Today, as since 1975 without much variation, the annual divorce rate is about 2 per 100 marriages. That level of "risk," when experienced for thirty-five years, does yield a likelihood of divorce of about 0.50.[1] Yet that same fact suggests that each year, an average of forty-nine out of fifty married couples choose to remain married, despite the relative ease of getting a divorce. Divorce rates are historically high by U.S. standards and higher here than in most any other developed country, but 2 percent a year does not seem like an epidemic.

Or consider the fact that from 1975 to 2000, roughly one quarter of all pregnancies were aborted. It is equally true that despite the relatively low cost of abortion and easy access to contraceptives and sterilization, for the past twenty years about 4 million babies have been born annually in the United States, and their mothers' education level in 2000 is much higher than that of mothers a half century earlier.[2]

For an economist, the interesting question is what functions are served by the social institutions of formal marriage and the broader unit of the family, and how these institutions compare with alternatives. The theme of this chapter is that these two institutions serve important functions for adults and children, and though there have been significant changes during the past half century, there is no clear evidence for the claim that the family or the institution of marriage is passé. If other institutions come along that better fulfill these functions, then marriage may become obsolete. But there is no evidence that this is likely. The changes in these institutions reflect changes in circumstances that alter their relative attractiveness. But I am getting ahead of my story.

The Lens of Economics

This chapter discusses some of the changes in family, marriage, and sexual behavior in recent decades in the United States through the lens of economics. To begin, it is useful to discuss what economics can and cannot contribute. Economics is best characterized not by its subject domain but by its way of thinking about human behavior.[3] It attempts to provide understanding about behavior and institutions through a few premises, supported by empirical evidence. The key premise is that choices or actions are strategic or purposive, best understood as the outcome of seeking some objective but constrained by the scarcity of one or more elements. The objectives reflect deeply held values; they typically include several distinct items that may be competitive and even conflicting. The elements of the relevant constraints may be material resources like income, skills, health, or information, or many other things necessary to achieve those objectives. These elements have prices that reflect their value, and these prices are set by formal or implicit "markets" through interactions among those competing to use the elements. These prices reflect the collective judgment of the elements' value and are important because they guide their use. These markets that set prices and allocate resources among competing objectives are what make the choices or actions social phenomena and make economics a *social* science.

This description of economics may seem abstract, but it emphasizes that economics is all about scarcity, about getting the best outcomes from limited resources. As a science of choices, economics is quite neutral about whether those objectives have inherent value or ethical worth. As a discipline, it cannot help us explain why we have "tastes" or preferences. But it can tell us how, given those preferences, certain changes in circumstances will affect behavior. As an inductive or empirical science, economics can help us understand why we behave the way we do, but it is not necessarily providing a defense of the status quo, just an explanation. Economists differ neither more nor less than any other group in what they value, and many of the differences in their policy pronouncements reflect these different opinions. For example, some think the inequality in household income in the United States should be lessened through governmental policy. Others see that inequality as a necessary by-product of the incentives that have generated the U.S. economy's remarkable engine of technical progress in the past century. However, much of the difference in policy advocacy by economists comes from another source—trying to address questions for which the evidence is too thin for a clear answer. This chapter may, alas, suffer that ill as well.

Nonetheless, economics can help us understand the changes in family and marriage by applying its premises to these social institutions.[4] I hope to back up this claim by first discussing the way an economist might use disciplinary tools to explain what each institution does, then consider how changes in the broader environment affect these institutions. For now, I will hold off on that point while reviewing the social institutions and describing their recent trends in the United States.

Marriage

First, we consider formal marriage. The core idea here is that each of us spends much of our time either working for pay or producing useful commodities in the nonmarket sector for our own consumption. These productive activities in the home, in leisure activities, in educational settings, and the like typically use money, time, effort, and know-how or technology. We are engaged in productive activities most of the time, and even sleeping or dining can be viewed as producing one of those elements we call an objective—good health results in part from adequate sleep and good nourishment, so we are "producing" health as we sleep and eat. We can perform most of these nonmarket productive activities alone, but for a lot of the products it is also feasible to engage in these productive activities with other people, and that can be more efficient as well as more pleasant. Cooking dinner is an example—one can do it alone, but for much less than double the effort or cost, one can cook for two and save time and money. There are a host of these "economies of scale." They motivate us to live together.

Take this idea of producing commodities that give us satisfaction a step further, and apply the production principles that work so well in a manufacturing plant, for example: It is resource saving if two workers specialize in separate tasks so that they become more skilled in them and avoid having to be equally good in all tasks. Similarly, in the home, it is efficient for one person to be organized in paying the bills and keeping track of the checking account, for example, while another focuses on gourmet menus or keeping the couple's social calendar straight.

Specializing in some skills while avoiding having to keep up in others makes sense if the two partners are going to be together for a long time, and thus longer-term marriage has some value over simple scale economies. Specialization in skills only pays off if the time horizon is long enough. Moreover, if we do make these investments in certain skills and dispense with others, we become dependent on having a partner with complementary skills. This, then, is a second reason for gains from marriage: specialization in the division of labor, and selective investment in complementary household skills. These are most important for activities where one person can substitute for another, as for the simple examples above.

Yet a third type of gain from a marriage seems to almost contradict the point about specialization. For many activities, one's time is not substitutable for another's, but rather one person's time in the activity enhances the usefulness of another's time in that same activity. Examples of these complementarities include having a good conversation, playing a good game of tennis, raising one's own child, and having sex. Here, investments are made in developing skills that complement, not substitute for, the partner's time. But like the substitutable skills, these investments also only pay off if the partnership remains intact; at least if it does not, one has an incentive to find a new partner with the same interests and skills as the last one, lest those investments in specific skills lose their value.

So, viewed through the lens of economics, one major function of marriage is that it facilitates several gains in home production and protects partners' coordinated investments in skills. The reason a person would marry is that gains result from simple scale economies (e.g., air conditioning can accommodate two almost as cheaply as one); from each partner's investment in specialized skills and trading the products of those skills; and from investing in complementary skills used in productive activities together, enhancing the products and satisfaction for both.

A skeptic might ask why, if these gains are so substantial, we do not normally see communes or groups larger than two adults. Two forces work against this. First, the quid pro quo from an equitable distribution of tasks and benefits in the home makes it difficult to oversee the trades and ensure their fairness in all the dimensions of family life when many traders become involved. For instance, "I will put up with your . . . if you will agree to let me choose . . ." becomes nearly impossible if it is my in-laws, your housing location preferences, and someone else's choice of artwork on the walls. It is then easier to invest in nearly fully specialized skills and trade their use for generalized money, and that is just how it works in the labor market, but not in the home. In the home, the currencies of the many trades between partners are quite varied and are valued differently by the different traders, so there is not a simple transitivity of payoff from one person to another. If we cannot use a common medium of exchange like money, we are better off not having too many people involved in the negotiation. The second reason for dyadic partnerships, not threesomes or more, is that one of the most tangible, delicate, and vital joint products of a marriage is one's own children, and this is a production process that biologically takes two, a heterosexual two, but not more.

The Family

Before exploring what this view of marriage tells us about the changes taking place in marital behavior, let us consider the other social institution, the family. While marriage involves two relatively equal adults, the family involves pairs or groups connected by blood or contract and often across generations. Using the demographer's notion of a nuclear family as the marriage partnership and offspring living under one roof, consider the whole family as a within- and across-nuclear-family and intergenerational blood-related unit. Three types of relationships can be viewed through the lens of economics: First is that between parents and children; second, that among related nuclear families at one point in time, such as adult siblings; and third, that across generations of family members over a wide span of time. Terms like "family values" refer to one or several of these distinct types.

The relationship between parents and children is frequently explored and of great importance. Here I limit the discussion to a few activities: One set of productive activities involves nurturing, training, and caring for dependent children from birth onward. Few obligations are of greater importance than parenting, providing for the healthy development of the child in psychological, social, economic, and many other dimensions. Adults choose to have children because of the satisfaction they bring, and parental expenditures of time and effort, money and inconvenience, and patience and encouragement are all part of productive parenthood. Parents differ, of course, in the resources they provide their children, their innate capabilities, and their psychological traits as well as material resources; they differ as well in their inclinations to use their resources for their children. Though the child's strict dependence on parents declines with age, in most families the flow of parental support probably continues throughout the lifetime. Children also make analogous expenditures of resources, patience, and effort in behalf of parents, differing of course in "age-appropriate" ways as both children and parents age.

From a life cycle perspective, it is not essential that a quid pro quo is met each year as parent and child interact. Over a lifetime, however, the flows of benefits and of costs may well balance out. There is much fascination among economists with the concept of an implicit contract between the generations that calls for parental investments in the younger generation during the period of the former's greatest earnings capabilities and the latter's greatest dependency as youth, in exchange for a payback during the period of the latter's adulthood when the parents experience dependency in old age. The nature of the economic functioning between these parent–child relationships is one of investment in youth and caring for dependents as youth and as elders.

The relationship among nuclear units within one family, as among the families of adult siblings, can be characterized as one of pooling resources to ensure against risks and enhancing efficiency in overcoming constraints. Given the long-term nature of the family bond and the depth of understanding, trust, and affection among these units—borne of a lifetime of common experiences and commitments—the extended family is well suited to provide support in times of unexpected need. This functioning is analogous to an insurance plan in which one pays premiums to pool risk and relies on the plan to help out with adverse events. That market solution of formal insurance has an informal analog in the extended family. There, albeit in terms typically less specific as to payment or protection and perhaps even unstated as to function, the family can often be counted upon for that same support during times of stress.

The function of overcoming financial constraints is similar: If one brother has a risky business venture and requires financial backing to get under way, or a family member needs a little more financing to make the down payment on the new home or tuition payment, he can often count on his extended family. Altruism and affection are only part of the reason. The long-term nature of the family bond suggests that the lender knows the borrower far better than a banker would and therefore can have not complete, but more, confidence in repayment, and typically has better access to detect shirking than would a market lender. So the extended family can provide the insurance and the lending that the market might offer but only at a higher cost. These, then, are two important functions of the extended family.

The third level of family functioning is across family members over a wider span of time. Pertinent here is the social biology of promoting one's genes in the gene pool, of a family dynasty that reflects the social status of the unit, or, less grandly, the idea of a family culture or the reputation of the family name. The traditions, expectations, and standards associated with a family have value and motivate its members' actions. We read much today about the "culture" of a corporation or college campus, about the core behaviors of an ethnicity or motivating beliefs of a religion. There may be a comparable "culture" to a family—the way a family raises its children and treats its elders, and its members' occupations, avocations, and style. Biographies of famous individuals often stress family expectations and intergenerational relationships in explaining their subject, and so do novels routinely. It is a mark of pride to be a member of some families, a point of embarrassment to be identified as a member of others. If there were no traditions that separated families and their reputations, our ideas about "the family" would be much less elevated or rich.

Sex

Whereas legal marriage and the broader dimensions of family are social institutions that perform specific functions and have value because they do so, "sex" is not analogous. Sex is typically undertaken in a dyadic partnership or alone, but it is not a social institution. It, too, serves several functions or yields several products. Elsewhere, I have suggested six jointly produced outcomes of sexual activity: physical pleasure, emotional satisfaction, intimate bonding with one's partner that may promote love, reputation or peer judgment, the probability of pregnancy, and the probability of transmission of disease.[5]

One might think that the functions of sex are transparent, and their relationship to marriage and the family self-evident, but I argue that this is not so. First, a plug for research and attention by scholars, researchers, and public intellectuals: There has been a persistent, many-decade political effort to discourage social-scientific research about sexual behavior, and as a result remarkably little is known about this salient aspect of life.[6] Those who have worked to understand sexual behaviors have often found it useful to couch their work in terms of a medicalization of sex, and so the work tends to focus on its various adverse outcomes: disease, unwanted fertility, and dysfunction. All this attention has given sex a bad name: the joys of sex are private and, probably blessedly, remain so, whereas many of the adverse consequences of sexual behavior become public and impose costs on us all. Thus, the joys of sex we keep to ourselves; the woes of sex we proclaim publicly. But sex is an important aspect of one's life, and its successful management is important for well-being. Individuals, personal advisers of all sorts, and policymakers must all make judgments about aspects of sexual life, so they should have better, more complete sources of information. The list of issues on which research is needed is quite long, but the absence of good data resources for their study makes this a challenging domain for research.[7]

How does sex affect marriage and family? I first consider four domains that link sex and marriage, and then links between sex and the extended family. One important linkage involves the quality of the partnership. The intimacy associated with partnered sexual behavior promotes a bond between partners as it affirms trust when one chooses to be exposed to risk of harm and the revelations of body and desires. This trust promotes love and affection. The respectful and effective use of this trust in giving pleasure expresses and promotes love.

Conversely, the disrespectful misuse of this trust is probably why there is so close an association between sexual behavior and personal ethics or social reputation. The exercise of sex in the absence of this delicate, vulnerable intimacy and trust is what is so unappealing about the depiction of sex in popular culture. The qualities of marital and of sexual partnerships are not identical, but surely they are usually closely related. The sexual dimension of a partnership is a factor in promoting its stability. The convenience, ease, safety, and effectiveness of sexual experience is one important function of marriage that links the two partners.

A second domain is investment in sexual skills, a topic seldom addressed and analogous to the issue of specialization in skills within the home. Like those more general skills that it behooves a couple to parcel out, specialize in, and gain from efficiency in coordinating, specific sexual skills are effective with one partner but may not be with another. Learning these spouse-specific skills in loving, and disinvesting from other sexually related skills like that of attracting a partner when one has been secured, involve the same incentives as any skill acquisition. The more focused the investment, the more effective—but only with the partner toward whom it is directed; some of those skills may have little value otherwise. Thus the decision to make these spouse-specific investments promotes longer partnerships. But the corollary is that if the duration is expected to be short, or the risk of dissolution is great, the incentives to make these investments are weak.

A third domain linking sexual and marital behaviors, of course, is fertility, a by-product of sexual activity traditionally linked to marriage largely because of its association with fertility. If the children are to be raised within the marital union, and if they are a likely result of sex, it makes sense to organize the sexual behavior around the context in which the child rearing can be effectively accomplished, that is, within marriage. Fourth and finally, just as logically and opposite in its influence, if promiscuous sexual behavior is highly risky in transmitting infectious diseases, then sexual behavior within the bounds of a monogamous relationship minimizes that risk and offers yet another function linking sex and marriage.

Sex plays a different role in family behavior: mainly, as a transmission of family culture or family values. For reasons left unexplored here, sexual behavior has major influence on one's own and one's peers' assessment of one's character. Mostly through example or indirect instruction, parents inform their children of what is appropriate sexual behavior, not so much in instruction about specific sexual skills as in the basics of respect for and sensitivity to others, avoidance of exploitation of trust, and the like.

Where families do not instruct children about the values they place on these behaviors, and where the children therefore do not receive that instruction within their family, and instead unavoidably get their instruction through peers and through public institutions such as the media, they do not acquire a sense of their family's position or values on appropriate sexual behavior. They formulate their own independent judgments that then have little tie to any family-based view except laissez-faire. In the absence of instruction, guidance, and encouragement in how these relationships should be managed, their sexual practices can be destructive and their ability to form and sustain lasting partnerships or friendships can be compromised. This is part of the culture of a family—its values as reflected in and transmitted to its offspring. The intimacy that typifies a family setting also has within it the capacity for abuse of the trust among members; in a small percentage of cases, there is pathology as the intimacy and trust within the family are violated through child or sexual abuse.

What Has Changed over the Past Half Century?

So the stage is set: I have sketched, from an economic perspective, several functions of marriage and of the family and the role sex plays within these two domains. The questions before us, then, are what has changed over the past half century in the patterns of these social institutions, and why. Obviously, this pair of questions cannot be given a simple, definitive answer, but I will attempt to sketch the outlines of a partial response. First, we must choose to focus on a few key changes in the pattern of these institutions, so I briefly describe some of the changes from 1950 to 2000.

During those fifty years, the inclination to marry, the proportion currently married, and the stability of existing marriages all declined, as shown in table 5.1. In the United States, the rate of marriage per 1,000 unmarried women age fifteen to forty-four years declined from 166 to 82; the median age at first marriage for women rose dramatically from twenty to twenty-five; the proportion of the population age fifteen and older that is currently married fell from 66 to 55 percent; and the annual divorce rate rose from 1 to 2 percent of marriages.[8]

A similarly dramatic pattern of change is found when we consider descriptions of the American family, as shown in table 5.2. The share of all households that are in fact "families" (i.e., groups bound by blood or contract, as distinct from other households) declined from 89 to 69 percent.

Table 5.1. Trends in Marriage in the United States, 1950–2000

Trend	1950	1960	1970	1980	1990	2000
Rate of marriage (per 1,000 unmarried women age 15–44 years)	166.4	148.0	140.2	102.6	91.3	81.5[a]
Median age at first marriage (women)	20.3	20.3	20.8	22.0	23.9	25.1
Percent of population currently married (women)	65.8	65.9	61.9	58.9	56.9	54.7
Rate of divorce (per 1,000 marriages)	10.3	9.2	14.9	22.6	20.9	19.5[a]

[a]Data are for 1996.

Sources: For the rate of marriage, see *Monthly Vital Statistics Report* 43, no. 12(S) (July 14, 1995): 7; for the rate in 1996, see U.S. Bureau of the Census, *Statistical Abstract of the United States: 2000*, table 143, p. 101, available at http://www.census.gov/statab/www/. For the age at first marriage, see U.S. Bureau of the Census, *Current Population Reports*, Series P20-537, table MS-2. For the percent of the population currently married, see U.S. Bureau of the Census, *Current Population Reports*, Series P20-537, table MS-2. For the rate of divorce, see *Monthly Vital Statistics Report* 43, no. 12(S) (March 22, 1995): 9; for the rate in 1996, see U.S. Bureau of the Census, *Statistical Abstract of the United States: 2000*, table 143.

Fertility, the principal product of the family, also declined—the fertility rate (the number of births per 1,000 women, age fifteen to forty-four) fell from 106 to 68. And much of the fertility now takes place outside the traditional marital union; the share of births to unmarried women rose from about 4 to 33 percent. The share of children under age eighteen living with two parents fell from 88 percent in 1960 to 69 percent by 2000. Though overall fertility rates have declined dramatically during the half century, the fertility rate among the unmarried has risen just as dramatically, even beginning to approach parity with the marital fertility rate. Finally, the labor force participation rate of married women with children under the age of six rose from 12 to 63 percent.

With regard to sexual behavior, it is much more difficult to get reliable data on trends because the subject has not been a focus of quantitative research, and government agencies and statistical surveys have typically avoided capturing information about sexual behaviors. One of the few dimensions of sexual behavior that has been documented over time is the typical age at which cohorts begin having sex. We know that this age has declined over the past several decades as age at puberty has correspondingly declined and as the onset of partnered sex has increasingly become disconnected from formal marriage.

Table 5.2. Trends in Fertility and Family Behavior in the United States, 1950–2000

Trend	1950	1960	1970	1980	1990	2000
Percent of households that are families	89.2	85.0	81.2	73.9	70.8	68.8
Fertility rate (births per 1,000 females age						
15–44 years)	106.2	118.0	87.9	68.4	70.9	67.5
Unmarried females	14.1	21.6	26.4	29.4	43.8	44.0
Births per 1,000 women age 15–19 years	—	89.1	68.3	53.0	59.9	47.7
Percent of births to mothers under age 18 years	—	—	6.3	5.8	4.7	4.1
Percent of births to unmarried females	3.9	5.3	10.7	18.4	28.0	33.2
Percent of children under age 18 years who						
live with two parents						
All	—	87.7	85.2	76.7	72.5	69.1
Whites	—	90.9	89.5	82.7	79.0	75.3
Blacks	—	67.0	58.5	42.2	37.7	37.6
Hispanics	—	—	77.7	75.4	66.8	65.1
Labor force participation rate of married females						
with children under age 6 years	11.9	18.6	30.3	45.1	58.9	62.8

Sources: For the percent of households that are families, see "America's Families and Living Arrangements, March 2000," in U.S. Bureau of the Census, *Current Population Reports*, Series P20-537, table HH-1. For the fertility rate, see *National Vital Statistics Report* 50, no. 5 (February 12, 2002): 27. For the fertility rate for unmarried females for 1950–60, see U.S. Bureau of the Census, *Statistical Abstract of the United States: 1969*, table 59, p. 50, available at http://www.census.gov/statab/www/; for 1990–2000, see U.S. Bureau of the Census, *Statistical Abstract of the United States: 2004–05*, table 79, p. 65, available at http://www.census.gov/statab/www/. For the percent of births of mothers under 18 years, see V. M. Fried, K. Prager, A. P. MacKay, and H. Xia, *Chartbook on Trends in the Health of Americans, Health, United States, 2003* (Hyattsville, Md.: National Center for Health Statistics, 2003), table 8, p. 106. For the percent of births to unmarried women for 1950–70, see U.S. Bureau of the Census, *Statistical Abstract of the United States: 1981*, table 98, p. 65, available at http://www.census.gov/statab/www/; for 1980–2000, see *National Vital Statistics Report* 50, no. 5 (February 12, 2002): table D, p. 9. For the percent of children under 18 years who live with two parents, see "America's Families and Living Arrangements, March 2000," in U.S. Bureau of the Census, *Current Population Reports*, Series P20-537, table CH-1. For the labor force participation rate of married females with children under 6 years, see U.S. Bureau of the Census, *Historical Statistics of the United States*, 134; and U.S. Bureau of the Census, *Statistical Abstract of the United States: 2000*, table 570, available at http://www.census.gov/statab/www/.

Only within the past decade, however, have data become available that show the sexual behaviors of the general population, so unfortunately few trends can be documented. Using a recent nationally representative data set with detailed information about sexual behavior, and relying on retrospective survey responses by adults at all ages up to sixty about their sexual behavior during adolescence, we can track a few aspects of sex and related fertility outcomes over much of the past half century, as shown in table 5.3, which reports both the rise in incidence of partnered sex before age eighteen and the off-

Table 5.3. A Few Trends in the Sexual Behaviors of Women in the United States before Their 18th Birthday, 1950–2000

Trend	1950	1960	1970	1980
Probability of giving birth[a]	11.7	10.5	9.6	12.9
Probability of having sex	29.2	30.9	44.4	63.1
Probability of conception, if sex	40.0	38.3	27.9	33.7
Probability of having abortion or miscarriage, if conception	0.0	11.2	22.6	39.3

[a]Probability of giving birth = $P_s{}^* P_{C|S}{}^* (1 - P_{AM|C})$.

Sources: Retrospective reports of women in the National Health and Social Life Survey; Robert T. Michael and Kara Joyner, "Choices Leading to Teenage Births" in *Sex, Love, and Health in America: Private Choices and Public Policies*, ed. Edward O. Laumann and Robert T. Michael (Chicago: University of Chicago Press, 2001), 83.

setting associated rise in fertility control. That evidence shows, interestingly, that while rates of sexual activity have risen, rates of avoidance of conception and of pregnancy termination have also risen, yielding practically no change over the decades in rates of teenage births.

This absence of a trend in the rate of teenage childbearing mirrors the national fertility data on this matter, despite all the public discourse about the subject. The pronounced trend toward younger age of first intercourse, seen in table 5.3 from retrospective reports, is also seen in many other surveys. For example, the share of women who report having had sex by age eighteen, for cohorts who were age twenty in the intervals 1958–60, 1970–72, 1985–87, and 1990–94, were 27, 35, 52, and 55 percent, respectively, according to a 2001 survey by the U.S. Department of Health and Human Services.[9]

Explanations for These Changes

In looking for explanations, the challenge is to identify forces that are not themselves determined by the changes we want to understand. It is too easy and ultimately unsatisfactory to claim, for example, that a social custom changed the value of marriage and promoted greater instability. That is nearly tautological and not informative. Similarly, without a cogent explanation for its development, it is not very enlightening to suggest that a social movement like feminism somehow promoted women's entrance into the workforce in the third quarter of the twentieth century and thereby caused the growth in female-headed families. One wants to identify exogenous changes in key forces within the system. An economist typically looks for changes in key prices and levels of wealth as influential factors because these reflect value and constrain behaviors. So the questions become: What are the major trends over the past half century in income and wealth, and what have been the major forces altering prices of key products or services?

At the risk of disregarding a host of other relevant factors, three key changes within the economy illustrate the argument that typifies the view of economists. First, household income rose substantially over the fifty years since 1950. Second, soon after 1950, the United States became the first economy dominated by the production of services rather than physical goods, and this, together with the century-long growth in the role of technology embedded in the machinery with which workers engage in production, increased the demand for technologically skilled workers whose human capital was far more important than their physical strength, thus neutralizing the earlier labor market preference for male workers. Third, the role of the government as a player in our lives expanded—both in setting important rules by which we live and performing some of the tasks we need addressed, notably in funding and providing formal education, and in extending its role in income and old-age security.

These three changes—in household income, in labor market demand for skills, and in government provision of a few services—are all reasonably "exogenous" to the pattern of family structure and marital decisions. How do they affect the social institutions of marriage and family? First, consider the growth of real income. As incomes rise, the demand for goods and services increases, but the demand does not rise in the same proportion for all items. Among the items with large relative increases in their demand, namely "luxuries," are services and more expensive or "higher-quality" goods. The increase in services fuels the growth in market demand for service workers and encourages the substitution of some household production into market production. This means that tasks formerly done at home when incomes were lower are now brought into the marketplace. This in turn encourages homemakers to enter the job market, which is one of several factors facilitating the movement of women into the labor market and larger investments in their human capital.

The shift into the labor market by many married women diminishes one key element of specialization within marriage, the "traditional" roles of one partner earning the dough and the other baking the bread. When both earn the income with which the bread is purchased, the benefits of a coordinated partnership decline. The decline in "gains" from that specialization between spouses diminishes one incentive for being married. Along the same lines, another luxury that can be afforded at higher levels of income is privacy, and so the gains from economies of scale, another reason for marrying, also decline as one's own privacy becomes more affordable.

A principal product from marriage is one's own children, and as their income rises, couples choose to spend more on each of their children. At higher levels of income, the couple spends more on their own consumption and on human capital investments, and they also do the same for their children. In effect, the "price" of a child rises with family income because of the choice of spending more per child. But that has the effect of discouraging having more children. This pattern is not limited to children; it is seen as well in the pattern of purchases of many consumer durable goods: As income rises, the percentage increase in the number of units of houses and cars, for example, is much smaller than that in the spending on each of those units; a tripling in income does not lead to a threefold increase in the number of houses or cars, even if it does lead to spending three or more times as much on houses or cars. That applies to children, too; most of the extra money goes into greater spending per child, not into more children.

The improvements in marketplace technology increased the demand for skills in workers and diminished the demand for physical strength. That in turn increased the incentive to invest in one's own and one's children's human capital, raising wage rates, time values, and income. These labor market changes are the mirror image of the changes accompanying the rise in household income, and they led to at least three important developments. First, the higher wages for all workers meant a greater incentive to enter the workforce for the family's second adult. This lowered the gains from specialization within the marriage—the "old-fashioned specialization" of Ozzie-employed-for-pay and Harriet-engaged-in-household-tasks gave way to less partner specialization. This transformation of the demand for labor to meet the growing needs of the service sector and its higher skill standards in turn promoted the education and employment of women. Second, this lowered the costs of becoming divorced because there was no longer one spouse without marketable skills wholly dependent on the other. Third, these higher wages and the move into the workforce increased the cost of bearing and raising children. So the number of children desired by many couples declined, fueling the half-century decline in birthrates and in the number of children per marriage.

So these developments lower the gains from being married because some functions move into the marketplace, the incentives to specialize in household tasks are reduced, there is greater personal but not familial security as each adult has marketable skills and earning potential, and child-rearing commitments are lessened when there are fewer children. There may have been salutary effects on individual economic security and identity, but these developments diminish both the role of formal marriage and the incentives to invest so heavily in spouse-specific skills that lose their value with divorce. The attractiveness of the institution of marriage declined because many of its functions in 1950 were gone by 2000. But marriages continue to take place because they still bring important gains, even if those gains are smaller. Any unexpected perturbation, however, is more likely now to render the "net gain" from marriage negative, making divorce more likely. The risk of divorce is higher because the types of spouse-specific skill investments that might further discourage divorce are also smaller. Couples hedge a bit on making these investments that add to their marriage, but these investments are lost if it dissolves, and so the incentives not to dissolve decline and the rates of dissolution rise.

The growth in government services furthered this process. Rather than reviewing the reasons for the growth in public provision of services, here I discuss two of them. The provision of education for children and of subsidized higher education in the form of state colleges and guaranteed student loans further encouraged the acquisition of marketable skills by all adults. As the instruction and education of young people and the care of preschool children become the responsibility of the schools or the government, the role of the family in these tasks declines. When governments attempt to supplement the family's efforts with their children—through school lunch programs, after-school efforts, sex education curricula, or any other program—that provision typically offsets some family efforts and diminishes that family function, at least at the margin.

It has always been the challenge of social policy that in providing support to those who have little—and making eligibility for that support conditioned on having little—that very policy is exactly what one would devise as a strategy for encouraging, not discouraging, being in that condition. A subsidy payable only if one has little encourages one to have little to get that subsidy. The logic here is quite clear. If a couple has made its decisions and allocated its resources and its efforts as best it can across all the things that matter to it, and then an outside force like the local government provides more of one of those many things, there will be an adjustment within the family.

Similarly, government provisions of income security lower the economic risks of being unpartnered and unemployed, especially when welfare policies provide larger payments to single parents. Also, the provision of old-age security to those who have paid into social security through payroll deductions made it feasible to enter the job market and to earn and secure retirement income with no reliance on one's children or extended family. Though that governmental provision may have great value to the couple, it will prompt a reallocation of some of the family's own efforts to other tasks to reestablish the right balance among all its competing ends. So a dollar spent by the outside group on one task does not in general yield a dollar's increment in that outcome, even if the value of the dollar is fully realized by the family. Many times, the dollar spent has a smaller value for any of several reasons, but even without any difference in the evaluation, the final impact of the transfer will generally involve a reallocation among several ends. In the process, however, both the usefulness of the marriage for these tasks and thus also the gains from it are diminished.

I have focused so far on the effects on marriage, but these three forces also adversely affect the functioning of the broader family. Consider, for example, the second of the three functions discussed above for the family, that of providing insurance and resource pooling across extended family members. If governments supplement that function by providing a minimal safety net for those unemployed or in bad health, and if it offers loan guarantees for schooling or startup entrepreneurship, though this may be designed to supplement the private provisions that include those from one family member to another, the fact of their provision diminishes the value of a close family tie. And what of the notion of a family culture across generations, a dynasty that for the wealthy may mean a family business, a multigenerational influence in a town or an industry, while for families with less financial resources it may mean a reputation or a set of customs, traditions, habits, and expectations? The smaller the number of children, the greater the instability of a marriage, and the increasing "blending" of families through remarriage, stepchildren, and half-siblings surely undercuts the incentives or raises the costs of securing these cross-generational family assets.

To take stock of the argument, these three exogenous changes have affected marriage and the family by altering their functions. As governments have taken over the tasks of providing some income security for low-income families and for the elderly, these functions of the family and the marital partnership have lost some of their importance. As the job market has attracted more second partners from marital unions and created incentives for greater skill acquisition, the gains from specialization in marriage have declined. This makes marriage less attractive and divorce more attractive. As incomes have risen, the benefits from economies of scale have lost some of their importance because adults can afford to live separately and enjoy their privacy. This is part of the story.

And what about sex? There is an important collateral and complementary story, I believe, about the role of sex over the past half century. The important changes here, too, were initiated by an exogenous technological development that began just after 1950, when the first application for a U.S. patent was made for an oral contraceptive. The pill was approved in the early 1960s and accompanied by the widespread medical adoption of the intrauterine device, followed in the early 1970s by the national legalization of abortion and the uses of both male and female sterilization. These changes truly constituted a "contraceptive revolution" that wholly transformed the risk of pregnancy among sexually active fertile adults.

To make clear just what a transformation this was for sexually active women, consider this: Using the best available contraceptive method in 1960 (the condom or diaphragm) at its observed use-effectiveness with an average frequency of sex, the probability of getting pregnant each month was 0.012; whereas using the oral contraceptive available by 1970 at its observed use-effectiveness, with the same frequency of sex, that probability was 0.0008. This means that if a fertile woman used that pre-pill technology for a twenty-year period of sexual activity, her expected number of conceptions was 2.3, and with 95 percent confidence she could expect to have between zero and 4.9 conceptions. That is a lot of uncertainty![10] If, instead, a fertile woman took the pill during twenty years of sexual activity, her expected number of conceptions was 0.2, and with a 95 percent confidence she could expect to have between zero and one conception.[11] The pill transformed the degree of uncertainty a woman faced, and the availability of legal abortion and sterilization essentially reduced that uncertainty to zero.

This transformation had, I have suggested elsewhere, four major effects on the family.[12] First, it provided women with the incentive to make expensive investments in their human capital because now they could, if they chose, be sexually active and not face a serious risk of bearing a child for any length period they did not want a pregnancy to interfere with their career. The growth in higher education of women, prompted by the changes in labor market demand, was greatly facilitated by the technological feasibility of the effective elimination of the risk of unwanted pregnancy. It had a profound influence in this fifty-year interval.

Second, the contraceptive revolution was unexpected, or its implications were surely not well understood by couples that married during the fifteen years or so following 1950. The unexpected nature of the changes was, as such events always are, highly destabilizing to marriages. People form marriages based on their best information about themselves, their partner, and the circumstances in which they will conduct their married lives. Much evidence suggests that any subsequent unexpected event destabilizes the match. It typically implies that at least one spouse could do better in competing for a spouse and that the marriage's terms need to be renegotiated, which frequently leads to dissolution. My estimate was that about half the doubling of the divorce rate from 1 to 2 percent in this fifty-year period, all of which occurred from 1965 to 1975, was associated with the unexpected nature of the contraceptive revolution.[13]

Third, the improved contraceptive technology helped couples reduce their fertility, and this lowered the benefits from marriage. Fourth, the decreased risk of pregnancy lowered at least one important risk of nonmarital sexual behavior by cutting the costs of sexual activity outside marriage for both unmarried and married adults. This further diminished the gains from marriage, because in earlier times sexual experiences were highly risky outside marriage and thus sex was one benefit of being married. And extensive extramarital partner searching, made less costly by the reduced risks of pregnancy, raises the likelihood that a preferred partner will be discovered as well as diminishing the incentives to invest in this-partner-specific skills. Perhaps the social and legal acceptance of greater diversity in sexual behavior and the increasingly public nature of explicit sexual behavior have affected the functions of both marriage and the family.

The contraceptive revolution also gave a woman increased control over her fertility because it required less cooperation from her partner, or even his knowledge of its use. That, and the additional education and enhanced career prospects for women, altered the balance of power toward women in their negotiations with men. Though giving women a stronger bargaining position that probably enhanced their well-being, this greater control over aspects of their lives also lowered the benefits of traditional 1950s-vintage marriage arrangements and made divorce more likely. It also increased income inequality across households by raising the income of two-earner families while creating many more lower-income female-headed families.[14] The assessment of these structural changes on general welfare will differ if we look only at money income and the rise in its inequality, or if we look also at the reduced inequality in individual security, control, and self-fulfillment. This is an example of what has been called "the money illusion": If we assess circumstances only in terms of their easily measured monetary aspects, we will fail to recognize many equally important but more difficult-to-measure features.[15]

Changed Functions But Still Functional

We have now come full circle: The three basic forces of technology, income growth, and expanded government may seem to have wholly undermined the institutions of marriage and the family. Public intellectuals who talk about the demise of the family may seem correct after all. But I do not think so. The functions of marriage have changed, and some have been taken over by the marketplace and the state; but there is nonetheless much evidence that marriage remains an important social institution with substantial payoffs. Consider the following four pieces of evidence.

First, while age at first marriage has risen dramatically, no birth cohort has yet reached the end of its period of fertility without a very large propor-

tion having been married. Of women age fifty-five to sixty-four in 2000, for
example, more than 95 percent had married at least once (see table 5.1). The
median age at first marriage has risen to unprecedented heights, but nearly
all U.S. women have married at some point before they turn fifty, at least for
now. That may change as the younger cohorts of today age, but we will just have
to wait and see.

Second, though divorce rates are high by historic standards, so are remarriage rates. To cite but one statistic, similar to the one just mentioned, in
1990, of those women age fifty to fifty-four who had ever divorced, 63.0 percent had also remarried at least once. So after having experienced marriage
and then its ending, two out of three women chose to marry again. That may
be seen as a rather strong endorsement of the institution. Again, of course,
these fifty- to fifty-four-year-old women in 1990 were in their early thirties
in 1970, which is early in the period of strongly declining rates of marriage.
So the picture may look quite different when we see the behavior of current
twenty-year-olds when they reach old age. But for now, there has not yet been
a cohort that passed through their fertile ages without a very large proportion
marrying and doing so again if the marriage ended.

Third, the decline in formal marriage does not imply a comparable decline in forming dyadic heterosexual partnerships. Today, however, many of
those partnerships are cohabitational unions instead of formal marriages.
Though there are substantial differences between the two types of partnerships, there is nevertheless evidence of a continued strong propensity to pair
off in adult living arrangements, as table 5.4 shows. On the basis of data collected in 1992 and asking adults up to the age of fifty-nine if and at what age
and in what form (marriage or cohabitation) they first formed a dyadic partnership with someone of the opposite sex, the pattern is quite revealing. If we
only look at formal marriages, women born in the decade 1933–42, compared
with those born in 1963–74, were far more likely to marry at a young age; their
reported behavior mirrors the official demographic statistics. But if we define the union to include both formal marriages and informal cohabitations,
there is practically no difference in the proportions that have paired off by age
twenty-five in those cohorts of women born three decades apart.

Fourth, though the evidence is only suggestive and subject to censoring
that might explain it away, married partners do report better sexual experiences than nonmarried adults and have more sex as well. Though sexual partnering outside marriage has become far more commonplace, the institution
continues to serve the function of sexual activity and satisfaction more effectively than any other.[16]

So, for several reasons, it may be too early to claim that marriage is passé.
The evidence just cited suggests that many, even most, adults still choose to

Table 5.4. Women in the United States Forming Dyadic Heterosexual Partnerships, by Age for Two Birth Cohorts, 1933–42 and 1963–74

Age (years)	Percent Married		Percent Married or Cohabiting	
	1933–42 Birth Cohort	1963–74 Birth Cohort	1933–42 Birth Cohort	1963–74 Birth Cohort
15	5	1	5	3
17	19	4	19	16
19	46	13	46	35
21	65	25	68	56
23	78	38	80	72
25	83	51	85	84

Source: National Health and Social Life Survey; see Robert T. Michael, John H. Gagnon, Edward O. Laumann, and Gina Kolata, *Sex in America* (Boston: Little, Brown, 1994), 98.

become married. And if the notion is expanded to include cohabiting couples, there is no overwhelming evidence of a reduced commitment to the institution of a paired live-in relationship. Moreover, in the sexual aspect of their lives, those with a monogamous long-term partner report being relatively satisfied with their lover and with their sex lives, compared with other adults.

What explains this revealed preference for marriage? The logic of the economic perspective is that while the functions of the institution may have changed during the past half century, they remain many and important. There are still the economies of scale, even though they may have less salience for adults with high levels of income; the complementary incentives to form a dyadic partnership and make investments in interests and skills that yield satisfaction from the interaction with that partner still exist and have considerable value, and sexual experiences are but one of these domains. Though the state has taken over some functions once expected of a partnership or family, it has not wholly replaced those familial functions, especially with respect to children. Marriage is still popular because it still meets many of the basic desires of adults.

Conclusion

While avoiding the temptation to offer projections about marriage and the family,[17] lest my message be interpreted as unduly positive, I note two broad current circumstances that are unequivocally disturbing. The first is the substantial inequality in economic well-being within the nation. The degree of earnings inequality has risen during the past quarter century so much as to offset the gains in reduced inequality over the preceding three quarters of the twentieth century.[18] Though the average, and even median, level of income has risen and is high by any comparative standard, the number of households considered impoverished is also disquietingly high.

The implications of that inequality can be seen in many ways, and one perspective is to consider the discrepancies in circumstances by race/ethnicity. Table 5.5 does so for a few of the same demographic circumstances reported above for 2000, but here displayed by race/ethnicity. It also shows 2000 median incomes and impoverishment rates for these groups. The levels of income by family type are far lower for blacks and Hispanics than for non-Hispanic whites. And even these figures hide part of the discrepancy because the distribution of the black households among the family categories shows much larger proportions in low-income categories; that is, for blacks, 28.2 percent of households are female-headed families, whereas for whites only 8.4 percent are female headed and their income levels are low. For blacks, 34.0 percent of all households are nonfamily units, whereas for whites only 11.3 percent are nonfamily units, and their income levels are lowest of all. By contrast, for blacks, 32.1 percent of the households are married-couple families, whereas for whites 55.0 percent are married couples, and their income levels are high.[19] If the fertility behaviors reported for the nation as a whole in the chapter's earlier tables were of concern, they are far more so for blacks, because table 5.5 shows the birthrates for very young women to be three times as high for blacks.

The second circumstance I note is the well-being of many children today. Again, there is enormous disparity among children. Many are doing phenomenally well in their schooling and in their social and emotional development; these children's prospects are breathtakingly favorable. But children at the other end of the continuum are in very poor shape, with bleak prospects. Look at the disparity in table 5.5 for children, again displayed by race/ethnicity, in terms of income or growing up in a two-parent family. Note three general conclusions from social science research about children. First, the evidence is strong that children benefit from being raised in family structures with two adults, especially their biological parents.[20] Second, the evidence is strong that investments in skills are far more efficacious when made at very young ages, and not made remedially at postschooling ages, because "learning begets learning."[21] Third, there is evidence that children "wanted" or planned before conception have better outcomes, including higher birthweight, less infant mortality, fewer developmental problems, less abuse and neglect, and greater investments and more parental attention.[22]

Table 5.5. A Snapshot of Disparity in the United States by Race/Ethnicity, 2000

Aspect of Disparity	Total	White[a]	Black	Hispanic
Median income (thousands of dollars)				
All households	42.2	45.9	30.4	33.5
All families	51.8	57.2	36.1	36.6
Married couples	59.3	62.1	50.7	41.1
Male only	42.1	45.7	37.0	39.0
Female only	28.1	33.2	21.7	23.7
All nonfamilies	25.4	26.3	20.6	21.3
Living in poverty (percent)				
All families	8.7	5.4	19.3	19.2
All married couples with children	6.0	3.7	6.7	16.8
All children	16.2	9.1	31.2	28.4
Birthrate for women age 15–17 years	27.4	15.8	52.0	60.0
Birthrate for women age 18–19 years	79.2	56.8	125.1	143.6
Percent of births to:				
Unmarried women	33.2	22.1	68.7	42.7
Women under 18 years of age	4.1	2.6	7.8	6.3

[a]Non-Hispanic whites.

Sources: For median income, see U.S. Bureau of the Census, *Income 2000*, table 1, available at http://www. census.gov/hhes/income/income00/inctab1.html. For the percent living in poverty, see U.S. Bureau of the Census, *Historical Poverty Tables*, table 4, available at http://www.census.gov/hhes/poverty/histpov/hstpov4. html. For the percent of all children living in poverty, see U.S. Bureau of the Census, *Historical Poverty Tables*, table 3, available at http://www.census.gov/hhes/poverty/histpov/hstpov3.html. For birthrates, see *National Vital Statistics Report* 50, no. 5 (February 12, 2002): table A, p. 4. For the percent of births to unmarried women, see *National Vital Statistics Report* 50, no. 5 (February 12, 2002): table 19, p. 49. For the percent of births to unmarried women under 18 years, see V. M. Fried, K. Prager, A. P. MacKay, and H. Xia, *Chartbook on Trends in the Health of Americans, Health, United States, 2003* (Hyattsville, Md.: National Center for Health Statistics, 2003), table 8, p. 106.

Although 75 percent of white children live in two-parent families, and of these only 3.7 percent are considered living in poverty, 62 percent of African American children live in female-headed families, and of these 41.0 percent live in poverty. These children are growing up apart from at least one of their natural parents and in circumstances considered to be inadequate to meet their families' financial needs. I suggested above at several points that the government has over the past half century provided some economic security against low income and the needs of old age, and has thereby taken over some of that traditional function of the family. Perhaps the amount of that governmental support has been sufficient to undercut the functioning of the family but not enough to meet the needs of those whose traditional families have weakened.

It is not clear that more government support is the best answer, because the family performs so many functions in addition to the basic economic ones that addressing the family's economic needs through governmental programs, without also addressing its diminished functionality, is not an attractive strategy. I suggest that perhaps the reduction in the family's basic economic functions, as supplemented by government transfer programs, has undermined the institution that effectively performs these other nurturing, care-giving, and love-encouraging duties. That is why I think it is premature to consider the family as outmoded. During the past half century, some of its functions have been reassigned to collective action through government—but not all have been, and not some of the most important ones. Further, the demands and attractiveness of the job market have encouraged changes that may have enhanced adults' well-being, but not so clearly children's. There remain many critically important functions that, to put the point neutrally, have not yet been reassigned to or assumed by any nonfamily social institution. Until they are, there are important functions for the family and for marriage, albeit some that may need to be redefined to include shorter-duration unions.

What is the role of public policy in this arena? A key goal of social policy is to set incentives and procedures to promote the common good. The most difficult challenge for makers of social policy related to family issues is not how to achieve a specific objective but rather what we consider to be the common good. The care of children is a fine example. Since 1996, the focus of federal social welfare policy has been to encourage parents to find employment and mothers to earn and therefore utilize substitute child care. This may be beneficial from the standpoint of the social cost of welfare transfers but not from that of children's well-being.[23]

As another example, consider that it would be technically relatively easy to lower the incidence of divorce in the United States if that were the agreed-on social objective. It could be accomplished by making divorce "more costly" in legal, material, and psychological terms through a variety of strategies. But is that in the interest of the common good? It may imply that youthful errors of judgment result in long periods of psychological or physical harm to one partner in a marriage. It may thwart the full expression of the individual's potential, unanticipated at the time of the marriage's formation. Few would argue that the current historically high rate of marital instability is itself attractive or appealing, yet many believe it is preferable to one in which errors of marital choice are irreversible.[24] One function of economics is facilitating the analysis of such alternatives. Economics can help both to analyze social policy choices and to provide guidance on achieving a specified objective, but it does not offer guidance on ranking social values or on justifying the expressed values reflected in behaviors. That is the business of the "religions of the Book" explored throughout this volume.

Notes

The author thanks Nancy Folbre for insightful comments on a draft of this chapter.

1. The probability of the event occurring is equal to $1 - (1 - 0.02)^{35}$.

2. E.g., the proportion of the U.S. female population with fewer than twelve years of schooling was about 62 percent in 1950, but by 2000 the proportion of the female population over twenty-five years of age who were not high school graduates was as low as 16 percent. Similarly, at the other end of the spectrum, in 1950 about 5 percent of the female population held college degrees; but by 2000, 24 percent had at least a college degree.

3. This discussion basically follows Becker's essay on the issue: Gary S. Becker, The Economic Approach to Human Behavior (Chicago: University of Chicago Press, 1976), chap. 1.

4. The interested reader is encouraged to look at Gary S. Becker, A Treatise on the Family (Cambridge, Mass.: Harvard University Press, 1991), a dense but thoroughly insightful and highly influential book that brings together many of Becker's important essays on aspects of marriage, divorce, and family behavior. Few scholars in any field with which I have familiarity so dominate the basic statements and insights as does Becker. Literally hundreds of useful studies have been undertaken to amplify, explore, qualify, and check on points in Becker's treatise. For a few summaries of aspects of this literature, see Yoram Weiss, "The Formation and Dissolution of Families: Why Marry? Who Marries Whom? And What Happens upon Divorce?" in Handbook of Population and Family Economics, vol. 1A, ed. Mark R. Rosenzweig and Oded Stark (New York: Elsevier, 1997), 81–123; and Joseph V. Hotz, Jacob A. Klerman, and Robert J. Willis, "The Economics of Fertility in Developed Countries: A Survey," in Handbook of Population and Family Economics, vol. 1A, 275–342.

5. Robert T. Michael, "Private Sex and Public Policy," in Sex, Love, and Health in America: Private Choices and Public Policies, ed. Edward O. Laumann and Robert T. Michael (Chicago: University of Chicago Press, 2001), 466.

6. Edward O. Laumann, John H. Gagnon, and Robert T. Michael, "A Political History of the National Sex Survey of Adults," Family Planning Perspectives 26 (January–February 1994): 34–38.

7. The list includes sex as an expression of adulthood; intimacy and sex, and sex without intimacy; the connections between ethics and sexual behavior, the role of sex in maintaining the quality of a partnership, and the production and maintenance of sexual skills; the reasons for the differences in salience of sex among adults; and personal sex, including thinking or fantasizing about sex.

8. Most of the data given in tables 5.1, 5.2, and 5.5 are from general sources, including U.S. Census Bureau, Statistical Abstract of the United States: 2001, 121st ed. (Washington, D.C.: U.S. Government Printing Office, 2001; and U.S. Department of Health and Human Services, Trends in the Well-Being of American's Children and Youth: 2001, Office of the Assistant Secretary for Planning and Evaluation (Washington, D.C.: U.S. Government Printing Office, 2002).

9. U.S. Department of Health and Human Services, Trends in the Well-Being of American's Children and Youth, 255.

10. These are calculated in this manner: Let p_i be the monthly probability of getting pregnant using contraceptive method i at its observed use-effectiveness. If no contraception is used, p is usually thought to be 0.2 per month for sexually active fertile couples. The mean length of the reproductive cycle, from the beginning of sexual activity to conception, through pregnancy, and postpartum infertility and back to the beginning of a fertile period once more, is $\mu_i = [(1-p_i)/p_i] + s$, where s is that period of infertility from conception through postpartum infertility. The length of s is often assumed to be 17 months, so for a fertile couple with no contraception, $\mu_{none} = (0.8/0.2) + 17 = 21$ months. Now, the expected number of children born to a woman with μ_i for 20 years or 240 months is $\mu_{Ni} = 240/\mu_i$, and its variance is $\sigma^2_N = 240[(1-p_i)/p_i^2]/\mu_i^3$.

11. A second fact that I find similarly compelling is the following. Studying the probability of a birth in the year, for women who had borne six children, Sanderson calculates that probability to have practically no variation in it from the period 1930 through 1960, despite the fact that that period included the very low birthrates of the Great Depression, the period of World War II and the postwar baby boom. He finds that probability of a seventh birth, indexed relative to 1960 = 100, remained in the range for a little over 100 to a little under 100 for each year despite the wide swings in fertility. But Sanderson shows that the index began to fall when the oral contraceptive came available and as quickly as 1966 that index of births to women with six live births had plummeted to 0.46. Warren C. Sanderson, *Towards Understanding the Fertility of American Women, 1920–1966* (Ph.D. diss., Stanford University, 1974).

12. Robert T. Michael, "Why Did the U.S. Divorce Rate Double within a Decade?" in *Research in Population Economics*, vol. 6, ed. T. Paul Schultz (Greenwich, Conn.: JAI Press, 1988), 367–99.

13. Ibid., 385.

14. Judith Treas and Robin Walther, "Family Structure and the Distribution of Family Income," *Social Forces* 56, no. 3 (1978): 866–80.

15. Robert T. Michael, "Money Illusion: The Importance of Household Time Use in Social Policy Making," *Journal of Family and Economic Issues* 17, no. 3/4 (1996): 245–60.

16. Robert T. Michael, John H. Gagnon, Edward O. Laumann, and Gina Kolata, *Sex in America* (Boston: Little, Brown, 1994), 112–25; and see Linda J. Waite and Maggie Gallagher, *The Case for Marriage* (New York: Doubleday, 2000).

17. Making successful projections about the future require two things: a reliable model of the determinants of the phenomenon of interest, (i.e., if we are interested in the future pattern of X, we first need a good relationship of $X = f(Y_1, Y_2, Y_3)$; and equally important, a reasonable understanding of the pattern of the explanatory variables into the future, (i.e., the trends forward in Y_1, Y_2, and Y_3). In the current context, we have neither, so I will not offer any projections.

18. Claudia Goldin and Lawrence F. Katz, "Decreasing (and Then Increasing) Inequality in America: A Tale of Two Half-Centuries," in *The Causes and Consequences of Increasing Inequality*, ed. Finis Welch (Chicago: University of Chicago Press, 2002), 37–82.

19. The numbers are as follows. For whites: 6,681,000 female-headed families, 43,624,000 married-couple households, and a total of 79,375,000 households in 2000. And for blacks: 3,762,000 female-headed families, 4,290,000 married-couple households, and a total of 13,355,000 households. Note, however, that the statement is still incomplete, because the nonfamily units are smallest and the married-couple units are the largest. Because the incomes reported here do not control for family size, they must be interpreted accordingly.

20. Greg J. Duncan and Jeanne Brooks-Gunn, eds., *Consequences of Growing Up Poor* (New York: Russell Sage, 1997).

21. James J. Heckman, "Policies to Foster Human Capital," *Research in Economics* 54 (1999): 3–56.

22. See the excellent summary in *The Best Intentions: Unintended Pregnancy and the Well-Being of Children and Families,* ed. Sarah S. Brown and Leon Eisenberg (Washington, D.C. : National Academy Press, 1995), chap. 3; and also see Michael Grossman and Theodore J. Joyce, "Unobservables, Pregnancy Resolutions, and Birthweight Production Functions in New York City," *Journal of Political Economy* 98, no. 5, part 1 (1990): 983–1007; and Michael Grossman and Theodore J. Joyce, "Pregnancy, Wantedness, and the Early Initiation of Prenatal Care," *Demography* 27, no. 1 (1990): 1–17.

23. P. Lindsay Chase-Lansdale, Robert A. Moffitt, Brenda J. Lohman, Andrew J. Cherlin, Rebekah Levine Coley, Laura D. Pittman, Jennifer Roff, and Elizabeth Votruba-Drzal, "Mothers' Transitions from Welfare to Work and the Well-Being of Preschoolers and Adolescents," *Science,* March 7, 2003, 1548–52.

24. See Steiner's discussion of the futility of setting a family policy: Gilbert Y. Steiner, *The Futility of Family Policy* (Washington, D.C. : Brookings Institution Press, 1981).

Chapter 6
The Family in Trouble: Since When? For Whom?

Claude S. Fischer and Michael Hout

Thinking about the family and the religions of the book brings to mind the stories of family trouble that fill the Bible. For example, Adam and Eve become homeless because they irritate the Landlord, and then one of their sons kills the other. Lot, in a drunken stupor, impregnates his daughters. Sarah is infertile into old age and in her jealousy gets Abraham to banish his concubine and his son to the desert. The twin sons of Isaac quarrel, and their mother connives with one to usurp the position of the other. And so on, from Genesis to King David and beyond. Families in trouble—indeed, dysfunctional families—are hardly new. Although in this chapter we do not deal with millennia, we do seek to put family troubles into a historical context.

In the effort to answer the questions of why American households are changing and what difference it makes, we see our responsibility as addressing a prior and fundamental question: *How* are American forms and norms of marriage and the family changing? In answering these questions, we shall suggest that some widespread worries about the family today may be founded on misunderstandings.

Many misunderstandings arise from false memories about American history, memories that credit an earlier time with more settled family life. In fact, with the exception of a brief period after World War II, Americans often fell short of their family ideal—the ideal of a happily married couple with children. Early in the twentieth century, numerous circumstances, from premature death to infertility, interfered with reaching that ideal. More recently, Americans have departed again from that ideal, many because they found new options and made alternative choices, options such as living longer and choices such as having fewer children or leaving bad marriages. How many of these choices should be considered "trouble" depends on one's perspective. We can value some of them as moral alternatives and valid aspirations—for example, to choose the way we live and with whom, and how to love and care responsibly for these people. Other Americans today have departed from the family ideal less from choice and more from constraint as a consequence of poverty and limited opportunities. In any case, the history of the family tells a story more complex than many appreciate.

In particular, a key concern we have is that discussion of family change often misses the questions "Since when?" and "For whom?" Consider the trend displayed in figure 6.1: It is consistent with the descriptions of "family trouble" in showing that the proportion of Americans age thirty to forty-four years who were living as single adults rose rapidly between 1960 and 2000.[1] These Americans were not married, nor in an extended family, but instead were living alone, or as single parents, or in a group situation, like roommates. The singles rose from 10 percent of their age group in 1960 to 30 percent in 2000. But if we look back to 1900 in figure 6.2, we see that this recent trend is a reversal of an older one. Moreover, if we were to correct the trend line's last two points, 1990 and 2000, for the fact that many of these supposed single people were actually cohabiting in a quasi-marriage, the end of the line would fall to about 20 percent, not much different than the percentages for 1900 and 1910. Indeed, we have reason to suspect that in 1900 some couples that reported themselves as married were, by modern definitions, really cohabiting. In many ways, it is the middle of the last century that is the aberrant period, not the last third of the century. This illustrates our concern about the question "Since when?"

Next, we address the question "For whom?" in figure 6.3. Here the gross pattern displayed in figure 6.2 is split by race, and we see a divergence between blacks and whites from 1900 to 2000. For African Americans, the percentage of thirty- to forty-four-year-olds living on their own went up 17 points over the century, from 25 to 42 percent, but it only went up eight points, from 18 to 26 percent, for whites. To add a further twist on the "For whom?" question, consider that the group that really expanded single living into a lifestyle was that of elderly women: Figure 6.4 shows that the percentage of elderly women living as singles almost doubled, from 26 percent in 1900 to 50 percent in 2000.

We have tried in this opening exercise to underline the point that simple impressions of family change may miss underlying complexities. We will return to the themes of "Since when?" and "For whom?" below. Before that, however, it is important to put those changes—changes in living out of marriage, in unwed motherhood, and in other statuses considered troubling—into a wider context of family change. We next discuss some of the major and less major changes in the American family recognized by demographers.

Overview of Family Changes

American family life changed in many ways in the twentieth century, but the severity of a change and the severity of the conversations about that change did not often match. As we shall see, some of the greatest changes involved the demography of the family and affected the elderly, while the much-discussed matters, such as family dissolution and family intimacy, were much more stable.

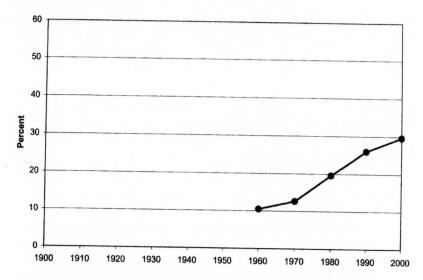

Figure 6.1. Percent of 30- to 44-Year-Olds Living as Singles, 1960–2000
Note: Singles are adults living alone, as single parents, or as nonrelatives in another's household.
Source: Steven Ruggles, Matthew Sobek, Trent Alexander, Catherine A. Fitch, Ronald Goeken, Patricia Kelly Hall, Miriam King, and Chad Ronnander, *Integrated Public Use Microdata Series: Version 3*, machine-readable database (Minneapolis: Minnesota Population Center, 2004), available at http://www.ipums.umn.edu/usa/.

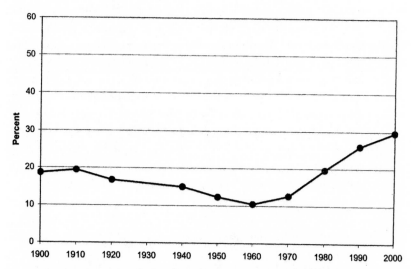

Figure 6.2. Percent of 30- to 44-Year-Olds Living as Singles, 1900–2000
Note: Singles are adults living alone, as single parents, or as nonrelatives in another's household.
Source: Steven Ruggles, Matthew Sobek, Trent Alexander, Catherine A. Fitch, Ronald Goeken, Patricia Kelly Hall, Miriam King, and Chad Ronnander, *Integrated Public Use Microdata Series: Version 3*, machine-readable database (Minneapolis: Minnesota Population Center, 2004), available at http://www.ipums.umn.edu/usa/.

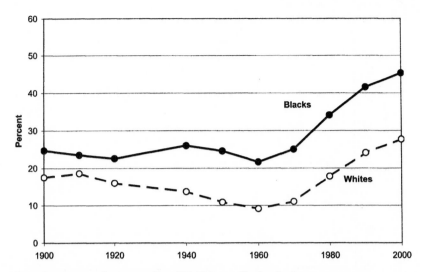

Figure 6.3. Percent of 30- to 44-Year-Olds Living as Singles, by Race, 1900–2000
Note: Singles are adults living alone, as single parents, or as nonrelatives in another's household.
Source: Steven Ruggles, Matthew Sobek, Trent Alexander, Catherine A. Fitch, Ronald Goeken, Patricia Kelly Hall, Miriam King, and Chad Ronnander, Integrated Public Use Microdata Series: Version 3, machine-readable database (Minneapolis: Minnesota Population Center, 2004), available at http://www.ipums.umn.edu/usa/.

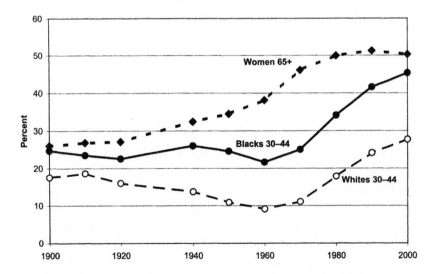

Figure 6.4. Percent of 30- to 44-Year-Olds Living as Singles, by Race, and Elderly Women, 1900–2000
Note: Singles are adults living alone, as single parents, or as nonrelatives in another's household.
Source: Steven Ruggles, Matthew Sobek, Trent Alexander, Catherine A. Fitch, Ronald Goeken, Patricia Kelly Hall, Miriam King, and Chad Ronnander, Integrated Public Use Microdata Series: Version 3, machine-readable database (Minneapolis: Minnesota Population Center, 2004), available at http://www.ipums.umn.edu/usa/.

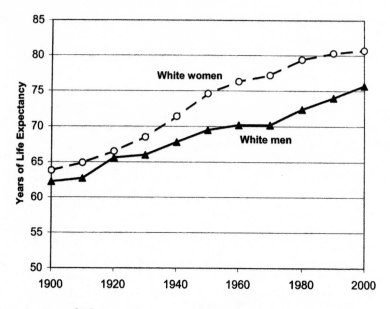

Figure 6.5. Years of Life Expected at Age 20, White Men and Women, 1900–2000
Source: National Center for Health Statistics via http://www.infoplease.com/ipa/A0005140.html.

Major Changes

Let us highlight the "big" changes in the American family over the century. The first one to note is basic and critical: Americans live a lot longer than they used to. Figure 6.5 shows the average life expectancy of white women and men who had already made it to the age of twenty.[2] A twenty-year-old white woman in 2000 could expect seventeen more years of life than could her ancestor in 1900; a twenty-year-old white man today could expect thirteen years more than a twenty-year-old man a century ago. (In addition to this change, there was an even greater expansion in the life expectancy of infants.) There are, as we shall see, profound implications to this greater longevity.

Add to this another major change—the reduction in the birthrate. The average number of births per woman, dated at the age she turned thirty, dropped steeply from 1900 to the 1940s, as shown in figure 6.6; if we could push back the view here to 1800, we would see a tilted line starting from about seven or eight births per woman in 1800 down to about two in 1940.[3] Again, the 1950s and early 1960s were unusual. Take out the anomalies—the drop in births during the Depression and World War II and the Baby Boom afterward—and we would see a smoothly declining curve from 1800 on; the last thirty years

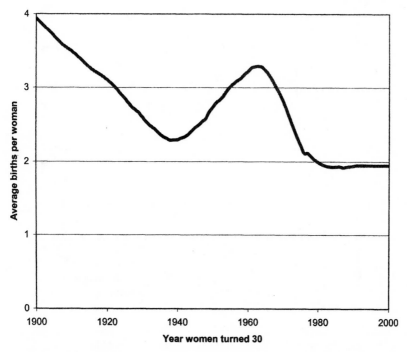

Figure 6.6. Number of Births over a Woman's Lifetime by Year of Her 30th Birthday, for Women Born 1870–1970.
Source: Steven Ruggles, Matthew Sobek, Trent Alexander, Catherine A. Fitch, Ronald Goeken, Patricia Kelly Hall, Miriam King, and Chad Ronnander, *Integrated Public Use Microdata Series: Version 3*, machine-readable database (Minneapolis: Minnesota Population Center, 2004), available at http://www.ipums.umn.edu/usa/.

are right on track. Women who were thirty years old around 1900 averaged four children apiece; women who were thirty years old around 2000 averaged two children apiece.

Extensions of life and reductions in births drove two other major changes: A large increase in the proportion of people fifty and older living in an "empty nest" (with just a spouse) and an increasing proportion of elderly Americans living alone. In 1900, about one in four of the elderly lived in one of these two circumstances; in 2000, more than three in four elderly people did so. These are enormous reversals in family life, shown in figure 6.7. Note that the biggest changes in family life, in Americans' living arrangements, during the twentieth century occurred for the elderly. The elderly today end their parenting much earlier in life, they have fewer children, and they live longer than the elderly a few generations ago. They also have more money and better health. They may also cherish their independence more than did the elderly of earlier eras.[4] Consequently, the elderly now live on their own instead of with

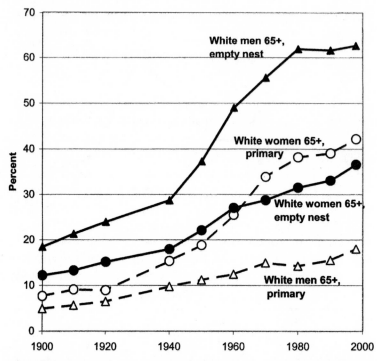

Figure 6.7. Percent of Elderly Who Live Either as "Primary Individuals" (dashed lines) or in an "Empty Nest" (solid lines), for White Men (triangles) and White Women (circles), 1900–98

Source: Steven Ruggles, Matthew Sobek, Trent Alexander, Catherine A. Fitch, Ronald Goeken, Patricia Kelly Hall, Miriam King, and Chad Ronnander, *Integrated Public Use Microdata Series: Version 3*, machine-readable database (Minneapolis: Minnesota Population Center, 2004), available at http://www.ipums.umn.edu/ usa/; Current Population Survey.

their children. Ironically, during the past thirty years, Americans have increasingly told pollsters that they think the aged should not live independently but should live with their children, but that trend emerged only because younger generations, not the elderly themselves, endorsed co-living.[5]

   The next big change is the enormous increase in the proportion of married women, and the proportion of mothers with children under six, working outside the home, shown in figure 6.8. In 1920, about 10 percent of married women officially worked; in 2000, more than 60 percent did. Note that the low percentages in the early part of the century are serious underestimates.[6] Nonetheless, the "real" trend is still a fundamental and sharp change. This trend, by the way, accelerated through the 1950s without pause. This transformation, too, had immense ramifications for our families, our children, and our culture—ramifications we have not yet fully absorbed.

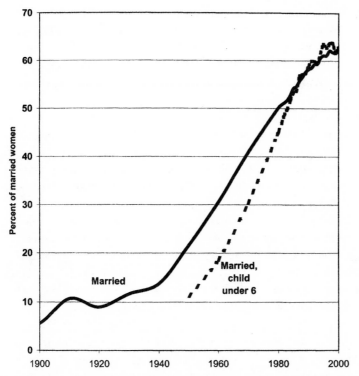

Figure 6.8. Percent of Married Women (and Married Women with a Child under 6) in the Labor Force, 1900–2000
Sources: U.S. Bureau of the Census, *Historical Statistics* and *Statistical Abstracts*.

These family changes, we submit, were the greatest in scale and probably in consequence. But there were also other noteworthy changes.

Modest Changes

One such change is the fluctuation in the age at which Americans married. First it dropped. American women marrying around 1900 tended to be about twenty-two years old; those marrying around 1950 tended to be about twenty, meaning that in the 1950s, about half of all brides were teenagers. This helps to explain the baby boom. Those marrying at the end of the century averaged twenty-four years of age on their wedding day, and a growing subgroup was marrying in their thirties.

Also, of course, the divorce rate increased. At the beginning of the century, there was roughly one divorce issued for every ten marriages performed. By the early 1990s, it was about one for every two, although the divorce rate has been dropping since roughly 1980.[7] This is a fivefold increase in divorce, but we do not call it a "big change." One reason is that rates of marriage dissolution did not change nearly as much. Early in the century, marriages broke up because a spouse died. If one combines dissolution by death with dissolution by divorce, the total stayed pretty constant to 1970, as rising divorce balanced out declining mortality. By 1980, rising divorce pushed the total dissolution rate about one-fourth over its historical level, but it has subsided some since then.[8] Another reason we do not stress divorce is that most divorced people remarry. As we saw above, in figures 6.1 and 6.2, the proportion of adults living unmarried did not increase nearly as much as the dramatic rise in the divorce rate would suggest. Many of those who do not remarry, it turns out, cohabit instead.

The increasing delay of marriage, in turn, contributed to higher rates of premarital sex. So, for example, about half of women who were teenagers in the 1950s were virgins at marriage, compared with under one-third of women who were teens in the 1970s.[9] The drop in virgin brides is, in part, simply the result of a longer time between puberty, which is now arriving earlier, and marriage, which is now arriving later. This change, by the way, also stopped or reversed in the 1990s.

Cohabitation, both before and after the first marriage, has increased significantly in the last few decades, as has popular tolerance of it. The proportion of American households at any one time with a cohabiting couple rose from under 1 percent in 1960 to a still low 5 percent in 2000. More important, half of married couples now begin their conjugal lives by cohabiting.[10]

A consequence of both delaying marriage and increasing divorce is the increase in children living with a single parent. We shall look more closely at this below, but the simple fact is that for the first half of the century, about 5 percent of American children were recorded as living with only a single parent, and more than 20 percent were doing so in 2000.

Finally in this list, survey data, which do not go back further than about 1960, show that Americans became in recent decades increasingly tolerant of these and related changes—of smaller families, of women working, of premarital sex, of cohabitation, and of single-parent families. That is, Americans increasingly accepted wider ranges of individual choices in how to form a family.

Minor or Minimal Changes

Many other aspects of the family changed little, as far as we can tell. Both marriage and children continue to be valued. Americans still say they want to marry. For example, in a 2001 Gallup survey, more than nine in ten teenagers said that they wanted to marry and to have children, an increase over a generation.[11] Single adults age twenty through twenty-nine fully endorsed marriage; 78 percent said that being married was a very important life goal, 88 percent said that they were confident of finding a suitable spouse when they are ready to marry, and 88 percent answered yes when asked if there was a unique "soul mate" for them "out there."[12]

Moreover, Americans do get married. The latest estimates are that 90 percent of women now about forty years old have married or will eventually marry, even if later in life. This is a marriage rate notably higher than that in the early part of the twentieth century or, for that matter, the mid–nineteenth century.[13] Another indicator of how Americans value marriage is that, despite increasingly tolerating premarital sex, Americans in recent decades have become less tolerant of extramarital sex. The thread connecting American attitudes on these subjects seems to be an increasing emphasis on freedom of choice combined with insistence on personal responsibility: Have premarital sex as you wish, marry as you wish, but if you marry, stay faithful.[14]

Finally, sociologists and historians have perused as many tea leaves as possible to see if they can spot a trend in familial intimacy, affection, and commitment. We can make no solid case one way or the other. What scholars can say with some confidence is that the standards and expectations for intimacy, affection, and commitment have increased. Whether in responses to survey data or in the complaints people list when in filing for divorce, Americans during the twentieth century demanded more companionship, warmth, and happiness in marriage.

What can we generalize about family change over the century? Here are a few defensible statements:

- Americans always preferred the household of a married couple with children.
- During the twentieth century, it became increasingly possible to have such a nuclear family. In the earlier years, many external events blocked that goal: premature death, ill health, economic dislocation, unplanned pregnancies, and infertility. These disturbances became less important. People have more control now. So more people spend more of their lives in marriage than was true a few generations ago.
- The second choice after a married-couple household has changed. In the first half of the century, people who could not—because they were spinsters or widows or orphans—be in a married-couple household lived instead with other relatives, or in institutional settings like poorhouses and orphanages. In recent decades, this has changed. People have been more able and perhaps more willing to choose other alter-

natives—if the married-couple arrangement was not available—to live alone, cohabit, or be a single parent.

· Other values such as personal attainment and independence, especially for women, increasingly competed with the goal of the married-couple household. Women's alternatives have expanded. Standards for a good marriage rose, and escapes from bad ones became easier. As a result, marriages are increasingly delayed or broken by choice rather than by external disruptions.

One consequence of these decisions can be trouble for the children. Children increasingly are living with a single parent outside a nuclear or an extended household. This is what we will look at more closely now.

Family Trouble: The Single-Parented Child

It is generally understood that children have easier lives and do somewhat better when they live with two parents instead of one.[15] Figure 6.9 shows the distribution of children, age birth to seventeen years, by their living arrangements across the century.[16] On top, we see the percentage who lived just with two parents and siblings (if any), the ideal nuclear family. In 1900, about 70 percent of children lived that way; another roughly 20 percent lived in an extended family that often included both parents.[17] The proportion in the nuclear family then rose to 78 percent by 1960 and then dropped down to 64 percent at the end of the century, a bit lower than it was 100 years before. (If we add cohabiting parents to married parents, then the 2000 figure is 66 percent.) These numbers unfortunately do not distinguish between children living with their original parents from those living in a stepfamily, and some literature suggests that stepparent families are less conducive to child welfare than having both original parents.[18] The long-term data we draw upon cannot distinguish biological from stepparents, but stepparents surely formed a larger portion of two-parent households recently than they did in the 1950s; whether stepparents were more common recently than in the early part of the century is not clear.

Until thirty years ago, children who were not in a nuclear family were likely to be in extended-family households, perhaps with a grandparent, uncle, or cousins—shown in figure 6.9 by a dashed line. Most of those households included both the child's two parents, at least early in the century, or one parent, more often now. Whether the extended household experience was better, the same, or worse than the two-parent household can be argued. The category of "other," shown at the bottom, refers to children living on their

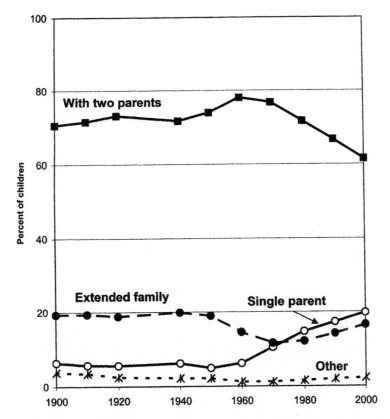

Figure 6.9. Percent of Children (Birth to Age 17), by Living Arrangement, 1900–2000
Source: Steven Ruggles, Matthew Sobek, Trent Alexander, Catherine A. Fitch, Ronald Goeken, Patricia Kelly Hall, Miriam King, and Chad Ronnander, Integrated Public Use Microdata Series: Version 3, machine-readable database (Minneapolis: Minnesota Population Center, 2004), available at http://www.ipums.umn.edu/usa/.

own or in some kind of group setting. Finally, we see—along a line connecting circles—the rise since 1960 in the proportion of children living with only one parent and no other relatives besides siblings. It had been under 10 percent for most of the century, took off in 1970, and reached 20 percent in 2000. This group and this last period is the subject of greatest public concern.[19]

The first question we have been raising is "Since when?" And we see here that the "when" is the 1950s. Indeed, if we were to push our view before 1900 back into the nineteenth century, we would quite likely see the bottom line, "other," keep going up and up as we move backward—backward into the era when children under eighteen, even many under twelve, were sent out of their homes to be farmhands, apprentices, and servants in other people's homes

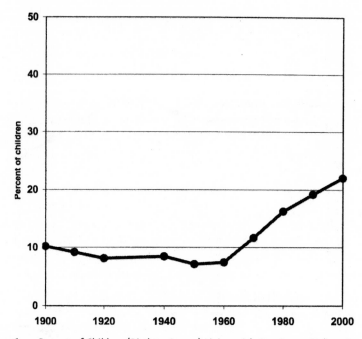

Figure 6.10. Percent of Children (Birth to Age 17) Living with One Parent Only or in "Other" Nonfamily Arrangement, 1900–2000
Source: Steven Ruggles, Matthew Sobek, Trent Alexander, Catherine A. Finch, Ronald Goeken, Patricia Kelly Hall, Miriam King, and Chad Ronnander, *Integrated Public Use Microdata Series: Version 3*, machine-readable database (Minneapolis: Minnesota Population Center, 2004), available at http://www.ipums.umn.edu/usa/.

and thus lived with neither parent nor extended kin but with "others." The 1950s may have been the decade with the least disruption to Victorian ideals of childhood in American history.

If comparing a couple of centuries is too long a period to make the point that we need to be specific about "when," then consider the last decade alone. The proportion of children living with fewer than two parents topped out at 32 percent in the mid-1990s (67 percent in 1995 for blacks) and dropped to 31 percent in 2002 (61 percent for blacks).[20] Other data also point to a recent decline in the behaviors that produce single-parent families, such as teen pregnancy and divorce, suggesting that we may have already seen the peak of one-parent households. So, again, we need to ask what we are using as historical comparisons and what is a reasonable comparison. Since when?

The other question we have been asking is "For whom?" Figure 6.10 focuses on the category of children living with only a single parent only or in one of those anomalous "other" settings. Then figure 6.11 shows us that the rise

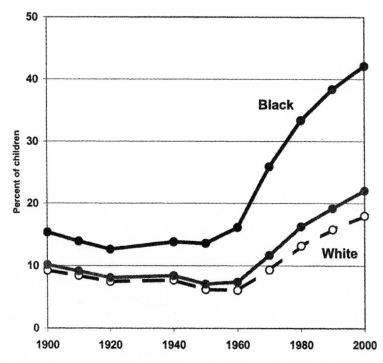

Figure 6.11. Percent of Children (Birth to Age 17) Living with One Parent Only or in "Other" Nonfamily Arrangement, by Race, 1900–2000

Source: Steven Ruggles, Matthew Sobek, Trent Alexander, Catherine A. Fitch, Ronald Goeken, Patricia Kelly Hall, Miriam King, and Chad Ronnander, *Integrated Public Use Microdata Series: Version 3*, machine-readable database. (Minneapolis: Minnesota Population Center, 2004), available at http://www.ipums.umn.edu/usa/.

in such children is disproportionately among black children. The black/white differential opened up in 1940 and then widened. Before 1940, white children were about 60 percent as likely as black children to be in a single-parent household; by the 1990s, they were about 40 percent as likely.[21] Single parenting has become disproportionately a "trouble" of the black community.

Sociologists believe that the trouble for black children, which accelerated in the 1950s and 1960s, coincides with increasing difficulties of black men in northern cities, which began with the loss of well-paying blue-collar jobs and then were compounded by rising drug use and crime. The result is that, though blacks and whites equally value the aspiration of getting married, blacks have become more disappointed with or even cynical about marriage.[22] That response may have taken on a life of its own, although there were signs in the late 1990s of marriage starting to rebound among African Americans.

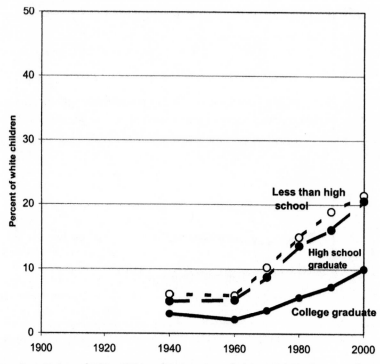

Figure 6.12. Percent of White Children (Birth to Age 17) Living with Single Parent, by Education of Parent, 1940–2000
Source: Steven Ruggles, Matthew Sobek, Trent Alexander, Catherine A. Fitch, Ronald Goeken, Patricia Kelly Hall, Miriam King, and Chad Ronnander, *Integrated Public Use Microdata Series: Version 3*, machine-readable database (Minneapolis: Minnesota Population Center, 2004), available at http://www.ipums.umn.edu/usa/.

Even among whites, there is a question "For whom?" Figure 6.12 divides white children up by the educational level of the head of their households, information available only since 1940. (For simplicity, the category of "some college" is not shown; their children fall in between the college and high school graduates.) It shows that children of college graduates have been affected only modestly by expanding single parenthood; the trend is specific to those without college educations. In another approach to the same question, David Ellwood and Christopher Jencks have shown that young white women with relatively little education tripled their propensity to be a single parent between the 1960s and 2000, while young white women with relatively much education saw no change—5 percent of the well-educated women were single mothers in the 1960s and 5 percent were single mothers in the 1990s.[23]

As in the case of African Americans, we suspect that this pattern is connected to the more difficult economic situation faced since the 1970s by couples with limited educations. Ironically, better-educated Americans are

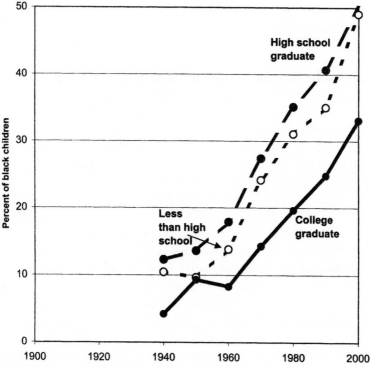

Figure 6.13. Percent of Black Children (Birth to Age 17) Living with Single Parent, by Education of Parent, 1940–2000

Source: Steven Ruggles, Matthew Sobek, Trent Alexander, Catherine A. Fitch, Ronald Goeken, Patricia Kelly Hall, Miriam King, and Chad Ronnander, *Integrated Public Use Microdata Series: Version 3*, machine-readable database (Minneapolis: Minnesota Population Center, 2004), available at http://www.ipums.umn.edu/usa/.

(slightly) more likely to resist the ideology that says that any marriage is better than none, but they are nonetheless more likely to achieve it.[24] Joshua Goldstein and Catherine Kenny found that these days, in a reversal of historical patterns, college-graduate women have a better chance of marrying than do women without a diploma.[25]

For African American children, the educational pattern is somewhat different. In figure 6.13, we see that black children of college graduates have been less likely to be in single-parent homes than other black children, but that the rates of all educational groups increased steeply. The percentage of black children of college graduates who lived in a single-parent household increased eightfold, almost 30 points, between 1940 and 2000, while the increase for white children of college graduates was threefold, 7 points.) Conversely, Ellwood and Jencks found that the one-third most-educated black women were not much more likely to be single parents in the late 1990s than in the late 1960s, which contradicts the story of figure 6.13.[26] Our data reinforce suggestions that middle-class black families have difficulty protecting their children from the spillover of social problems from lower-income black communities.

Economics is not all that is involved in the growth of single parenting. Changes in the specifics of single parenthood—the who and the when—parallel both cultural as well as material changes; they thereby tell us something about the "why." The 1960s as a cultural phenomenon shaped family life through rapid ideological shifts concerning gender, sex, and rights of personal fulfillment. That helps account for some of the timing and the growth in single parenting even among white elites; it happened quickly around 1970, a pattern consistent with a change in preferences. For example, in just the four years between July 1969 and July 1973, the percentage of Americans who said that premarital sex was "wrong" dropped 21 points; in the subsequent nearly three decades, it dropped only another 9 points.[27]

Yet material conditions also matter. For example, in the early 1970s, college graduates were notably more liberal on premarital sex than were high school graduates or high school dropouts; but, as we saw, it is not the children of college graduates who ended up in one-parent homes. At the same time, blacks' attitudes about premarital sex became more conservative; yet it was black children who increasingly ended up in one-parent homes.[28] We know that blacks and whites without college degrees suffered from stagnating or even declining men's incomes in this same period, even as women's earnings grew. And we know that economically marginal men tend to leave fatherless children behind. That economic strain must be part of the "why." And it reminds us of the strains that disrupted many families in the early part of the century.

Conclusion

The effort we have gone through to look at who was affected when by family troubles is more than an accounting exercise. The numbers help us understand why these changes occurred and, potentially, what levers of influence exist. For example, the historical data going back to the early part of the twentieth century make it difficult to explain family change as a linear consequence of "modernity." Classic sociological theories of the family, notably those of the 1950s, claim that the family lost its functions to the state and other institutions and therefore became weaker. But the nonlinear changes in the family cast doubt on such an explanation; for example, people are as or more likely to marry now as they were a century ago. The internal variations we have tracked also lead us to question such explanations. It is, after all, the most advantaged among us who have most embraced nonfamilial opportunities, sending children off to college and purchasing family services such as food, cleaning, child care, and parenting advice. Yet the most advantaged have been the least affected by family troubles. The data also cast doubt on simple economic explanations of family patterns. For example, the notion that people have children to serve as their old-age insurance runs up against the contradiction that Americans indulged in a huge baby boom just after the U.S. government set up public old-age insurance.[29] History speaks to us.

When we put "family troubles" in historical perspective, we learn a few broad lessons. One is that troubles with marriage and parenting are concentrated among Americans with disadvantages. These Americans would live the 1950s ideal if they could, but they often cannot. In this way, they are like many Americans a century ago, whose family aspirations were blocked by death, disease, and disaster. Not many advantaged Americans have such problems. As we saw, in 2000, only one in ten white children with a college-educated parent as head of household lived in a single-parent home.

Another lesson is that, for more advantaged Americans, being unwed, childless, or divorced is less a matter of malign fate and more a matter of new opportunities. Increasing affluence and improving health have made more choices more available to more people. These people choose to delay marriage, to have fewer children, and to live apart from those children when they age. These choices are not "family troubles," except insofar as one assumes that people not living in a nuclear family are ipso facto troubled. To be sure, trouble in the form of divorce or single parenting does occasionally visit such people these days. We might best understand the family troubles that some of the advantaged face as a by-product of cultural shifts, such as the increasing freedom that individuals have to make personal, self-expressive choices in sex, marriage, and the family. And these are cultural shifts we typically approve. For example, vastly more wives work than before and vastly more Americans approve. In 1938, about one in four Americans said that it was okay for a wife to work if her husband could support her; by the 1990s, more than three in four did.[30] Yet such expansions of personal autonomy for the well-off can carry costs, one of which is increasing divorce and another is increasing numbers of children being single parented. Our moral burden, then, is to deal with the side effects, such as single parenting, of the changes we desire, such as more options for women.

Finally, we learn that America's social history is more complex and nuanced than many a simple gloss would have it. For example, every year the Bureau of the Census announces and newspapers report that a smaller percentage of American homes are occupied by nuclear families. True, but what does that mean? It largely means that more homes are occupied by still-vibrant older couples or singles whose youngest child left home before the parents turned fifty and who have thirty years of life to go. Increasing life spans have also meant that Americans spend more years knowing their aging parents, watching their children grow up, and sharing the company of a spouse.[31] So with regard to family troubles, we do need to ask "Since when?" and "For whom?"

Notes

This chapter draws on a longer work: Michael Hout and Claude S. Fischer, "American Households through the Twentieth Century," Working Paper, USA: Century of Difference Project, University of California, Berkeley (http://ucdata.berkeley.edu/rsfcensus), funded by the Russell Sage Foundation. Readers interested in further documentation for the points made here should consult that source. The authors acknowledge the research assistance of Jon Stiles and Gretchen Stockmayer, and helpful comments by Steven Tipton.

1. Our data largely come from the U.S. censuses for 1900 through 2000—except for 1930, which has only just been released. These raw files have been compiled and made available as the Integrated Public Use Microdata Series; see Steven Ruggles, Matthew Sobek, Trent Alexander, Catherine A. Fitch, Ronald Goeken, Patricia Kelly Hall, Miriam King, and Chad Ronnander, *Integrated Public Use Microdata Series: Version 3*, machine-readable database (Minneapolis: Minnesota Population Center, 2004), available at http://www.ipums.umn.edu/usa/.

2. These numbers are from the National Center for Health Statistics, available at http://www.infoplease.com/ipa/A0005140.html.

3. That longer line is unavailable because earlier data use the number of children under five per the number of women age fifteen to forty-four. See U.S. Census Bureau, *Historical Statistics of the United States* (Washington, D.C.: U.S. Government Printing Office, 1977), 54; and subsequent *Statistical Abstracts*.

4. Frances E. Kobrin, "The Fall in Household Size and the Rise of the Primary Individual in the United States since 1940," *Journal of Marriage and the Family* 38 (May 1976): 233–39.

5. Authors' analysis of the General Social Survey (GSS) item "AGED," http://csa.berkeley.edu:7502/archive.htm.

6. For one, many wives worked informally in family businesses—farms, in particular. Others "took in" work, such as laundry, that they may not have reported. Also, we have reason to suspect that "respectable" families underreported the wives' work.

7. The gross divorce rate in 1979 was 5.3 per 1,000 Americans; it was 4.1 in 2000 (http://www.cdc.gov/nchs). Joshua R. Goldstein, "The Leveling of Divorce in the United States," *Demography* 36 (August 1999): 409–14, finds that this was a meaningful social change, not a statistical fluke.

8. These calculations are summarized in Andrew J. Cherlin, *Marriage, Divorce, Remarriage*, rev. ed. (Cambridge, Mass.: Harvard University Press, 1992), 25. The rate of dissolution from the 1860s through 1970 was about 33 to 34 dissolutions per 1,000 marriages; it rose to a peak of 41 around 1980 and declined to 39 by 1989.

9. Edward Laumann, John H. Gagnon, Robert T. Michael, and Stuart Michaels, *The Social Organization of Sexuality* (Chicago: University of Chicago Press, 1994), 197–99, 213–14; see also Sandra L. Hofferth, Joan R. Kahn, and Wendy Baldwin, "Premarital Sexual Activity among American Teenage Women over the Past Three Decades," *Family Planning*

Perspectives 19 (March 1987): 46–53. On early twentieth-century premarital sexuality, see, e.g., Daniel Scott Smith, "The Dating of the American Sexual Revolution" in *The American Family in Social-Historical Perspective*, 2nd edition, ed. Michael Gordon (New York: St. Martin's Press, 1978), 426–38; Amara Bachu, "Trends in Marital Status of U.S. Women at First Birth: 1930 to 1994," *Current Population Reports*, Special Studies (Washington, D.C.: U.S. Bureau of the Census, 1999), 23–197; and Stuart N. Seidman and Ronald O. Rieder, "A Review of Sexual Behavior in the United States," *American Journal of Psychiatry* 151 (March 1994): 330–41.

10. Lynne M. Casper and Suzanne M. Bianchi, *Continuity and Change in the American Family* (Thousand Oaks, Calif.: Sage Publications, 2002), chap. 1.

11. Linda Lyons, "Kids and Divorce," Gallup Online, http://www.gallup.com.

12. Kelley Maybury, "I Do? Marriage in Uncertain Times," Gallup Online, http://www.gallup.com.

13. Joshua R. Goldstein and Catherine T. Kenny, "Marriage Delayed or Marriage Forgone? New Cohort Forecasts of First Marriage for U.S. Women," *American Sociological Review* 66 (August 2001): 506–19. Goldstein and Kenny project current women's experiences into the twenty-first century. On longer historical comparisons, see Catherine A. Fitch and Steven Ruggles, "Historical Trends in Marriage Formation: The United States 1850–1990," in *The Ties That Bind: Perspectives on Marriage and Cohabitation*, ed. Linda J. Waite (New York: Aldine de Gruyter, 2000), 59–89. The percentage of never-married women in Charleston and Boston circa 1845 was higher than now; see Jane H. Pease and William H. Pease, *Ladies, Women, and Wenches: Choice and Constraint in Antebellum Charleston and Boston* (Chapel Hill: University of North Carolina Press, 1990).

14. On this and other attitude items, see Arland Thornton and Linda Young-Demarco, "Four Decades of Trends in Attitudes toward Family Issues in the United States," *Journal of Marriage and the Family* 63 (November 2001): 1009–38.

15. Sara McLanahan, "Life without Father: What Happens to the Children?" *Contexts* 1 (spring 2002): 35–44, provides an overview. The literature is large and controversial, but we assume that, other things being equal, a one-parent family as less desirable for children.

16. The numbers exclude from the base the few zero- to seventeen-year-olds who were in married couples with no children households—i.e., young brides and grooms. "Other" includes the very tiny fraction who were on their own and a small percentage who were in some form of "shared quarters."

17. Census data show that 84 percent of children in 1900 lived with two parents, suggesting that most of the children in extended households (seven of ten) had both parents there. U.S. Bureau of the Census, "Historical Living Arrangements of Children," http://www.census.gov/population/socdemo/child/p70-74/tabo2.xls.

18. E.g., Andrew J. Cherlin and Frank F. Furstenberg Jr., "Stepfamilies in the United States: A Reconsideration," *Annual Review of Sociology* 20 (1994): 359–81; McLanahan, "Life without Father."

19. Census Bureau calculations show that the percentage of children living with one or neither parent was 13 to 17 percent from 1900 through 1970, then rose to 31 percent by 2000. U.S. Bureau of the Census, "Historical Living Arrangements of Children"; plus 2000 Current Population Survey.

20. These figures are based on slightly different data, "Table CH-1: Living Arrangements of Children under 18 Years Old: 1960 to Present," http://www.census.gov, drawn from the *Current Population Survey* and more recent data from the same source. These data count children living in extended households with a parent or two as living with a parent or both.

21. On this point, see also Fitch and Ruggles, "Historical Trends," 65.

22. This summary statement is supported by the many ethnographies of poor African Americans. It also shows up in survey data. The GSS asked unmarried people in the 1990s, "If the right person came along, would you like to be married?" There was no difference between blacks and whites (either a raw difference, or after statistical controls). Blacks were even slightly more likely to say that a bad marriage was better than no marriage. But on questions such as whether married people were happier than unmarried people, whether personal freedom was more important than marriage, whether people who want children should wait to get married, and whether single mothers can raise children as well as married couples, blacks were noticeably more skeptical about the marriage option. Authors' analysis of the GSS.

23. David T. Ellwood and Christopher Jencks, "The Growing Differences in Family Structure: What Do We Know? Where Do We Look for Answers?" John F. Kennedy School of Government, Harvard University, July 2001, fig. 1.

24. In GSS data, educational attainment is positively associated (controlling for race, age, and gender) with saying that one would not marry even if the right person came along and with denying that a bad marriage is better than no marriage (authors' analysis).

25. Goldstein and Kenny, "Marriage Delayed."

26. Ellwood and Jencks, "Growing Differences," fig. 2.

27. In 1969, 68 percent said it was wrong for "a man and a woman to have sexual relations before marriage"; in 1973, 47 percent did; in 2001, 38 percent did. Similarly, Americans' ideal family size dropped sharply in those few years. Between 1936 and 1967, the percentage of Americans who said that three or more children was ideal ranged from 61 to 77 percent; in 1967, it was 70 percent. But in 1973, it was 43 percent, a 27-point drop in six years. After 1973, that percentage ranged from 28 to 42; Lydia Saad, "Majority Considers Sex before Marriage Morally Okay," http://www.gallup.com.

28. Authors' analysis of the GSS item "PREMARSX": Among whites under sixty-five years of age, the percentage who said that premarital sex was "not wrong at all" was, in the early 1970s, 39 percent for college graduates, 31 percent for high school graduates, and 25 percent for high school dropouts. (By the late 1990s, the percentages were virtually identical, at 51, 48, and 49.) Similarly, white attitudes toward premarital sex became more liberal between 1970 and 2000. Among white women under sixty-five, "not wrong at all" answers increased steadily from 25 percent in the early 1970s to 46 percent in the late 1990s. Conversely, black women under sixty-five hit a high point of 54 percent "not wrong at all" in the late 1970s and dropped to 36 percent in the late 1990s. Yet black rates of single-parented children increased until the mid-1990s.

29. Similarly, scholars of the fertility decline that began in the nineteenth century have found simple economic explanations insufficient.

30. The GSS asked Americans whether the women's movement had improved, worsened, or not affected the lives of particular groups. Moderate pluralities to large majorities said "improved" in answers referring to questions about effects on "homemakers," working-class women, professional women, and even children. People were evenly split as to whether men benefited or lost from the women's movement (authors' analysis).

31. Susan Cotts Watkins, Jane A. Menken, and John Bongaarts, "Demographic Foundations of Family Change," *American Sociological Review* 52 (June 1987): 346–58.

Part III

I Do, I Don't: Reasons and Rites for and against Marriage and Family Life

Chapter 7
Marriage and Responsible Fatherhood: The Social Science Case and Thoughts about a Theological Case

Linda J. Waite and William J. Doherty

Marriage in the contemporary world is a social institution and a legal contract between two individuals to form a sexual, productive, and reproductive union. Through the marriage, this union is recognized by the family, society, religious institutions, and the legal system. Marriage defines the relationship of the two individuals with each other, with any children they might have, with their extended families, with shared property and assets, and with society generally. It recognizes the paternity of the father and defines his responsibilities to the mother and child. It also defines the relationship of others, including social institutions, with the married couple.

In recent decades, this idea of marriage as a social institution and central legal contract has been challenged by the view that marriage should be seen as a personal lifestyle to be entered and exited freely. From this perspective, parenthood should not necessarily be linked to marriage, and marriage should not be privileged over other adult intimate arrangements.[1] In addition to libertarian ideological grounds, this view of marriage has been based on two empirical assumptions that we challenge in this chapter: the idea that marriage does not contribute to the well-being of married people, and women in particular; and the idea that good coparenting—and fathering in particular—can be disentangled from marriage. We begin with an overview of marriage as a social institution, and we then review the research on the benefits of marriage. We next address evidence for the role of marriage in responsible fathering. Finally, we briefly address moral and theological issues in the connection between marriage and fathering.

The key features of marriage include a legally binding, long-term contract; sexual exclusivity; coresidence; shared resources; and joint production. Spouses acquire rights and responsibilities with marriage, which are enforceable through the legal systems and through social expectations and social pressure.

Legal Aspects of Marriage

"Marriage" differs from other, less formal relationships primarily in its legal status. Marriage is a legally binding contract. As such, the treatment of marriage in the law shapes the institution, and recent changes in family law appear to have made marriage less stable. Historically, in the United States and many other countries, both secular and religious law generally viewed marriage vows as binding and permanent. The marriage contract could only be broken if one spouse violated the most basic obligations to the other and could be judged "at fault" in the breakdown of the marriage.[2]

Beginning in the mid-1960s, however, states of the United States substantially liberalized and simplified their divorce laws. One key feature of these changes was a shift from divorce based on fault or mutual consent to unilateral divorce, which required the willingness of only one spouse to end the marriage. Most states also adopted some form of the resulting "no-fault" divorce, which eliminated the need for one spouse to demonstrate a violation of the marriage contract by the other. The shift to unilateral no-fault divorce laws was accompanied by a surge in divorce rates in the United States. At least some of the increase in divorce rates appears to have resulted directly from the shift in the legal environment in which couples marry and decide to remain married, or in which they divorce.[3] The link between divorce rates and laws that permit unilateral divorce has led several states to develop more binding alternative marriage contracts, such as "covenant marriage."

Key Features of the Institution of Marriage

Permanence, joint production, coresidence, and the social recognition of a sexual and child-rearing union are perhaps the most important characteristics of the institution of marriage.[4] These features lead to some of the other defining characteristics of marriage. Because two adults make a legally binding promise to live and work together for their joint well-being, and to do so ideally for the rest of their lives, they tend to specialize, dividing between them the labor required to maintain the family. This specialization allows married men and women to produce more than they would if they did not specialize. The coresidence and resource sharing of married couples lead to substantial economies of scale; at any standard of living, it costs much less for people to live together than it would if they lived separately. These economies of scale and the specialization of spouses both tend to increase the economic well-being of family members living together.

The institution of marriage assumes the sharing of economic and social resources and coinsurance. Spouses act as a small insurance pool against life's uncertainties, reducing their need to protect themselves by themselves against unexpected events. Marriage also connects spouses and family members to a larger network of help, support, and obligation through their extended family, friends, and others. The insurance function of marriage increases the economic well-being of family members.[5] The support function of marriage improves their emotional well-being.[6]

The institution of marriage also builds on and fosters trust. Because spouses share social and economic resources, and expect to do so over the long term, both gain when the family unit gains. This reduces the need for family members to monitor the behavior of other members, increasing efficiency.[7]

The Benefits of Marriage

As a result of the features just discussed, marriage changes the behavior of spouses and thereby their well-being. Married people tend to have better physical and emotional health than single people, at least in part because they are married.[8] The social support provided by a spouse, combined with the economic resources produced by the marriage, facilitate both the production and maintenance of health. Married men and women report higher levels of sexual activity and sexual satisfaction than single men and women. The specialization, economies of scale, and insurance functions of marriage all increase the economic well-being of family members, and the increase is typically quite substantial. Generally, married people produce more and accumulate more assets than unmarried people.[9] And children raised by their married parents experience better outcomes, on average, than those raised in other situations.

Next, we describe the benefits provided by marriage on each of these dimensions and discuss possible explanations for the better outcomes shown by married people.

Emotional Health

Mental and emotional well-being are important components of health and necessary ingredients to a happy life. And these advantages seem to accrue more often to the married than to those who are single. Married men and married women show better emotional health than those who are not married, on average, reporting less depression, less anxiety, and lower levels of other types of psychological distress than those who are single, divorced, or widowed.[10] When social observers first noted this pattern, they wondered whether simply living with another person, which almost all married persons do, was the source of the psychological health of the married. Perhaps living alone causes distress, and those unmarried men and women living with others get the psychological benefits of marriage. Walter Gove and Michael Hughes tested this idea by comparing married adults and unmarried adults who lived alone with those who lived with someone else; they found that living with someone did not provide the same boost in psychological well-being as being married. Single adults were more depressed than married adults, and living with others did not solve the problem.[11]

A number of recent studies have attempted to assess the mental health consequences of marriage and divorce, and to separate these from the selection of emotionally healthy individuals into marriage and distressed or unhealthy individuals out. These studies followed individuals over time as some marry, some divorce, and some retain their previous marital status. Consistently, transitions into marriage improve mental health, on average, for both men and women, and transitions out of marriage decrease it.[12] Robin Simon finds that divorce increases symptoms of emotional distress among both women and men, but women show greater increases than men in depressive symptoms following divorce. Both men and women who divorce report a significant increase in alcohol abuse. Simon also finds that men and women who divorced reported more depression and more alcohol problems earlier than those who remained married, which she interprets as evidence that low levels of emotional well-being are both a cause and a consequence of disruption.

The better emotional health of married people results, at least in part, from the social support marriage offers. Almost by definition, married people share their lives with their spouses to a much greater extent than single adults share their lives with the people they live with. Roommates, parents, and adult children all have their own separate lives to a much greater extent than spouses do. Even parents and children are supposed to be more independent of each other emotionally and financially, at least once they are all adults, than we expect husbands and wives to be. So in marriages that are working reasonably well, husbands and wives have a built-in confidant to offer them support to an extent not generally available to those who are single. Good marriages provide the partners with a sense of being cared for, esteemed, loved, and valued as a person. And no matter what else is going on in life, these feelings make problems easier to bear.

But the psychological benefits of marriage come only from good-enough marriages—those rated by the individual as "happy" or "very happy." A bad marriage—one rated as not too happy or not at all happy—actually makes things worse. Not surprisingly, men and women in the relatively small number of unhappy marriages show more psychological distress than do single people.[13] People who say that their relationships are unhappy, that they would like to change many aspects of their relationship, and that they often consider leaving their spouse or partner have higher distress levels than people without partners at all.[14] If a good marriage is a source of support and intimacy, an unhappy marriage is a source of pain and self-doubt.

Physical Health and Longevity

People in good physical health feel fit and energetic, without pain, disability, or symptoms of disease. Good health means more than just the absence of disease or its symptoms; it means feeling robust and strong. Good health is a resource. It gives people access to activities and achievements that they value. And most people badly want to be free from pain, fatigue, and symptoms of disease. But men and women who are married are more likely to get the "benefits" of good physical health than are the unmarried. For example, Waite and Hughes find that among men and women at midlife, those who were married and living only with a spouse (and, perhaps, children) reported significantly better physical health and were less likely to have a condition that limited their mobility than unmarried adults and those in more complicated living arrangements.[15]

Health Behaviors

Married people, especially married men, show better health behaviors than those who are not married. One out of four young single men reported in a recent national survey that they drink enough to cause them problems at work or problems with aggression. Young married men the same age, who were also similar in race and level of education, showed substantially fewer problems with alcohol. Single men no doubt see more problems from drinking because they drink more, almost twice as much as married men. One out of four married men drink so little that they qualify as "abstainers"; only one out of six or seven single men drink this little.[16] Divorced and widowed men also show substantially more problems with alcohol than married men.[17]

Single men do not just drink more than married men. They also are more likely to drink and drive, more likely to get into fights, and more likely to take risks that increase the chances of accidents and injuries.[18] Alcohol plays a role in many of these behaviors. People drink and drive when they need to get home after an evening of drinking somewhere else. And excessive drinking can precipitate fights, arguments, and accidents. Some people drink to deal with depression, anxiety, or other emotional problems; heavy drinking reduces depression in the short run but increases it in the long run.[19]

Marriage seems to discourage these unhealthy behaviors. Single men who are heading toward marriage reduce their drinking up to a year before the ceremony, so that although they start with the same heavy drinking patterns as their friends who stay single, by the time they marry they drink much less than they did a year earlier. At the same time, the alcohol consumption of young men who stay single remains high and they continue to experience problems from drinking. Young men who were light drinkers, moderate drinkers, and heavy drinkers prior to marrying *all* drink less after they marry than they did before.[20] Marriage also seems to benefit women during the young adult years, when they are most likely to smoke, drink heavily, and use drugs. Although young women less often drink or drink heavily than young men, and less often use cocaine or marijuana, those who marry reduce these negative behaviors dramatically compared with those who stay single.[21]

One important avenue through which marriage improves women's health and longevity appears to be income. Women with income in excess of their own earnings rate their health as better than women without these added financial resources.[22] And married women's longer lives seem to result in large part from the greater financial resources that husbands bring.[23]

Marriage also gives women access to private health insurance, an increasingly precious commodity in the contemporary United States. Hahn showed that just over half of divorced, widowed, and never-married women had private health insurance, compared with 83 percent of married women.[24] Women with private health insurance rate their health significantly higher than women without it. Insurance coverage improves health directly by giving women access to health care services, and it improves psychological health by giving people a sense of security about their health care.[25]

Catherine Ross and her colleagues summed up the evidence on the relationship between marital status and longevity: "Compared to married people, the nonmarried . . . have higher rates of mortality than the married: about 50 percent higher among women and 250 percent higher among men."[26] The unmarried face especially high mortality rates for causes of death that have a large behavioral component, such as suicide,[27] accidents, lung cancer, and cirrhosis.

All marriages are not equal. The quality of the relationship between the spouses makes a difference. Couples whose marriages improve over time also see improvements in the physical health of husband and wife, primarily through the improvements in psychological well-being that accompany better marriage quality.[28]

How Does Marriage Improve Health?

How does marriage improve health? For one thing, marriage provides individuals—especially men—with someone who monitors their health and keeps track of things like their diet, smoking, and exercise, and who encourages them to take care of themselves.[29] As part of the marriage bargain, spouses give each other some say over how they live their lives together. They also give each other some power over the parts of their lives that take place outside the marriage, for example, their work lives. A wife can remind a husband to order the low-fat entree at dinner. A husband can urge his wife to see a doctor about that bump on her leg. Spouses can beg, nag, cajole, or threaten each other to encourage good health practices like healthy eating, or to discourage bad health practices like smoking. Married people tend to eat meals together, which generally improves both the quality and nutritional value of the meals that men eat. The social lives of married people generally revolve around alcohol to a much smaller extent than does the social life of single men. And married people tend to sleep and eat on a more regular schedule than do singles, in part because they coordinate these activities with another person. Nutritious and regular meals, regular sleep, and moderate amounts of alcohol are all important components of a healthy lifestyle.[30]

Neither sex has a monopoly on healthy nagging. Both husbands and wives can encourage and support the healthy lifestyle choices of their partners. In reality, though, wives more often provide this marriage benefit for their husbands than they receive it. The sociologist Debra Umberson found that married men are much more likely than single men to report that someone monitors their health. That person is almost always their wife, although sometimes it is their mother. Married women do not report any more health monitoring than single women. Eight out of ten married men say that their wife tells them or reminds them to do something to protect their health, which Umberson calls "social control of health behavior." Six out of ten married women say their husband does this for them. For wives, their parents and children often substitute for husbands as advocates for healthier living. As a result, marriage provides less social control of health practices for women than for men.

The task of keeping an eye on their husband's health seems to fall to wives because, according to Umberson, women generally know more about health-related issues than men, are more likely to monitor their own health, and are less likely to engage in risky health behaviors than are men. Wives tend to be responsible for shopping and preparing food, and for keeping track of health supplies and prescriptions. Traditionally, wives have also seen to the emotional health of family members, providing nurturing and caring. Nursing sick family members was, historically, an essential function of families performed almost exclusively by women.[31] Traditional female roles empha- size this caring, emotionally supportive aspect of women's behavior, giving women license to concern themselves with their husband's health, and giv- ing men license to cede authority over these behaviors to their wives. For the husbands and wives who get health advice and even nagging, the effects are important. Umberson identified spouses who said that someone tells them or reminds them to do something to protect their health and compared their health behaviors three years later with those of married people who did not have this support. The supported and monitored husbands and wives reduced their cigarette smoking, and the supported and monitored wives increased their average hours of sleep and their physical activity.[32]

Marriage and the parenthood that often accompanies it also seem to pro- vide individuals with a sense of meaning in their lives. Husbands and wives in good marriages realize that their partners' well-being depends on them. They recognize how devastated their family would be by their illness, injury, or death, and this realization makes them more cautious and careful. The ob- ligation that married people feel to their partner inhibits them from driving dangerously, drinking excessively, or failing to take their medication. It gives them the incentive to take care of their health, so that they can meet their ob- ligations to those who are counting on them.[33] Married people seem to moni- tor their own health more closely because of their sense of responsibility for others. And they allow their partner to monitor their health on their behalf. A husband may respond more positively to his wife's urgings to take care of himself because he knows that she and their children depend upon him, and because he knows that she is concerned for his welfare.

A good marriage also gives people someone they can count on for help, moral support, advice, and a shoulder to cry on. This social support helps individuals deal with stress, bolstering both physical and emotional health. Support can take the form of help in a crisis. A wife might help her husband in a job search by making telephone calls and contacting friends and relatives who might know of work. A husband might help his wife restore computer files that she accidentally destroyed as a major project deadline approached. Support can also take the form of encouragement and sympathy, as when a husband listens to his wife's complaints about her boss. Both kinds of support make things better.

Marriage improves health by giving people access to an intimate rela- tionship. Although many people get support from friends, parents, lovers, roommates, or even their lawyers or therapists, married men and women generally have much more supportive intimate relationships than single peo- ple,[34] because every married person has a spouse, and what spouses provide is unique and uniquely valuable. Intimate relationships give people the feeling that they are not facing problems alone, that someone important to them cares and will help. Intimacy fosters feelings of self-esteem and mastery.[35] In a study of depression, the sociologists Ron Kessler and Marilyn Essex find that the intimacy of relationships with spouses and other important confidants is such an important resource that in its absence almost nothing else helps and in its presence almost nothing else hurts. The resource of intimacy is one of the most important benefits of marriage.

Feeling that one is loved and cared for improves emotional well-being, decreasing depression and anxiety and increasing psychological resources such as self-esteem, mastery, and confidence. The intimacy and emotional support that are part and parcel of a good marriage, then, lead to better emotional health in husbands and wives. They also seem to lead to better physical health. Emotional health and resources may affect how physically healthy people feel by improving the way their body functions; emotional health seems to help in maintaining proper neuroendocrine reactivity. It also improves immune function, especially cellular immunity. People with strong networks of social support are less likely to get colds after exposure than people with less support.[36] Emotional health gives people the resources and support to undertake and continue with a healthy lifestyle, which directly improves their physical health.[37]

Sex

In most societies, marriage circumscribes a large majority of sexual relationships. Data from the United States show that almost all married men and women are sexually active and almost all have only one sex partner—their spouse. Married men and women report substantially higher levels of sexual activity than single people, as one might expect. But frequency of sex is even higher for those who are living together. According to the 1992 National Health and Social Life Survey, cohabiting men and women make love on average between seven and seven and a half times a month, compared with between six and seven times for married people.[38] The slight advantage in sexual quantity holds even after we take into account the age of the individuals and the length of the relationship. Men and women report the most sex in the early years of a marriage or cohabitation, and most couples who live together either marry or break up within a few years. Unmarried men and women have much lower levels of sexual activity than the married, in part because a substantial minority have no sex partner at all. Just under a quarter of the unmarried men and a third of the unmarried women who were not cohabiting at the time of the survey had no sex partner in the previous year.

Norms about the relationship between sex and marriage have changed a great deal in recent years. For example, only a minority of Americans now view premarital sex as always wrong. But within this sea of sexual change, the norm of marital faithfulness has changed very little. Almost all people who are married or even living with someone say they expect the relationship to be sexually exclusive. In the National Health and Social Life Survey, 94.6 percent of cohabitors and 98.7 percent of married people expect their partner to be sexually faithful to them.[39] Married men and women are more likely than those who are cohabiting to live up to this ideal. The National Health and Social Life Survey shows the percentages of men and women born between 1963 and 1974 who had another sexual partner in addition to their spouse while married—9.9 percent of men and 6.2 percent of women—compared with the much higher percentages of those who had a secondary sex partner while cohabiting—24.2 percent of men and 11.3 percent of women. Four percent of married men compared with 16 percent of cohabiting men say that they had another sexual partner in the past year. Thirty-seven percent of single men in an ongoing sexual partnership without cohabitation had another sex partner at the same time as their girlfriend in the past year. Only one married woman in a hundred said that she had an affair in the past year, compared with 8 percent of cohabiting women and 17 percent of single women in an ongoing sexual relationship.[40]

Renata Forste and Koray Tanfer find strikingly similar figures in the National Survey of Women.[41] Married women in their survey were least likely to have had a secondary sex partner—4 percent, compared with 20 percent of cohabiting women and 18 percent of dating women. Women's behavior changed dramatically when they married, with a huge decline in the chances of having a secondary sex partner. Forste and Tanfer conclude that marriage itself increases sexual exclusivity; cohabitation is no better than "dating" on this dimension.

Married men and women also report higher levels of emotional satisfaction from their sexual relationship than do otherwise similar cohabiting or single adults. Waite and Joyner find that married women and married men are more emotionally satisfied with sex, even after one takes into account their demographic and background characteristics, than are those in any other type of relationship except single people who expect their current relationship to last a lifetime.[42] For women, marriage itself, with the public, socially supported lifetime commitment it represents, seems to increase emotional satisfaction with sex. For men, marriage seems to increase emotional satisfaction with sex by increasing emotional investment in the relationship, which itself increases sexual satisfaction. Both men and women report greater emotional satisfaction with sex when they are in a "long-term" relationship, although for women, only a lifetime commitment is long enough, whereas for men, a somewhat shorter time horizon is sufficient.

How Does Marriage Change Sexual Behavior and Satisfaction?

Finding a partner and negotiating a sexual relationship requires resources such as time, money, and social capital. Because the process of finding new partners is costly, it makes better sense for individuals to gratify their emotional and physical needs in an ongoing partnership than to keep switching partners. In addition, individuals in ongoing relationships invest in skills that enhance the emotional and physical pleasure of a particular partner. Sex with the partner who knows what one likes and how to provide it is bound to be more satisfying than sex with a partner who lacks such skills and experience. Individuals have more incentive to invest in partner-pleasing skills if they expect a relationship to last. A long-term orientation toward a relationship—commitment—increases willingness to accommodate the needs of a partner and may lead people to derogate alternative partners.[43] Marriage signals commitment to the relationship, both to the partner and to others. And this commitment is legally, religiously, and socially enforceable, although the availability of unilateral divorce has reduced the extent to which this is true.

Marriage as a social institution offers guidelines with respect to sexual conduct, among other things. In most times and places, the marriage contract binds the partners together in a long-term, sexually exclusive contract, as expressed by marriage vows in many religions. More recently, this institution has also emphasized the emotional bond between partners.[44] Although cohabitation and marriage both offer sexual access, they differ in important ways. The institution of marriage, with the social and legal contract that is its foundation, legally binds the partners to a lifetime commitment, barring divorce. Cohabitation carries no explicit commitment to stay together for the long term. Unless they are engaged, the fact that cohabiting partners are not married to each other signals both to each other and to those around them a lower level of commitment to each other and to the relationship, at least by one of the partners. Suggesting this is the case, partners in cohabitation frequently bring different expectations for its future.[45] Cohabitors report a lower quality of relationship than do married couples, but only if they do not have plans to marry.[46]

Because of their greater commitment, married couples have more of an incentive to develop "relationship-specific capital," which includes learned skills that make a particular relationship better but are generally less useful in alternative relationships.[47] Pleasing a partner sexually is one such skill. Married couples also have more of an incentive than do cohabiting couples to remain sexually exclusive, and they have more social support and social pressure to do so. As Posner argued, the emotional investment in companionate marriage makes extramarital sex "an inferior substitute for marital sex."[48]

Children

Children raised by their own married parents do better across a range of outcomes than children who grow up in other living arrangements, on average. There is evidence that the former are less likely to die as infants,[49] enjoy better health during childhood,[50] and even survive longer into old age.[51] They complete more years of schooling. They are less likely to drop out of high school, are less likely to be idle as young adults, and are less likely to have a child as an unmarried teen.[52] Children who grow up in stable homes also tend to have better mental health than their counterparts who have gone through the experience of a parental divorce. Using seventeen-year longitudinal data from two generations, Amato and Sobolewski find that the weaker parent–child bonds that result from marital discord mediate most of the association between divorce and the subsequent mental health outcomes of children.[53]

Andrew Cherlin and his colleagues find that children whose parents would later divorce already showed evidence of more emotional problems even before the divorce, which suggests that marriage dissolution tends to occur in families that are troubled to begin with.[54] However, they also find that the gap continues to widen subsequent to the divorce, suggestive of a causal effect of family breakup on mental health. Summing up his overall assessment of the studies in this field, Cherlin concludes that growing up in a nonintact family can be associated with short- and long-term problems, partly due to the effects of family structure on the child's mental health, and partly due to inherited characteristics and their interaction with the environment.[55]

Career Success

Married men earn substantially more than otherwise similar unmarried men. The wage premium married men receive is one of the most well-documented phenomena in social science, in this country and in many others. Married men earn at least 10 percent more than single men and perhaps as high as 40 percent more. Economists call this the "marriage premium." Women get no wage premium and pay no wage penalty for being married.[56] Although high-earning men are more likely than others to get married, marriage itself seems to increase earnings.[57]

The longer a man is married, the greater the wage premium he receives. One recent study of younger men, for example, found that married men in their twenties and early thirties earned $11.33 an hour, while single men earned $10.38, and divorced or separated men earned $9.61.[58] For older men, the wage gap between husbands and bachelors is even larger. A study of men age fifty-five to sixty-four years found that married men earned 20 to 32 percent more than their nonmarried counterparts.[59] A rigorous and very thorough statistical analysis by Korenman and Neumark reports that married white men earn 11 percent more than their never-married counterparts, controlling for all the standard human capital variables.[60] Between 50 and 80 percent of the effect remains, depending on the specification, after correcting for selectivity into marriage based on characteristics such as attractiveness or personality that researchers do not observe but potential partners certainly do.

Economists generally agree that the greater productivity of married men plays a substantial role in their higher earnings. This productivity boost comes with the more settled, stable lifestyle of marriage, with its regular hours, adequate sleep, and decent meals. It also may come directly from the productivity-enhancing efforts of the wife herself, assisting her husband with his tasks for work, giving advice, or taking on other household duties that allow him to focus on his job.[61]

Wealth

Married people have, on average, substantially greater assets and wealth than people with similar levels of education and earnings who are not married. The economists Joseph Lupton and James Smith estimated wealth and assets for individuals in their early fifties through early sixties interviewed as part of a large national survey, the Health and Retirement Survey. They included real assets such as a house or apartment, second home, farm or ranch, or mobile home. They also included other real estate; vehicles; business equity; individual retirement account or Keogh account; stocks, trusts, or mutual funds; checking, saving, or money market funds; certificates of deposit; government savings bonds or Treasury bills; other bonds; and other savings and assets. They deducted the value of first and second mortgages, home equity loans, mortgages on second homes, and other debt.

Lupton and Smith found that, on average, a married couple's net worth is substantially greater than that of unmarried people. Because there are two adults in married-couple families and only one unmarried adult, we might expect greater wealth simply because married couples pool resources. But even when Lupton and Smith divided the assets of married couples in half, their wealth still exceeded that of all other types of unmarried adults. For example, married couples in their study had a median net worth of $132,200, which amounts to $66,100 per person. Separated adults, who had a median net worth of only $7,600, were the worst off of all unmarried adults. But even widowed people, with a median net worth of $47,275, had substantially lower wealth than married people who were similar to them in other ways.

Some of the greater wealth of married couples results from their higher earnings—but not all of it. Even at the same level of earnings, married couples have more assets because they save more. Lupton and Smith also found that people who divorced lost assets. For example, a married head of household who divorced lost about a third of his net wealth over a five-year period, whereas a divorced person who married doubled his or her wealth over the same period. This research also showed what the researchers call the "shockingly low" net worth among both separated and never-married black and Hispanic adults and point to the low levels of marriage among blacks and Puerto Ricans as one cause of the very substantial racial and ethnic disparities in financial well-being.

How Does Marriage Improve Wealth and Asset Accumulation?

The legally enforceable lifetime agreement that underlies marriage gives partners the long time horizon needed to allow them to specialize, splitting life's tasks between them to maximize efficiency. This specialization allows married adults to produce more, working together, than they would if each of them did everything alone. Married couples also get the economies of scale that come from sharing a house or apartment. The most recent estimates suggest that two can live as cheaply as 1.65 if they live together. Of course, the economies of scale that come with marriage also accrue to roommates, cohabiting partners, or siblings who live together. But most people are unenthusiastic about sharing a bathroom and kitchen with someone of whom they are not particularly fond or do not know fairly well, limiting the availability of the economies of scale from shared living arrangements.

Married people are also much more likely than unmarried people to receive money from family, perhaps because parents and in-laws see married couples as a stable unit, and cohabiting partners as not really members of the family. Marriage also increases wealth by increasing savings; Lupton and Smith found that even at the same level of family income, married adults accumulated assets at a much faster rate than otherwise similar unmarried people.[62] Something about being married encourages saving and asset accumulation.

Finally, spouses act as a small insurance pool, protecting each other from the full effect of life's uncertainties. If one becomes ill or disabled, the other can often provide care and take over more of the household duties. If one spouse becomes unemployed, the other may work more to help out. Kotlikoff and Spivak calculated how much spouses gain from pooling their risks in marriage.[63] Just getting married creates an annuity value that is equal to increasing one's wealth by 12 to 14 percent at age thirty and by 30 percent at age seventy-five, compared with staying single. We do not count these windfalls in wealth from marriage in any official statistics, so the astoundingly greater wealth of the married that we noted above is really even bigger than it looks.[64]

Do Married People Do Well Because Successful People Get Married?

Cross-sectional differences in both emotional and physical health, wealth, and career accomplishments between the married and divorced are sizable but may result from the selection of the healthy and successful into marriage and the unhealthy failures out of it. Many recent studies have addressed this selection by following individuals over time, to assess the relationship between changes in marital status and in their well-being. These studies consistently find that selection into or out of marriage does not account for the better physical[65] or psychological[66] health of married men or married women. It accounts for about half of the higher earnings of married men.[67] Something about being married, and something about being unmarried, affects health and well-being.

Marriage and Fatherhood: The Social Science Data

Until the 1970s, fathers were pretty much invisible in social science research, with most studies of parent–child relationships focusing on mothers. Fathers were seen as breadwinners and backup parents.[68] This changed with the major increases in divorce rates and nonmarital childbearing during the 1970s and 1980s. Fathering could no longer be taken for granted, and researchers turned their attention to fathering both inside and outside marriage. In the past decade in particular, the evidence linking active fathering to the status and quality of marriage has become increasingly compelling. Here we summarize that research literature, starting with fathering that begins outside marriage.

Studies have shown a strong negative effect of nonmarital fathering on the father's involvement and the father–child bond. Children born outside marriage almost always reside with their mothers. If the fathers do not live with the mother and child, their presence in the child's life is often marginal. Even when fathers are active for a time, they later tend to withdraw. Lerman, using data from a nationally representative group of more than 600 unwed fathers, found that about three-fourths of young fathers who did not reside with their children at birth never lived in the same household with them.[69] About 50 percent of these fathers visited their child once a week, but about 20 percent never visited or visited once a year. The pattern over time was toward less contact as the children got older. This is the consistent finding of research on fathering that begins outside of marriage.

The same pattern applies to the quality of the father–child relationships outside marriage. Furstenberg and Harris, reporting on their twenty-year follow-up of unmarried African American parents in Baltimore (a group that was generally representative of African American unmarried parents nationally), found that only 13 percent of the young adults reported a strong bond with their biological father if he had not lived with them.[70] Even for those who had lived with their father, only 50 percent reported a strong bond. Some critics of the emphasis on fathering point to the availability of surrogate fathers in children's lives. Furstenberg and Harris examined this phenomenon and reported sobering findings. After examining bonds with stepfathers and other male figures in the child's life, they summarized their findings in this way: "Taking all these father figures into account, just 1% of the children had a strong relationship with two or more fathers, 30% reported a strong tie with at least one, and 69% had no father figure to whom they were highly attached."[71]

One objection to an emphasis on "married fatherhood" argues that it is residential fathering that counts, not whether the father is married to the mothers. Indeed, in more than 25 percent of nonmarital births, the parents are cohabiting.[72] In these cases, as one would expect, fathers are far more present in their children's lives. However, studies indicate that cohabiting couples have high breakup rates, and those who go on to marry have higher divorce rates.[73] Therefore, even when the father lives with the mother of the child, his ongoing presence in the child's life is often fragile. Although the number of nonmarital births has increased dramatically since the 1960s, an even greater number of children live with a single parent subsequent to divorce. In 85 to 90 percent of cases, these children reside with their mothers. Research has documented a declining presence of noncustodial fathers over the years after a divorce. One national study of school-aged children found that, two years after a divorce, about half had not seen their father for a year.[74] In a later study, Nord and Zill found that about one-third of divorced fathers did not spend time with their children in the previous year.[75] In general, although fathers' involvement after divorce seems to be increasing and some fathers are quite involved with their children after a divorce, the predominant pattern among noncustodial fathers is one of gradual withdrawal from their children's lives.[76]

The consequences of divorce for the quality of father–child relations are as sobering as the consequences for the level of contact. Zill, Morrison, and Coiro followed a large national sample of children and parents through the young adulthood of the children.[77] Even after adjusting for a variety of demographic factors and academic test scores, these researchers found increasing alienation of divorced fathers from their children, as measured by the children's descriptions of these relationships. Among eighteen- to twenty-two-year-olds, 65 percent of those whose parents had divorced reported a poor relationship with their father, compared with 29 percent of those whose parents had not divorced. The data also showed poorer relationships with mothers after divorce, but the effect for fathers was stronger. Remarriage of one of the parents made things worse; 70 percent of children of divorce and remarriage reported a poor relationship with their father. Amato and Sobolewski reported similar findings for the negative effects of divorce on father–child relationships in young adulthood.[78]

We have shown thus far how fathering is strongly influenced by whether the father is married to the child's mother. We next show that when the father is married to the mother, there is a strong relationship between the father's involvement and the quality of marital relationship. In fact, a number of studies have shown that the quality of father–child relations both inside and outside marriage is more highly correlated with the quality of the coparental relationship than is true for the mother–child relationship.[79] Fathers appear to withdraw from their child when they are not getting along with the mother, whereas mothers do not show a similar level of withdrawal. This is one way to understand the tendency of fathers to remove themselves from their children's lives after a breakup with the mother, especially if they have a negative relationship with the mother.[80] As Furstenberg and Cherlin have asserted, for many men, marriage and parenthood are a "package deal."[81]

To adapt an old phrase about sons and daughters, one might say that in contemporary American culture, a woman is a mother all her life, but a man is a father only if he has a wife. What is more, if a man has a wife but does not get along with her, he is around but not such a good father. We turn now to the moral and theological issues raised by this analysis.

The Moral and Theological Underpinnings of Married Fatherhood

We have argued that the problem of absent and underinvolved fathers in today's world stems in large part from the decline of marriage as a venue for bearing and raising children. That is why anything that strengthens healthy marriage is likely to promote responsible fathering. However, there is also an urgent need to articulate the moral and theological underpinnings of fathering inside and outside marriage, because fathers and mothers are making decisions every day about whether to bear children outside marriage and whether to end a marriage with children. Both are moral decisions that affect the children and other stakeholders. As useful as social science data can be for informing these decisions, our data are probabilistic, based on averages, and not refined enough to determine complex individual decisions. Social science does not have the wherewithal to ground fathering ethically in terms of moral "oughts" not only because of the limitations of its data but also because of its allegiance to the idea of value-free theories and objective data.

An illustration of this point is an ongoing debate in the field about whether fathers make distinctive contributions to the well-being of their children, beyond an economic support that could be provided by the government.[82] Although most scholars have concluded that fathers make important psychosocial contributions in addition to economic contributions,[83] there remain skeptics. This issue of how important fathers are for children is connected with feminist concerns about constraining women in making decisions about bearing children outside marriage and about leaving a bad relationship with the father of their child. It is also connected to concerns of advocates of lesbian marriage, who fear that an emphasis on the role of fathers is a way to disparage families with two mothers.[84]

The best we can do within the social science paradigm to resolve these debates is to examine the empirical data. An example is Amato and Rivera's study of the question of whether fathers in married households contribute anything to children's well-being beyond mothers' contributions.[85] In other words, if children in two-parent families do better than children in one-parent families, maybe it is because these mothers are better mothers, not because the fathers make distinctive contributions. Amato and Rivera argued that the only way to determine if fathers add something of value is to see if their parenting behavior relates to children's adjustment after controlling for mothers' behavior. Stated differently, do fathers count after you subtract what mothers contribute? The good news is that the researchers found that fathering does indeed contribute to children's well-being even after controls for mothering. Parenthetically, it is interesting that no researcher has thought to ask the question of whether mothers add anything of value beyond what fathers contribute to children's well-being, a reflection of what Phares has termed a "matricentric" approach of researchers to parenting.[86]

What if Amato's data had turned out differently? What if researchers could not demonstrate that fathering is "value added" for children, at least beyond economic support? In this case, should prospective fathers use social science research to guide their decisions about what kind of fathers to be? Should they wait until social scientists arrive at a firmer consensus, in the meantime making sure they write a check for their child each month? These questions point to the poverty of the ethical underpinnings of social science when it comes to fathering and marriage. Social science research for the most part reflects an implicit utilitarian or consequentialist ethic, focusing on the measurable benefits—material or psychosocial—for individuals or society. As important as empirical findings are, they do not provide the ethical depth to guide either individual decisions or social policy. Surely a moral sense within most individuals and public officials would lead us to assert the importance of fathers' lifelong commitment to the emotional and material well-being of their children, and a similar commitment to their wife.

Outside marriage, the same moral sense would assert the same degree of commitment to one's children and a modified but nevertheless strong obligation to supporting the mother of one's children even if there is no marriage. Few of us would question this moral sense on the basis of the latest findings from social science, although it is to be hoped that the specific ways we act on this moral sense will be influenced by social science findings—for example, that married fatherhood is better for children than nonmarried fatherhood and that authoritative fathering (a combination of warmth and firmness) is best for children. In other words, social science is better at answering the question "How can I be a good father?" than the question "Why should I be a good father when I have competing priorities in my life?"

If social science lacks sufficient ethical grounding, why not turn to philosophical ethics as a primary resource to ground an ethic of fathering? Although we are not professional ethicists, our sense is that philosophical ethical traditions have not adequately engaged the question of duties and virtues in family relationships. For example, John Rawls, the twentieth century's most eminent philosopher of justice in social relations, based his theory on independent moral agents not tied to particularistic commitments such as a marriage or parenting.[87] Philosophers as different as the feminist Margaret Walker[88] and the neo-Aristotelian Alasdair MacIntyre[89] have taken contemporary philosophy to task for ignoring the contexts of dependency and interdependence in human life. In other words, philosophy, with its universalizing tendencies, has not been up to the task of understanding something as grounded as fathers' moral obligations to their children or spouses and coparents' obligations to each other.

We suspect that only our Western theological traditions have the necessary resources to ground an ethic of responsible fathering in the context of marriage. Because we are not professional theologians, we can only point in the direction of what this grounding might be. The theological tradition of "covenant" in Judaism and Christianity appears to be a potentially fertile source for an ethic of fatherhood and also of marriage. This tradition evolved out of biblical ways of understanding God's relationship with God's people, an unbreakable bond based on mutual promises and bearing important obligations. As examined by scholars such as Browning,[90] Stackhouse,[91] and Witte,[92] the covenantal tradition offers a way to think about fathering and marriage that transcends utilitarian and consequentialist thinking. Here are several covenantal ideas based on Stackhouse's work that could be applied to fathering[93]:

- It is voluntarily entered, but then obligatory.
- It has both private and public dimensions, defining both a personal identity and role, and a social institution with many stakeholders.
- It is unbreakable, in principle; in practice, it is breakable only for powerful reasons and with legal approval.
- It is holy; in secular usage, one could say that the father–child covenant has profound moral and spiritual roots.

The father–child covenant, seen from this perspective, is binding on men who father a child, irrespective of law, economic circumstances, and the relationship with the mother. Conversely, millennia of human experience and a wealth of contemporary research studies indicate that this father–child covenant is best enacted in the context of a good marriage for the well-being of the child, mother, father, and community. Thus does research on the health consequences of marriage and the marital underpinnings of responsible fathering join with our Western religious traditions to make the case for marriage and married fatherhood.

Notes

This chapter was supported in part by the Alfred P. Sloan Center for Parents, Children, and Work at the University of Chicago and by the Agricultural Experimentation Station at the University of Minnesota.

1. William J. Doherty and J. S. Carroll, "Marriage and Couples Education in Historical and Ideological Perspective" in *Marriage, Health, and the Professions*, ed. Don S. Browning, John Wall, William J. Doherty, and Stephen Post (Grand Rapids: William B. Eerdmans, 2002), 208–32.

2. Milton C. Regan Jr., "Postmodern Family Law: Toward a New Model of Status," in *Promises to Keep: Decline and Renewal of Marriage in America*, ed. David Popenoe, Jean Bethke Elshtain, and David Blankenhorn (Lanham, Md.: Rowman & Littlefield, 1996), 157–86.

3. Leora Friedberg, "Did Unilateral Divorce Raise Divorce Rates? Evidence from Panel Data," *American Economic Review* 88 (1998): 608–27.

4. Linda J. Waite and Maggie Gallagher, *The Case for Marriage: Why Married People Are Happier, Healthier and Better Off Financially* (New York: Doubleday, 2000).

5. Lawrence J. Kotlikoff and Avia Spivak, "The Family as an Incomplete Annuities Market," *Journal of Political Economy* 89 (1981): 372–91.

6. John Mirowksy and Catherine Ross, *Social Causes of Psychological Distress* (New York: Aldine de Gruyter, 1989).

7. Gary S. Becker, *A Treatise on the Family* (Cambridge, Mass.: Harvard University Press, 1991).

8. Mirowksy and Ross, *Social Causes;* Waite and Gallagher, *Case for Marriage.*

9. Joseph Lupton and James P. Smith, "Marriage, Assets, and Savings," in *Marriage and the Economy*, ed. S. Grossbard-Shechtman (Cambridge: Cambridge University Press, 2003), 129–52.

10. Mirowksy and Ross, *Social Causes.*

11. Walter R. Gove and Michael Hughes, "Possible Causes of the Apparent Sex Differences in Physical Health: An Empirical Investigation," *American Sociological Review* 44 (1979): 126–46.

12. Allan V. Horwitz, Helene Raskin White, and Sandra Howell-White, "Becoming Married and Mental Health: A Longitudinal Study of a Cohort of Young Adults," *Journal of Marriage and the Family* 58 (1996): 895–907; Nadine F. Marks and James D. Lambert, "Marital Status Continuity and Change among Young and Midlife Adults: Longitudinal Effects on Psychological Well-Being," *Journal of Family Issues* 19 (1998): 652–86; Robin W. Simon, "Revisiting the Relationship among Gender, Marital Status, and Mental Health," *American Journal of Sociology*, 107 (2002): 1065–96.

13. About 3 percent of respondents to the General Social Survey between 1972 and 2000 rate their marriage as "not too happy," and 97 percent rate their marriage as "somewhat or very happy."

14. Catherine E. Ross, "Reconceptualizing Marital Status as a Continuum of Social Attachment," *Journal of Marriage and the Family* 57 (1995): 129–40.

15. Linda J. Waite and Mary Elizabeth Hughes, "At Risk on the Cusp of Old Age: Living Arrangements and Functional Status among Black, White, and Hispanic Adults," *Journal of Gerontology: Social Sciences* 54.B (1999): S136–S144.

16. Carol Miller-Tutzauer, Kenneth E. Leonard, and Michael Windle, "Marriage and Alcohol Use: A Longitudinal Study of 'Maturing Out,'" *Journal of Studies on Alcohol* 52 (1991): 434–40.

17. Debra Umberson, "Family Status and Health Behaviors: Social Control as a Dimension of Social Integration," *Journal of Health and Social Behavior* 28 (1987): 306–19.

18. Jerald G. Bachman, Katherine N. Wadsworth, Patrick M. O'Malley, Lloyd D. Johnson, and John E. Schulenberg, *Smoking, Drinking, and Drug Use in Young Adulthood* (Mahwah, N.J.: Lawrence Erlbaum Associates, 1997); Catherine E. Ross, John Mirowksy, and Karen Goldsteen, "The Impact of the Family on Health: Decade in Review," *Journal of Marriage and the Family* 52 (1990): 1059–78; Umberson, "Family Status."

19. Douglas A. Parker, Elizabeth S. Parker, Thomas C. Harford, and Gail C. Farmer, "Alcohol Use and Depression Symptoms among Employed Men and Women," *American Journal of Public Health* 77 (1987): 704–7.

20. Bachman et al., *Smoking, Drinking, and Drug Use;* Miller-Tutzauer et al., "Marriage and Alcohol Use."

21. Bachman et al., *Smoking, Drinking, and Drug Use.*

22. Beth A. Hahn, "Marital Status and Women's Health: The Effect of Economic Marital Acquisitions," *Journal of Marriage and the Family* 55 (1993): 495–504.

23. Lee A. Lillard and Linda J. Waite, "'Til Death Do Us Part: Marital Disruption and Mortality," *American Journal of Sociology* 100 (1995): 1131–56.

24. Hahn, "Marital Status."

25. Ibid.

26. Ross, Mirowsky, and Goldsteen, "Impact of the Family on Health."

27. Jack C. Smith, James A. Mercy, and Judith M. Conn, "Marital Status and the Risk of Suicide," *American Journal of Public Health* 78 (1988): 78–80.

28. K. A. S. Wickrama, Frederick O. Lorenz, Rand D. Conger, and Glen H. Elder Jr., "Marital Quality and Physical Illness: A Latent Growth Curve Analysis," *Journal of Marriage and the Family* 59 (1997): 143–55.

29. Ross, "Reconceptualizing Marital Status"; Umberson, "Family Status"; Debra Umberson, "Gender, Marital Status and the Social Control of Health Behavior," *Social Science and Medicine* 34 (1992): 907–17.

30. Lisa F. Berkman and Lester Breslow, "Social Networks and Mortality Risk," in *Health and Ways of Living: The Alameda County Study* (New York: Oxford University Press, 1983), chap. 4.

31. Vern Bullough and Bonnie Bullough, *The Care of the Sick: The Emergence of Modern Nursing* (New York: Prodist, 1978).

32. Umberson, "Gender, Marital Status."

33. Walter Gove, "Sex, Marital Status, and Mortality," *American Journal of Sociology* 75 (1973): 45–67; Umberson, "Family Status."

34. Ronald C. Kessler and Marilyn Essex, "Marital Status and Depression: The Importance of Coping Resources," *Social Forces* 61 (1982): 484–507.

35. Leonard I. Pearlin and Joyce S. Johnson, "Marital Status, Life Strains and Depression," *American Sociological Review* 42 (1977): 704–15.

36. Sheldon Cohen, William J. Doyle, David P. Skoner, Bruce S. Rabin, and Jack M. Gwaltney Jr., "Social Ties and Susceptibility to the Common Cold," *Journal of the American Medical Association* 227 (1997): 1940–44.

37. Terry E. Duncan and Edward McAuley, "Social Support and Efficacy Cognitions in Exercise Adherence: A Latent Growth Curve Analysis," *Journal of Behavioral Medicine* 16 (1993): 199–218.

38. Edward O. Laumann, John H. Gagnon, Robert T. Michael, and Stuart Michaels, *The Social Organization of Sexuality: Sexual Practices in the United States* (Chicago: University of Chicago Press, 1994).

39. Laumann et al., *Social Organization.*

40. National Health and Social Life Survey, 1992, in *Social Organization,* by Laumann et al., tables 5.9A and 5.9B.

41. Renata Forste and Koray Tanfer, "Sexual Exclusivity among Dating, Cohabiting, and Married Women," *Journal of Marriage and the Family* 58 (1996): 33–47.

42. Linda J. Waite and Kara Joyner, "Emotional and Physical Satisfaction in Married, Cohabiting and Dating Sexual Unions: Do Men and Women Differ?" in *Sex, Love, and Health in America: Private Choices and Public Policies,* ed. E. Laumann and R. Michael (Chicago: University of Chicago Press, 2001), 239–69.

43. Laumann et al., *Social Organization.*

44. Andrew J. Cherlin, *Marriage, Divorce and Remarriage* (Cambridge, Mass.: Harvard University Press, 1992).

45. Larry L. Bumpass, James A. Sweet, and Andrew Cherlin, "The Role of Cohabitation in Declining Rates of Marriage," *Journal of Marriage and the Family* 53 (1991): 913–27.

46. Susan L. Brown and Alan Booth, "Cohabitation versus Marriage: A Comparison of Relationship Quality," *Journal of Marriage and the Family* 58 (1996): 668–78.

47. Carmela Chiswick and Evelyn Lehrer, "On Marriage-Specific Human Capital: Its Role as a Determinant of Remarriage," *Journal of Population Economics* 3 (1990): 193–213.

48. Richard A. Posner, *Sex and Reason* (Cambridge, Mass.: Harvard University Press, 1992), 112.

49. Trude Bennett, Paula Braveman, Susan Egerter, and John L. Kiely, "Maternal Marital Status as a Risk Factor for Infant Mortality," *Family Planning Perspectives* 26 (1994): 252–56, 271.

50. Ronald Angel and Jacqueline Lowe Worobey, "Single Motherhood and Children's Health," *Journal of Health and Social Behavior* 29 (1988): 38–52.

51. J. S. Tucker, H. S. Friedman, J. E. Schwartz, et al., "Parental Divorce: Effects on Individual Behavior and Longevity," *Journal of Personality and Social Psychology* 73 (1997): 381–91.

52. Sara McLanahan and Gary D. Sandefur, *Growing Up with a Single Parent: What Hurts, What Helps* (Cambridge, Mass.: Harvard University Press, 1994).

53. Paul R. Amato and Juliana Sobolewski, "The Effects of Divorce and Marital Discord on Adult Children's Psychological Well-Being," *American Sociological Review* 66 (2001): 900–21.

54. Andrew J. Cherlin, Lindsay Chase-Lansdale, and C. McRae, "Effects of Parental Divorce on Mental Health throughout the Life Course," *American Sociological Review* 63 (1998): 239–49.

55. Andrew J. Cherlin, "Going to Extremes: Family Structure, Children's Well-Being, and Social Science," *Demography* 36 (1999): 421–28.

56. J. Waldfogel, "The Effect of Children on Women's Wages," *American Sociological Review* 62 (1997): 209–17.

57. Kermit Daniel, "The Marriage Premium," in *The New Economics of Home Behavior*, ed. Mariano Tommasi and Kathryn Ierulli (Oxford: Oxford University Press, 1995), 113–25.

58. These are sample means for white men age twenty-four to thirty-one years, in 1989 dollars. See J. S. Gray, "The Fall in Men's Return to Marriage: Declining Productivity or Changing Selection?" *Journal of Human Resources* 32 (1997): 481–504.

59. Robin L. Bartlett and Charles III Callahan, "Wage Determination and Marital Status: Another Look," *Industrial Relations* 23 (1984): 90–6.

60. Sanders Korenman and David Neumark, "Does Marriage Really Make Men More Productive?" *Journal of Human Resources* 26, no. 2 (1991): 282–302.

61. Shoshana Grossbard-Shechtman, *On the Economics of Marriage: A Theory of Marriage, Labor and Divorce* (Boulder, Colo.: Westview Press, 1993).

62. Lupton and Smith, "Marriage, Assets."

63. Kotlikoff and Spivak, "Family."

64. Ibid.

65. Lee A. Lillard and Constantijn Panis, "Marital Status and Mortality: The Role of Health," *Demography* 33 (1996): 313–27.

66. Horwitz, White, and Howell-White, "Becoming Married"; Marks and Lambert, "Marital Status"; Simon, "Revisiting the Relationship."

67. Daniel, "Marriage Premium."

68. J. H. Pleck, "Paternal Involvement: Levels, Sources, and Consequences," in *The Role of the Father in Child Development*, 3rd edition, ed. M. E. Lamb (New York: Wiley, 1997).

69. Robert I. Lerman, "A National Profile of Young Unwed Fathers," in *Young Unwed Fathers: Changing Roles and Emerging Policies*, ed. Robert I. Lerman and T. J. Ooms (Philadelphia: Temple University Press, 1993), 27–51.

70. F. F. Furstenberg Jr. and K. M. Harris, "When and Why Fathers Matter: Impacts of Father Involvement on the Children of Adolescent Mothers," in *Young Unwed Fathers*, ed. Lerman and Ooms, 117–38.

71. Furstenberg and Harris, "When and Why Fathers Matter," 126.

72. Larry Bumpass and Hsien-Hen Lu, "Trends in Cohabitation and Implications for Children's Family Contexts in the United States," *Population Studies* 54 (2000): 29–41.

73. Larry L. Bumpass, James A. Sweet, and Andrew Cherlin, "The Role of Cohabitation in Declining Rates of Marriage," *Journal of Marriage and the Family* 53 (1991): 913–27; A. DeMaris and V. Rao, "Premarital Cohabitation and Subsequent Marital Stability in the United States: A Reassessment," *Journal of Marriage and the Family* 54 (1992): 178–90.

74. F. F. Furstenberg and C. W. Nord, "Parenting Apart: Patterns of Childrearing After Marital Disruption," *Journal of Marriage and the Family* 47 (1985): 893–904.

75. C. W. Nord and N. Zill, *Non-Custodial Parents' Participation in Their Children's Lives: Evidence from the Survey of Income and Program Participation* (Washington, D.C.: U.S. Department of Health and Human Services, 1996).

76. P. R. Amato and S. J. Rejac, "Contact with Nonresident Parents, Interparental Conflict, and Children's Behavior," *Journal of Family Issues* 15 (1994): 191–207; J. A. Seltzer, "Relationships between Fathers and Children Who Live Apart: The Father's Role after Separation," *Journal of Marriage and the Family* 53 (1991): 79–101.

77. N. Zill, D. R. Morrison, and M. J. Coiro, "Long-Term Effects of Parental Divorce on Parent–Child Relationships, Adjustment, and Achievement in Young Adulthood," *Journal of Family Psychology* 7 (1993): 91–103.

78. Amato and Sobolewski, "Effects of Divorce and Marital Discord."

79. J. Belsky and B. L. Volling, "Mothering, Fathering, and Marital Interaction in the Family Triad During Infancy," in *Men's Transitions to Parenthood: Longitudinal Studies of Early Family Experience*, ed. P. W. Berman and F. A. Pedersen (Hillsdale, N.J.: Lawrence Erlbaum Associates, 1987), 37–63; M. J. Cox, M. T. Owen, J. M. Lewis, and V. K. Henderson, "Marriage, Adult Adjustment, and Early Parenting," *Child Development* 60 (1989): 1015–24; S. S. Feldman, S. C. Nash, and B. G. Aschenbrenner, "Antecedents of Fathering," *Child Development* 54 (1983): 1628–36; R. Levy-Shiff and R. Israelashvili, "Antecedents of Fathering: Some Further Exploration," *Developmental Psychology* 24 (1988): 434–40.

80. C. R. Ahrons and R. B. Miller, "The Effect of the Postdivorce Relationship on Paternal Involvement: A Longitudinal Analysis," *American Journal of Orthopsychiatry* 63 (1993): 441–50.

81. F. S. Furstenberg and A. J. Cherlin, *Divided Families: What Happens to Children When Parents Part* (Cambridge, Mass.: Harvard University Press, 1991).

82. A. J. Walker and L. A. McGraw, "Who Is Responsible for Responsible Fathering?" *Journal of Marriage and the Family* 62 (2000): 563–69.

83. J. H. Pleck, "Paternal Involvement: Levels, Sources, and Consequences," in *Role of the Father in Child Development*, ed. Lamb, 63–103; Ross D. Parke, *Fatherhood* (Cambridge, Mass.: Harvard University Press, 1996).

84. Walker and McGraw, "Who Is Responsible?"

85. Paul R. Amato and F. Rivera, "Paternal Involvement and Children's Behavioral Problems," *Journal of Marriage and the Family* 61 (1999): 375–84.

86. V. Phares, "Conducting Nonsexist Research, Prevention, and Treatment with Fathers and Mothers: A Call for Change," *Psychology of Women Quarterly* 20 (1996): 55–77.

87. John Rawls, *A Theory of Justice* (Cambridge, Mass.: Harvard University Press, 1971).

88. Margaret U. Walker, *Moral Contexts* (Albany: State University of New York Press, 2003).

89. Alasdair MacIntyre, *After Virtue: A Study in Moral Theory,* 2nd ed. (Notre Dame, Ind.: University of Notre Dame Press, 1997).

90. Don S. Browning, *Marriage and Modernization* (Grand Rapids: William B. Eerdmans, 2003).

91. Max L. Stackhouse, *Covenant and Commitments* (Louisville: Westminster John Knox Press, 1997).

92. John Witte Jr., *From Sacrament to Contract: Marriage, Religion, and Law in the Western Tradition* (Louisville: Westminster John Knox Press, 1997).

93. Stackhouse, *Covenant and Commitments.*

Chapter 8
The Changing Pathway to Marriage: Trends in Dating, First Unions, and Marriage among Young Adults

Barbara Dafoe Whitehead

Scores of television reality shows, self-help books, and websites have sprung up in recent years to cater to the seemingly inexhaustible popular appetite for advice on finding a mate. Yet research has lagged behind the popular culture. With the exception of studies of cohabitation and dating violence, empirical investigations into contemporary patterns of dating and mating among young adults have been scant.

Similarly, recent grassroots and policy initiatives aimed at strengthening marriage have generally ignored the topic of mate selection. As the sociologist Norval Glenn has observed, these efforts tend to focus on teaching communication and relationships skills to engaged or married couples rather than on promoting good choices of a life partner. Yet, as he notes, making the right choice of a marriage mate is at least as important in marital success as learning how to get along with each other once the choice of a mate has been made.[1]

There are good reasons why the dating and mating behavior of young adults has been neglected. In the past, when young people married shortly after finishing formal education, they tended to seek and often to find their future marriage partner among the school population of peers. Thus for researchers interested in young people's choice of a partner, the student population was the relevant population to study. Also, the conduct of dating usually occurred within the catchment area of the school campus where researchers happened to be located as well. It was relatively easy to study students' romantic relationships, and, not surprisingly, much of the earlier research on mate selection focused on dating among college students.

Today, however, young people are less likely to regard their undergraduate years as the time when they will seek and find a marriage mate. More are postponing the search for a life partner until older ages. By the time they begin to search for someone to marry, they have left the campus for the work world. This poses greater difficulties for researchers. It is more time consuming and expensive to study the dating relationships of young working singles who are geographically dispersed among the broad population of working-age adults.

At the same time, the population and romantic aims of young dating singles have become more diverse. Same-sex as well as opposite-sex romantic relationships are now part of the youthful dating scene. People seek partners for a wide variety of intimate arrangements, ranging from casual sexual relationships to future marriage. The partner market itself has diversified to include single parents and divorced people as well as the never-married young. Finally, new technologies and market-based methods of mate selection are changing the conduct of romantic relationships. To cite just one example, the Internet has affected the size, scope, and composition of the mating market as well as the matchmaking process itself. But we do not yet have reliable studies on the impact of this new technology on dating and mating behavior, mate selection, or the choice of a marriage partner.

Even without a robust body of social science evidence, however, it is fair to say that the traditional pathway into marriage is changing. So, too, are traditional attitudes about the timing, purpose, and expectations for marriage. The social institutions that once guided young adults' path into marriage are losing influence. New technologies and commercial services are emerging to take their place. Today's young adults stand at the forefront of all these changes.

This chapter describes some key trends in youthful opposite-sex romantic relationships as they affect the pathway into marriage. Given the limitations of current knowledge, my aims are modest. I approach the topic by focusing on three areas: (1) demographic trends in the timing and sequencing of benchmark events preceding entry into first marriage, (2) young adults' attitudes toward marriage, and (3) trends in the youthful courtship system itself. Finally, I consider the implications of these trends for those who are involved in guiding, teaching, or directly preparing young adults for marriage.

Demographic Trends

For most of the past century, and certainly before that time, marriage was one of the most important rites of passage. It accomplished several goals associated with growing up: an economic transition from the parental household to an independent household, a psychosexual transition merging two separate lives into one family, and a social and legal transition from single to married status. Today, as demographic trends suggest, the sequence and timing of marriage in the early adult life course are changing, with the result that marriage is losing its role as the key event marking the transition to adulthood.

Delay of First Marriage until Older Ages

For today's young adults, the path from single life into married life is more prolonged than it used to be. Since the beginning of the last century, the median age of first marriage for men and women has ranged between the late teens and early twenties. Even as recently as 1970, the median age of marriage was 23.2 years for men and 20.8 years for women. Today, however, the median age has risen to 26.8 for men and 25.1 for women. Among the college-educated young, the age of first marriage is estimated to be at least a year or two older. As a consequence of the delay of marriage, the proportion of men and women who are not yet married during the traditional "marrying years" has risen dramatically in the past thirty years. Between 1970 and 2000, the proportion of never-married women age 20 to 24 doubled from 36 percent in 1970 to 73 percent in 2000, while the proportion of never-married men age 20 to 24 increased from 55 percent in 1970 to 84 percent in 2000.[2]

The trend toward older age at first marriage has altered the early adult life course. What was once a fleeting few years of single life between graduation day and wedding day has lengthened into a new life stage that might be called "twentyhood." For some young adults, and especially the college-educated young, this stage can stretch out for as much as a decade after college graduation and before first marriage.

Lengthening Time Span between First Sexual Intercourse and First Marriage

For women in past generations, the timing of first sexual intercourse was closely connected to the timing of first marriage.[3] Ninety percent of women born between 1933 and 1942 were either virgins when they married or had their first intercourse with the man they married.[4] Today, the timing of first sex is more widely separated from the timing of first marriage. The age of first sexual intercourse for young women is about seventeen years, while the median age of first marriage is twenty-five.[5] So for a growing percentage of young women today, there is at least a seven- or eight-year span of time between first sexual intercourse and first marriage. Because college-educated women are likely to marry at slightly older ages than their less-well-educated peers, the time span between the two milestone events may be even greater for them.

Equally important, the normative connection between first sexual intercourse and marriage has weakened. For women in past generations, premarital sex was truly premarital; it was an initiatory event closely associated with entry into first marriage. Today, that is far less likely to be the case. Among women born in the 1960s, for example, only 10 percent were married when they first had sexual intercourse.[6] Young women today are also less likely to marry their first sexual partner than women in previous generations.

Indeed, though today's young women may not be continuously sexually active or partnered during the years between first intercourse and first marriage, they are more likely to engage in sex as part of a romantic relationship without any intention, promise, or expectation of future marriage. In a nationally representative Gallup survey of young adults age twenty to twenty-nine years commissioned by the National Marriage Project (NMP) in 2001, close to eight out of ten (78 percent) agreed that "it is common these days for people my age to have sex just for fun, and not expect any commitment beyond the sexual encounter itself," and more than half (54 percent) agreed there are people with whom they would have sex even though they have no interest in marrying them.[7] Simply put, for many young adults, sex is an expected part of dating relationships; it has lost its close connection to the timing of marriage as well as to the choice of a partner for marriage.

Cohabitation as the First Living-Together Union

If the normative connection between first sexual intercourse and first marriage has weakened, so, too, has the connection between first opposite-sex living-together union and first marriage. In the past, couples used to marry in order to live together. Today, couples are living together in order to decide whether they should marry or as an alternative to marriage. As recently as three decades ago, cohabitation was a socially marginal practice for opposite-sex couples. Today, it has become mainstream. The number of unmarried, opposite-sex-partner households is 4.9 million today, compared with fewer than 500,000 in 1970. A majority of young women today will live with a partner before they are married, either with the person they eventually marry or another opposite-sex partner.

Not surprisingly, among young adults, cohabitation has become a socially accepted and even socially expected precursor to marriage. In the NMP/Gallup survey, 62 percent of young adults said that living together before marriage is a good way to avoid divorce, and more than four in ten agreed that they would only marry someone who agreed to live with them first.

Cohabiting Unions and Orientation to Marriage

Many people assume that cohabiting unions are all the same. However, with respect to their orientation to marriage, this seems not to be the case. Cohabiting unions can have very different aims and purposes when it comes to choosing someone to marry. To illustrate, let me identify four types of co-habiting unions, each with a distinctive orientation toward mate selection and marriage: (1) nonnuptial cohabitation, (2) prenuptial cohabitation, (3) opportunistic cohabitation, and (4) courtship cohabitation.[8]

Nonnuptial cohabitation. This type of living-together union is an alternative to marriage. Nonnuptial cohabitation is essentially marriage for opposite-sex couples that do not seek or believe in the institution of marriage. Nonnuptial cohabiting partners have chosen each other as mates and are committed to a future together, but they have chosen not to marry. In countries like Sweden, such nonnuptial cohabiting unions are typically long lasting, stable, and include virtually all the social benefits of marriage. However, in the United States, the Scandinavian type of cohabitation is fairly rare. Only about 10 percent of cohabiting unions in the United States last five years or longer.[9]

Prenuptial cohabitation. This type of living-together union involves couples that are planning to marry in the near future and may have set their wedding date. They are living together before they marry—perhaps to fix up the house they plan to live in as a married couple, to save money that otherwise would be spent on separate households, or to spend time together to plan the wedding itself. Prenuptial cohabitors have chosen each other as life partners and have made public their intentions to marry. Thus prenuptial cohabitation is a relatively short-term arrangement designed to lead to marriage.

Opportunistic cohabitation. This living-together union is for couples that are romantically involved and want to share rents, living expenses, and household efficiencies but are not considering marriage to each other or to anyone else. These opportunistic cohabiting unions are popular among young adults who want to maintain a high degree of personal mobility and freedom in their near-term future. They provide the means for young couples to gain some of the sexual, economic, and domestic advantages of marriage before they are ready to choose a marriage partner or think seriously about marriage. In this sense, opportunistic cohabiting relationships can be thought of as part of a strategy to delay marriage but not as part of the process of choosing a marriage partner.

Courtship cohabitation. This is a living-together union for couples that are romantically involved and want to explore their potential for marriage. For many dating couples, cohabitation fulfills a traditional function of courtship, namely, getting to know the habits, disposition, and character traits of a romantic partner in order to test mutual compatibility for marriage. However, unlike traditional courtship, this new kind of courtship involves sharing a roof and bed. As noted above, sex is a common part of young adults' dating relationships. Couples can become passionately involved sexually before they have gone through the slower process of gaining trust, familiarity, and knowledge of each other, and of each other's families. Consequently, they turn to living together as a way to gather information about their partner's character, habits, interests, daily routines, and family background. Some of the young college-educated women I have interviewed firmly believe that "you can't tell whether your boyfriend is 'husband material' on the basis of the idealized image he sets forth on a date or on the basis of the good sex you have together. You have to observe him in everyday household life as well."[10]

Further, some young working singles contend that living together provides a regular time and place to be together after long workdays, something that is harder to schedule and achieve by living apart and dating. Finally, as noted above, young adults view cohabitation as a means of avoiding a bad marriage and preventing eventual divorce, should they eventually marry each other, though this view is not borne out by the available evidence. In fact, a substantial body of evidence indicates that couples that live together before marriage are more likely to break up after marriage than those that do not.[11]

With respect to marriage, nonnuptial and prenuptial cohabitation stand at opposite poles. The nonnuptial union is formed explicitly and deliberately as an alternative to traditional marriage or, some might even say, as a critique of it. At the opposite pole, the prenuptial union is a step leading to marriage.

In opportunistic and courtship cohabitation, couples choose to live together for reasons that have more to do with current circumstances than with future plans. They enter these unions without any long-term commitment to each other and with the notion that the unions will dissolve, whenever they cease to "work" for one or both partners.

With respect to orientation toward marriage, however, the two types differ. In the case of opportunistic cohabitation, there is no intention of marriage. These cohabiting unions are designed for people who want to remain free to move on. Indeed, the low-commitment and time-limited nature of opportunistic cohabitation is its principal attraction and rationale. Courtship cohabitation, conversely, is more oriented toward marriage. It is a process of testing a romantic partner's suitability for a long-term partnership, and possibly for marriage. A high percentage of cohabiting unions apparently fulfill this function. For all cohabiting unions, the most recent estimates suggest that about 55 percent of cohabiting couples marry, and 40 percent end within five years of the beginning of the cohabitation.[12] For first-time cohabiting unions, a recent report estimates that "58 percent of cohabitations that have lasted at least three years have made the transition to marriage by that time and 70 percent of cohabitations that have lasted for five years have made the transition by that time."[13] (Estimates of the percentage of cohabiting partnerships that lead to marriage vary, depending on the data source and whether the partnerships are first-time cohabitations or all cohabitations.)

Nonetheless, this new form of courtship leaves a high degree of uncertainty as to its purpose and outcome. In traditional courtship, a set of well-defined rules and rituals marks the progress, or lack of progress, in the romantic relationship. Each step toward marriage carries wider public recognition, broader prerogatives and obligations, and more symbols of the couple's mutual commitment to each other. Moreover, the purpose of traditional courtship is to find a marriage partner, and this orientation toward marriage shapes the expectations, behavior, and pacing of a romance. Couples have to demonstrate their readiness and worthiness for marriage, not only to each other but also to parents, family, and friends. Except in times of war or emergency, they are expected to spend time getting to know each other and to observe each other in a variety of social and family settings before marrying. In traditional courtship, people who are considering marriage to each other are slower to engage in sex; more likely to seek someone without previous sexual partners or children; and more likely, especially if they are religiously observant, to wait to have sex until they are married.[14]

In courtship cohabitation, there are no formal rules or rituals marking entry into the union. The decision to live together is private. It is sometimes made casually, hastily, or expediently. People can move in together without any serious discussion, public announcement, or mutual understanding as to its meaning, purpose, or likely duration.

Further, though a high percentage of cohabiting unions lead to marriage, courtship cohabitation is more indeterminate in its orientation toward marriage than traditional courtship. Its purpose is to test compatibility and commitment for a future partnership—perhaps a "long-term relationship"; perhaps marriage; or perhaps, if things do not work out romantically, living together as roommates. As a consequence, it is easy for a couple to decide to live together yet at the same time harbor very different expectations for the future of their relationship. This may be why one of the most hotly debated "relationship issues" among cohabiting women is "When do I bring up the subject of marriage?"

Young Adults' Attitudes toward Marriage

I now turn to young adults' attitudes toward marriage. Here I will draw primarily upon the NMP/Gallup survey.

Marriage as an Intimate Relationship

Young adults today prize marriage as a personal life goal and as the ultimate expression of commitment. A majority of single adults (56 percent) say they expect to be married to one person for a lifetime. They also place a high value on intimacy and friendship in marriage. An overwhelming majority—94 percent of the men and women surveyed—say that they want to marry someone who is a "soul mate" and best friend; and 88 percent agree that there is a special person, a soul mate, waiting for them somewhere.

To be sure, this is not entirely new. In the Western tradition, there is a long-standing ideal and aspiration for romantic friendship in marriage.[15] However, today's young adults seem to be notching up their expectations for a soul mate to an even higher level. They are seeking emotional intimacy above more traditional marriage goals such as becoming a full-fledged adult, gaining social acceptance, or getting ahead economically. For example, though both men and women believe that marriage will improve their economic standing, more than eight in ten (81 percent) young women agree that it is more important to them to have a husband who can communicate about his deepest feelings than to have a husband who makes a good living.

At the same time that young men and women express a heightened desire for emotional intimacy in marriage, however, they see a diminished role for marriage in its institutional aspects. For them, many of the larger social, economic, religious, and public purposes associated with marriage are receding or entirely missing. To state the case more starkly, the men and women surveyed think of marriage as a private intimate relationship that is emotionally deep but socially shallow. Let me cite some evidence for these views.

The Shift Away from Marriage as a Child-Rearing Institution

Although 60 percent agree that people who want children ought to get married, only 16 percent of young adults agree that the main purpose of marriage these days is to have children. Fewer than half (44 percent) think that having a child outside marriage is wrong. Forty percent of young single women agree with the statement that "you would consider having a child on your own if you hadn't found the right man by your mid-thirties."

The Shift Away from Marriage as an Economic Partnership

Rather than seeing marriage as a means to gaining economic independence from parents, the young adults surveyed expect to gain economic independence on their own before entering marriage. Eighty percent of never-married young adults surveyed agree that "educational pursuits or career developments come before marriage at this time in your life." An even higher proportion (86 percent) agree that "it is extremely important to you to be economically set before you get married." It is noteworthy that young women are as likely as young men to agree with this statement. Partly, this trend seems to represent changing patterns of education and work. More women are going on to higher education—outnumbering men on most undergraduate campuses—and also spending more years as working singles before marriage. During this longer period of youthful adult singlehood, they acquire debts, a higher income, and sometimes assets of their own. Thus they tend to think about their economic lives and fortunes in individual terms.

In part, this trend also seems to reflect a keen awareness of the instability of marriage, and particularly an awareness among young women of their vulnerability, should they depend on marriage for their economic security. Overall, slightly more than half of all singles surveyed (52 percent) and an even higher percentage of those in their late twenties (60 percent) agree that one of their biggest concerns about marriage is the possibility that it will end in divorce. Notably, a large majority of the young women (82 percent) surveyed now agree that "it is unwise to rely on marriage for financial security." Given their professed anxiety about divorce and given the persistently high divorce rate, the young people surveyed may regard the economic strategy of building social capital through a long-lasting marital union as risky compared with the economic strategy of acquiring individual capital by investing in one's own education and career advancement. When a marriage breaks up, the reasoning goes, the resources invested in the marriage are put at risk but not the resources invested in one's own human potential. No one can take away what is in your head or on your résumé. Thus greater security comes from the investments you make in yourself.

The Shift Away from Marriage as a Public Institution

Young adults tend to see marriage as a private, intimate partnership between two consenting adults. Eight out of ten agree that marriage is nobody's business but that of the two people involved. Further, a substantial proportion agree that the government should not be involved in licensing marriage or in privileging marriage above opposite-sex cohabiting relationships.

The Shift Away from Marriage as a Religious Institution

More precisely, this is a decline in the importance of sharing the *same religious traditions and faith.* Fewer than half (42 percent) of single young adults believe that it is important to find a spouse who shares their own religion. In an entirely unscientific study I have conducted of two dating websites aimed at the educated elite, I have found further evidence of this attitude.[16] The majority of personal ad placers do not mention religion at all. Good health habits such as nonsmoking, fitness, and athleticism, along with compatibility with pets, rank among the most commonly favored characteristics. Those who do cite religion as a desirable characteristic nonetheless seem to want their ideal mate's religious faith to be as syncretic and blandly "spiritual" as possible. For example, one personal-ad placer preferred a "Protestant as long as you're not a Bible thumper"; another was looking for a "realistic Catholic"; another characterized her faith as "Episcopalian with Buddhist sensibilities"; yet another described herself as "Jewish but not very." Admittedly, my findings would have been different had I surveyed the dating websites for singles seeking someone of their own religious faith, such as http://www.J-Date.com for Jewish singles, http://www.avemariasingles.com for Catholic singles, and http://www. findachristian.com for evangelical Protestant singles.[17] Nonetheless, among many well-educated young singles today, and especially those identifying themselves as liberal Protestants, the requirement of a shared religious faith seems to be a relatively unimportant factor in searching for a partner.

A Shift in the Place of Marriage in the Early Adult Life Course

In the transition to adulthood, marriage used to be an early step. Now it comes later in the sequence of events. After the completion of formal schooling, the first step in the transition, today's young men and women focus on achieving certain individual life goals—getting out of debt; getting ahead in work; and gaining personal life experience, including having experience with more than one romantic partner. A National Opinion Research Center (NORC) study based on data from the 2002 General Social Survey found evidence supporting this new sequence. Overall, people place finishing schooling, being financially independent, living on one's own, and obtaining full-time employment well ahead of marriage as key steps toward achieving adulthood.

Within this strong social consensus, however, the NORC study reveals some notable differences. The young and never married favor earlier transitions to financial independence, living away from parents, and working full time and later transitions to getting married and having children than do older adults and the widowed and married. The college-educated class favor later transitions in all domains, including finishing education at the age of twenty-three or twenty-four years and getting married at about twenty-seven.[18]

The delay of marriage until older ages has some positive effects on marital stability. Teenage marriages are at a substantially higher risk of divorce than first marriages of people in their twenties or older. About one-half of teen marriages (among women age nineteen and twenty years) will end in divorce in fifteen years, compared with one-third of marriages for women over twenty.[19] Indeed, one recent study found that the increase in the median age of first marriage is the single most important factor in the recent leveling of divorce rates.[20] Putting off marriage to gain additional education beyond high school has advantages for women as well. Women with at least a baccalaureate degree are more likely to marry and less likely to divorce or separate than women of lesser educational attainment.[21]

However, there are some negative effects associated with putting off marriage until substantially older ages. With a longer period of sexually active single life before first marriage, the likelihood of having multiple sex partners and of cohabiting increases, and these behaviors are associated with increased risk of divorce. Among sexually active singles, marital delay also increases the risks of unwed parenthood, and unwed parenthood significantly reduces the chances of ever marrying, especially for women. Despite more tolerant attitudes toward unwed parenthood, a recent study finds that having children is still one of the least desirable characteristics a potential marriage partner can possess.[22]

In addition, there is reason to believe that the delay of marriage favors men's timetable for married parenthood over that of women. Men can postpone marriage and still gain many of the sexual and domestic advantages of marriage, including the caretaking of a female partner, without risking their future chances of having biological children. Declines in fertility begin earlier for women than for men, though men's fertility is hardly as eternal as the stories of late-in-life celebrity fathers might suggest. Finally, a cycle of low-commitment partnerships followed by breakups may contribute to an overall climate of gender mistrust, cynicism, and disappointment among single men and women, making them more leery of the commitment to marriage.

Trends in Youthful Courtship

During the first two-thirds of the last century, a system of romantic courtship oriented toward marriage was firmly in place. The system was designed for the population of never-married opposite-sex young people, and its clear intent was pairing off people for marriage. As the cultural historian Beth L. Bailey has argued, this system was so broad and comprehensive that it could be described as national in its scope and influence. It provided a set of rules, conventions, and practices that nearly everyone recognized and most followed. She writes: "The rules were constantly reiterated and reinforced. The sameness of the message was overwhelming. Popular magazines, advice and etiquette books, texts used in high school and college marriage courses, the professional journals of educators who taught the courses, all formed a remarkably coherent universe."[23] Though these rules may seem narrow and

stifling to people today, she notes, they nonetheless provided a clear and coherent guide to dating and mating. No one suffered confusion about what the
standards for courtship were, what the consequences for violating the standards might be, or what the purposes and ends of courtship were.

This "national" courtship system was supported by the three central
youth-shaping institutions in the society: the family, the school, and the faith
community. Parents influenced youthful dating activities by overseeing their
offsprings' social activities and by guiding them into peer groups, private or
parochial schools, and colleges, where they were likely to meet someone with
a similar religious or social background.

For a growing number of young people in the mid–twentieth century,
coeducational residential colleges functioned as effective marriage markets
by bringing together a population of never-married peers who were closely
matched in educational aspirations and socioeconomic background. Campus
life encouraged couple dating. Until the mid-1960s, faculty and administra-
tors supervised collegiate social life in loco parentis. Further, the campus-
based system established both the timetable and goal for romantic relationships. It was widely understood that the purpose of coed dating was to find
someone to marry—and, especially for women, usually by graduation day.

Finally, when young people married shortly after they finished formal
schooling and when their parents paid for, planned, and "ran" weddings, their
connection to their family's faith community remained relatively undisrupted.
They stayed within or returned to the fold for marriage preparation and for the
wedding itself. To be sure, interfaith marriages—as well as family politics, war-
time, or simple logistics—sometimes required alternative arrangements. But
for most of the last century, the population of marriage-minded young adults
remained within the influence and reach of their family's faith community.

None of these three youth-shaping institutions has nearly as much influence on mate selection today. Today's unmarried young adults are geographically, socially, and emotionally removed from all three. As we have seen,
young people now seek economic and residential independence from their
parents well before they begin to look for a marriage mate, much less marry.
College graduates may pursue work or graduate study far from home. And the
coed college, with its densely concentrated, geographically localized pool of
never-married peers, does not function as effectively as a marriage market
as it once did. Couple dating has been replaced by coed group socializing, accompanied by casual sexual relationships, variously termed "scooping, clock-
ing, hooking, scamming, scrumping, mashing and shacking," as well as by the
occasional longer-term partnership.[24]

By the time young singles begin to search seriously for a spouse, many
have graduated and left the campus community. They are spending their days

in the workplace and their evenings in private residences. Beyond bars and nightclubs (arguably not the best place to search for a future marriage mate), they have limited opportunities and occasions for peer socializing. Increasingly—because of time pressures, a lack of opportunities and places to meet other young singles, and especially because of the rootlessness and mobility of these early adult years—many are turning to the Internet to search for romantic partners.

Finally, faith communities are losing influence over the mating behavior and choices of the young. For one thing, many young adults, and especially young single men, are among the least religiously observant individuals in the population. For another, some religious communities have not reached out to, or perhaps fully recognized, the growing population of young working singles in their midst. Religiously observant singles have told me that they often feel invisible in their family-oriented faith communities. And lastly, religious prohibitions against premarital sex and cohabitation may make it more difficult to reach those young adults who have engaged in such behavior in the past or may be living together currently but nonetheless plan to marry.

Even those singles who have not engaged in premarital sex or cohabitation are frustrated. As some complain, their own faith communities fail to recognize how a prolonged singlehood poses greater challenges to people who want to follow church teachings on sex and marriage. As one such woman puts it: "Delaying marriage forces many Christian singles into the abstinence marathon against which every cell in their bodies revolts."[25]

As a further challenge to the influence of traditional social institutions, the mating market itself is globalizing. Thanks to study and travel abroad, the growing popularity of Internet dating, and the expansion of an international workplace, young Americans are meeting and marrying people from diverse backgrounds and often non-Western religious and cultural traditions. As a romantic trend, of course, love across cultural and national boundaries has its charms and delights. Nevertheless, the growing globalism in mating markets creates new challenges for successful mate selection. Opposites may attract, but they do not always live together harmoniously, especially when a couple has sharply discrepant cultural ideas about gender roles, child rearing, religious faith, and family obligations to in-laws and kin.

Implications for Marriage and Marriage Preparation

Finally, I consider the implications of these findings for parents, teachers, counselors, clergy, scholars, and especially for those who are actively engaged in preparing young adults for future marriage. Providing a system for successful mate selection is one of the fundamental tasks of a society. Indeed, the task of pairing off men and women for the purposes of marriage and parenthood is so important that no known society leaves it up to lone individuals wandering around on their own. But for many marriage-minded young singles today, that seems to be exactly what is happening. Finding a suitable person to marry has become a do-it-yourself project, a trend that makes the process of finding a mate more prolonged, confusing, difficult, and at least potentially less successful.

Given the lengthening pathway to marriage, a trend that is unlikely to change direction, what can be done to foster success in mate selection? One step is to do a better job of educating young adults about choosing a life partner. For reasons I have suggested, the social institutions that have been the traditional custodians of a body of thought, knowledge, and practice on marriage have less influence on youthful mating behavior. The entertainment media and the market fill the vacuum. Many young adults get their ideas about sex, love, and relationships from television shows like *Friends, Sex and the City,* and *The Bachelor.* As a consequence, misconceptions abound, especially when it comes to the effects of casual sex, cohabitation, and unwed parenthood on marital matching. Young adults are likely to see these behaviors as having a positive or null effect on the future choice of a marriage partner, when in fact the evidence suggests that all three are likely to have negative effects on successful marital matching and future marital stability. At the very least, there should be stronger educational efforts to correct such misconceptions.

In addition to disseminating accurate information about mate selection, it would also be helpful to gain a better understanding of the role of the Internet in matchmaking. Online dating is now more than a fad or a curiosity. It has become a mainstream practice among young working singles. More than half the members of Match.com, one of the biggest and most profitable dating websites, are under the age of thirty.[26] Indeed, this new technology is likely to have as revolutionary an impact on youthful patterns of dating and mating as the automobile did in 1920s and the birth control pill did in the 1960s. But little is known about the impact or effectiveness of the Internet on marital matching. Psychologists, software designers, and market researchers are gathering data on the people who use dating websites, but so far marriage researchers have not measured the impact of this technological innovation on mate selection.

Another positive step would be to identify and support social networks that would foster effective marital matching among the population of young working singles. Once out in the work world, singles have too little time and too few suitable places to meet other singles. Moreover, given the diversity of partnering goals among today's population of dating singles, marriage-minded singles may also have difficulty locating partners who are interested in matrimony rather than casual sex or a "long-term relationship." As Norval Glenn has persuasively argued, better "marriage market circulation" might occur if people and institutions shared and disseminated information about the places where marriage-minded singles could meet.[27]

Some groups of work colleagues and friends are beginning to share this kind of information informally. For example, I interviewed several young women lawyers in Dallas who were involved in a Habitat for Humanity project sponsored by their firm. They were busy spreading the word among their single friends that Habitat sites attracted altruistic single male lawyers who knew how to use a power saw—apparently an attractive combination of brains, brawn, and benevolence in their eyes.

Yet another step would be to encourage faith communities to take into account the trend toward a longer pathway to marriage and to consider its implications for teachings on premarital sex and cohabitation. This is not to say that there should be a retreat from such religious teachings, but it is to suggest that there must be fuller recognition of the changing circumstances of young people's lives and a greater effort to provide practical supports to help them live up to the teachings of their faith.[28]

Clearly, these steps are small and merely suggestive. The larger and still unanswered question is whether families, as well as educational and religious institutions, will be able to come up with innovative ways to support successful mate selection and marriage among the population of young working singles, or whether they will surrender this crucial social task to the market.

Notes

1. Norval D. Glenn, "A Plea for Greater Concern about the Quality of Marital Matching," in *Revitalizing the Institution of Marriage for the Twenty-First Century: An Agenda for Strengthening Marriage,* ed. Alan J. Hawkins, Lynn D. Wardle, and David Orgon Coolidge (Westport, Conn.: Praeger, 2002), 45–46.

2. U.S. Bureau of the Census, *America's Families and Living Arrangements: Population Characteristics, 2000,* Current Population Reports P20-537, prepared by Jason Fields (Washington, D.C.: U.S. Bureau of the Census, 2001), 9.

3. Data are presented for women since changes in recent decades have been more significant for them than for men. In timing of first intercourse and number of sexual partners, women's formative sexual experiences are becoming more like men's, though men still have sex at slightly younger ages and with more sexual partners. Edward O. Laumann, John H. Gagnon, Robert T. Michael, and Stuart Michaels, *The Social Organization of Sexuality: Sexual Practices in the United States* (Chicago: University of Chicago Press, 1994), 324–27.

4. Robert T. Michael, John H. Gagnon, Edward O. Laumann, and Gina Kolata, *Sex in America: A Definitive Survey* (Boston: Little, Brown, 1994), 97.

5. Kristin A. Moore, Anne K. Driscoll, and Laura Duberstein Lindberg, *A Statistical Portrait of Adolescent Sex, Contraception and Childbearing* (Washington, D.C.: National Campaign to Prevent Teen Pregnancy, 1998), 3.

6. R. Kelly Raley, "Recent Trends and Differentials in Marriage and Cohabitation," in *The Ties That Bind: Perspectives on Marriage and Cohabitation,* ed. Linda J. Waite (New York: Aldine de Gruyter, 2000), 32.

7. Barbara Dafoe Whitehead and David Popenoe, "Who Wants to Marry a Soulmate?" in *The State of Our Unions 2001* (Piscataway, N.J.: National Marriage Project, Rutgers University, 2001). Hereafter, the survey will be identified as the NMP/Gallup survey. Except where otherwise noted, attitudinal findings are based on this study.

8. This typology is intended only for the purposes of analyzing these select characteristics. It should not be taken as an empirical description of cohabiting unions, nor should it be considered as inclusive of all possible types of cohabiting unions. I am excluding two other common types: opposite-sex cohabiting unions with children, a family arrangement that has increased 850 percent since 1960; and opposite-sex cohabiting unions between older widowed or divorced individuals who live together rather than marry to avoid tax, inheritance, or pension complications.

9. Pamela J. Smock, "Cohabitation in the United States: An Appraisal of Research Themes, Findings, and Implications," *Annual Review of Sociology* 26 (2000): 3.

10. Barbara Dafoe Whitehead, *Why There Are No Good Men Left: The Romantic Plight of the New Single Woman* (New York: Broadway Books, 2002), 119–20.

11. Most scholars agree that the increased divorce risk for cohabiting couples is partially due to "selection effect," the fact that people who live together before marriage have different characteristics than those who do not, and it may be these characteristics, and not the experience of cohabitation per se, that leads to future marital instability. However, there is also evidence to support the idea that cohabitation itself fosters habits and behaviors that are detrimental to marriage. What can be said for certain is that no evidence has yet been found that those who live together before marriage have stronger or longer lasting marriages than those who do not. See "Unmarried Cohabitation," in *The State of Our Unions 2003,* ed. David Popenoe and Barbara Dafoe Whitehead (Piscataway, N.J.: National Marriage Project, Rutgers University, 2003); available at http://marriage.rutgers.edu.

12. Smock, "Cohabitation in the United States," 3.

13. W. D. Bramlett and W. D. Mosher, "Cohabitation, Marriage, Divorce and Remarriage in the United States," *Vital Health Statistics* (National Center for Health Statistics) 23, no. 22 (2002): 12.

14. See the discussion in Laumann et al., *Social Organization of Sexuality,* 506–8.

15. See, e.g., Jean H. Hagstrum, *Esteem Enlivened by Desire: The Couple from Homer to Shakespeare* (Chicago: University of Chicago Press, 1992).

16. The two websites are http://goodgenes.com and http://rightstuffdating.com. Both restrict membership to graduates or faculty in a handful of elite higher educational institutions.

17. "Surfing for Your Soulmate," a multifaith guide to dating websites, can be found at http://www.beliefnet.com.

18. Tom W. Smith, *Coming of Age in 21st Century America: Public Attitudes towards the Importance and Timing of Transitions to Adulthood,* GSS Topical Report 35 (Chicago: National Opinion Research Center, University of Chicago, 2003).

19. Naomi Seiler, *Is Teen Marriage a Solution?* (Washington, D.C.: Center for Law and Social Policy, 2002), 8.

20. Tim B. Heaton, "Factors Contributing to Increasing Marital Stability in the United States," *Journal of Family Issues* 23 (2002): 392–409.

21. U.S. Bureau of the Census, *Number, Timing and Duration of Marriages and Divorces: 1996,* Current Population Reports P70-80, prepared by Rose M. Kreider and Jason M. Fields (Washington, D.C.: U.S. Bureau of the Census, 2002), 8.

22. Gayle Kaufman and Frances Goldscheider, "Willingness to Stepparent: Attitudes toward Partners Who Already Have Children," paper delivered at the 2003 American Sociological Association meeting; available at http://www.asanet.org/convention/2003/program.html.

23. Beth L. Bailey, *From Front Porch to Back Seat: Courtship in Twentieth Century America* (Baltimore: Johns Hopkins University Press, 1988), 8.

24. Arthur Levine and Jean Cureton, *When Hope and Fear Collide: A Portrait of Today's College Students* (San Francisco: Jossey-Bass, 1998), 109–10. For a portrait of college women's attitudes toward dating relationships, also see Norval Glenn and Elizabeth Marquardt, *Hooking Up, Hanging Out and Hoping for Mr. Right: College Women on Dating and Mating Today* (New York: Institute for American Values, 2001).

25. Debbie Maken, "How Churches Have Failed Singles," http://www.beliefnet.com/story/130/story.

26. Anna Mulrine, "Love.com," *U.S. News & World Report,* September 29, 2003, 52–58.

27. Glenn, "Plea for Greater Concern," 55–57.

28. See Michael G. Lawler, "Becoming Married in the Catholic Church: A Traditional Post-Modern Proposal," *INTAM Review* 7 (2001): 37–54, for one theologian's well-argued proposal for church recognition of cohabitation as part of a marriage process.

Chapter 9
American Middle-Class Families:
Class, Social Reproduction, and Ritual

Bradd Shore

This chapter is part of a larger effort to understand how the traditional functions of myth and ritual in helping to make shared meaning and produce social coordination in communities are being carried out in contemporary American middle-class working families, especially dual-wage-earner families juggling work and home life.[1] Studying myth and ritual in contemporary American families is necessarily somewhat different from comparable research in the kinds of places that have conventionally been the fieldwork sites for anthropologists. Indeed, myth and ritual might seem at first glance like a peculiar subject matter in the context of an agenda for understanding the challenges of contemporary American dual-earner families. The notion that myth and ritual are marginal to modern life is itself a kind of "myth" of modernity that serves to mask the actual importance that these practices have in contemporary family life. When we look at the developmental cycle of American family structure, myth and ritual can be shown to have a special significance in the constitution of American family life.

When a new family is formed in any society, it faces not only the practical challenges of providing food and shelter for its members but also the less commonly recognized challenge of creating a new miniature society with a distinctive set of traditions and coordinating practices. In many societies, the new family unit immediately becomes a part of an encompassing family and descent group, and it simply replicates or continues the traditions and practices of the older group. But where, as in the contemporary United States, new families generally set themselves up as autonomous or semiautonomous units, living apart from the families in which the new bride or groom grew up, the task of creating a new family culture is a major challenge of family making. New parents bring with them a stock of understandings and practices from their own childhood families, many of which will be used in making the new family. But despite these important imported resources from older family ties, the ritual life of a new family will depend upon ongoing negotiations between parents, the gender and role system that is adopted by the new family, and the character of the community in which the family resides. The shape of a particular family's ritual life will also depend on the specific circumstances of individual families, including work patterns, numbers of children, economic status, and the health status of family members.

However they do it, successful families have to create a meaningful order of myths and rituals for themselves. No family will simply reproduce the structure of stories and rituals that the parents experienced as children. The creation of a family in the United States is in great part the orchestration of routines and stories that give the family a functional and also distinctive character.

Middle-Class Families

Our focus is not just on the American family, but more specifically on middle-class families. But what makes a family "middle class"? Social class is notoriously confused in American discourse. Though issues connected with gender and race are common topics of discussion in the United States, class status remains a far more equivocal and ambiguous issue, particularly for the middle class. Class presupposes significant social distinctions, but the utility of the concept seems questionable when about 80 percent of Americans identify themselves as middle class.[2] If self-identification is employed as the basis of class, then the vast majority of Americans would seem to fall into "a rather amorphous and hence universalistic and culturally neutral middle."[3]

But the idea that the United States is an essentially classless or a one-class society is misleading. Americans do not generally speak of themselves in class terms. This silence about class is not an insignificant aspect of race in America. The anthropologist Sherry Ortner has suggested that "class is central to American social life, but it is rarely spoken in its own right. Rather it is represented through other categories of social difference: gender, ethnicity, race, and so forth."[4]

Middle-class identity in America tends to be expressed through the language of social status and especially through discourses on consumption. Claiming middle-class status both reveals and conceals aspects of actual social position in America. It reveals something important about the social and economic aspirations of an individual. But the blanket term "middle class," extended as it is in American usage, also serves to mask significant differences in actual economic status and social power. When so many people whose actual economic status and social power are so different are lumped together under one class category, we have a right to wonder what work that category is actually doing.

Part of the significance of the label "middle class" is its close association with consumption habits and aspirations. Middle-class identity is deeply intertwined with consumer identity, leading Marilyn Strathern to call it "the plasti-class," suggesting the conflation of class status and credit status.[5] Credit cards in the United States are often marketed as class status markers as much as pragmatic consumption tools.[6] With middle-class status so deeply linked to consumption behavior, marketers have an interest in promoting the widest possible extension of middle-class identity, and hence promoting the idea that class status is a reflection of one's consumption patterns rather than some sort of social essence: "The fact that a majority of Americans self-identify as middle class indicates that the media, in addressing and largely representing the middle class, or at least an imagined idea of the middle class, effectively constitutes its audience regardless of incomes, job status, educational levels, and lifestyles. This is not, in other words, a chicken-and-egg problem, but a media-fabricated social imaginary."[7] In other words, though it does point to an important American concept, the term "middle class" also serves to conceal a variety of important social distinctions at the same moment as it appears to be revealing one.

This conceptual confusion in the use of the term is linked to the fact that "middle class" actually conflates distinct income groups (e.g., those earning $25,000 a year and those earning ten times that), labor groups (e.g., wage earners, salaried workers, industrial workers, craft workers, service workers, managers, and entrepreneurs), and what Max Weber called "status groups."[8] In spite of these ambiguities, and keeping in mind the important elements of "false consciousness" implied by claims of middle-class status, this broad and almost ubiquitous extension of middle-class status is a significant fact of American life. Middle-class status takes its part in a class system in American life that begs for clarification. We can distinguish four hierarchically ordered status groups in the United States that we can use as a baseline model of American class structure. They are not precisely income groups, rather they are framed by distinct self-identities and different worldviews.

At the upper end of the "class" spectrum are a relatively small number of "old families," which consider themselves to be the upper crust of American life. Often but not always wealthy, these families do not use wealth per se as a distinctive marker of their status, because parvenus and "new money" may be recognized by these families as possessing even greater wealth than themselves, but not their social status or position. This traditional elite status group in American life is generally white, Anglo-Saxon, and Protestant (WASP). These elites do not generally consider wealthy or socially and politically prominent non-WASPs to be genuine peers. Though most of these families are relatively wealthy, and some are influential, wealth and social achievement are not by themselves the most important criteria for upper-class status. Upper-class status is framed as ascribed and inherited rather than achieved, attributed to birth, "blood," social connections to the right ancestors, clubs, families, schools, and a sense of authentic "style" that is held to be largely unattainable and inimitable by outsiders and parvenus.

At the other end of the class spectrum is America's "underclass," perennially unemployed or marginally employed, poorly educated, and often ethnically marked communities of those who have little hope of economic advancement. They are generally the most vulnerable segment of American society, subject to violence and many kinds of major health risks. This underclass is not populated just by the unemployed. According to the political scientist John Schwartz:

> More than 12 million full-time year round workers are paid wages beneath those needed to support a minimally decent standard of living for households with children. Two-thirds of workers who start at subpar wages are unable to lift themselves up to a decent wage even after a decade of full-time work.[9]

Struggling to put food on the table and keep a roof over their heads, the American working poor along with the perennially unemployed are not a statistically insignificant part of our population, but they are often ignored by social policy analysts. Their economic vulnerability means that most of them experience life outside of the aspirations and goals of the American middle class.

The third American status group are blue-collar workers. In the United Kingdom, they are known as the "working class."[10] More than a lower-middle-range income group, blue-collar communities are defined by a distinctive set of social values and by relatively flat status aspirations and educational goals. Blue-collar workers often assume that what was good for them and their parents is good for their children. In this important sense, members of the blue-collar class are distinct from the middle class by the absence or muting of values stressing social climbing or economic and career advancement. Often socially conservative, blue-collar communities tend to be tight-knit and marked by a strong and self-conscious identity. Their residential patterns and social networks are also characteristically distinct from those of the middle class.[11]

From a purely income perspective, there is some overlap between blue-collar workers and the middle class.[12] In some communities, blue-collar workers may have higher incomes than some middle-class workers, as in the case of a community in which factory workers are paid higher wages than the salaries of local school teachers. The major differences between blue-collar and middle-class communities are more matters of self-identification and social aspiration. Most Americans identify themselves as middle class. Despite, or perhaps because of, this extensive identification with middle-class status, the middle class as a group has been notoriously hard to define or pin down, though people often do not have a hard time identifying particular individuals as middle class. Perhaps this is because "middle class" is as much a state of mind as it is an economic or income status. In contemporary America, "middle class" tends to be defined not so much by any stable "status" but in terms of social and economic aspirations and attitudes. This is why "middle class" is not easily pigeonholed in terms of income or any neat cluster of ascribed characteristics. Because of the aspirational basis of middle-class identity, Americans from a wide range of income groups identify themselves as middle class. To be middle class is to be mobile, to aspire to economic and social upward mobility, to see one's life as a ladder.

Middle-class identity assumes generational discontinuity and upward mobility. One's own social and economic status should ideally be higher than one's parents' status. One's children are expected to exceed their parents' social and economic status. Middle-class status is calculated on a fine gradient of status markers rather than in simple class terms. The status markers from the middle class are generally framed in terms of consumption patterns. Major emphasis is given to visible signs of economic achievement, such as neighborhood, house, membership in the right clubs or churches, furnishings, and, above all, cars. In the General Motors model lines of cars, there is rank ordering in a chain of increasing social prestige.[13] But all kinds of consumption patterns enter into the complex calculus of rising class status. This is why it is so difficult to distinguish status level from income for the middle class. Unlike the ascribed characteristics that govern upper-class identity, middle-class status inevitably engages the best markers of status that money can buy.

In the context of this discussion, it should be clear why middle-class status is so complex and ambiguous in America. Whereas other classes seem to be more or less aware of the class structure of the United States and see themselves in conscious relation to one or more other classes, members of the middle class seem to focus their attention on competitive relations with other members of their own class. The emphasis on internal status competition contributes to the muting among the middle class of awareness of class relations in general.

The middle class is also structurally different from the other classes. Whereas the other three class statuses are generally defined by fairly fixed or ascribed criteria, and thus approximate what we normally think of as "groups," the middle class is far more amorphous and unstable. Middle-class status engages a dynamic and always relative calculus of comparative mobility as measured by a wide variety of consumption patterns. A person or family may enter the middle class, just as one may fall from it.[14] In relation to family life, the relatively dynamic and aspirational character of middle-class identity has important implications for the structure and developmental trajectory of middle-class families. The stress on the generational discontinuity of social and economic status in middle-class life leads naturally to the question of the distinctive structure of middle-class American families.

Middle-Class Family Structure

Demographic changes in the contemporary American family have been well documented. Recent census figures document the long-term rise in the divorce rate, the entailed increase in single-parent households, the gradual decline in average number of children per household, the increase in the number of people living alone, a growing number of families with same-sex couples, an increase in families with no children, a steady rise of the number of dual-wage-earner families, and a growing number of families where the adults work nontraditional hours and complementary rather than parallel schedules.[15]

But to an anthropologist, these important changes are taking place within a distinctive and enduring type of family system that has not generally been recognized and analyzed as an important feature of working-families issues. Generally, the literature on working families has simply taken for granted the nature of the American middle-class family system. But the American family is a distinctive type of family system that takes its place among a wide variety of family systems that exist in human societies. Understanding the character of the American family from this comparative perspective provides us with an eye-opening view of some of the key aspects of contemporary family life. Moreover, one cannot understand the role of ritual and myth in modern families apart from an understanding of the structural and developmental characteristics of this family type over time.

The American middle-class family is often classified as a "nuclear family" system. The nuclear family is not a generic or universal type of family system. The most basic unit of family life is generally considered to be the mother and her offspring, which is sometimes called the "elementary family." Though economic globalization is making it increasingly common throughout the world, it is important to remember that the nuclear family is far from a universal type of social organization.

Nuclear families are units of a couple and their offspring. The normative and idealized form of the nuclear family is that of a monogamous, heterosexual couple and their offspring. Though this is still the modal family type in the

United States, we are experiencing a considerable variation in the constitution of the American nuclear family. The latter third of the twentieth century saw increases in single-parent families, blended families (the union of two single-parent units), and families with two parents of the same sex.

Despite these important variations in American family structure, the middle-class nuclear family has a number of important characteristics that we generally take for granted but need to be examined. First, it is a kind of genealogical isolate, a highly atomized family structure that is generally not deeply embedded in any encompassing kin or descent groups. This atomism is implied by our kin terminology, which is classified by anthropologists as "an Eskimo terminology." This kind of terminology isolates lineal kin (mother, father, brother, sister, grandparent, grandchild) from collateral kin (cousin, aunt, uncle, niece, nephew). It distinguishes relatives by generation but not by maternal or paternal line (i.e., it distinguishes uncle from nephew and mother from grandmother, but not mother's brother from father's brother: uncle).

The effect of this isolation is to carve out of the potential universe of kin a relatively isolated unit that is not structurally embedded in wide or deep relations with kin beyond three lineal generations defined by grandparents, parents, and children. This is not to say that Americans do not have strong sentimental and even practical attachments with those that they consider their "extended family," but that there are very few structural links of an enduring nature that tie the nuclear family to a wider universe of kin. Throughout the world, most families are embedded in encompassing descent groups that are based upon common economic holdings, such as land, houses, or joint economic enterprises. These encompassing descent groups exercise considerable authority and influence over the lives of their members. By contrast, American middle-class families are adapted to a kind of economic individualism, with the parental unit controlling its own household economy and functioning, and exercising primary authority over the welfare and socialization of its offspring.

American middle-class families do not generally have much genealogical depth; most members do not know their relatives beyond the grandparent generation. Nor do they interact with collateral relatives more than one generation out, that is, beyond the first cousins. There are exceptions to this, and some regional variations. The existence of family circles, cousin clubs, family reunions, and periodic gatherings with more distant kin, and the growing interest in family genealogy, suggest strong interest in overcoming the inherent isolation of this family unit. However, in this case the exception proves the rule and only underscores the lack of explicit structural links tying American nuclear families to wider networks of kin and descent units.

The Developmental Cycle of the American Family

Some of the most important characteristics of the middle-class family become clear only when we turn away from the relatively static picture that we have presented thus far of the American family system and focus instead on what anthropologists call its "developmental cycle."[16] The notion that every type of family system has a distinctive developmental cycle was developed by British social anthropologists and is particularly associated with Jack Goody.[17] Some of the important variations in family structure evident within any given community at a given time are due not so much to differences in basic family structure as to differences in the developmental phase that different families are in. Every kind of family system has a distinctive developmental trajectory and goes through characteristic phases.

The nuclear family system that is characteristic of the American middle class develops in a very distinctive way over time. We can begin, somewhat arbitrarily, with a newly married couple. Though American couples may reside at any given time with the parents of either the husband or the wife, this is not the ideal situation, and middle-class parents (whether married or single, straight or gay) strive to establish their own independent residence as soon as possible. Returning "home" to Mom and Dad in this context suggests dependency, which implies failure to become an adult. Moving on implies the first stage of moving up.[18] The implication is clear and important. The couple does not conceive of itself as continuing the family of either the husband or the wife. Nor is it establishing a branch of any other family. The couple is beginning a completely new family. This means that the effective life of any given middle-class family is about one-and-one-half generations. This nuclear family life span encompasses the raising of young children up until the age when they themselves leave home to establish their own families, as well as a period of involvement of young children with grandparents.

The developmental goal of the American middle-class family is thus to produce viable offspring who will be capable of eventually leaving their natal households and setting up families of their own. Families whose children cannot do this are considered in popular parlance "dysfunctional" or at least relatively unsuccessful by middle-class standards. The implications are hard to miss: *The American middle-class family is one of the few family systems in the world whose developmental trajectory is, in an important sense, to self-destruct.* In this context, the maintenance of ties of kin dependency outside the context of the nuclear family becomes problematic and a source of considerable ambivalence for family members.

As a family matures, consider how the meaning of "my family" changes. In the early stages of creating a family, and particularly before children enter the picture, a couple is likely to retain their close ties with their natal families, which scholars sometimes call "the family of orientation." In this case, "my family" would refer to their own parents and siblings. Following the birth or adoption of a child, Americans consider the couple now as its own "family." Indeed, the old euphemism for pregnancy, which represented the woman as being "in a family way," suggests the importance for Americans of children in the creation of a family. In this context, it is interesting to note that single parenthood does not seriously compromise a unit as a family in the same way that childlessness does.[19]

Both in terms of the socialization of children and the development of the family as a unit, the ideal for the middle-class family is a high degree of autonomy. Separation occurs not only by the new family unit in relation to its parental units, but also within the new family, as children come into the picture. Though many families are not able to afford a big enough house to give each child his or her own room, this remains an ideal for middle-class families. This separation of children from their parents is modeled in a number of ways in the American middle-class family. Perhaps most obvious is the ideal of providing infants with their own room as soon as possible.

This ideal of "a space of their own" for children is a key theme of middle-class family life throughout its development. In my interviews with middle-class families, the privileged space in the house for many kids was not the public space in which they actually spend much of their time but rather the private, often secret spaces that are uniquely theirs. Every child I interviewed reported having some kind of private hideout either inside the house in an attic, basement, or closet, or in some kind of constructed space outside the house such as a "fort," a "tree-house," a "playhouse," or other hideout. Parents I have interviewed also remember having such spaces in their childhood homes. Such secret spaces continue to be important for American middle-class children until they can claim their own room as a private and inviolable space. So long as parents and older siblings have free access to their bedrooms, children often create a separate space of privacy.

Providing or creating private space within family space is not the only way that Americans prepare their children to leave the nest. Rituals of detachment are commonplace in American middle-class family life. The aspirational mobility of the middle-class family means that moving from one place to another—it is to be hoped, but not necessarily, "moving up"—is a common experience of middle-class family life. Thus perpetual displacement is tied paradoxically to nostalgic notions of "home" as twin aspirations of the "American dream." For adults, this ever-present possibility of having to move means balancing defenses against attaching oneself too strongly to a community with learning how to quickly "become involved" in community life.

For kids, this displacement involves managing the uncomfortable status of "the new kid on the block" and "the new kid in the class." In *Falling from Grace: Downward Mobility in the Age of Affluence,* Katherine Newman describes this quintessentially middle-class experience of moving to a new community:

> Like many other executive families, they were newcomers to suburban New York. Only two years before, David's firm had transferred him from its California branch to its New York headquarters. The move east held the promise of a more important executive job for David and the taste of real affluence. The transition had not been easy, since the social barriers of suburban society were hard to penetrate. Making new friends was no small accomplishment, and after two years there were only a few they could count as close. But they weren't the kind of old friends one could lean on in a crisis, and this surely was a crisis.
>
> Their two teenage children were equally disoriented. Like most kids, they had opposed moving away from the place where they had grown up. They made no secret of their fury at being disrupted in the middle of high school, exiled to a new state where they knew no one. The girl had become rather withdrawn. The boy had worked hard to make new friends, leaning on his father's prestige as a company executive as an avenue into the status-conscious cliques of the local high school. When his son first arrived, as David put it, "No one would even talk to him. He was looked upon as a transient. Everyone else in his school had been in the same area since grammar school." The son's efforts to break into the networks met only with mild success, and even then it took nearly the entire two years before he felt on solid social ground. He had finally reached the comfortable plateau when David lost his job. The whole family was thrown into turmoil, and the prospect of moving surfaced once again.[20]

In addition to the major pattern of recurrent home displacement, middle-class family life is filled with smaller rites of detachment. Middle-class Americans are prepared for separation early, starting with their being placed in their own cribs, preferably in their own rooms, as soon as practically possible after birth. These rites of detachment continue throughout the life course in the form of sleep-away parties; childhood traditions of "running away from home;" going away to camp during the summer, where learning to overcome "homesickness" is an important goal; and, finally, going off to a college at least far enough away from home not to have to live with one's parents, a feared dependency status probably associated with both a failure to achieve adulthood and with blue-collar rather than middle-class values. Though children sometimes do live at home during college years, or during the early years of work, this is an awkward status that may satisfy poorly articulated or understood needs for attachment to family but is nonetheless understood by middle-class society as a sign that one has failed to achieve adult status.

The recognition by children that their natal house is not going to be their permanent home may be communicated early on by parents and children alike in these "detachment rituals." It is also perpetuated by a variety of American "popular myths" about family, such as adolescents complaining but actually bragging about how dysfunctional their family is to friends, or competing to see who has the worst parents, and for parents lamenting to peers about the terrible teens and how they cannot wait to get them out of the house. Of course, like all myths, these tales may contain some truth, but they also provide a set of shared cultural reference points for both parents and children that actually scaffold the difficult job of detaching from one another.

Most young families seem to be relatively unaware of the implications of these practices and beliefs until the children reach their teenage years and "the empty nest" scenario looms. These years in the life of a maturing family are sometimes characterized as the "terrible teens," and they are often the site of difficult negotiations between parents and growing children concerning issues of autonomy. Parents are often conflicted. Their genuine concerns for the safety and welfare of their teenage children, and their often inarticulate desires to hold onto their children, are in tension with their recognition that they have to prepare their children to be on their own. Everyone has to learn to "let go," and family rituals and myths are geared to helping them through this difficult process. Though teenagers are generally not so open about their own ambivalence, I would expect that similar mixed feelings about autonomy and dependency are present in many of the children as well.

Whether they are headed to college or directly to the working world, eventually middle-class children are propelled out of their natal houses and into increasingly "independent living." More than one informant has described for me their traumatic moment of realization that they no longer had a home. For children who go away to college, that realization often occurs in their third or fourth year of school, when they return home for vacation to discover that their bedroom has been turned into a guest room and that their childhood "stuff" has been put away in the attic.

Of course family ties do not disappear when the kids leave home. The dissolution of the natal family is a gradual process that has many phases. But the meaning of "family" is forever changed when the kids move out. In a sense, the parents are left with the same kind of ambiguity they experienced before the birth of their children. Is a couple with no children in their empty nest still "a family"? Once their children establish families of their own, just what and where is that original family? Are they now members of their children's "extended family"? Who will visit whom, and what does it mean for the complex negotiations that are at stake? For women, these issues often revolve around control of food production and other nurturing acts. For men, the issue becomes: Who is the head of what family, and how do we know?

Families with adult children are not simply affected by the fact that the unit no longer resides together under one roof. The very existence and meaning of the old family unit is put into question by the fact that the children are beginning the process by which the primary meaning of family will shift from their natal family to the family that they are about to make.

Just what happens to the old family in this developmental process? From the point of view of the parental generation, their family still exists, though in a dispersed state. Family ties are maintained by telephone and e-mail communication, by periodic visits, and, significantly, by a cycle of ritual celebrations such as holidays and family life events like funerals and birthdays that bring dispersed family members together. Gradually, however, the get-togethers are reframed, and what was once considered as "the kids coming home" gradually becomes "the children coming for a visit," and eventually "going to visit the grandchildren." We might call this gradual displacement and reversal of roles "the King Lear scenario."

From the perspective of the children, their focus gradually shifts to thinking about reestablishing themselves as independent adults. This process began in the teenage years, when many of them sought increasing freedom to be away from home and with peers rather than parents. It culminates eventually in the establishment of a fully autonomous residence. At this stage of their lives, the locus of "family" and "home" begin to diverge. Though the "family" will continue to mean parents and siblings until they have their own children, the term "home" becomes crucially ambiguous and can refer either to the natal family setting or to their new residence. This shift in the meaning of "my home" portends a future shift in the meaning of "my family." The family has been successful in its mission. It has not been continued, extended, or reproduced. It has been, for the most part, replaced.

The Growing Importance of Ritual and Myth

These distinctive characteristics of middle-class families have important implications for the place of ritual and myth in American family life. In this context, we might well ask what holds families together. What exactly are the ties that bind? The oldest answer is sex and child care. In evolutionary terms, the human family was initially tied together by erotic attraction. With the loss of the estrus cycle of seasonal mating, and the possibility of year-round sexual access, hominids had the biologically grounded basis of a perpetual bond between mates that allowed a functional and stable family unit to develop for the socialization and protection of offspring. Families are also held together by sentimental bonds, guaranteed by the elaboration of what psychologists call "attachment," though family life also produces a wide range of negative and ambivalent emotions in addition to attachment.

Along with these emotional bases of family life, families are functional units held together by ties of practical interdependence. The family is the most basic instance of a group integrated by what Émile Durkheim termed "organic solidarity,"[21] a division of labor in which individuals with specialized roles exchange labor and come to depend on one another for that which each can contribute to the whole. Most families have a relatively elementary division of labor, by gender and age. Sharing common interests in producing and raising children, protecting them from harm, and provisioning the household with food, shelter, and other necessities, all families are to some extent pragmatic units with common material interests. This is, of course, the case for American middle-class families, whose existence rests as much on shared practical and economic interests as on sentiments.

In most family systems, these pragmatic interests transcend the life of a single household. Their members (often sets of brothers, or of sisters—in matrilineal societies) share enduring common interests in a wide variety of practical resources, including land, houses, animals, seeds, tools, forms of secret knowledge, ritual magic, and offspring. The continuity of the descent group beyond the life of a single family rests on these enduring pragmatic interests. In addition to these interests, the continuity and solidarity of families are maintained by its rituals and myths, which provide the basis for the symbolic continuity of the group. Human communities are constituted as both pragmatic and symbolic orders, and generally the two dimensions reinforce one another.

The same is true for American middle-class families. But the relative importance of the pragmatic and the symbolic ties changes over the developmental life of any given family. Modern middle-class families are notable for their relative absence of enduring joint property or economic interests. Modern families are organized on the basis of economic individualism, private rather than communal ownership of property, and the commodification of land, houses, and other property. These resources may well be inherited or passed down by family members, but property is rarely jointly owned by a sibling set, unless the family legally incorporates. Unless the family establishes a joint family business, whether a large and complex enterprise or a small family-run business, siblings share few or no enduring pragmatic ties after they leave home. Family interdependence remains only as a set of diffuse and not always reliable expectations about helping out family members with financial, emotional, or labor support in times of need.

As the family matures and children prepare to leave the nest, its pragmatic life weakens. Though adult children may continue to count on parental
economic help from time to time, the practical ties that reinforced the unity
of the family unit gradually lose force as the constituting basis of the family.
In the absence of strong pragmatic ties, joint ownership of property, and coresidence, what guarantees the continuity of any family unit? To a surprising
degree, the answer is myth and ritual.

Family continuity is maintained in part by narratives of various kinds:
Family talk, family stories, and family gossip become the life blood of an essentially dispersed family group. The family comes to be linked through its
flow of words as much as anything else. "Keeping in touch" by phone, e-mail,
letters, and periodic visits becomes increasingly important as the practical
interests of the group are diminished. Moreover, American families become
increasingly dependent on their ritual traditions to keep them going. Birthdays, anniversaries, deaths, and weddings as well as the important "home-
coming" rituals of families (most notably Thanksgiving, Christmas, and, for
Jews, Passover) become the lifeblood of family continuity. But rather than
serving symbolically to reinforce the pragmatic interests that constitute the
material basis for the family, rituals come to be the constituting condition for
the continued existence of the family. Over the course of their developmental
histories, *American families shift from being a basically pragmatic order to being an almost exclusively ritual and mythic order.* The work that parents—largely
mothers—do in establishing family ritual and memory traditions early in the
life of the family will not only serve the children as an important framework
for their childhood memories but will also establish the basis for whatever
enduring joint life this family will have once the children leave home.

The somewhat surprising conclusion is that ritual and myth are not just
important for middle-class families but crucial factors in its very constitution.
The structure and developmental trajectory of middle-class families give ritual and narrative a particularly important role in underwriting the continuity
of the family, especially in its mature form, when the children leave home.[22]
As the pragmatic basis of family life for any middle-class family weakens, the
slack is largely taken up by talk, stories, and celebrations. Beginning as a mix
of sentimental attachments and practical interests, the family ends up as almost entirely a product of its ritual performances.

Meaning Making

One of the consequences of being culture-bearing and culture-creating
animals is that humans are compelled to seek meaning in their lives.[23] Find-

ing the significance of our actions in some grander scheme of things is second
nature for humans. Ritual and myth are basic to the way humans create and
update meaning in their lives. What exactly is "meaning?" Though it appears
to be a somewhat elusive concept, "meaning" is not impossible to define. To
experience something as meaningful is to experience it as a kind of remembering. When something becomes meaningful for us, it is perceived as a kind
of repetition or near repetition of something already known. Something alien
becomes familiar. This happens by a process of reframing. Something gains
an expanded context in relation to which it is knowable. Rather than being
an isolated experience, a meaningful event becomes more than itself. It becomes an instance of something more general, a distinct kind of experience,
something like (though not always exactly like) what we have already been
through.

Ritual and myth provide the basis for this kind of reframing of experience. Rituals and myths are not simply specific actions and stories. They are
also generalized templates for action and story, the framework for canonical events. In this sense, myths and rituals have a crucial ambiguity. They are
halfway between specific events and general forms—human speech and activity on the way to becoming shared institutions. This distinctive formalized
character of ritual and myth sets them apart from ordinary action and speech
as marked action frames. Myth and ritual are foundational modes of narrative
and action, which are relevant to a whole range of specific events. They provide many of the general models humans use to interpret the ongoing events
of their lives, the general forms that help us make sense of the particular moments of our lives.

This special character of ritual and myth means that they play an important role in memory, and in the complex relationship between personal
memory and social memory.[24] Human memory works in relation to pre-
stored mental schemas that serve both to frame and sometimes to distort how
we remember specific events.[25] These schemas may be highly idiosyncratic,
but often they are conventional mental models derived from a shared environment. Rituals and conventional stories are two of the most important
ways in which such shared schemas get produced and transmitted within a
community. The highly formalized character of rituals and myths means that
they take on considerable power by framing how events come to be recalled
by people. In this sense, the complex fabric of family routines, rituals, and
stories that helps make up a "family culture" provides much of the framework
for what family members will remember of their family life.

When adults look back on their childhood, two kinds of memories will
be salient in what psychologists term "autobiographical memory."[26] On the
one hand, there are the unique memories of emotionally salient events such

as deaths, births, accidents, major storms, and any other incidents that stand out from the normal flow of life's experiences.[27] On the other hand, memories of family life will often be framed in more general terms than particular events, and expressed as habitual forms of action such as "When I was young we used to. . . ." These are not actually part of event memory but rather what Connerton has called "habit memory."[28] These kinds of generalized memories of one's earlier life are a product of two important kinds of activity: routines (rituals) and canonical stories (myths).[29]

To the extent that family life is always becoming memory, and thus family history, it rests inevitably on the routines and stories that are the foundation of its enduring character. As we have seen, this is especially true in American middle-class families, in which these structured memories gradually become the sole basis of the continuity of a family as its members move on.

Myth, Ritual, and the Challenges of Work and Family Life

This special place of myth and ritual in the constitution of autobiographical memory and in meaning making more generally has important implications for the study of modern family life. Myth and ritual are key resources that families deploy in meeting the challenges of constructing a coherent set of stories and practices in the making of a modern family. The traditional work of myth and ritual is seriously affected by the significant changes contemporary families have experienced in the allocation of their time to work, family, and civic life; by new trends in scheduling patterns at home, at work, and at school; by the effects of mass media; and by changing communication technologies.

At the heart of ritual and myth are issues of social coordination. Ritual promotes coordination in activities,[30] and both ritual and myth promote coordination of perspective. Coordination does not imply perfect overlap or exact replication, but only a significant degree of joint attention and mutuality of reference to important aspects of experience. But coordination is also at the heart of the juggling problem and the time bind that have come to define the life of the modern working family.[31]

A majority of American middle-class families have two working parents, and an even larger percentage, including single-parent families, have no parent whose primary job is running the household and looking after the children. Increasingly, the traditional nine-to-five work schedule is giving way to a whole variety of nontraditional schedules, including night work, shift work, flex-time work, and part-time work. Increasingly, couples are working very different work schedules in large part because of child care concerns.[32]

Family members may be seen to be increasingly segregated into distinct experiential niches, even though they may appear to live in the same place. People sitting together in a room but tuned into different media or engaged in telephone conversations or Internet chat-room discussions are in an important sense not really together. The extreme market segmentation of television and movies means that parents and children are not actually living in the same world so far as media messages are concerned. Even norms of accepted activity scheduling separate the generations, with teenagers increasingly comfortable with a social life that begins after midnight. Once upon a time, some degree of family coordination was guaranteed by an implicit social contract that acknowledged periods set aside for family activities—mainly dinner time and weekends. But it is now common for kids' sports activities or office meetings to run into dinner time or to take up much of the weekend, so that "family time" is transformed into serial eating, with parents juggling the multiple and conflicting obligations of their workplaces and their children's activities. Increasingly, everyone seems to have a highly individualized schedule, oriented toward the coordination of the team, the workplace, or the club, but not the family. The implications of these transformations not simply for pragmatic coordination of activities but also for the equally important work of coordinated meaning making need a whole range of good empirical studies.

Equally pressing is the need to understand the effect of changes in communication. Modern information technology has had an enormous impact on the very meaning of "being together." Computers, mobile phones, voice mail, and pagers have all made it possible for us to be "in touch" without actually being in the same place or even in the same time frame. Virtual togetherness is real and has increased our ability to keep in almost constant "touch" with family members and friends to a degree not possible in a purely flesh-and-blood world. But virtual connection is a far cry from the ordinary sense of being together. Linked together in dense networks of electronic channels, providing a world of powerful shared media messages as well as interpersonal communication links, people are experiencing radically new ways of "sharing" experiences and information. How these changes have affected people's view of their world and their relationships has yet to be adequately studied.

The Social Distribution of Ritual

Though it is probably not the case that ritual is less important in contemporary American life than in other times and places,[33] it is undoubtedly true that the social distribution of ritual has undergone significant change. Robert Putnam has stressed the dramatic contraction over the past fifty years of the

202 • Bradd Shore

third arena of American life after home and work: civic life and voluntary associations.[34] In his famous community study of Newburyport, Massachusetts, prior to World War II, W. Lloyd Warner documents in detail the large number of civic events and rituals that the average citizen of "Yankee City" attended in the course of a year,[35] confirming the durability of Alexis de Tocqueville's early observation about the special importance of voluntary organizations in American life.[36]

Contributing to this contraction of civic life in contemporary America are two important factors. The first is the postwar growth of the suburbs, which replaced small towns and cities as the communities of choice for middle-class families. Suburbs are generally designed as self-contained communities, often with their own governance structure and social institutions. Though they may try to mimic traditional communities, they are actually private rather than civic communities and do not provide any genuinely public or civic space where a larger community can form. Suburbs tend to be zoned for cars rather than pedestrians, and they do not provide casual access to public physical spaces or commercial areas where people can congregate beyond their immediate communities.[37] The spatial layout implies a kind of protective privatization as opposed to civic congregation.[38] The simultaneous growth of shopping malls replacing the "downtown" of a town or city represents a parallel privatization of space and the loss of a sense of being part of a civic community.

The second factor contributing to the shrinking of American civic life has been the transformation of the culture of work in American life and the return of mothers to the workplace. With families struggling to juggle the demands of children, home, and work, little time or energy is left for civic involvements beyond the family.[39] How much time is left for family activities is currently under study at the Center for Myth and Ritual in American Life (MARIAL Center) at Emory University. Of particular interest is the fate of the family dinner. This is particularly salient both because of the general symbolic significance of eating together but also because the family meal is one of the few times when families can talk as families. Several MARIAL Center researchers are studying family conversations at dinnertime, both to understand how much family communication is going on in working families around the dinner table and also because the amount and specific type of family talk is hypothesized to be a key variable in the emotional resilience of children.[40]

Ritual has not disappeared from American life, but it appears to have shifted significantly in its social distribution. Civic ritual has in great part contracted and been replaced by increasingly privatized routines and rituals. Our research at the MARIAL Center is just beginning to uncover some of these shifts in the distribution of our ritual lives. Many questions remain to be answered. With the blurring of the boundaries between home and work,[41] how much of our ritual life has shifted from the family to the workplace?[42] Modern media and communication devices make possible new forms of "virtual ritual," experiences that we "share" with others, such as watching the same television shows, that do not require us to actually be together. What ritual functions are served by television situation comedies, football games, or movies that may be watched alone but provide a common framework for ritualized encounters around the water cooler the day after?[43]

Finally, there is the generally unrecognized importance of purely personal rituals. These include all those small habitual activities that each of us takes for granted as part of a normal day or week, and that we notice only when they are disrupted. "Having my morning coffee" or "reading my paper" or "watching my favorite TV show" may sound petty when compared with the major social events that normally go under the label of "ritual," but such minor personal rituals are far more important to an individual's sense of having a coherent life than we normally acknowledge. The interesting question is whether such personal rituals have taken on increasing importance as civic rituals have contracted. This privatization of ritual would be consistent with the privatization of our community lives.[44]

Conclusion

We have seen that there are a number of compelling reasons why the study of ritual and myth needs to be recognized as a central aspect of the study of modern families. The particular structure of American middle-class families, as revealed by their developmental cycle, suggests that family rituals are not just accidental aspects of family life but over time have come to be the constituting condition of the continuity of the family. American families are not structural appendages of larger family systems or simply a new generation of an old family. Each family unit must constitute itself anew. The building blocks of this new family unit include its stories and its routines.

Other than its material bases—shelter, food, transportation—ritual and myth are the most important resources that parents must produce in making a viable new family. We have seen how important ritual and myth are as resources for meaning making and for producing a coherent set of family memories. And we have identified numerous ways in which changes in contemporary family and work life as well as changes in mass media and communication technology have affected the content and distribution of ritual and myth.

From a practical point of view, focusing on the importance of myth and ritual in the constitution of meaningful family life has a number of advantages. Many of the social, economic, and demographic forces that are shaping modern work and family life are remote and elusive for affected families. Most of us do not feel that we have the power to significantly affect government labor laws or company policies. Faced with an increasingly onerous "time bind," people may feel out of control, with little sense that there is much they can do to make their lives easier. But this is not true when it comes to shaping the rituals and myths in our lives. We all have considerable control over the rituals we enact together and some control over the stories by which we make sense of our lives. Though ritual and myth may seem a bit abstract as resources, understanding their importance in our family lives gives us perhaps our single most powerful tool for reshaping our lives together in a constructive way.

At first glance, it might well appear that bringing the study of ritual and myth into the arena of work and family research represents an odd marriage. But it should be clear by now that the real puzzle is why the important relation between the study of ritual and myth and the study of working families was not recognized long ago.

Notes

1. To support the effort, the Alfred P. Sloan Foundation in 1999 established, through a generous grant to Emory University, the Center for Myth and Ritual in American Life (MARIAL Center), as one of seven U.S. research and training Centers on Working Families.

2. Paul Fussel, *Class: A Guide through the American Status System* (New York: Touchstone Books, 1983), 44.

3. Lorraine Delia Kenny, *Daughters of Suburbia: Growing Up White, Middle-Class, and Female* (New Brunswick, N.J.: Rutgers University Press, 2000), 71.

4. Sherry Ortner, "Reading America: Preliminary Notes on Class and Culture," in *Recapturing Anthropology: Working in the Present*, ed. Richard Fox (Santa Fe, N.M.: School of American Research Press, 1991), 164.

5. Marilyn Strathern, *After Nature: English Kinship in the Late Twentieth Century* (Cambridge: Cambridge University Press, 1992).

6. Given the high rate of consumer debt in the United States linked to the proliferation of credit cards, this association of class and credit status in America suggests that we consider "middle-class" to be not so much an income bracket as a "consumption bracket."

7. Kenny, *Daughters of Suburbia*, 71.

8. Max Weber, *Economy and Society: An Outline of Interpretive Sociology*, trans. Ephraim Fischoff (Berkeley: University of California Press, 1978).

9. John E. Schwartz, "The Hidden Side of the Clinton Economy," *Atlantic Monthly*, October 1998, 18–21; quoted in Theda Skocpol, *The Missing Middle: Working Families and the Future of American Social Policy* (New York: W. W. Norton, 2000), 5.

10. Katherine Newman, *Falling from Grace: Downward Mobility in the Age of Affluence* (Berkeley: University of California Press, 1999 [1988]), chap. 6.

11. Elizabeth S. Bott, *Family and Social Network: Roles, Norms, and External Relationships in Ordinary Urban Families* (New York: Free Press, 1971).

12. Interestingly, blue-collar status is generally limited to white people of various

ethnic affiliations. It would appear that African Americans who might otherwise be counted as blue-collar in terms of work status, social values, or residential status consider themselves to be middle class (Riche Barnes Daniel, personal communication).

13. The emergence of the car as a status symbol can be traced to the marketing genius of Alfred Sloan at General Motors, who developed a collection of car companies into a huge company whose lines of cars were neatly ordered in a chain of increasing social prestige. One could mark one's progress up the social ladder through one's automobile purchases while staying with the same company. In contrast, Henry Ford concentrated on perfecting efficient mass production techniques and increasing worker efficiency. Insisting that the Model T was good enough for everyone, he resisted building other models until his son Edsel finally got him to relent. Thus it might be said that while Ford got everyone on the move physically, it was GM that got everyone to link this ideal of physical mobility with emerging notions of ubiquitous social mobility.

14. Newman, *Falling from Grace.*

15. Harriet B. Presser, "Toward a 24-Hour Economy: The U.S. Experience and Implications for the Family," in *Challenges for Work and Family in the 21st Century,* ed. Dana Vannoy (New York: Aldine de Gruyter, 1998), 39–47.

16. Anthropologists term this pattern of establishing new and independent households at marriage "neolocal residence."

17. Jack Goody, *The Developmental Cycle in Domestic Groups* (Cambridge: Cambridge University Press, 1958).

18. Interestingly, this is close to the definition that sociobiologists have given to the notion of genetic "fitness," which they propose as an actual motivation underlying human social organization and individual competitive reproductive strategies. Robert Trivers, *Selected Papers of Robert Trivers* (Oxford: Oxford University Press, 2002); Richard Dawkins, *The Selfish Gene* (Oxford: Oxford University Press, 1989).

19. Though the single-parent family has been much discussed and studied, the same cannot be said for the childless family, which remains both understudied and seriously anomalous in our culture, despite the increase in the number of couples who are choosing not to have children.

20. Newman, *Falling from Grace,* 3–4.

21. Émile Durkheim, *The Division of Labor in Society* (New York: Free Press, 1984).

22. That ritual and myth do not just have symbolic value but can actually constitute the basis of a social group's existence may seem counterintuitive. But there are other important examples of this constitutive role for ritual. Clifford Geertz argues that the nineteenth-century Balinese polity was actually a "Theater State," and that its court rituals were an important basis of political power and not just an expression of power; Clifford Geertz, *Negara: The Theatre State in Nineteenth-Century Bali* (Princeton, N.J.: Princeton University Press, 1980). Steven Mullaney likewise argues for the fundamental political function of the ritual circuits that Queen Elizabeth I made around her kingdom, and the importance of ritual performance to political power that underlay Elizabeth's fascination with and her fear of the stage; Steven Mullaney, *The Place of the Stage: License, Play, and Power in Renaissance England* (Chicago: University of Chicago Press, 1988).

23. Clifford Geertz, "Thick Description: Toward an Interpretive Theory of Culture," in his *Interpretation of Cultures* (New York: Basic Books, 1973), chap. 1; Jerome Bruner, *Acts of Meaning* (Cambridge, Mass.: Harvard University Press, 1990); Bradd Shore, *Culture in Mind: Cognition, Culture and the Problem of Meaning* (New York: Oxford University Press, 1996), chap. 13.

24. Shore, *Culture in Mind*.

25. Frederic C. Bartlett, *Remembering: A Study in Experimental and Social Psychology* (New York: Macmillan, 1932).

26. M. A. Conway and D. A. Bekerian, "Organization in Autobiographical Memory," *Memory and Cognition* 15 (1987): 119–32; Daniel Schacter, *Searching for Memory: The Brain, the Mind, and the Past* (New York: Basic Books, 1996).

27. Although such event-memories often make a deep and ineradicable impression, they are also subject to various kinds of memory distortion; Schacter, *Searching for Memory*.

28. Paul T. Connerton, *How Societies Remember* (Cambridge: Cambridge University Press, 1989).

29. Bruner, *Acts of Meaning*.

30. Roy Rappaport, *Pigs for the Ancestors: Ritual in the Ecology of a New Guinea People* (New Haven, Conn.: Yale University Press, 1968).

31. Arlie Russel Hochschild, *The Time Bind: When Work Becomes Home and Home Becomes Work* (New York: Henry Holt, 1997); Juliet Schor, *The Overworked American: The Unexpected Decline of Leisure* (New York: Basic Books, 1991).

32. Presser, "Toward a 24-Hour Economy"; Harriet B. Presser, "Nonstandard Work Schedules and Marital Instability," *Journal of Marriage and the Family* 62 (February 2000): 93–110.

33. So important is ritual for humans that it probably does not make sense to assume that ritual per se is more important for one community than another.

34. Robert Putnam, *Bowling Alone: The Collapse and Revival of American Community* (New York: Simon & Schuster, 2000).

35. W. Lloyd Warner, *Yankee City* (New Haven, Conn.: Yale University Press, 1963).

36. Alexis de Tocqueville, *Democracy in America* (New York: J. and H. G. Langley, 1841).

37. Ray Oldenburg, *The Great Good Place: Cafés, Coffee Shops, Community Centers, Beauty Parlors, General Stores, Bars, Hangouts and How They Get You Through the Day* (New York: Paragon Books, 1989); James Howard Kunstler, *The Geography of Nowhere: The Rise and Decline of America's Man-Made Landscape* (New York: Simon & Schuster, 1993).

38. This trend toward privatization has intensified in recent years in the proliferation of "private gated communities."

39. Schor, *Overworked American;* Hochschild, *Time Bind;* Putnam, *Bowling Alone*.

40. Robyn Fivush, J. Bohanek, R. Robertson, and M. Duke, "Family Narratives and the Development of Children's Well-Being," in *Family Stories and the Life Course: Across Time and Generations,* ed. M. W. Pratt and B. H. Fiese (Mahwah, N.J.: Lawrence Erlbaum Associates, 2004).

41. Hochschild, *Time Bind*.

42. Charles Jandreau, "Social Rituals and Identity Creation in a Middle Class Workplace," MARIAL Working Paper 014-02, 2002.

43. It appears that much of the appeal of the hit television sitcom *Seinfeld* has to do with the recounting by groups of friends of famous episodes. Knowledge of *Seinfeld* episodes constitutes a kind of virtual ritual object with the same effects on promoting coordination of perspective as more traditional kinds of ritual objects. Indeed, the content of many of *Seinfeld*'s funniest episodes emphasizes apparently trivial experiences that are not normally mentioned by people, but that are immediately recognizable as shared private experiences. This odd mix of highly private yet highly shared and recognizable experiences reproduces at the level of content the odd but potent synthesis of private and public ritual that is represented by media-based social rituals.

44. The limiting case of highly personalized ritual is the pathological role of private ritualization in obsessive compulsive disorder. The fiftyfold increase in diagnosis of this disorder during the same period that civic ritual was contracting opens to question whether one form of ritual may act as a compensation for another; Diana Smay, "The Disease of Ritual: Obsessive Compulsive Disorder as an Outgrowth of Normal Behavior," MARIAL Working Paper 004-01, 2001.

Part IV
Blessed Yoke and Fragile Freedom

Chapter 10
The Heart of the Matter: The Family as the Site of Fundamental Ethical Struggle

Jean Bethke Elshtain

Why is the family debate so heated? Why do the same arguments appear over and over again, whatever the state of the empirical evidence? Why does the ideological cri de coeur so often substitute for careful argument in discussions of the family? In this chapter, I argue that we can understand the volatility and intractability of the family debate because the family generates so much heat. It is the site of our deepest longings and most terrifying fears. Families decoct and intensify every basic human urge, from our most generous capacities to give life to and sustain others, to our most passionate desires to dominate. As Saint Augustine taught so many centuries ago, the *libido dominandi*—or lust to dominate—is a restless engine that never sleeps. The family is not immune. If the urge to dominate or to manipulate is curbed in favor of loving authority, families will nurture us, care for us, and mold us in ways that send us forth into the world well equipped for its complexities, tests, dilemmas, and possibilities. But, as we all know, if children are subjected to systematic humiliation, apathy-inducing neglect, and soul-killing cruelty, they are sent into the world in ways that reproduce such horrors and damage children— often irreparably.

The family debate is so intractable in part because so many find it difficult if not impossible to do what scholars are supposed to do—to stand somewhat outside themselves and to look dispassionately, in the best sense of that word, at the complex evidence ready-to-hand. And if you take a good, hard look, it turns out we actually do know a few things, including something about optimal child-rearing arrangements for a society organized such as ours. This is a society that values education and work; a society laced through and through with the constitutive norms of both equality and human freedom; and a society that, at its best, nurtures its vulnerable, and none is more vulnerable than the newborn child. It is that epicenter from leftover but not left-behind issues having to do with families that we, as adults, often find so frightening to focus on. For when you focus on children, on that soft-shelled baby, it does things to your view of adult freedom and adult responsibility. It reminds you that no decent human being can or should remain as free and as carefree as before, once he or she takes on the responsibility for a child.

Even as all the pressures and possibilities of a life decoct to that throbbing point of origination, the family, so all the pressures and possibilities of our culture do as well. I am going to take up four of these essential points of contact between broad cultural forces and family life. If we think about these forces in and through a family lens, it helps us to understand the forces themselves better. The four are:

1. The public and the private as refracted in our liberal society.
2. Genetic technology and human reproduction, or revisiting questions of biology and nurture.
3. The pervasive influence of television, film, music, the Internet, and literature—in a word (or two) popular culture.
4. The demands of work life, including the stress of two-income family life on marriages and children, or economics.

Let me add that there are many ways you could place the family in the center of things as a powerful magnet around which nearly everything sooner or later collects. Philosophically, one could look at what is called "the particular" and "the universal." One could approach the matter teleologically: Is there some actualization of family immanent, as Hegelians might say, within its very form? One could look through the lens of "liberalism" and "communitarianism." One could take up, as I and others have from time to time, the family as connected to and a part of a democratic civil society. I am going to be more modest here and stand down from the lofty heights to grub about on the hardscrabble of where the family meets various understandings of itself.

Public and Private

The public and the private are inevitable within, and vital to, any liberal democratic form of politics. That does not make sorting it all out simple. As I argued two decades ago in *Public Man, Private Woman: Women in Social and Political Thought,* images of public and private are "necessarily tied to views of moral agency; evaluations of human capacities and activities, virtues, and excellence; assessments of the purposes and aims of alternative modes of social organization."[1] Clusters of images concerning the excellences of men and women are part of this story. Public and private are twin force fields that help to create a moral environment for individuals, singly and in groups; to dictate norms of appropriate or worthy action; and to establish barriers to action, particularly in areas such as the taking of human life, the regulation of sexual relations, the promulgation of familial duties and obligations, and the arena of political responsibility. Public and private are embedded within a dense web of associational meanings and intimations and linked to other basic notions: nature and culture; male and female; as well as views of work and ideas about authority, community, death, and God. In Western culture, public and private are fundamental, not incidental or tangential, ordering principles.

Part of what has thus been ordered is a general view of what is political and what is not; what belongs under the purview of politics and what does not; what in principle should be included under the political label and what should be off-limits; and what activities or relationships not now included under politics or public life can and should be thus incorporated.

Why is this central to how we think about families? Let us tie together several strands. One problem with the 1970s feminist slogan "the personal is political" is that it helped to underwrite two problematic trends: (1) a politics of subjectivism in which the individual makes no distinction between her inner barometer and the public world; and (2) a politics that obliterates privacy altogether in favor of an overweening public aim, or, alternatively, that creates zones of privacy, legally and politically sustained, that are nonetheless labeled entirely off-limits to public concern. Let us reflect for a moment on the totalizing urge behind a collapse of the public into the private that works either to eliminate the private or, alternatively, to make certain aspects of what is called privacy nigh-sacrosanct.

Imagine an ordinary family, by which I here mean parents and children. Then think about it as a magnet drawing public and private issues into its orbit. Sexual intimacy seems a clear candidate for inclusion under "privacy." So let us further assume the general correctness of the view that sexual intimacy belongs in bedrooms, not boardrooms nor public streets, or even the Oval Office. That is the easy part. It is much harder to deal with how much of the "world" comes in through the front door and how much of the "public" flows into the "private." What are the demands the public can make of the private?

There have been two broad sorts of feminist answers to this query. One feminist strand insisted that everything private was grist for the public mill. A second strand demanded political sanction of zones declared off-limits altogether to public concern. In the latter, politics polices the perimeter of the private, making sure government does not enter. Closer examination reveals that this strategy seems to apply principally to one highly fraught issue: abortion. Here the reigning feminist view is that government should have no say over one's body, ergo, the "abortion option" is a nigh-sacrosanct right. Yet the law, which is certainly not exempt from politics, sanctioned such privacy in the first place, which means the law can amend or alter it at any time. There is no wall around privacy, for good and for ill. For good, in that we have come to see issues like child or spouse abuse as appropriately matters of public concern. For ill, in that we may consistently fail to discern any concern for the "public" good or "common" good in whether or not fetuses, the unborn, can be aborted at *any* stage of pregnancy and for *any* reason.

For example: If we may compel Christian Scientist parents to seek medical treatment for their children—going so far, in some cases, as to make children wards of the court and to negate the parents' preemptory rights in this regard because the well-being of children is an overriding good—then we can certainly decide as a society that at a certain point in pregnancy, the well-being of the child-to-be trumps the mother's (belated) decision to terminate the pregnancy.

Once you open up these matters to public scrutiny, you cannot assume that one ideological or ethical take on the issues will triumph on every occasion. Americans seem to discern, in growing numbers according to surveys, that a privacy right cannot comprehensively cover certain highly fraught issues. They discern this because they see fragile newborns when they think of unborn fetuses; because something of the caring and compassionate dimensions of our natures is triggered by such images. Suffice it to say, there is no bright line separating definitively public and private. Some of the activities that take place under cover of privacy may be corrosive of public life, so they cross over into a public concern. But there is no a priori way to parse this.

The upshot is that one must grapple honestly with these issues. The family becomes the centerpiece in an ongoing, deeply contentious cultural debate and political struggle about how much the public or political should define, control, and intrude into the private. Sometimes help in this matter comes from unexpected quarters. Consider a powerful essay, "What Does It Mean to Tell the Truth?" by the anti-Nazi German theologian Dietrich Bonhoeffer.[2] Bonhoeffer writes about the truths that guide human life within what he calls "the mandates" given by God in the areas of family life, culture, and government. He offers the example of a child who heatedly denies a teacher's accusation. The zealous teacher asks "whether it is true that the father often comes home drunk. It is true, but the child denies it."[3] The child speaks a deeper truth, Bonhoeffer insists, than the accusatory teacher. The teacher has strayed into territory that is not her rightful domain. The teacher's question constitutes illegitimate prying in a public setting. The child gestures to a protective urge generated by the God-sanctioned mandate to the family. The child possesses a wisdom the teacher lacks.

If we pull back the scrim on what goes on within the household entirely, we commit an egregious harm. Some activities cannot flourish in the glare of publicity. But if we do not pull back that scrim a bit from time to time, much that is harmful not only to private but to public goods may also be permitted to flourish. The family is the magnet. The disputes are endless and essentially contested in a society organized, as is ours, in ways that require a public/private distinction but leave it to citizens to sort out exactly where the lines are to be drawn—within a framework of constitutional restraints, of course. There is simply no way to make these disputes go away once and for all, and that is one reason family life is the heart of the matter.

Genetic Technology and Human Reproduction: The Family and Nature

What a hornet's nest is here disturbed! Human embodiment, human creatureliness, human finitude—these are matters many do not want to think about. The helplessness of infants and their demand on adult love and care remind us of all three and compel us to focus on the best environments within which that human vulnerability can be honored, respected, and turned into durable strengths. Radical feminists of the era in which I came of age politically insisted that the only way to achieve women's equality was to eradicate nature, or biological imperatives, as well as the family. The "natural," they insisted, divided us into male/female. That divide, even before the patriarchalists began to "construct" social worlds to serve their interests, was itself oppressive. Why? Because women bore children. That was a mark of inequality as such and that must end.[4]

The repugnance at embodiment was palpable in such arguments, together with an extraordinarily naive gullibility about the wonders of a future in which technological instrumentalities would have replaced what was routinely called the "barbarism" and brutality of human birth.[5] Something of this attitude lingers in current paeans to genetic engineering and the prospect of genetic perfection that, oddly enough, now indict nature as not so much cruel as sloppy. Nature makes us imperfect; genetic technology will perfect us. We call upon the laws of nature, manipulated by humans, either to destroy imperfect fetuses or to manufacture perfect fetuses. Either way, we reject nature or the natural as any sort of standard.

The heart of the matter lies in a loss of appreciation of the nature of human embodiment, which is heavily decocted within the family: sexual intimacy, conception, birth; human illness and decrepitude; human mortality; bodily injuries and ailments—all are concatenated within this complex institution. Our bodies both limit and are the modality of human freedom. Anyone can see this in a child's delight at motion—the first tentative, then the more confident steps, then, finally, running and the look of terror on a child's face when he or she realizes, "I cannot stop running, I might fall." Freedom and flight, the possibility of loss of control, are here on display in their original or most basic form.

Our society teaches us that control is what it is all about. But the body does not bend entirely to our wills. The heart of the matter lies in a loss of appreciation of the nature of human embodiment, something families do not let us forget. We are loathe to grant the status of givenness to any aspect of ourselves, despite the fact that human babies are wriggling, complex little bodies preprogrammed with all sorts of delicately calibrated reactions to the human relationships, that "nature" presumes will be the matrix of child nurture. If we think of bodies concretely in this way, we are then propelled to ask ourselves questions about the world little bodies enter: Is it welcoming, warm, responsive? But if we tilt in the biotech constructivist direction and proclaim that our bodies are whatever we make of them, then the body is raw material to be worked on and worked over. The familial and cultural surround in which bodies are situated fades from view as the Body gets enshrined as a kind of messianic project. One might tag this view "genetic fundamentalism," for we are invited to pay less attention to socially shaping better child-rearing environments and more attention to genetically perfecting human products as an act of voluntary design.

The body we currently inhabit becomes the imperfect body, the one our families know all about, the one subject to chance and the vagaries of life, including illness and aging. This body is our foe. The new body to come is to be our gleaming fabrication. For soon, surely, we will have found a way around the fact that our poor foremothers and forefathers, living in a less enlightened era than our own, took for granted—that the body must weaken and one day pass from life to death. The future perfect body will not be permitted to falter. So we devise multiple strategies to fend off aging. We represent aging bodies as those of teenagers with gleaming gray hair. Rather than approaching matters of life and death with humility, knowing that we cannot cure the human condition, we seek cures in the assumption that the more we control the better.

The current cloning debate focuses all these energies, anxieties, and fantasies like a laser beam on the family. This is the gravamen of Leon Kass's powerful arguments against cloning. He points out that merely technical or meliorist approaches "all ignore the deeper anthropological, social, and indeed ontological meanings of bringing forth new life. To this more fitting and profound point of view, cloning shows itself to be a major alteration, indeed, a major violation of our given nature as embodied, gendered, and engendering beings—and of the social relations built on this natural ground."[6]

If we move in the direction of cloning, a direction that advocates such as the law professor Laurence Tribe have advanced as part of the zone of human privacy and choice, Kass warns that we enter a world in which unethical experiments "upon the resulting child-to-be" are conducted. We deprive a cloned entity of a "distinctive identity not only because he will be in genotype and appearance identical to another human being, but, in this case, because he may also be twin to the person who is his 'father' or 'mother'—if one can still call them that." We deliberately plan situations that we know from incontrovertible empirical evidence are not optimal arenas for the rearing of children, namely, family fragments that deny relationality or shrink it. We "enshrine and aggravate a profound and mischievous misunderstanding of the meaning of having children and of the parent-child relationship. . . . Cloning is inherently despotic, for it seeks to make one's children . . . after one's own image . . . and their future according to one's will."[7]

You cannot talk about contemporary and promised future techniques of controlling and manipulating human birth without tending to the family, for once again, it is also the heart of this matter. Bonhoeffer understood this. In "The Natural" in his unfinished *Ethics,* he tells us that humans possess only a "relative freedom" in natural life and there are "true and . . . mistaken uses of this freedom."[8] If we destroy the natural, we destroy freedom. If we misuse or distort nature, we misuse or distort freedom. This distortion is on display in the contempt shown for ordinary embodiment, and it violates, he argues, the Christian teaching that rejects the view that the body is simply a prison for the immortal soul. For our bodies are ends in themselves. Nowhere is this more evident than in families and the intense focus on the preciousness of the body of this singular, unique child given to us to sustain and to love.

Popular Culture

Pop culture bashing is popular, but I do not think it is very helpful. Instead, one should focus on what fears the family draws down upon itself where popular culture is concerned. We have some pretty good ideas of what these are. Parents fear they are losing their children to an excessively materialist, frequently violent, hypersexualized culture. This culture is represented to children through all the media to which they are exposed—television, music, film, the Internet. Parents have some measure of control over the films their children see. But even G-rated films partake of some of the qualities parents most fear.

For example, contrast such classic Disney films as *Snow White* with current Disney fare. I am thinking of *Hercules;* you may have your own favorite or unfavorite example. Hercules looks like Arnold Schwarzenegger on steroids, and I hope you take the full force of that. The female in question looks like a

Barbie doll who has had multiple breast implants. The film is riddled with double-entendres, winks and nods, and lots of sexual heat. Yet this is okay for our four-year-olds.

My concern is not about the overhyped innocence of children. Children are not innocent in the moral sense. Children exhibit rage, jealousy, and plenty of ordinary garden-variety malevolence in their dealings with others. But children are innocent in the ways in which noncombatants in time of war are innocent: They do not have the power to defend themselves. That is why parents must be the first line of defense. That is why those who proclaim loudly children's rights where access to all forms of media is concerned are so wrong. Parental fears are magnified daily given stories about Internet pedophiles and predators and plans hatched in Internet chat rooms for a teenager to "hook-up" with some real but fictitious person he or she has "met" on the Internet.

The disembodiment of contemporary communication, particularly where the Internet is concerned, is arguably more insidious over the long run to our sense of integrity toward the family and the complex, intimate relations it enhouses than are the annoying bulging biceps and bursting breasts of recent Disney films. And, truth be told, I am not that worried about a popular rap artist like Eminem, either. The energy and anger in his songs is an intelligible human response, however troubling aspects of it might be to real human situations. (Although, it must be said, there is some rap and hip-hop that, in its violence and misogyny, must be opposed. But as with everything else, not all rap is created alike.)

In a nutshell: I do not think popular culture has simply gone to hell or is taking us there. But I do believe contemporary technologies pose a challenge if not a threat to the concrete, embodied nature of family relations, as well as those of friendship, pedagogy, and so on. The family decocts concrete embodiment in a particularly potent way. Let us turn to Bonhoeffer again. In *Life Together,* written in 1938, when the world was collapsing all around him, he meditated on the theme of community.[9] Community cannot exist without the physical presence of others, he argued. Why? He responds theologically, "Because a human being is created as a body; the Son of God appeared on earth in the body for our sake and was raised in the body. In the sacrament the believer receives the Lord Christ in the body, and the resurrection of the dead will bring about the perfected community of God's spiritual-physical creatures."[10]

Through his discussion of one concrete community, Bonhoeffer helps us to criticize what he calls all spurious forms of idealism that invite us to live in a psychic or disembodied "reality" like cyberspace, in a "dream world . . . and to abandon ourselves to those blissful experiences and exalted moods that sweep over us like a way of rapture."[11] Real communities make real demands on us, and they include those who are weak and vulnerable. The concrete, nitty-gritty, tactile nature of real community is far different from that reality called "virtual." The danger here is that to the extent children are invited to live in virtual reality, then to that extent the friction of the real world where human wills clash—and it is in families that we learn to mediate this clash—may be lost on them. Some of the cyberspace scenarios extol as the manifest virtue of cyberspace the fact that all boundaries disappear—between self and other, male and female, anything and everything. We can be anyone we want. We can go anywhere we want. We can do anything we want. Yet the burden of parents is precisely teaching children that this is *not* the way of the world.

Does it seem exaggerated to suggest that to the extent we become adept at imagining a world in which all boundaries disappear, then to that extent the boundaries that exist in reality will come to seem insupportable? We will want to wish such boundaries away, too, if we can. Cybercommunity is a form of modern gnosticism: Everything exists in abstract messages purified of their taint by the embodied, the material, the carnal. The embodied, the material, and the carnal are what families are all about. With other media, we are not so much invited to escape reality altogether as to engage it, at least much more so than in cyberspace. Negotiating all of this is part of a parent's task. That requires time. Time requires presence—the actual physical presence of embodied adults, of mothers and fathers—and time is what we seem to have so little of. This brings me to my final point of contact between the family as a magnet and the wider society, the world of work and time.

The World of Work and the World of Love

The goal of feminism—the goal of liberal, not radical, feminism—was to "free" women of household obligations so they could work outside the home, in the wage-labor system. (Whether this is a worthy ideal of freedom is a debate in and of itself, but it is not one that I will take up here.) Another part of this ideal was that men would then be obligated to spend more time in the home. Somehow this would all even itself out in the ideal scenarios that required massive government-funded day care centers to care for the children as moms and dads busied themselves in paid work life. The overriding presumption was, and is, that leaving home to work for pay is bound to be more "fulfilling" than staying home with young children. As a culture, we were urged to convince ourselves that this would also be better for the children.

It has not quite worked out as planned. That is not entirely correct; some of it has. The wage gap between male and female workers has nearly closed.

With same-age workers under the age of fifty years, it has either disappeared nearly altogether or women now earn more than men. Most of the remaining wage gap can be explained by the fact that more women than men continue to choose to work part time. As male wages have stagnated, women's wages have risen for more than a decade at a rate above the rate of inflation. Jared Bernstein of the Economic Policy Institute (described by the *New York Times* as a "liberal research group in Washington" that monitors the workforce) notes: "The wage trends for men are unequivocally bad." Even with the current economic downturn, "women's wages are still growing."[12] The reasons for all of this are complex. Much of it has to do with the shift to a service economy and the massive loss of industrial jobs held by males at relatively high wages won by unions.

Is this a feminist victory? I cannot say. But what this does tell us is that men and women alike are caught up in the economic scramble; hence, the tensions of making provision for families in between the demands of work. In other words, feminists who care about families should not look at the statistics about rising female wages and falling male wages and declare victory, for a number of reasons. Victory in behalf of what? It is of course the case that you cannot educate people and then expect them not to use their educated powers to their fullest. But the vast majority of the jobs we are talking about have to do with what jobs have always done: Pay the rent or the mortgage, buy the food and the clothes, set aside some for a rainy day, try to save for the children's educations. We are told on pretty good authority that the average worker today spends 163 hours more a year working than in 1980, that is, a whole month stolen from family, church, community, and citizenship. Some 71 percent of school-age children have no parent at home full time compared with 43 percent in 1970, yet only 13 percent of mothers with preschool-age children say they want to work full time. Moreover, our tax code remains biased against parents, although this is getting better. But, truth be told, we have a culture tilted against concrete, hands-on time spent with children.[13] We rationalize our way out of this with great cunning. But the kids know better.

Some years ago, the notion of "quality time" gained credence. It is surely no coincidence that "quality time" emerged in tandem with rising misgivings about spending less and less time with our children and increasingly giving our children over to others to care for. So celebrants of the zeitgeist hit on the idea of quality time, different from that old-fashioned sort of time with its complex, natural rhythms that flowed and bumped along as hours unfolded in which the task at hand might be work or play, baking cookies or learning how to ride a bike, reading a book, taking a bath, taking a "time out," watching Mom or Dad in the kitchen, Mom or Dad gardening, doing homework, doing nothing but doing it in one another's company. No, quality time was that little window of opportunity that opened between 7:00 and 8:30 P.M., after a rushed dinner and before being sent to bed.

Why the rush? The answer is obvious. Because every adult in the home and the neighborhood was now in the paid labor force, children either fended for themselves during the hours of danger left unsupervised after school hours, or they awaited a harried parent at "after care." Mom or Dad raced home, raced through supper, and were then enjoined to engage in that magical moment of quality time. Somehow the snatches of quality time here and there made up for all the time apart, all the absences, all the harried bits and pieces that make up the ever more typical day of ever more typical American parents. As the economist Allan Carlson has pointed out, modern capitalism and modern states have a "vested interest" in family disaggregation, a point made interestingly enough by conservatives and Marxists alike: "Family bonds interfere with the efficient allocation of human labor, and household production limits the sway of a money-based economy."[14] Much of what we have measured as economic growth over the past forty years, Carlson continues, "has simply been the transfer of remaining household tasks uncounted in monetary terms—home cooking, child care, elder care—to external entities such as Burger King, corporate day-care centers, and state-funded nursing homes."[15]

This is called progress. Is it? Quality time is part and parcel of a monetizing of everyday life. Time is parceled out into measurable, hence more efficient chunks—and families are notoriously inefficient. There are many wonderful day care centers, of course, staffed by loving if notoriously underpaid people. Many of these are church based. I have no interest in criticizing either day care workers or overworked parents. But if we think of the family as that magnet drawing the tensions of the society into its very heart, then it obliges us to raise questions about our priorities and the many ways we fool ourselves into thinking things are better than they really are.

Love—family love, not the errant, foolish, venal nonsense on television now in those bachelor and bachelorette "reality-based" programs—involves tough-minded, hard work. Loving children, as caring mothers and fathers throughout the years have recognized, is about profound attention. Attention requires being there. One must be cued in to the nuances of the child's needs as these change, sometimes from day-to-day in the case of babies and toddlers. We say the devil is in the details. So is love. Love is not a sentiment. It is a craft. It is a craft practiced in the family. It is learned there, or it is not learned at all. I submit that we are forgetting this craft of love, in part because the nature of economic life is driving us away from it. In our frenzied lives, we cannot spend the time and attention it requires. Love is the heart of formation, of what it means to initiate children into a way of life, to help them to understand what a decent, loving life is all about.

We want to believe that we are doing the right thing. We give our children so many choices nowadays, we explain. But a two-year-old does not need five dozen options. He or she needs trust and love and the confidence that we are competent to do God's work on earth by holding and nurturing those born of our own acts of co-creation. This is the product of that attunement to the nitty-gritty details, to time in all its complexity, for it takes time to learn what children need, time to tend to these tasks. We all need this sort of loving attention paid to us. The dignity of the human person lies in the fact that we are beings to whom a certain loving attention is owed. And that really is the heart of the matter, finally.

Conclusion: Not Yet an Ethical Polity

In *Public Man, Private Woman,* almost a quarter of a century ago now, I described the goal of a critical and ethical feminism as one of moving us toward an ethical polity. We are not there yet. And, of course, we never will be—not in a perfect sense. But I submit that looking at how the family is faring helps us to think about how near or far lies that ethical polity. The family is rather like the canary down the mine shaft: It gives us an early warning system of societal stresses and strains, of where things are wounded and broken and need to be healed or mended.

A central feature of this ethical polity I characterize as the redemption of everyday life, of its simple joys and pleasures tethered to recognition of the inherent dignity of everydayness, of the doing of simple tasks in peace, by which I mean a form of Augustinian "right order." Let me conclude with words drawn from the final pages of that book.

My ideal is the preservation of a tension between diverse spheres and competing ideals and purposes. There is always a danger that a too strong and overweening polity would swamp the individual, as well as a peril that life as lived in a polity such as our own will decivilize us. That is, the crises of our time may erode within us the possibility of civic virtue as we increasingly come to substitute private pleasures and asocial inwardness for any sort of public involvement and obligation to others. Within an ethical polity the individual would, or could, have many irons in the fire. The prevailing image of the person would be that of a human being with a capacity for self-reflection as to the ends and means of public and private action. Such persons could tolerate the ineradicable tension between public and private imperatives, thought and action, aesthetic standards and ethical principles. He or she could distinguish between those conditions, events, or states of affairs that are part of a shared human condition—grief, loss through death, natural disasters, and decay of the flesh—and those human-made injustices that can be remedied or that one can work to remedy. Above all, the human being within the ethical polity never presumes that ambivalence and conflict will one day end, for he or she has come to understand that such ambivalence and conflict are the wellspring of a life lived reflectively and that we are all enriched by the messy reality that is our lot. A clear notion of what ideals and obligations are required to animate an authentic public life, an ethical polity, must be adumbrated: authority, freedom, public law, civic virtue, the ideal of the citizen—all those beliefs, habits, and qualities that are integral to a political order.

We will have kept the moral wager and affirmed our humanity only if, with Albert Camus, we refuse to capitulate to the plague. We must embrace a politics of limits. There are things we must not do, for in so doing we will not only further cheapen already fragile human ties in the present but also undermine the very humanitarian ends we claim to seek. Each of us has the responsibility to make judgments between competing visions of the political imagination, rejecting those that tap primitive rage from those that have as their template our earliest memories of needs met and succor provided within a social context that was our secure universe. Only in this way can envisagements of hope and compassion—private and public ideals that the more clamorous pictures of the rageful would expunge from our world—be kept alive.[16]

The family embodies the coming together of all these hopes and fears. That is why it is the heart of the matter.

Notes

1. Jean Bethke Elshtain, *Public Man, Private Woman: Women in Social and Political Thought* (Princeton, N.J.: Princeton University Press, 1981), 4.

2. Dietrich Bonhoeffer, "What Does It Mean to Tell the Truth?" in *Ethics* (New York: Touchstone Books, 1995), 358–76.

3. Ibid.

4. See, e.g., Shulamith Firestone's radical feminist "classic," *The Dialectic of Sex: The Case for Feminist Revolution* (New York: Bantam Books, 1972), 7–8, which speaks of a biological "tyranny" of men over women, with the division of human beings into males and females constituting a "fundamental inequality" that she extends into the nonhuman animal kingdom. Others making related arguments in this era include Ti-Grace Atkinson, "Theories of Radical Feminism," in *Notes from the Second Year: Women's Liberation*, ed. Shulamith Firestone, n.p.; and Susan Brownmiller, *Against Our Will: Men, Women, and Rape* (New York: Simon & Schuster, 1975). Brownmiller speaks of a biologically given male propensity to rape. Her argument is that all men are rapists in situ. But that is like saying all women are prostitutes or child murderers in situ. Because some men and women murder and some women sell their bodies does not mean that all men and women are propelled in such a direction and must be coercively held in check lest they kill, murder, prostitute themselves, and so on. Once you start arguing from biological reductionism

and your view of biology is itself crudely reductionistic, you wind up committing all manner of error and folly.

5. On birth as "barbaric" see Firestone, *Dialectic of Sex*, 201. It is important to remember that this text and others were not marginal documents but hailed as essential to women's liberation. They were required reading in courses, and it was regarded as dangerously heretical to parse such texts critically, as I learned early on in my teaching experience in the 1970s.

6. Leon Kass, "The Wisdom of Repugnance," *New Republic,* June 2, 1997, 20.

7. Ibid., 22–24.

8. Bonhoeffer, *Ethics.*

9. The community in question, for Bonhoeffer, was the Christian community of seminarians at a site called Finkenwalde. He and his seminarians of the Confessing Church that had split off from the so-called Deutsche Christen (the official Lutheran Church) shared a life together until the Gestapo forced the closing of their community.

10. Dietrich Bonhoeffer, *Life Together: Prayerbook of the Bible,* in *Dietrich Bonhoeffer's Works,* trans. Martin Kaske and Ilse Tödt and gen. ed. Wayne W. Floyd Jr. (Minneapolis: Fortress Press, 1996–), vol. 5, 29.

11. Ibid.

12. Quoted by David Leonhardt, "Gap between Pay of Men and Women Smallest on Record," *New York Times,* February 17, 2003, A15.

13. Sylvia Ann Hewlett and Cornel West, *The War against Parents* (Boston: Houghton Mifflin, 1998).

14. Allan Carlson, "Toward a Family-Centered Economy," *New Oxford Review,* December 1997, 28–35, at 29.

15. Ibid.

16. Elshtain, *Public Man, Private Woman*, 351–52.

Chapter 11
Inside the Preindustrial Household: The Rule of Men and the Rights of Women and Children in Late Medieval and Reformation Europe

Steven Ozment

In 1960, the French cultural historian Philippe Ariès (1914–84) published the most influential twentieth-century study of Western family life. This book, which was translated into English with the title *Centuries of Childhood,* described the transformation of a traditional work-centered household into a modern nesting home.[1] His was a story of a family that loved its children too little becoming one that loved them too much. That evolution began with the discovery that a child was not a small adult, but a twig that might be bent, and it ended with previously indifferent parents becoming often smothering ones. By both liberating childhood from neglect and robbing it of its informality and joy, this victory of nurture over nature and regimentation over freedom was said to be widespread by the late seventeenth century.

Ariès thus put the history of the family on a continuum, yet he described its forward movement as both gain and loss. Following his lead, historians and the general public have embraced the belief in progressive family development, while at the same time ignoring its downside. By the late 1970s, the English historian Lawrence Stone unfolded 350 years of seamless English family history between 1450 and 1800, beginning with a cold and distant medieval household and ending with a loving and sharing modern family. Between 1450 and 1800, the English household is said to have evolved from low to "steep gradient affect."[2]

Today, the history of the family is still written from bad parents to better ones and from abused children to loved ones. The agent of change has been sentimentality, or what Al and Tipper Gore have called being "joined at the heart,"[3] affective relationships from which both sharing spouses and loving parents have evolved. Unlike the Gores, who are sympathetic to families past and present, many historians portray the history of the family as a horror story only recently relieved. The editor of the *Journal of Psychohistory,* Lloyd DeMause, has gone so far as to offer a prize to anyone who can show him "one 'good mother' prior to the eighteenth century . . . who would not today be incarcerated for child abuse."[4]

Even the best present-day guild historians find the Arièsian myth of parental ineptitude and unrecognized, or suppressed, childhood irresistible. The editors of a recent multivolume history of the family between 1500 and the present promise the reader a revision of the "myth of the family in pre-industrial Europe"—apparent relief for historiographically maligned spouses and parents living in the centuries before 1700. The myth they have in mind is the belief that most people in the past were married, which they were not; lived in large, stable patriarchal families, which they did not; and valorized men over women, the old over the young, and first-born children over younger, which is only half true. The first volume, devoted to early modern Europe, documents a society of comparatively small families, with five to six children on average, male heads of household who were not always "despots with absolute powers," and youth who had a say about whom they married.[5]

The authors also present a variety of preindustrial households that anticipate rather than contradict those we know today. In addition to nuclear families, there were cohabiting singles without children, conjugal pairs living with resident kin, two or more related families housed under the same roof, and married sons rearing new generations in the homes of their parents. In Europe's large cities before the fifteenth century, the unmarried population exceeded the married, and single-person households outnumbered nuclear families.[6]

Having promised a needed revision of the history of family life, the editors surprise the reader by dating the progressive span of the preindustrial family from the late seventeenth century, exactly where Ariès had pegged it. That conclusion not only contradicts some of the research presented by the contributors; it also ignores other studies, particularly in German lands, that have compellingly documented modern characteristics within the late medieval family.[7]

The culprit said to prevent an earlier appearance of the modern family is also that of the 1960s: patriarchy, particularly in the form of the Protestant paterfamilias. As the editors put it:

A patriarchal model of authority was everywhere dominant with a hierarchy of roles and positions defined on the basis of age, sex, and birth order. At the top was a male, the father and husband. A rigid separation of roles divided husband and wife. Parents trained the children from a young age to be submissive and docile. Children, kept at a distance and shown little trust, learned to see themselves as different and inferior.[8]

Although the Reformation successfully implemented numerous reforms of the estate of marriage—an appreciation of its civil nature, the reduction of alleged impediments (incest prohibitions), the abolition of celibacy, and the recognition of divorce—the editors proclaim its true legacy to be the "notion of the husband and father as family head."[9] Together with the demotion of the Virgin Mary from supreme divine intercessor to one among many biblical models of faith, the rise of the Protestant paterfamilias in home, church, and state seems indeed to have challenged the most liberal domestic teaching of the medieval church: its consensualist definition of marriage. Because the medieval church recognized the binding power of private vows made by men and women of marriageable age and without disqualifying impediments, modern historians have praised its teaching as liberating contemporary youth from parental and societal control of their marriage options—the very patriarchy they see the Protestant reformers successfully reinstating in the sixteenth century.[10] But this perceived liberality was not without self-interest. It allowed the church to inject itself directly into the family circle: Consensual marriage made Rome the paterfamilias.

New research has reopened three issues of family history in late medieval and Reformation Europe, which a majority of historians, arguably prematurely, have deemed to be settled: How patriarchal were these centuries, how free were women and children, and what model of life did they bequeath to us?

The Reformation and Marriage

The major reason modern historians believe the preindustrial family was a less successful domestic institution than its modern counterpart is the comparative absence, or inadequacy, of sources that reveal the inner life of that family. Conversely, a major reason why the family seems to have made such great strides by the late seventeenth century is the increased availability of such sources. Because history is what historians say it is, what they read and value as primary evidence makes all the difference in how the past is portrayed and evaluated. Historians working in neglected family archives have found a more competent family life than historians whose primary data are demographic and legal. Thanks to the growth of vernacular schools and the availability of cheap ink and paper, growing numbers of literate urban dwellers were able to document and preserve their own family histories. Collections of diaries and letters, account books and chronicles, and personal relics and memorabilia leave a deep, familiar record of burgher family life. Beyond the family's portrayal in contemporary literature, theology, and law—which, in varying degrees, is abstract from daily life—family archives give historians more immediate access to the family circle, and one that is less given to didactics, ideals, and norms. Supplemented by social-historical studies, which reconstruct the surrounding workaday world and its popular culture, these first-person sources allow us to be the proverbial fly on the wall of history.[11]

In addition to the exploitation of new sources, an accurate picture of the preindustrial family also awaits an end to the scapegoating of the Reformation as the great enemy of modernity. In an age of confident liberal democracy, an era of acclaimed patriarchy, misogyny, and political absolutism can only be caricatured, not deeply studied. Such a description of the Reformation era says more about the success of modern liberation movements in constructing their own sympathetic prehistories than it does about the era itself. In its own element, Reformation Europe was as bold an attempt at domestic social reform as it was at ecclesio-religious reform. Before the Reformation had legal standing in a single town or territory, the German reformers, believing the life of the family to be in as dire straits as that of the medieval church, addressed numerous tracts and treatises to marriage formation, household management, spousal harmony, and the rearing and schooling of children.

The Right to Marry

In the early 1520s, Martin Luther assailed what he called the "confusion, abuses, and false situations" surrounding the estate of marriage and family due to the "lax authority" of church and state. He had in mind the disruptions of peoples' lives brought about by unbiblical celibacy, private consensual vows of marriage, multiple impediments to marriage, and the absence of a Christian right to divorce and remarry. The year 1523 saw the beginning of Protestant attacks on nunneries and encouragement of parents to remove daughters from cloisters, a prelude to the latter's dissolution in Protestant lands. In a pamphlet titled *Why Nuns May Leave Cloisters with God's Blessing,* Luther urged parents to "liberate" daughters confined there prematurely or against their will, and allow them to marry.[12] At issue was not the denial of a religious lifestyle appealing to women who would otherwise have been trapped in domestic service or an unwanted marriage. At stake was a nun's right, at any point in her life, to abandon a lifestyle she may not have freely chosen, or one that had since lost its appeal. As one sixteenth-century pamphleteer made the case for choice: "Let [religious women] stay in the cloister only so long as they freely choose, and when one wishes no longer to remain, let her follow the example of her friends, take a husband, and serve her neighbor in the world."[13]

Although many devout nuns left cloisters in Protestant lands kicking and screaming, there are enough examples of renegade nuns eagerly departing them to substantiate such pleas. In cases where the cloister was rejected out of personal unhappiness with celibacy, or a reevaluation of the religious life in light of Protestant critique, release was indeed a liberation. For orphaned nuns with no place to go and for those determined to remain in the religious life out of conscience, Protestant cities provided accommodations in token convents. However, the entry of new recruits into such institutions was strictly forbidden, which allowed the convents to die a natural death with their last devout residents.

In addition to making marriage legal for the clergy and the religious, the Reformation also made it easier for the laity to enter and, under certain conditions, to dissolve. The Protestant reform of marriage was part and parcel of a larger program of civic reform intent on expanding the basic freedoms of the individual. In the same year that Luther urged parents to remove their children from cloisters, he called on lay congregations to appoint, at their own initiative, evangelical pastors in place of Roman priests.[14] At the same time, he denied rulers any legitimate power to command the laity in matters of religious belief.[15] The reformers also campaigned for new schools, which in Luther's words would put before children "the character, life, counsels, and purposes . . . of the whole world . . . [allowing them to] draw the proper inferences and . . . take their own place in the stream of human events."[16]

Consent and Publicity

As regards the tie that binds, Wittenberg completely agreed with Rome that free consent between a man and a woman made a true marriage in the eyes of God. In these early centuries, arranged marriages were exceptional and not the rule. Catholic and Protestant youth rather welcomed parental counsel and family support when choosing a mate.[17] Although Protestants insisted on parental consent for a licit marriage, that did not mean that a marriage was impossible without it. Given Rome's long-standing sanction of clandestine marriages based on private vows, Protestant and Catholic parents alike found themselves outflanked by willful youth prepared to exchange secret vows, engage in private sex, and become publicly pregnant. As Luther put it: "Where matters go beyond mere engagement, and the two have secretly become one flesh, it is right to allow them to remain united and to withhold the hand of parental authority."[18]

If, in the history of the family, children have parents they do not deserve, it is also true that parents have children who are unworthy of them. In the past, recalcitrant youth wrecked the best-laid plans of devoted parents, embarrassed and shamed them, and threatened their livelihood and even lives. Although as capable of sentimentality as their modern counterparts, late medieval parents had no illusions about children: These parents were prepared both to save their children from themselves and to protect themselves from their children. Their realism in this matter was not farther away than everyday experience. Here is a list from the reformed Nürnberg Code of 1479 citing ten legal grounds for disinheriting a child, each of which was the medieval parent's worst nightmare:

1. Wanton assault on a parent.
2. Plotting, or undertaking, grave mischief against a parent.
3. Falsely accusing a parent of a capital crime [innocent parents died at the stake after being accused of witchcraft by their children].[19]
4. Attempting to take a parent's life by poison, or other means.
5. Sexual assault on a stepmother by a stepson.
6. Refusal to make bail, or ransom, for an imprisoned, or captive, parent.
7. Preventing a parent from freely making a last will and testament.
8. Predatory madness [insanity] directed at a father by a son.
9. A daughter's willful rejection of marriage and the pursuit of a promiscuous life in its place.
10. Embracing a heresy, when one's family is Christian.[20]

Not So Tough Love

At the Council of Trent in the mid–sixteenth century, Rome agreed with Wittenberg that both the intent of a couple to marry and the event itself must be publicized. This allowed the exposure of a compromised marriage and a proper recording of the union. Though consensual vows made a true marriage in heaven, only a witnessed exchange of vows could secure a marriage on Earth. By that assertion, Rome backed away from the litigious, clandestine marriages that its sanction of private vows had enabled for centuries. While holding firm on the sufficiency of consent, the Tridentine decree *Tametsi*, enacted in 1563, required couples to announce their intention to marry several weeks before the event (banns) and to exchange their vows in the presence of a priest and other witnesses. Although no mention was made of parental consent, Rome no less than Wittenberg and Geneva preferred and expected such publicity.

As long as consent alone made a binding marriage, parental hands could be tied. Yet both church and state encouraged parents to be proactive in the best interests of their children. Neither side, however, condoned a father's denial of marriage to a child, or the coercion of a child into an unwanted marriage—though a father might properly foil a perceived bad or foolish marriage. Luther advised fathers to apprise their children of their realistic choices, but then to "forgo paternal right and authority" by leaving the final decision to them. The best marriage was one desired by all sides, parents and children alike, or, as Luther stated in the title of the tract in which he gave such counsel: "Parents should neither compel nor hinder the marriage of their children, and children should not become engaged without their parents' consent." As for parents who would deny their children their hearts' desire or force them to marry someone they had "no heart for," Luther instructed such youth to flee the parental home, appeal to legal authority, and marry whomever they pleased.[21]

In condemning clandestine marriages, the reformers did not intend either to replace a consensual marriage with a parentally coerced one or to willfully deprive youth of its freedom and joy. The same was true of Trent's reattachment of publicity to a binding marriage. Both confessions recognized that physical attraction, love, and loyalty between the bride and the bridegroom served the material and social interests of a marriage by promising to keep the couple happy, together, and prolific.

The great burden of clandestine marriages was not the constraint of patriarchy but the pain and embarrassment such marriages created for parents, children, and society when unknown, unapproved, unpublicized, and uncorroborated marriage vows were litigated in court by couples that no longer shared, if ever they had, the same memory of the climactic consensual event.[22] In court testimony, secret vows revealed nothing so much as a seduction strategy and pretext for premarital sex, resulting in what critics called "superficial and unheeding" marriages, assuming such relationships ended in a proper marriage at all.[23] If the medieval church's recognition of binding marriages without "parental consent, clerical participation, witnesses, or consummation"[24] gave medieval youth a modern freedom, it also encouraged in them an all too familiar licentiousness.

Unobstructing Marriage

For Protestants, the recognition of secret vows was only one of several church laws diminishing marriage and family. Canon law had extended impediments of affinity and consanguinity, so-called incest prohibitions, to the seventh degree of relationship before the Fourth Lateran Council, meeting in 1215, rolled them back to four—which was still double the biblical number recognized in Leviticus 18. Luther scorned the authors of such laws as "merchants selling vulvas and genitals."[25] By encouraging exogamy over endogamy—that is, marrying out of one's community rather than within it—Rome's list of impediments seemed to serve purposes beyond religion. One historian has speculated that such barriers were intended to restrict the concentrated growth of noble families, thus making it easier for the church to remain a contender with the aristocracy.[26]

Protestants also saw no biblical basis for, nor any pastoral advantage in, clerical celibacy, while foreseeing all its problems down to the present day. Celibacy, they forewarned, was a prelude to "whoring and sodomy," a lifestyle disrupting both the emotions and the mission of the clergy, both of which the estate of marriage was said to remedy and to serve.[27]

Although less easily permitted in the sixteenth century, divorce with freedom to remarry was another novel Protestant reform. All the reformers recognized adultery and desertion as primary grounds, while some added new ones. Among these were life-threatening abuse and refusal of sex—the latter because it increased the temptation of whoring, adultery, and spousal abandonment. The Swiss reformer Huldrych Zwingli thought that unbelief was also a proper ground, whereas the Strasbourg reformer, Martin Bucer—the most Protestant on the subject—was prepared to recognize divorce by "mutual consent and repudiation,"[28] an apparent early recognition of what today we call irreconcilable differences. Arguing that no "fully confirmed" marriage existed where there was not a "true assent of hearts," Bucer urged his parishioners to attest publicly to the legality and truth of their marriages with a wedding feast and privately with "plenty of carnal intercourse."[29]

In its first decade, the Reformation was more a catalyst for domestic, religious, and political freedoms than an agent of hierarchical repression in home, church, and state. The reformers supported the right of monks and nuns to leave cloisters and to marry, of lay congregations to choose and to depose their clergy, of citizens and subjects to resist the state's impositions on conscience and church, of spouses to divorce and remarry, and of children to flee an unbearable, forced marriage.

The Rights of Women

If the test of women's equality in history is equivalent legal standing with men, sexism was alive and well in the Renaissance and Reformation.[30] If, however, the test is the self-fulfillment of women's lives at work and at home, then "sexism" may be the wrong word. There is no gainsaying that men, until recent times, enjoyed civic freedoms and opportunities denied to women, particularly in politics and government. However, in evaluating women's lot in the past, the more pertinent question is not whether the man was the head but, to borrow a line from a perceptive recent movie, *My Big Fat Greek Wedding*, whether the woman was the neck that turns the head. Drawing on biblical and classical authorities, learned theologians and licensed witch-hunters portrayed women misogynistically as being less in control of their emotions than men and, hence, more likely to succumb to temptation and sin.[31] Such doubts and suspicions were not, however, shared throughout society. The average merchant did not begin and end his day by explaining to his wife his superiority and her inferiority.

Despite the higher legal standing of men and the exclusion of women from politics and government, the records of family archives suggest a high incidence of companionable marriages in burgher society—housemothers who were equivalent partners with housefathers, together sharing authority and responsibility in both the family household and workshop.[32] Women managed households, reared and educated children, and worked outside the home in almost as many industries as men.[33] In the fourteenth and fifteenth centuries, they filled their own trades, mostly in the clothing and food industries, and shared many others with men. Women were butchers, ironmongers, and skinners as well as silk weavers, embroiderers, and hatmakers.[34] Although the buck stopped at the male head of household, a real husband or boss was arguably the captain of a team that conjointly ran a household, raised a family, and operated a home-based business, with each member contributing to all these tasks.[35]

At Work

The centuries immediately preceding the Reformation were exceptionally good ones for working women, who entered trades, cloisters, and beguinages in record numbers. Some historians describe these centuries as the best for working women prior to the twentieth.[36] That became possible during the thirteenth and fourteenth centuries, when crusades and plague reduced the numbers of skilled men available to industry, while the demand for finished goods remained high. As a result, both single and married women gained exceptional opportunities to learn and practice a skilled trade.

Given the difficulty of creating a new household in the best of times, the shrinkage of marriageable males contributed to a predominance of the single over the married life.[37] Most women who worked outside the home were single. During the thirteenth and fourteenth centuries, large numbers from the upper classes and the nobility entered religious convents and church-supported beguinages. In the cities of northern Germany, Holland, and Belgium, thousands of beguines lived in designated houses in groups as small as 4 and larger than 100, some of whom gained significant wealth and local influence, particularly in the yarn and silk industries.[38] Cloistered women shared in productive work beyond their prayers, gardening, slaughtering, sewing, washing, and cooking—and not just for themselves, but also for visiting and supervisory male brothers from neighboring monasteries who also received their services.[39]

At Law

If not completely on the scale of men, late medieval women possessed significant protections and privileges at law. A wife shared civil rights and freedoms with her husband by virtue of their marriage contract, and the consent on which that contract was based remained operative throughout the marriage. As a rule, the husband managed the property a wife brought into the marriage and any new property she acquired during it. He could not, however, dispose of that property, nor of any new property the two acquired together, without her consent.[40] Within the household, a wife shared authority with her husband, commanding laborers and servants and monitoring the behavior of household members. Marriage also gave propertied widows passive citizenship, guaranteeing them the same protections enjoyed by their husbands but generally denied to nonpropertied men and their spouses.[41]

Although a wife might discuss civic and political matters with a husband, and thereby privately influence his views and actions, she did not have the right to vote or hold political office. As a rule, she had a voice of her own only within the household. However, if she was employed in a regulated trade, and thus legally responsible for her business transactions, she could speak in a court of law independently of her husband, or a court-appointed spokesman.[42]

Legally under her husband's authority, a wife was subject also to his discipline, which in some law codes before the fifteenth century included a nonreciprocal right to execute her, should she be caught in a willful act of adultery.[43] In all other common criminal and property matters, women had ready access to the courts. Rape, including that of prostitutes, was everywhere a capital crime. And when the evidence was insufficient to render a clear verdict, one fourteenth-century German code, in a principled grasp at justice, allowed the plaintiff or her stand-in to seek a divine resolution by a duel. The accused male was made to fight from a waist-deep hole in the ground, armed with a short wooden club, while his accuser circled him freely with a sling made by placing a large stone in her scarf or sash.[44]

How far a woman might go at law in these early centuries was demonstrated when the twenty-five-year-old daughter of the imperial mayor of Schwäbisch Hall, seemingly against all odds, challenged her powerful father in imperial, territorial, and local courts. In the 1520s, he had banished her from his household after discovering simultaneous sexual liaisons with two men, bringing shame and embarrassment on him, as well as disgracing herself. Assisted by sympathetic relatives, she accused her father of denying her a proper marriage, and she sued him for abandonment and support. In retaliation, he took her captive in his home, and kept her under house arrest, during which she was routinely chained to a table. Escaping with the assistance of a servant, she brought new charges of paternal abuse and denial of inheritance in an on-and-off litigation that lasted for more than twenty years. Although she died before the final disposition of her case, she did recover a part of what was hers, and if she had not insisted on full and complete restitution, she might have gotten more.[45]

All things considered, the legal position of women in late medieval and early modern Europe was variable. At one end of the spectrum, we find a far-reaching, gender-based subordination of women to male authority, while at the other, there was an equivalent legal status for women engaged in either their own or their husband's trade. In between were numerous relaxations of domestic male rule and a pragmatic sharing of household authority and responsibility, much like that of modern couples.[46] What we do not find in the households of old Europe are women passively on the sidelines pitying themselves. Amid the documentation portraying these centuries as first steps toward women's liberation are popular depictions of subjugated husbands doing laundry under a wife's finger, or stick. Also revealing are popular portrayals of spousal battles over the pants or the keys, the symbols of authority within the household.[47] In one early-sixteenth-century woodcut, the prudent housewife with her wooden spoon stands side by side with a lawyer with his law books and a Jewish merchant with his bags of money as one of the big three, who are said to "truly rule the world."[48]

Equilibrium

For urban women who married, homemaking and child rearing were a full-time career and cannot be compared to Betty Friedan's comparatively idle modern counterpart. Especially in the countryside, food had to be grown and harvested, raised and slaughtered, prepared and served—and that was just one task of homemaking. In craft households, wives manufactured and distributed products. In merchant households, they received and delivered imports. In both instances, they kept careful records of their transactions.[49] With the possible exception of aristocratic wives confined in isolated castles, who were the least engaged of preindustrial women, women in the past did not view themselves as "mere wives."[50]

In family archives and letters, the private relationship between spouses gives every evidence of accommodation, mutual respect, and power-sharing—a private parallel to the public acceptance of women in trades and industries in the workaday world. As Eileen Power pointed out in her 1970s study of medieval women, a woman's standing in the past changes with the sources one consults.[51] If contemporary literature and theology seem hateful and dismissive of women (misogynistic), and legal codes condescending and protective (sexist), first-person descriptions of actual courtship, marriage, and parenting suggest true partnerships.[52] Drawing on sources closer to the family circle, the hearty new genre of "couples history" has documented enough loving marriages and parents in premodern Europe to claim the editor of the *Journal of Psychohistory*'s prize several times over.

Beginning in the fifteenth century, examples of spousal and parental love fill family archives, attesting to the Reformed poet Johann Fischart's late-sixteenth-century description of contemporary marriage by analogy with the sun and the moon. Although in size and power the sun (the husband) exceeds the moon (the wife), they do not exist in a fixed hierarchical relationship. They rather coexist in equilibrium, a cyclical relationship that gives each his, or her, own place and time.[53]

Martin Luther's wife, Katherine von Bora, oversaw a household of six children and ran successful home-based businesses beyond it. She refurbished the cloister that served as their home to accommodate rent-paying boarders, while also profitably developing its herbal gardens, vineyards, and brewery. Her famous husband's respect was conveyed on those occasions when he called her "Mr. Kathy" or praised her facility with the German language over his own. At the end of his life, he refused to appoint a male trustee to manage his estate on her behalf after his death, saying that she could manage it herself.[54]

Christoph Scheurl, Nürnberg's city counsel and a diplomat, and his wife Katherine were a loving couple and attendant parents. In the 1530s, after twelve miscarriages and stillbirths, they celebrated late in life—he then in his early fifties, she in her early forties—the successful births, two years apart, of two sons. For the next ten years, on the day of each boy's birth, the father recorded their progress to date in detailed descriptions that were both clinical and from the heart. For the modern reader who thinks the distant past is a parental dark age, the father's words are best simply quoted. On the first birthday of their eldest son, Georg, Christoph writes:

This Sunday, April 19, my dear son Georg is one year old. So far, he is hearty. . . . Only his teeth, of which there are five and a half (the upper front two being great shovels) have caused him to run a temperature. . . . He has a large, strong head, likes to laugh, and is a happy, high-spirited child. He can say "da, da," extends his little hand to Father, and point to . . . birds on the window. He likes to go out into the open air. When he sees Father washing his hands, he must wash his too and splash about in the sink. He also takes after his father in liking horses.

There are ten warts on his body, which . . . is a sign of long life, as is also the soft spot that can still be felt on his head. . . . He is a fast eater and drinker. By no means will he sit or otherwise remain still in his chair, but he bends over double, as he struggles against it. Otherwise he does not whine. . . . He freely allows the nurse to suckle him and points out the chair to her. He loves her very much, as she does him. He goes happily to Father and loves him too. Moreover, he is Father's every joy, delight, and treasure. Father will say to him: "Georg, be a bad one," and he then wrinkles up his nose and sneers. If Father coughs, he coughs too; and he can sit only beside Father. He can understand and duplicate an action [once it has been shown him]. In sum, Georg Scheurl, by his bearing, gestures, and role playing, presents himself at one year as a plucky, resolute child. He is learning to use his hands now and really likes to go through books, letters, and papers; he throws up his arms and shrieks with joy.[55]

The Scheurl archives also document parental competition for the boys' affections. When their second son turned two, the father wrote of him and the mother: "He is a beautiful, happy, sweet boy, who loves Father very much, and falls on him with wide-open mouth and kisses him. He is dearly loved by Father in return. Less exuberantly, he also loves Mother very much, and he has great affection for horses as well."[56]

Irrepressible Marriage

What jobs in industry did for the self-esteem of working women outside the home, the sharing of household authority and home workshop responsibility did for women who were homemakers and coworkers in their husband's trade. By its reform of marriage and projection of attractive family models in their own lives, the reformers aided and abetted the transition from a predominantly single to a predominantly married society. By the fifteenth century, both the appeal of marriage and the social problems created by its denial were visible in the litigation of clandestine marriages and the sizable numbers of clergy living in concubinage, a practice both tolerated and punished by the church.[57]

Although counterintuitive at first glance, the irrepressible appeal of marriage and family in these centuries was broadcast far and wide by the lifestyles of those who appear to have denied it most emphatically: cloistered nuns and cloistered monks. To all appearances, religious women pursued single, nonprocreative lives within a distinctive woman's place. But metaphorically and psychologically, the cloistered life was modeled not on the single life but on that of marriage and family. A novice nun entering a cloister did not assume the roles of an independent single woman but rather those of a faithful wife and doting mother. Nuns were first and foremost brides of Christ and mothers of God, with wedding rings on their fingers and baby Jesus dolls in their laps to show it. Conformity of mind and will with their divine Husband and his divine Mother was their life's goal, their earnestness made clear by fantasies of spiritual wedlock and motherhood.[58]

In the fifteenth century, a parallel cult of Joseph sprang up within the monastic life—both a veneration and a spiritual imitation of Jesus' earthly father. Like the nuns who identified with Mary, there were monks who became fathers of Christ in a similar metaphorical-psychological way.[59] The religious of both genders also literally received their nieces and nephews into their cloisters, where they stayed overnight, or for several days, sharing both a familial and a religious life, as happened frequently with the Scheurl boys, who had aunts in neighboring convents. For the religious who worked in foundling homes, the parenting experience was even more direct and literal.[60]

By constructing the religious lives of men and women around prominent images of marriage and parenthood, the medieval church responded with insight and kindness to the ineradicable human need to pair and to nurture, even among those who fled the companionship and progeny of marriage altogether.

For the Protestant reformers, this indirect accommodation of the married lifestyle deep within the cloister was another indictment of celibacy, now coming from the heart of the medieval church itself. Many Protestants had lived a previously celibate life, and they drew from their own loneliness and temptation in the cloister what they deemed to be an obvious truth: The single, nonprocreative life was both against and beyond human nature and the Bible, a lifestyle Luther deemed only one in a thousand might achieve and happily maintain. In the 1520s, Andreas Karlstadt, the author of the first major Protestant tract on the subject, juxtaposed alternatives this way: "Marriage produces children, rears them in the faith, makes adults of them, cultivates the earth, and is vigilant in charity, whereas celibacy very often destroys boys and girls and makes deserts upon the earth."[61]

In the early 1700s, the Anglican priest Jeremy Taylor elaborated the alternatives after a century of successful Protestant criticism and clerical marriage:

Celibacy, like an insect in the heart of an apple, dwells in solitude: but marriage, like the useful bee, builds a house, gathers sweetness from every flower, labours, forms societies, sends out colonies, feeds the world with delicacies, obeys the sovereign, keeps order, exercises many virtues, promotes the interest of mankind, and is that state of good things to which God hath designed the present constitution of the world.[62]

Modern society also has sizable numbers of single, nonprocreative individuals and couples that reject the companionship and progeny of traditional marriage yet still have an irrepressible need to bond and to nurture. Unlike their counterparts in the medieval convent and monastery, whose pairing and nurturing was confined to metaphor and fantasy (rings, dolls, and stories), modern singles live together in groups of friends, who often pair off and have children out of wedlock. Modern gays and lesbians not only enter into private unions, they also become biological parents through artificial insemination and sperm donation or adoption while demanding the legal rights and the sacramental rituals of heterosexual marriage. Because of the perceived threat such unions pose to the procreative nuclear family, and the concern many have over the parental model gay and lesbian parents present to presumed heterosexual adoptees, such unions and family creation are highly controversial. These prominent examples of single, nonprocreative individuals rejecting the companionship and progeny of traditional marriage, yet manifestly seeking companionship and progeny in other forms, strikingly attest to the abiding familial core of humankind.

Conclusion

The history of the family is one of small, complex households networking largely on their own. At least since the late Middle Ages, nuclear and extended families have been effective competitors with overarching religious, political, and social institutions that would control and dominate the cellular worlds and networks families create. In ways we do not fully understand, what families make of their offspring simply by being there is more deeply ingrained than what larger institutions inculcate over longer periods of time and at greater expense.

Today, many observers—some gleefully, some with grief—believe that the family is in its last throes, fragmenting before our eyes. History suggests, however, that the family has never been as domineering as its critics allege nor as fragile as its defenders fear. The family has always been a work in progress, arranging itself in a variety of households, as it picks and chooses, ignores and rejects, what a presumed magisterial society, or culture, prescribes for it or attempts to impose upon it. Whether functional or dysfunctional, traditional or alternative, what distinguishes the family is its undying independence and longevity. Family is there when one arrives and when one departs, the first and last social institution people see. And by comparison with its competitors, it is one that neither forgets names nor treats its members as ciphers.

Notes

1. Philippe Ariès, *Centuries of Childhood: A Social History of the Family,* trans. Robert Baldick (New York: Vintage, 1962); Steven Ozment, *Ancestors: The Loving Family in Old Europe* (Cambridge, Mass.: Harvard University Press, 2001).

2. Lawrence Stone, *The Family, Sex, and Marriage in England, 1500–1800,* abbr. ed. (New York: Harper & Row, 1977).

3. Al and Tipper Gore, *Joined at the Heart: The Transformation of the American Family* (New York: Henry Holt, 2002).

4. Lloyd DeMause, "The Evolution of Childrearing," *Journal of Psychohistory,* 28 (2001): 363. In 1974, DeMause posited six "improving modes of parent–child relations" in history, stretching from antiquity, when parents practiced infanticide, to the twentieth century, when, after two millennia, they became "helpful" to their children. DeMause, ed., *The History of Childhood: The Untold Story of Child Abuse* (New York: Bedrick Books, 1974), 1.

5. David I. Kertzer and Marzio Barbagli, *History of the European Family, I: Family Life in Early Modern Times, 1500–1789* (New Haven, Conn.: Yale University Press, 2001), x–xii.

6. Ibid., x–xii, xvii. For examples of single-parent households, see *Three Behaim Boys: Growing Up in Early Modern Germany,* ed. Steven Ozment (New Haven, Conn.: Yale University Press, 1990). On the ascendancy of the single over married life, see Heide Wunder, *"Er ist die Sonn," Sie ist der Mond: Frauen in der Frühen Neuzeit* (Munich: Beck, 1992), 59–63, 267–68, trans. as *He Is the Sun, She Is the Moon: Women in Early Modern Germany,* trans. Thomas Dunlap (Cambridge, Mass.: Harvard University Press, 1998); Ozment, *Ancestors,* 33–36.

7. See esp. Mathias Beer, *Eltern und Kinder des späten Mittelalters in ihren Briefen . . .* (1400–1550) (Nürnberg: Stadtarchiv, 1990); Mathias Beer, "Private Correspondence in the Reformation Era: A Forgotten Source for the History of the Burgher Family," *Sixteenth Century Journal* 32 (2001): 931–52; Steven Ozment, *Flesh and Spirit: Private Life in Early Modern Germany* (New York: Viking, 1999); Nicholas Orme, *Medieval Children* (New Haven, Conn.: Yale University Press, 2001); and Eamon Duffy, "The Cradle Will Rock," *New York Review of Books,* December 19, 2002, 61–63. On this approach to family history, known as the "Sentiments School," see Michael Anderson, *Approaches to the History of the Modern Western Family, 1500–1914* (New York: Cambridge University Press, 1995), chap. 3.

8. Kertzer and Barbagli, *History,* xxviii.

9. Ibid., xxv–xxvi, via Lawrence Stone. Jeffrey Watt claims that Protestant reformers "did little to change medieval Catholic attitudes toward women [also believing them to be] by nature inferior," while eliminating many avenues of religious expression important to women, "most notably the nunnery." Citing the feminist excesses of Susan Karant-Nunn, Watt claims the Reformation "relegated women to the roles of wives and mothers . . . and

may [even] have undermined the acceptability of a woman working outside the family." Jeffrey Watt, "Impact of the Reformation," in Kertzer and Barbagli, *History*, 151–52.

10. Kertzer and Barbagli, *History*, xxiv.

11. Wunder, *"Er ist die Sonn"*; Robert W. Scribner, *Popular Culture and Popular Movements in Reformation Germany* (London: Hambledon, 1987); Natalie Z. Davis, *Society and Culture in Early Modern France* (Stanford, Calif.: Stanford University Press, 1975).

12. Steven Ozment, *When Fathers Ruled: Family Life in Reformation Europe* (Cambridge, Mass.: Harvard University Press, 1983), 16–25.

13. Ibid., 18, 192. The treatise appeared in 1524 under the pseudonym Noricus Philadelphus.

14. Martin Luther, "Christian Congregation or Community Has the Right and Power to Judge All Doctrine and Appoint and Depose Its Own Teachers," discussed in Steven Ozment, *Protestants: The Birth of a Revolution* (New York: Doubleday, 1992), 136–37.

15. Martin Luther, "On Temporal Power: To What Extent It Can Be Obeyed?" in *Luther's Works*, ed. W. I. Brandt (Philadelphia: Fortress Press, 1962), vol. 45, 75–131.

16. Martin Luther, "To the Councilmen of All Cities in Germany That They Establish and Maintain Schools," in ibid., vol. 45, 368–70.

17. Watt, "Impact," 140–41.

18. Martin Luther, "Parents Should Neither Compel Nor Hinder the Marriage of Their Children," in *Luther's Works*, vol. 45, 391; Ozment, *When Fathers Ruled*, 39–41.

19. Wolfgang Behringer, "Kinderhexenprozesse," *Zeitschrift für Historische Forschung* 16 (1989): 31–47.

20. "Nürnberger Reformation," in *Quellen zur neueren Privatrechtsgeschichte Deutschlands*, ed. Wolfgang Kunkel (Weimar: H. Böhlaus Nachfolger, 1932–42), vol. 1, no. 15.2, 19–20.

21. Luther, "That Parents," 391–93. For examples of youthful initiative and success in choosing a spouse, see Beer, *Eltern und Kinder*, 97–112; Ozment, *When Fathers Ruled*, 31; Ozment, *Three Behaim Boys*, chap. 1; and Ozment, *Flesh and Spirit*, chap. 1.

22. According to Watt, whose examples are French, Protestants hated clandestine marriages because they "undercut parental authority;" yet "the young people of Reformation Europe, Catholic and Protestant, welcomed the input of their parents in choosing spouses," making arranged marriages "exceptional" in France. Watt, "Impact," 129, 140, 142.

23. On fifteenth-century French litigation, see Beatrice Gottlieb, "The Meaning of Clandestine Marriage," in *Family and Sexuality in French History*, ed. Robert Wheaton and Tamara K. Hareven (Philadelphia: University of Pennsylvania Press, 1980), 50–65. On the German litigation, see Walther Köhler, *Zürcher Ehegericht und Genfer Konsistorium*, 2 vols (Leipzig: M. Heinsius Nachfolger, 1932–42), vol. 1, 85–89; and Ozment, *When Fathers Ruled*, 28–29, 34–35.

24. Lloyd Bonfield, "Developments in European Family Law," in *History*, ed. Kertzer and Barbagli, 96.

25. Ozment, *When Fathers Ruled*, 45.

26. Bonfield, "Developments," 96–99; Jack Goody, *Development of Family and Marriage in Europe* (New York: Cambridge University Press, 1983). See the criticism of David Herlihy, *Medieval Households* (Cambridge, Mass.: Harvard University Press, 1985), 11–13.

27. Ozment, *When Fathers Ruled*, 4–7; Ozment, *The Age of Reform (1250–1550): An Intellectual and Religious History of Late Medieval and Reformation Europe* (New Haven, Conn.: Yale University Press, 1980), chap. 12.

28. Watt, "Impact," 131–32.

29. Ozment, *When Fathers Ruled*, 63.

30. This is as Natalie Z. Davis argued long ago in "City Women and Religious Change in 16th Century France," in *A Sampler of Women's Studies*, ed. D. G. McGuigan (Ann Arbor: Center of Continuing Education of Women, University of Michigan, 1973), 35–37.

31. The famous fifteenth-century witch manual the *Malleus Malificarum* deemed witchcraft a womanly rather than a manly art. On gender prejudices, see Ian MacLean, *Renaissance Notion of Woman* (New York: Cambridge University Press, 1980); and Brian Levack, *The Witch-Hunt in Early Modern Europe* (London: Longman, 1987).

32. See esp. the pioneering work of Beer, *Eltern und Kinder*, 141–78.

33. It is an overstatement to say that Protestant reformers "accepted without question that women by nature were inferior." Watt, "Impact," 151. Men in all ages have recognized that women possess abilities and strengths that are different from their own and no less God pleasing.

34. Eileen Edna Power, *Medieval Women: A Social History of Women in England, 450–1500* (New York: St. Martin's Press, 1995), 51–52.

35. Ibid.; Steven Ozment, *Magdalena and Balthasar* (New York: Simon & Schuster, 1986), chap. 3; Georg Steinhausen, *Der Kaufman in der Deutschen Vergangenheit* (Leipzig: E. Diedrichs, 1899).

36. "In den Städten des hoch Mittelalters waren die frauen generell von keinem Gewerbe ausgeschlossen, zu dem ihre Kräfte ausreichten." Gabriele Becker, Silvia Bovenschen, and Helmut Brackert, *"Aus der Zeit der Verzweiflung": Zur Genese und Aktualität des Hexenbildes* (Frankfurt: Suhrkamp, 1977), 63–64; see also Anke Wolf-Graf, *Die verborgene Geschichte der Frauenarbeit: Eine Bildchronik* (Weinheim: Beltz, 1983), 30–71.

37. Wunder, *"Er ist die Sonn,"* 59; Ozment, *Ancestors*, 33.

38. Wolf-Graaf, *Verborgene Geschichte*, 52; Herbert Grundmann, *Religious Movements in the Middle Ages*, trans. Steven Rowan (South Bend, Ind.: University of Notre Dame Press, 1995); Ozment, *Ancestors*, 25.

39. "Nuns maintained a household of servants, ran a farm, looked after estates, bought and sold accounts . . . combining the functions of Martha and Mary, no less a housewife than her neighbors." Power, *Medieval Women*, 85; Ozment, *When Fathers Ruled*, 15–16.

40. Gerhard Köbler, "Das Familienrecht in der spätmittelalterlichen Stadt," in *Haus und Familien in der spätmittelalterlichen Stadt*, ed. Alfred Haverkamp (Cologne: Böhlau, 1984), 155–56.

41. Gernot Kocher, "Die Frau in spätmittelalterlichen Rechtsleben," in *Frau und Spätmittelalterlicher Alltag: Internationaler Kongress Krems an der Donau 2. bis 5. Oktober 1984* (Vienna: Verlag der Österreichischen Akademie der Wissenschaften, 1986), 480–81.

42. Peter Ketch, *Frauen im Mittelalter: Frauenbild und Frauenrechte in Kirche und Gesellschaft: Quellen und Materialen* (Düsseldorf: Schwann, 1984), vol. 2, 179–80. "Dennoch bot schon damals die 'Berufstätigkeit' der Frau einen ersten Ansatzpunkt für ihre Befreiung von der männlichen Vorherrschaft." Becker, Bovenschen, and Brackert, *"Aus der Zeit,"* 49.

43. Kocher, "Die Frau," 478–81.

44. E.g., the *Sachsenspiegel*, composed between 1215 and 1235. Illustration in Ketch, *Frauen im Mittelalter*, vol. 2, 165.

45. Steven Ozment, *The Bürgermeister's Daughter: Scandal in a Sixteenth Century Town* (New York: HarperCollins, 1997).

46. Kocher, "Die Frau," 485.

47. Ozment, *Ancestors*, illustration 3.

48. Max Geisberg, *The German Single-Leaf Woodcut: 1500–1550*, IV, ed. Walter L. Strauss (New York: Hacker Art Books, 1974), 1436.

49. Ozment, *Magdalena & Balthasar.*

50. Wunder, *"Er ist die Sonn,"* 94–96, 267–68.

51. Power, *Medieval Women,* 85.

52. Beer, *Eltern und Kinder,* 151ff.

53. Wunder, *"Er ist die Sonn,"* 73, 265, 167; Ozment, *Ancestors,* 37–38.

54. Ozment, *Ancestors,* 32; Ozment, *Protestants,* 159–62.

55. Ozment, *Flesh and Spirit,* 98–99.

56. Ibid., 115.

57. For examples of the latter, see Steven Ozment, *The Reformation in the Cities* (New Haven, Conn.: Yale University Press, 1975), 59–60.

58. Claudia Opitz, "Zwischen Fluch und Heiligkeit:: Kinderlose Frauen im Späteren Mittelalter," in *Frauen, die sich keine Kinder wünschen,* ed. Barbara Neuwirth (Vienna: Weiner Frauenverlag, 1988), 84, 105, 109–111.

59. Ozment, *Ancestors,* 59, 62; M. Liberman, "Pierre D'Ailly, Jean Gerson et le culte à san Joseph," *Cahiers de Josephologie* 1 (1953): 319–22; 14 (1966): 271–314; 15 (1967): 5–113. Bertrand de Margerie, "St. Joseph, modèle et médiateur du mariage spirituel avec la Vierge Marie," *Cahiers de Josephologie* 42 (1994): 19–52. Joseph Seitz, *Deutsches Anteil an der Verehrung des heiligen Joseph: Ein Rückblick und Ausblick,* n.p. 1912.

60. Ozment, *Flesh and Spirit,* chap. 2; Herlihy, *Medieval Households;* Shulamith Shahar, *Childhood in the Middle Ages* (New York: Routledge, 1990), 122–26; David Herlihy, *Opera Muliebria: Women and Work in Medieval Europe* (Philadelphia: Temple University Press, 1990), 29–30.

61. Ozment, *Age of Reform,* 384.

62. Ibid., 389.

Chapter 12
Retrieving and Reconstructing Law, Religion, and Marriage in the Western Tradition

John Witte Jr.

A century ago, Friedrich Nietzsche made a dire prediction about the fate of the Western family. Every millennium, he said, has chosen an ever smaller unit to organize its people. Two millennia ago, Jews, Greeks, and Romans put the people, polis, and empire first. Last millennium, the tribe and the clan became the basic units of social life. In the current millennium, marriage and the family have emerged as the foundation of Western culture. But this will not last, Nietzsche predicted. In the course of the twentieth century, "the family will be slowly ground into a random collection of individuals," haphazardly bound together "in the common pursuit of selfish ends" and in the common rejection of the structures and strictures of family, church, state, and civil society. The "raw individual" will be the norm and the nemesis of the next millennium.[1]

Nietzsche's grim prophesies about the fate of the Western family have proved painfully prescient—as other chapters in this volume document.[2] My task in this chapter is to briefly map how we got from earlier teachings that placed marriage and the family at the cornerstone of Western culture to modern teachings that give new preeminence to individual autonomy and sexual liberty. My further task is to hold up several traditional ideas and institutions of marriage and the family that are worth retrieving and reconstructing for our use in this new century.

The Western tradition of marriage and the family, I argue, was forged out of two main theological sources—one rooted in Christianity and one in the Enlightenment. Each tradition has contributed a variety of familiar legal ideas and institutions about marriage and the family—some overlapping, some conflicting. It is in these overlapping, creatively juxtaposed legal contributions of the Christian and Enlightenment traditions that one sees some of the ingredients of a third way respecting marriage and the family. These are outlined in the last section of this chapter.

Marriage and the Family in the Christian Tradition

The Western Christian tradition has, from its beginnings, viewed marriage from at least four perspectives.[3] Marriage is a contract, formed by the mutual consent of the marital couple and subject to their wills and preferences. Marriage is a spiritual association, subject to the creed, code, cult, and canons of the religious community. Marriage is a social estate, subject to special state laws of property, inheritance, and evidence, and to the expectations and exactions of the local community. And marriage is a natural institution, subject to the natural laws taught by reason and conscience, nature and custom.

These four perspectives are in one sense complementary, for they each emphasize one aspect of this institution—its voluntary formation, its religious sanction, its social legitimation, and its natural origin, respectively. The four perspectives have also come to stand in considerable tension, however, for they are linked to competing claims of ultimate authority over the form and function of marriage—claims by the couple, the church, the state, and nature and nature's God. Some of the deepest fault lines in the historical formation and the current transformations of Western marriage ultimately break out from this central tension of perspective. Which perspective of marriage dominates a culture, or at least prevails in an instance of dispute—the contractual, the spiritual, the social, or the natural? Which authority wields preeminent, or at least peremptory, power over marriage and family questions—the couple, the church, the state, or God and nature operating through one of these parties?

Catholics, Protestants, and Enlightenment exponents alike have constructed elaborate models to address these cardinal questions. Each group recognizes multiple perspectives on marriage but gives priority to one of them. Catholics emphasize the spiritual (or sacramental) perspective. Protestants emphasize the social (or public) perspective. Enlightenment exponents emphasize the contractual (or private) perspective. In broad outline, the Catholic model dominated Western marriage law until the sixteenth century. From the mid–sixteenth to the mid–nineteenth centuries, Catholic and Protestant models, in distinct and hybrid forms, dominated Western family law. In the past century, the Enlightenment model has emerged, in many instances eclipsing the theology and law of Christian models. A snapshot of each tradition follows to come to terms with a bit of the theological and legal pedigree of modern marriage and the family.

The Catholic Inheritance

The Roman Catholic Church first systematized its theology and law of marriage in the course of the twelfth and thirteenth centuries.[4] For the first time in that era, the church integrated earlier legal and theological teaching into an understanding of marriage as a natural, contractual, and sacramental unit. First, the church taught, marriage is a natural association, created by God to enable man and woman to "be fruitful and multiply" and to raise children in the service and love of God. Since the fall into sin, marriage has also become a remedy for lust, a channel to direct one's natural passion to the service of the community and the church.

Second, marriage is a contractual unit, formed by the mutual consent of the parties. This contract prescribes a lifelong relation of love, service, and devotion for each spouse and proscribes unwarranted breach or relaxation of their connubial and parental duties. Third, marriage, when properly contracted between Christians, rises to the dignity of a sacrament. The temporal union of body, soul, and mind within the marital estate symbolizes the eternal union between Christ and his church. Participation in this sacrament confers sanctifying grace upon the couple and the community. Couples can perform this sacrament privately, provided they are capable of marriage and comply with the rules for marriage formation.

This sacramental theology placed marriage squarely within the church's social hierarchy. The church claimed jurisdiction over marriage formation, maintenance, and dissolution. It exercised this jurisdiction through both the penitential rules of the internal forum and the canon law of the external forum.

The church did not regard marriage and the family as its most exalted estate, however. Though a sacrament and a sound way of Christian living, marriage was not considered to be so spiritually edifying. Marriage was a remedy for sin, not a recipe for righteousness. Marriage was considered subordinate to celibacy, propagation less virtuous than contemplation, marital love less wholesome than spiritual love. Clerics, monastics, and other servants of the church were to forgo marriage as a condition for ecclesiastical service. Those who could not were not worthy of the church's holy orders and offices.

Upon this conceptual foundation, the medieval Catholic Church built a comprehensive canon law of sex, marriage, and family life that was enforced by a hierarchy of church courts throughout Christendom. Until the sixteenth-century Protestant Reformation, the church's canon law of marriage was the West's preeminent marriage law. A civil law or common law of marriage, where it existed, was usually supplemental and subordinate.

Consistent with the naturalist perspective on marriage, canon law punished contraception, abortion, infanticide, and child abuse as violations of the natural marital functions of propagation and child rearing. It proscribed unnatural relations, such as incest and polygamy, and unnatural acts, such as bestiality and buggery. Consistent with the contractual perspective, canon law ensured voluntary unions by annulling marriages formed through mistake, duress, fraud, or coercion. It granted husband and wife alike equal rights to enforce conjugal debts that had been voluntarily assumed, and it emphasized the importance of mutual love among the couple and their children. Consistent with the sacramental perspective, the church protected the sanctity and sanctifying purpose of marriage by declaring valid marital bonds to be indissoluble and by annulling invalid unions between Christians and non-Christians or between parties related by various legal, spiritual, blood, or familial ties. It supported celibacy by annulling unconsummated vows of marriage if one party made a vow of chastity and by prohibiting clerics or monastics from marriage and concubinage.

The medieval canon law of marriage was a watershed in the history of Western law. On the one hand, it distilled the most enduring teachings of the Bible and the Church Fathers and the most salient rules of earlier Jewish, Greek, and Roman laws. On the other hand, it set out many of the basic concepts and rules of marriage and family life that have persisted to this day—in Catholic, Protestant, and secular polities alike. Particularly, the great decree *Tametsi,* issued by the Council of Trent in 1563, codified and refined this medieval law of marriage, adding the rules that marriage formation requires parental consent, two witnesses, civil registration, and church consecration. A 1566 Catechism commissioned by the same council, and widely disseminated in the Catholic world in multiple translations, rendered the underlying sacramental theology of marriage clear and accessible to clergy and laity alike.

The Protestant Inheritance

The Protestant reformers of the sixteenth and seventeenth centuries supplanted the Catholic sacramental model of marriage and the family with a social model.[5] Like Catholics, Protestants retained the naturalist perspective of the family as an association created for procreation and mutual protection. They retained the contractual perspective of marriage as a voluntary association formed by the mutual consent of the couple. Unlike Catholics, however, Protestants rejected the subordination of marriage to celibacy and the celebration of marriage as a sacrament. According to common Protestant lore, the person was too tempted by sinful passion to forgo God's remedy of marriage. The celibate life had no superior virtue and was no prerequisite for clerical service. It led too easily to concubinage and homosexuality and impeded too often the access and activities of the clerical office. Moreover, marriage was not a sacrament. It was an independent social institution ordained by God, and equal in dignity and social responsibility with the church, state, and other social units. Participation in marriage required no prerequisite faith or purity and conferred no sanctifying grace, as did true sacraments.

Calvinist Protestants emphasized that marriage was not a sacramental institution of the church but a covenantal association of the entire community. A variety of parties played a part in the formation of the marriage covenant. The marital couple swore betrothals and espousals before each other and God—rendering all marriages triparty agreements with God as party, witness, and judge. The couple's parents, as God's "bishops" for children, gave their consent to the union. Two other people, as God's "priests" to their peers, served as witnesses to the marriage. The minister, holding the spiritual power of the Word of God, blessed the couple and admonished them in their spiritual duties. The magistrate, holding the temporal power of the sword, registered the parties and their properties and ensured the legality of their union.

This involvement of parents, peers, ministers, and magistrates in the formation of a marriage was not an idle or dispensable ceremony. These four parties represented different dimensions of God's involvement in the marriage covenant, and they were thus essential to the legitimacy of the marriage. To omit any party was, in effect, to omit God from the marriage covenant. Protestant covenant theology thus helped to integrate what became universal requirements of valid marriage in the West after the mid–sixteenth century— mutual consent of the couple, parental consent, two witnesses, civil registration, and church consecration.

As a social estate, Protestants taught, marriage was no longer subject to the church and its canon law but to the state and its civil law. To be sure, church officials should continue to communicate biblical moral principles respecting sexuality and parenthood. Church consistories could serve as state agents to register marriages and to discipline infidelity and abuse within the household. All church members, as priests, should counsel those who seek marriage and divorce, and cultivate the moral and material welfare of baptized children, as their congregational vows in the sacrament of baptism required. But legal authority over marriage, most Protestants taught, lay principally with the state, not the church.

Despite the bitter invectives against the Catholic canon law by early Protestant theologians—symbolized poignantly in Martin Luther's burning of the canon law and confessional books in 1520—Protestant rulers and jurists appropriated much of the traditional canon law of marriage and the family. Traditional canon law's prohibitions against unnatural sexual relations and acts and against infringements of the procreative functions of marriage remained in effect. Canon law procedures treating wife and child abuse, paternal delinquency, child custody, and the like continued. Canon law impediments that protected free consent, that implemented biblical prohibitions against marriage of relatives, and that governed the relations of husband and wife and parent and child within the household were largely retained. These and many other time-tested canon law rules and procedures were as consistent with Protestant as with Catholic theology, and they were transplanted directly into the new state laws of marriage in Protestant Europe.

The new Protestant theology of marriage, however, also yielded critical changes in this new civil law of marriage. Because the reformers rejected the subordination of marriage to celibacy, they rejected laws that forbade clerical and monastic marriage and that permitted vows of chastity to annul vows of marriage. Because they rejected the sacramental concept of marriage as an indissoluble bond, the reformers introduced divorce in the modern sense— on grounds of adultery, desertion, cruelty, or frigidity—with a subsequent right to remarry at least for the innocent party. Because persons by their lustful nature were in need of God's soothing remedy of marriage, the reformers rejected numerous canon law impediments to marriage not countenanced by scripture.

After the sixteenth century, these two Christian models of marriage lay at the heart of Western marriage law. The medieval Catholic model, confirmed and elaborated by the Council of Trent, flourished in southern Europe, Spain, Portugal, and France, and their many transatlantic colonies. A Protestant social model rooted in the Lutheran two kingdoms theory dominated portions of Germany, Austria, Switzerland, and Scandinavia together with their colonies. A Protestant social model rooted in Calvinist covenant theology came to strong expression in Calvinist Geneva, and in portions of Huguenot France, the Pietist Netherlands, Presbyterian Scotland, and Puritan England and New England. A Protestant social model rooted in an Anglican theology of the overlapping domestic, ecclesiastical, and political commonwealths dominated England and its many colonies all along the Atlantic seaboard.

The Early American Distillation

These European Christian models of marriage were transmitted across the Atlantic to America during the great waves of colonization and immigration in the sixteenth to eighteenth centuries. They provided much of the theological foundation for the American law of marriage until well into the nineteenth century.

Catholic models of marriage, though not prominent in early America, came to direct application in parts of the colonial American South and Southwest.[6] Before the United States acquired the territories of Louisiana (1803), the Floridas (1819), Texas (1836), New Mexico (1848), and California (1848), these colonies were under the formal authority of Spain and the formal jurisdiction of the Catholic Church. Most of the areas east of the Mississippi River came within the ecclesiastical provinces of Santo Domingo or Havana; most of those west came within the ecclesiastical province of Mexico. Catholic clergy and missionaries taught the sacramental theology of marriage. The ecclesiastical hierarchy sought to enforce the canon laws of marriage, particularly the decree *Tametsi* issued by the Council of Trent in 1563.[7]

To be sure, there was ample disparity between the law on the books and the law in action, particularly on the vast and sparsely populated frontier. Religious and political authorities alike often had to recognize the validity of private marriages formed simply by mutual consent, particularly if the union had brought forth children. Yet the church hierarchy sought to enforce the marital formation rules of *Tametsi*—mutual consent of the couple, parental consent on both sides, two witnesses to betrothals and espousals, and priestly consecration in the face of the church (or, in the absence of a priest, which was not uncommon, a substitute "marital bond" pending later consecration). Privately or putatively married couples that had defied these rules sometimes faced sanctions. Intermarriage between Catholics and non-Catholics, in open defiance of the sacrament, led to involuntary annulment of the union and the illegitimating of children born of it. Ecclesiastical authorities also grudgingly acceded to the reality of divorce and remarriage, particularly in distant regions to the north and west that lay beyond their practical reach. Yet their persistent teaching was that a marriage, once properly contracted, was an indissoluble union to be maintained until the death of one spouse.

With the formal acquisition of these territories by the United States in the nineteenth century, jurisdiction over marriage shifted to the U.S. Congress and, after statehood, to state governments. These new civil governments at first rejected much of the inherited Catholic tradition of marriage, reflecting the growing anti-Catholicism of the day. Particularly the Catholic Church's administration of marriage laws and the canonical prohibitions on religious intermarriage and on divorce and remarriage were written out of the new state laws almost immediately. But the Catholic clergy in these territories were generally left free to teach the doctrines and retain the canons of marriage for their own parishioners. Marriages contracted and consecrated before Catholic priests were eventually recognized in all former Spanish colonies in America. The Catholic hierarchy was generally free to pass and enforce new rules for sex, marriage, and family life to guide their own faithful and to advocate state adoption of these rules. Many basic Christian marital norms thereby found their way into American common law, particularly with the exponential growth of American Catholicism in the later nineteenth century.

Protestant models of marriage were much more influential in shaping early American marriage law. By the American Revolution of 1776, the Atlantic seaboard was a checkerboard of Protestant pluralism. Lutheran settlements were scattered throughout Delaware, Maryland, Pennsylvania, and New York.

Calvinist communities (Puritan, Presbyterian, Reformed, and Huguenot) were strong in New England, and in parts of New York, New Jersey, Pennsylvania, and the coastal Carolinas and Georgia. Evangelical and Free Church communities (Baptists, Methodists, and Quakers especially) found strongholds in Rhode Island and Pennsylvania and were scattered throughout the new states and far onto the frontier. Anglican communities (after 1780 called Episcopalian) were strongest in Virginia, Maryland, Georgia, and the Carolinas but had ample representation throughout the original thirteen states and beyond.

These plural Protestant polities, though hardly uniform in their marital norms and habits, were largely united in their adherence to basic Protestant teachings. Though embracing many of the same basic Christian norms of sex, marriage, and domestic life taught by Catholics, they rejected Catholic sacramental views of marriage and ecclesiastical jurisdiction over marital formation, maintenance, and dissolution. They encouraged ministers to be married. They permitted religious intermarriage. They truncated the law of impediments. They allowed for divorce on proof of fault. They encouraged remarriage of those divorced or widowed.

One issue, however, divided these Protestant communities rather sharply: jurisdictional conflicts over marriage and divorce. New England Calvinist communities, from the beginning of the colonial period, allowed eligible couples to choose to marry before a justice of the peace or a religious official. Anglican communities, following the *Book of Common Prayer*, insisted that such marriages be contracted "in the face of the church" and be consecrated by a properly licensed religious official. Calvinist communities in the North granted local civil courts jurisdiction over issues of divorce, annulment, child custody, and division of the marital estate. Anglican communities in the South insisted that only the legislature should hear and decide such cases.[8] These jurisdictional differences between North and South were eventually smoothed over in the nineteenth century—with the Mid-Atlantic and Midwestern states often providing examples of a middle way between them. The New England way ultimately prevailed.

Aside from this jurisdictional difference, however, a common "Protestant temperament" attended much of the American legal understanding of marriage in the nineteenth and early twentieth centuries.[9] Most common law authorities accepted Protestant social models of marriage that placed special emphasis on the personal felicity, social utility, and moral civility of this godly institution. Joseph Story, for example, one of the leading American jurists of the nineteenth century, wrote repeatedly that marriage is "more than a mere contract." He elaborated on this sentiment in 1834, arguing that marriage might best be viewed as a balance of natural, social, and spiritual contracts:

Marriage is treated by all civilized societies as a peculiar and favored contract. It is in its origin a contract of natural law. . . . It is the parent, and not the child of society; the source of civility and a sort of seminary of the republic. In civil society it becomes a civil contract, regulated and prescribed by law, and endowed with civil consequences. In most civilized countries, acting under a sense of the force of sacred obligations, it has had the sanctions of religion superadded. It then becomes a religious, as well as a natural and civil contract; . . . it is a great mistake to suppose that because it is the one, therefore it may not be the other.[10]

Chancellor James Kent, one of the great early systematizers of American law, wrote about the spiritual and social utility of the marriage contract:

The primary and most important of the domestic relations is that of husband and wife. It has its foundations in nature, and is the only lawful relation by which Providence has permitted the continuance of the human race. In every age it has had a propitious influence on the moral improvement and happiness of mankind. It is one of the chief foundations of social order. We may justly place to the credit of the institution of marriage a great share of the blessings which flow from the refinement of manners, the education of children, the sense of justice, and cultivation of the liberal arts.[11]

W. C. Rogers, a leading jurist at the end of the nineteenth century, opened his oft-reprinted treatise on the law of domestic relations with a veritable homily on marriage:

In a sense it is a consummation of the Divine to "multiply and replenish the earth." It is the state of existence ordained by the Creator, who has fashioned man and woman expressly for the society and enjoyment incident to mutual companionship. This Divine plan is supported and promoted by natural instinct, as it were, on the part of both for the society of each other. It is the highest state of existence . . . the only stable substructure of our social, civil, and religious institutions. Religion, government, morals, progress, enlightened learning, and domestic happiness must all fall into most certain and inevitable decay when the married state ceases to be recognized or respected. Accordingly, we have in this state of man and woman the most essential foundation of religion, social purity, and domestic happiness.[12]

Likewise, the U.S. Supreme Court spoke repeatedly of marriage as "more than a mere contract," "a Godly ordinance, a sacred obligation."[13] In *Murphy v. Ramsey* (1885), one of a series of cases upholding the constitutionality of antipolygamy laws, the Court declared:

For, certainly, no legislation can be supposed more wholesome and necessary in the founding of a free, self-governing commonwealth . . . than that which seeks to establish it on the basis of the idea of the family, as consisting in and springing from the union for life of one man and one woman in the holy estate of matrimony; the sure foundation of all that is stable and noble in our civilization; the best guarantee of that reverent morality which is the source of all beneficent progress in social and political improvement.[14]

The Court elaborated on these sentiments in *Maynard v. Hill* (1888), which upheld a new state law on divorce, holding that marriage was not a "contract" for purposes of interpreting the prohibition in Article I.10 of the U.S. Constitution: "No State shall . . . pass any . . . Law impairing the Obligation of Contracts." After rehearsing at length the theological and common law authorities of the day, the Court declared:

[W]hilst marriage is often termed . . . a civil contract—generally to indicate that it must be founded upon the agreement of the parties, and does not require any religious ceremony for its solemnization—it is something more than a mere contract. The consent of the parties is of course essential to its existence, but when the contract to marry is executed by marriage, a relation between the parties is created which they cannot change. Other contracts may be modified, restricted, or enlarged, or entirely released upon the consent of the parties. Not so with marriage. The relation once formed, the law steps in and holds the parties to various obligations and liabilities. It is an institution, in the maintenance of which in its purity the public is deeply interested, for it is the foundation of the family and society, without which there would be neither civilization nor progress.[15]

Not only the basic theology but also the basic law of marriage inherited from earlier Protestant models found their way into early American law. With ample variations across state jurisdictions, a typical state statute in the nineteenth century defined marriage as a permanent monogamous union between a fit man and a fit woman of the age of consent, designed for mutual love and support and for mutual procreation and protection. The common law required that betrothals be formal, and, in some states, that formal banns be published for three weeks before the wedding. It required that marriages of minors be contracted with parental consent on both sides and that all marriages be contracted in the company of two or more witnesses. It required marriage licenses and registration and solemnization before civil and/or religious authorities. It prohibited marriages between couples related by various blood or family ties identified in Mosaic law. The common law discouraged—and, in some states, annulled—marriage where one party was impotent, sterile, or had a contagious disease that precluded procreation or gravely endangered the health of the other spouse. Couples that sought to divorce had to publicize their intentions, to petition a court, to show adequate cause or fault, and to make permanent provision for the dependent spouse and children. Criminal laws outlawed fornication, adultery, sodomy, polygamy, incest, contraception, abortion, and other perceived sexual offenses against the natural goods and goals of sex and marriage. Tort laws held third parties subject to suit for seduction, enticement, loss of consortium, or alienation of the affections of one's spouse.[16]

Marriage in the Enlightenment Tradition

The Enlightenment understanding of marriage was adumbrated in the eighteenth century, elaborated on theoretically in the nineteenth century, and implemented legally in the twentieth century.[17] Exponents of the Enlightenment introduced a theology of marriage that gave new, and sometimes exclusive, priority to the contractual perspective. The essence of marriage, they argued, was not its sacramental symbolism, its covenantal association, or its social utility for the community and commonwealth. The essence of marriage was the voluntary bargain struck between the two married parties. The terms of their marital bargain were not preset by God or nature, church or state, tradition or community. These terms were set by the parties themselves, in accordance with general rules of contract formation and general norms of civil society. Such rules and norms demanded respect for the life, liberty, and property interests of other parties, and compliance with general standards of health, safety, and welfare in the community. But the form and function and the length and limits of the marital relationship were to be left to the private bargain of the parties—each of whom enjoyed full equality and liberty, both with each other and within the broader civil society. Couples should now be able to make their own marriage beds and lie in them or leave them as they saw fit.

The Contract Model of Marriage

This contract model of marriage, already adumbrated ambivalently by John Locke in his *Two Treatises of Government* (1690), was elaborated in endless varieties and combinations in the eighteenth and nineteenth centuries.[18] The Enlightenment was no single, unified movement but a series of diverse ideological movements in various academic disciplines and social circles throughout Europe and North America. For all the variations on its basic themes, however, the Enlightenment was quite consistent in formulating marriage as a contract and quite insistent on reforming traditional marriage laws along contractarian lines.

It must be emphasized that the inspiration for this model was not simply ideological fiat. The Enlightenment model was aimed at the abuses that sometimes attended traditional Christian doctrines of marriage in action. The traditional doctrine of parental consent to marriage, for example, gave parents a strong hand in the marital decisions of their children. Some enterprising parents used this to coerce their children into arranged marriages born of their own commercial or diplomatic convenience, or to sell their consent to the highest bidder for their child's affections. The traditional doctrine of church consecration of marriage gave clergy an effective instrument to probe deeply into the intimacies of their parishioners. Some enterprising clergy used this as a means to extract huge sums for their marital consecration, or to play the role of officious matchmaker in callous defiance of the wills of the marital parties or their parents. The traditional doctrine of common law coverture, which folded the person and property of the wife into that of her husband, gave husbands the premier place in governing the household. Some enterprising husbands used this as a license to closely control the conduct and careers of their wives, or, worse, to visit all manner of savage abuses upon them and upon their children, often with legal impunity. The traditional doctrine of adultery imposed upon innocent children the highest costs of their parents' extramarital experimentation. Children conceived of such dalliances were sometimes aborted in vitro or smothered on birth. If they survived, they were declared bastards with severely truncated civil, political, and property rights. It was, in part, these and other kinds of abuses manifest in the Christian models of marriage in action that compelled Enlightenment exponents to strip marriage and its law to its contractual core.

Exponents of the Enlightenment advocated the abolition of much that was considered sound and sacred in the Western legal tradition of marriage. They urged the abolition of the requirements of parental consent, church consecration, and formal witnesses. They questioned the exalted status of heterosexual monogamy, suggesting that such matters be left to private negotiation. They called for the absolute equality of husband and wife to receive, hold, and alienate property; to enter into contracts and commerce; and to participate on equal terms in the workplace and public square. They castigated the state for leaving annulment practice to the church, and they urged that the laws of annulment and divorce be both merged and expanded under exclusive state jurisdiction. They urged that paternal abuse of children be severely punished and that the state ensure the proper nurture and education of all children, legitimate and illegitimate alike.

Although this contractarian gospel for the reformation of marriage was too radical to transform much of American law in the nineteenth century, it anticipated much of the agenda for the reform of American marriage law in the twentieth century. The reform proceeded in two waves. The first wave, which crested from 1910 to 1940, was designed to bring greater equality and equity to the traditional family and civil society, without denying the basic values of the inherited Western tradition of marriage. The second wave, which crested from 1965 to 1990, seemed calculated to break the preeminence of traditional marriage and the basic values of the Western tradition that have sustained it.

The First Wave of Legal Reforms

In the early part of the twentieth century, sweeping new laws eventually broke the legal bonds of coverture that bound the person and property of a married woman. A married woman eventually gained the right to hold independent title and control of, and exercise independent contractual and testimonial rights over, the property she brought into the marriage or acquired thereafter. She also gained the capacity to litigate in respect of her property, without interference from her husband. As their rights to property were enhanced, married women slowly gained several broader rights: to pursue higher education; to join learned societies; to join trade and commercial guilds and unions; to participate in various professions and occupations; and ultimately to vote in political elections—all of which had been largely closed to them, by custom or statute.

Other new laws provided that, in cases of annulment or divorce, courts had discretion to place minor children in the custody of that parent best suited to care for them. This reversed the traditional presumption that child custody automatically belonged to the father, regardless of whether he was at fault in breaking the marriage. The wife could now gain custody after marriage, particularly when children were of tender years or when the husband was found to be cruel, abusive, or unfit as a caretaker. Courts retained the traditional power to order guilty husbands to pay alimony to innocent wives; they also gained new powers to make other "reasonable" allocations of marital property to the innocent wife for child support.

Other new laws granted greater protection to minor children, within and outside the household. Firm new laws against the assault and abuse of children offered substantive and procedural protections to children, particularly those who suffered under intemperate parents or guardians. Ample new tax appropriations were made available to orphanages and other charities catering to children. Abortion and infanticide were subject to strong new criminal prohibitions. Child labor was strictly outlawed. Educational opportunities for both boys and girls were substantially enhanced through the expansion of public schools. Illegitimate children could be more easily legitimated through the subsequent marriage of their natural parents, and eventually also through adoption by any fit parent, even if not a blood relative. Annulments no longer rendered the children born of a putative marriage illegitimate, particularly if the child remained in the custody of one parent.

This first wave of legal reforms sought to improve traditional marriage and family life rather than abandon it. Most legal writers in the first half of the twentieth century still accepted the traditional Western ideal of marriage as a permanent union of a fit man and fit woman of the age of consent. Most accepted the classic Augustinian definition of the marital goods of *fides, proles, et sacramentum*—sacrificial love of the couple, benevolent procreation of children, and structural stability of marriage as a pillar of civil society. The primary goal of these early reforms was to purge the traditional household and community of its paternalism and patriarchy and thus render the ideals of marriage and family life a greater potential reality for all.

The Second Wave of Legal Reforms

The same judgment cannot be so easily cast for the second wave of legal reforms, which crested from 1965 to 1990. Since the 1960s, American writers have been pressing the Enlightenment contractarian model of marriage to more radical conclusions. The same Enlightenment ideals of freedom, equality, and privacy that had earlier driven reforms of traditional marriage laws are now being increasingly used to reject traditional marriage laws altogether. The early Enlightenment ideals of marriage as a permanent contractual union designed for the sake of mutual love, procreation, and protection are slowly giving way to a new reality of marriage as a "terminal sexual contract" designed for the gratification of the individual parties.[19]

The Uniform Marriage and Divorce Act (1987)—both a barometer of enlightened legal opinion and a mirror of conventional custom on marriage—reflects these legal changes. The act defines marriage simply as "a personal relationship between a man and a woman arising out of a civil contract to which the consent of the parties is essential."[20] Historically, valid marriage contracts required the consent of parents or guardians, the attestation of two witnesses, church consecration, and civil licensing and registration. The act requires only the minimal formalities of licensing and registration for all marriages, and parental consent for children under the age of majority. Marriages contracted in violation of these requirements are presumptively valid and immune from independent legal attack, unless the parties themselves petition for dissolution within ninety days of contracting marriage.[21] Historically, impediments of infancy, incapacity, inebriation, consanguinity, affinity, sterility, frigidity, and bigamy, among several others, would nullify the marriage or render it voidable and subject to attack from various parties. It would also expose parties who married in knowing violation of these impediments to civil and criminal sanctions. The act makes no provision for sanctions and leaves the choice of nullification to the parties alone. The act does confirm the traditional impediments protecting consent—granting parties standing to dissolve marriages where they lacked the capacity to contract by reason of infirmity, mental incapacity, alcohol, drugs, or other incapacitating substances, or where there was force, duress, fraud, or coercion into entering a marriage contract.[22] But the act limits the other impediments to prohibitions against bigamy and marriages between "half or whole blood relatives" or parties related by adoption.[23] And, in many states that have adopted the act, all impediments, save the prohibition against bigamy, are regularly waived in individual cases.

These provisions of the Uniform Marriage and Divorce Act reflect a basic principle of modern American constitutional law, first articulated clearly by the U.S. Supreme Court in *Loving v. Virginia* (1967): "The freedom to marry has long been recognized as one of the vital personal rights essential to the orderly pursuit of happiness by free men. Marriage is one of the 'basic civil rights of man,' fundamental to our very existence and survival. . . ."[24] Using that principle, the Court has struck down, as undue burdens on the right to marry, a state prohibition against interracial marriage, a requirement that noncustodial parents obligated to pay child support must receive judicial permission to marry, and a requirement that a prisoner must receive a warden's permission to marry.[25] This same principle of the freedom of the marital contract, the act's drafters report, has led state courts and legislatures to peel away most traditional formalities from marriage formation.

The Supreme Court has expanded this principle of the freedom of the marital contract into a more general right of sexual privacy within the household. In *Griswold v. Connecticut* (1965), for example, the Court struck down a state law banning the use of contraceptives by a married couple as a violation of their freedom to choose whether to have or to forgo children.[26] In a 1972 case, the Court stated its rationale clearly: "The marital couple is not an independent entity with a mind and heart of its own, but an association of two individuals, each with a separate emotional and intellectual makeup. If the right of privacy means anything, it is the right of the *individual,* married or single, to be free from unwanted governmental intrusion into matters so fundamentally affecting the person as the decision whether to bear or beget a child."[27]

In *Roe v. Wade* (1973), the Supreme Court extended this privacy principle to cover the right of abortion by a married or unmarried woman during her first trimester of pregnancy—without interference by the state, her husband, parent, or other third party. Still today, a married woman cannot be required to obtain permission from her husband to have an abortion.[28] In *Moore v. East Cleveland* (1978), the Court struck down a municipal zoning ordinance that impaired members of an extended family from living together in the same household.[29] In *Kirschberg v. Feenstra* (1981), the Court struck down a state statute that gave the husband as "head and master" of the family the right unilaterally to dispose of property held in common with his wife.[30] In all such cases, the private contractual calculus of the parties was considered superior to the general state interest in the health, safety, and welfare of its citizens.

State legislatures and courts have extended these principles of the freedom of the marital contract and sexual privacy to other aspects of marriage. Many states, for example, have abandoned their traditional reticence about enforcing prenuptial and marital contracts. The Uniform Premarital Agreement Act, adopted in nearly half the states today, allows parties to contract, in advance of their marriage, all rights pertaining to their individual and common property and "any other matter, including their personal rights and obligations, not in violation of public policy or a statute imposing a criminal penalty."[31] This act does prohibit courts from enforcing premarital contracts that are involuntary, unconscionable, or based on less than full disclosure by both parties. But within these broad strictures, marital parties are left free to define in advance their own personal and property rights during marriage or in the event of separation, dissolution, or divorce.

Similarly, many states have left marital parties free to contract agreements on their own, or with a private mediator, in the event of temporary or permanent separation. The Uniform Marriage and Divorce Act provides that "parties may enter into a written separation agreement containing provisions for disposition of property owned by either of them, maintenance of either of them, and support, custody, and visitation of their children." Such agreements are presumptively binding on a court. Absent a finding of unconscionability, courts will enforce these agreements on their own terms, reserving the right to alter those contract provisions that bear adversely on the couple's children. If the separation ripens into divorce, courts will also often incorporate these separation agreements into the divorce decree, again with little scrutiny of the contents of the agreement.

The same principles of freedom of contract and sexual privacy dominate contemporary American laws of divorce. Until the mid-1960s, a suit for divorce required proof of the fault of one's spouse (e.g., adultery, desertion, or cruelty), and no evidence of collusion, connivance, condonation, or provocation by the other spouse. Today, this law of divorce has been abandoned. Every state has promulgated a "no-fault divorce" statute, and virtually all states allow for divorce on the motion of only one party. Even if the innocent spouse forgives the fault and objects to the divorce, the courts must grant the divorce if the plaintiff insists. The Uniform Marriage and Divorce Act and fifteen states have eliminated altogether consideration of the fault of either spouse—even if the fault rises to the level of criminal conduct. The remaining states consider fault only for questions of child custody, not for questions of the divorce itself.

Virtually all states have also ordered a one-time division of marital property between the divorced parties. Parties may determine their own property division through prenuptial or separation agreements, which the courts will enforce if the agreements are not unconscionable. But without such an agreement, the courts will simply pool the entire assets of the marital household and make an equitable division of the collective property. These one-time divisions of property have largely replaced traditional forms of alimony and other forms of ongoing support—regardless of the fault, expectations, or needs of either party.

These two reforms of the modern law of divorce served to protect both the privacy and the contractual freedom of the marital parties. No-fault divorces freed marital parties from exposing their marital discords or infidelities to judicial scrutiny and public record. One-time marital property divisions gave parties a clean break from each other and the freedom to marry another. Both changes, together, allowed parties to terminate their marriages as easily and efficiently as they were able to contract them, without much interference from the state or from the other spouse.

These principles of contractual freedom are qualified in divorce cases involving minor children. The fault of the marital party does still figure modestly in current decisions about child custody. The traditional rule was that custody of children was presumptively granted to the mother, unless she was found guilty of serious marital fault or maternal incompetence. Proof of marital fault by the husband—particularly adultery, homosexuality, prostitution, or sexual immorality—virtually eliminated his chances of gaining custody, even if the wife was also at fault.

Today, the court's custodial decisions are guided by the proverbial principle of the "best interests of the child." According to the Uniform Marriage and Divorce Act, courts must consider at once the child's custodial preferences, the parents' custodial interests, "the interrelationship of the child with his [or her] parent or parents," "the child's adjustment to his [or her] home, school, or community," and "the mental and physical health of all parties involved."[32] "The court shall not consider the conduct of a proposed custodian that does not affect his relationship to the child," the act concludes, setting a high burden of proof for the party who wishes to make their spouse's marital fault an issue in a contested custody case. Under this new standard, the presumption of maternal custody is quickly softening, and joint and shared custody arrangements are becoming increasingly common.

Signposts of a Third Way

A Hegelian might well be happy with this dialectical story. Christian models of marriage that prioritized religious norms and ecclesiastical strictures squared off against Enlightenment models of marriage that prioritized private choice and contractual strictures. Christianity was exposed for its penchant for paternalism and patriarchy, and it lost. The Enlightenment was embraced for its promise of liberty and equality, and it won. Thesis gave way to antithesis. Such is the way of progress.

The story is not so simple, however. It is true that the Enlightenment ideal of marriage as a privately bargained contract between husband and wife about all their rights, goods, and interests has largely become a legal reality in America. The strong presumption today is that adult parties have free entrance into marital contracts, free exercise of marital relationships, and free exit from marriages once their contractual obligations are discharged. Parties are still bound to continue to support their minor children, within and outside marriage. But this merely expresses another basic principle of contract law—that parties respect the reliance and expectation interests of their children, who are third-party beneficiaries of their marital or sexual contracts.

It is equally true, however, that the undue contractualization of marriage has brought ruin to many women and children.[33] Premarital, marital, separation, and divorce contracts too often are not arms-length transactions, and too often are not driven by rational calculus alone. In the heady romance of budding nuptials, parties are often blind to the full consequences of their bargain. In the emotional anguish of separation and divorce, parties are often driven more by the desire for short-term relief from the other spouse than by a concern for the long-term welfare of themselves or their children. The economically stronger and more calculating spouse triumphs in these contexts. And in the majority of cases today, that party is still the man—despite the tempting egalitarian rhetoric to the contrary.

"Underneath the mantle of equality [and freedom] that has been draped over the ongoing family, the state of nature flourishes," Mary Ann Glendon writes.[34] In this state of nature, contractual freedom and sexual privacy reign supreme. But also in this state of nature, married life is becoming increasingly "brutish, nasty, and short," with women and children bearing the primary costs.

The very contractarian gospel that first promised salvation from the abuses of earlier Christian models of marriage now threatens with even graver abuse.

What is the way out of this dilemma? Surely, part of the way forward is to look backward—back to the sources of our marriage traditions, but now newly enlightened! The achievements of the Enlightenment in reforming the traditional theology and law of marriage cannot be lost on us. It took the contractual radicalism of the Enlightenment to force the Western tradition to reform itself—to grant greater respect to the rights of women and children, to break the monopoly and monotony of outmoded moral and religious forms and forums respecting sexuality, marriage, and the family. It took the bold step of stripping marriage and its law to its contractual core for the Western tradition to see the need to reform its basic doctrines of parental consent, church consecration, male headship, child illegitimation, and the like. Though some religious traditions may have retrieved or conceived their own resources to achieve these reforms, it was the Enlightenment critique that forced these traditions to reform themselves and the state to reform its laws. This was no small achievement.

Just as the Enlightenment tradition still has much to teach us today, so do the earlier Catholic and Protestant traditions of the West. First, these Western Christian traditions have seen that a marriage is at once a contractual, religious, social, and natural association, and that to survive and flourish, it must be governed both externally by legal authorities and internally by moral authorities. From different perspectives, Catholic and Protestant traditions have seen that a marriage is an inherently communal enterprise, in which couples, magistrates, and ministers must all inevitably cooperate. After all, marital contracts are of little value without courts to enforce them. Marital properties are of little use without laws to validate them. Marital laws are of little consequence without canons to inspire them. And marital customs are of little cogency without natural norms and narratives to ground them.

The modern lesson in this is that we must resist the temptation to reduce marriage to a single perspective or forum. A single perspective on marriage—whether religious, social, or contractual—does not capture the full nuance of this institution. A single forum—whether the church, state, or the household itself—is not fully competent to govern all marital questions. Marriage demands multiple forums and multiple laws to be governed adequately. American religious communities must think more seriously about restoring and reforming their own bodies of religious law on marriage, divorce, and sexuality, instead of simply acquiescing in state laws. American states must think more seriously about granting greater deference to the marital laws and customs of legitimate religious and cultural groups that cannot accept a marriage law of the common denominator or denomination. Other sophisticated legal cultures—Denmark, England, India, and South Africa—grant semiautonomy to Catholic, Hindu, Jewish, Muslim, and Traditional groups to conduct their subjects' domestic affairs in accordance with their own laws and customs, with the state setting only minimum conditions and limits. It might well be time for America likewise to translate its growing cultural pluralism into a more concrete legal pluralism on marriage and family life.[35]

Second, the Western tradition has learned to distinguish between betrothals and espousals, engagements and weddings. Betrothals were defined as a future promise to marry, to be announced publicly in the local community and to be fulfilled after a suitable waiting period. Espousals were defined as the present promise to marry, to be celebrated in a public ceremony before civil and/or religious officials. The point of a public betrothal and waiting period was to allow couples to weigh the depth and durability of their mutual love. It was also to invite others to weigh in on the maturity and compatibility of the couple, to offer them counsel and commodities, and to prepare for the celebration of their union and their life together thereafter. Too long an engagement would encourage the couple to fornication. But too short an engagement would discourage them from introspection. Too secret and private a marriage would deprive couples of the essential counsel and gifts of their families and friends. But too public and routinized a marriage would deprive couples of the indispensable privacy and intimacy needed to tailor their nuptials to their own preferences. Hence the traditional balance of engagement and wedding, of publicity and privacy, of waiting and consummating.

The modern lesson in this is that we must resist collapsing the steps of engagement and marriage, and restore reasonable waiting periods between them, especially for younger couples. Today, in most states, marriage requires only the acquisition of a license from the state registry followed by solemnization before a licensed official—without banns, with little waiting, with no public celebration, and without notification of others. So sublime and serious a step in life seems to demand a good deal more prudent regulation than this. It may well not be apt in every case to invite parents and peers, ministers and magistrates to evaluate the maturity and compatibility of the couple. Our modern doctrines of privacy and the disestablishment of religion militate against this. But especially in the absence of such third parties, the state should require marital parties themselves to spend some time weighing their present maturity and prospective commitment. A presumptive waiting period of at least ninety days between formal engagement and wedding day seems to be reasonable, given the stakes involved—particularly if the parties are under twenty-five years of age. Probationary waiting periods, particularly for younger parties, are routinely required to enter into a contract for a home mortgage, or to procure a license to operate a motor vehicle or handgun. Given the much higher stakes involved, marital contracts should be subject to at least comparable conditions.

Third, the Western tradition has learned to distinguish between annulment and divorce. Annulment is a decision that a putative marriage was void from the start, by reason of some impediment that lay undiscovered or undisclosed at the time of the wedding. Divorce is a decision that a marriage once properly contracted must now be dissolved by reason of the fault of one of the parties after their wedding. The spiritual and psychological calculus and costs are different in these decisions. In annulment cases, a party may discover features of their marriage or spouse that need not, and sometimes cannot, be forgiven—that they were manipulated or coerced into marriage; that the parties are improperly related by blood or family ties; that the spouse will not or cannot perform expected connubial duties; or that the spouse misrepresented a fundamental part of his or her faith, character, or history. Annulment in such instances is prudent and sometimes mandatory, even if painful.

In divorce cases, by contrast, the moral inclination, if not imperative, is to forgive a spouse's infidelity, desertion, cruelty, or crime. Divorce, in such instances, might be licit, or even prudent, but it often feels like, and is treated as, a personal failure even for the innocent spouse. The historical remedy was often calculated patience; one spouse's early death was the most common cure for broken marriages. In the modern age of fitness and longevity, patience is not so easily rewarded.

The modern lesson in this is that not all marital dissolutions are equal. Today, most states have simply collapsed annulment and divorce into a single action, with little procedural or substantive distinction between them. This is one (largely forgotten) source of our exponentially increased divorce rates; historically, annulment rates were counted separately. This is one reason that religious bodies have been largely excluded from the marital dissolution process; historically, annulment decisions could be made by religious bodies and then enforced by state courts. And this is one reason that no-fault divorce has become so attractive; parties often have neither the statutory mechanism nor the procedural incentive to plead a legitimate impediment. Parties seeking dissolution are thus herded together in one legal process of divorce—subject to the same generic rules respecting children and property, and prone to the same generic stigmatizing by self and others.

Fourth, the Western tradition has learned, through centuries of hard experience, to balance the norms of marital formation and dissolution. There was something cruel, for example, in a medieval Catholic canon law that countenanced the easy contracting of marriage but provided for no escape from a marriage once properly contracted. The Council of Trent responded to this inequity in the *Tametsi* decree of 1563 by establishing several safeguards to the legitimate contracting of marriage—parental consent, peer witness, civil registration, and church consecration—so that an inapt or immature couple would be less likely to marry. There was something equally cruel in the rigid insistence of some early Protestants on the reconciliation of all married couples at all costs—save those few that could successfully sue for divorce. Later Protestants responded to this inequity by reinstituting the traditional remedy of separation from bed and board for miserable couples incapable of either reconciliation or divorce.

The modern lesson in this is that rules governing marriage formation and dissolution must be balanced in their stringency—and separation from bed and board must be maintained as a release valve. Stern rules of marital dissolution require stern rules of marital formation. Loose formation rules demand loose dissolution rules, as we see today. To fix the modern problem of broken marriages requires reforms of rules at both ends of the marital process. Today, many states have sought to tighten the rules of divorce without giving corresponding attention to the rules of marital formation and separation. Such efforts, standing alone, are misguided. The cause of escalating divorce rates is not only no-fault divorce, as is so often said, but also no-faith marriage. Both marital formation and dissolution rules must be adjusted together, as is the case in some of the recent covenant marriage legislation.

Fifth, the Western tradition has recognized that marriage and the family have multiple goods and goals. This institution might well be rooted in the natural order and in the will of the parties. Participation in it might well not be vital, or even conducive, to a person's salvation. But the Western tradition has seen that the marriage and family are indispensable to the integrity of the individual and of the preservation of the social order.

In Catholic and Anglican parlance, marriage has three inherent goods, which Saint Augustine identified as *fides, proles, et sacramentum.*[36] Marriage is an institution of *fides*—faith, trust, and love between husband and wife, and parent and child, that goes beyond the faith demanded of any other temporal relationship. Marriage is a source of *proles*—children who carry on the family name and tradition, perpetuate the human species, and fill God's church with the next generation of saints. Marriage is a form of *sacramentum*—a symbolic expression of Christ's love for his church, even a channel of God's grace to sanctify the couple, their children, and the broader community.

In Lutheran and Calvinist parlance, marriage has both civil and spiritual uses in this life. On the one hand, the family has general "civil uses" for all persons, regardless of their faith. Marriage deters vice by furnishing preferred options to prostitution, promiscuity, pornography, and other forms of sexual pathos. Marriage cultivates virtue by offering love, care, and nurture to its members and by holding out a model of charity, education, and sacrifice to the broader community. Ideally, marriage enhances the life of a man and a woman by providing them with a community of caring and sharing, of stability and support, of nurture and welfare. Ideally, marriage also enhances the life of the child, by providing it with a chrysalis of nurture and love, with a highly individualized form of socialization and education. It might take a village to raise a child properly, but it takes a marriage to make one.

On the other hand, the family has specific "spiritual uses" for believers—ways of sustaining and strengthening them in their faith. The love of wife and husband can be among the strongest symbols we can experience of Yahweh's love for his elect, of Christ's love for his church. The sacrifices we make for spouses and children can be among the best reflections we can offer of the perfect sacrifice of Golgotha. The procreation of children can be among the most important words we have to utter.[37]

Notes

This chapter is adapted, in part, from my *From Sacrament to Contract: Marriage, Religion, and Law in the Western Tradition* (Louisville: Westminster John Knox Press, 1997).

1. This is from a letter of August 1886, quoted in Friedrich Merzbach, *Liebe, Ehe, und Familie* (Berlin: Duncker and Humblot, 1958), 113.

2. In this volume, see the introduction and chapters 4 by Wuthnow, 7 by Waite and Doherty, 8 by Whitehead, 10 by Elshtain, and 13 by Browning.

3. John Witte Jr., *From Sacrament to Contract: Marriage, Religion, and Law in the Western Tradition* (Louisville: Westminster John Knox Press, 1997), hereafter *FSC*; a shorter version of this work appeared in *First Things* 125 (October 2002): 30–41. The reference here is to *FSC*, 1–12.

4. *FSC*, 16–41; James A. Brundage, *Law, Sex, and Christian Society in Medieval Europe* (Chicago: University of Chicago Press, 1987); Theodor Mackin, *Marriage in the Catholic Church*, 2 vols. (New York: Paulist Press, 1982–84); George Hayward Joyce, *Christian Marriage: An Historical and Doctrinal Study*, 2nd ed. (London: Sheed & Ward, 1948).

5. *FSC*, 42–193, 226–68; chapter 11 in this volume by Ozment; Steven E. Ozment, *When Fathers Ruled: Family Life in Reformation Europe* (Cambridge, Mass.: Harvard University Press, 1983); Ozment, *Ancestors: The Loving Family in Old Europe* (Cambridge, Mass.: Harvard University Press, 2001); John Witte Jr., *Law and Protestantism: The Legal Teachings of the Lutheran Reformation* (Cambridge: Cambridge University Press, 2002), 199–256; John Witte Jr. and Robert M. Kingdon, *Sex, Marriage, and Family in John Calvin's Geneva* (Grand Rapids: William B. Eerdmans, 2004).

6. Hans W. Baade, "The Form of Marriage in Spanish North America," *Cornell Law Review* 61 (1975): 1–89.

7. This was not true of American Catholic communities, outside Spanish territory, where the decree *Tametsi* was not in effect. They thus continued to recognize the pre-Tridentine Catholic canon law that a secret marriage formed by mutual consent was valid, even without priestly consecration. This disparity continued among some American Catholics until the Tridentine legislation was written into the 1918 Code of Canon Law.

8. George Elliott Howard, *A History of Matrimonial Institutions*, 3 vols. (Chicago: University of Chicago Press, 1904).

9. Philip Greven, *The Protestant Temperament: Patterns of Child-Rearing, Religious Experience, and the Self in Early America* (Chicago: University of Chicago Press, 1977).

10. Joseph Story, *Commentaries on the Conflict of Laws, Foreign and Domestic, in Regard to Contracts, Rights, and Remedies*, 2nd ed. (Boston: Hillard Gray and Co., 1834), sec. 108.

11. James Kent, *Commentaries on American Law*, 12th edition, ed. Oliver Wendell Holmes Jr. (Boston: Little, Brown, 1896), vol. 2, 76.

12. W. C. Rogers, *A Treatise on the Law of Domestic Relations* (Chicago: Flood, 1891), sec.2.

13. *Maynard v. Hill*, 125 U.S. 190, 210–11 (1888); *Reynolds v. United States*, 98 U.S. 145, 165 (1879); *Murphy v. Ramsey*, 114 U.S. 15, 45 (1885); *Davis v. Beason*, 133 U.S. 333, 341–42 (1890).

14. *Murphy v. Ramsey*, 114 U.S. at 45.

15. *Maynard v. Hill*, 125 U.S. at 210–11.

16. Chester Vernier, *American Family Laws: A Comparative Study of the Family Law of the Forty-Eight States*, 5 vols. (Stanford, Calif.: Stanford University Press, 1931–38).

17. FSC, 194.–215, 268–73.

18. John Locke, *Two Treatises of Government* [1690], ed. Peter Laslett (Cambridge: Cambridge University Press, 1960), I.9, I.47, I.98, II.2, II.77–83.

19. Carole Pateman, *The Sexual Contract* (Stanford, Calif.: Stanford University Press, 1988).

20. Uniform Marriage and Divorce Act, 9 U.L.A. 147 (1987), sec. 201; hereafter UMDA.

21. Ibid., secs. 202–8.

22. Ibid., secs. 207–8.

23. Ibid., sec. 207.

24. *Loving v. Virginia*, 388 U.S. 1, 12 (1967).

25. Ibid.; *Zablocki v. Redhail*, 434 U.S. 374 (1978); *Turner v. Safley*, 482 U.S. 78 (1987).

26. U.S. 479 (1965). This holding was extended to protect access of unmarried couples, and minors, to contraceptives: *Eisenstadt v. Baird*, 405 U.S. 438 (1972); *Carey v. Population Services International*, 431 U.S. 678 (1977).

27. *Eisenstadt v. Baird*, 405 U.S. at 543 (1972).

28. U.S. 113 (1973); upheld in *Planned Parenthood v. Casey*, 112 S.Ct. 2791 (1992); *Stenberg v. Carhart*, 530 U.S. 513 (2000).

29. U.S. 494 (1977).

30. U.S. 455 (1981).

31. Uniform Premarital Agreement Act, sec. 3.

32. UMDA, sec. 402.

33. Lenore J. Weitzman, *The Divorce Revolution: The Unexpected Social and Economic Consequences for Women and Children* (New York: Free Press, 1985); Barbara Dafoe Whitehead, *The Divorce Culture: How Divorce Became an Entitlement and How It Is Blighting the Lives of Our Children* (New York: Alfred A. Knopf, 1997); Paul R. Amato and Alan Booth, *A Generation at Risk: Growing Up in an Era of Family Upheaval* (Cambridge, Mass.: Harvard University Press, 1997). In this volume, also see chapter 6 by Michael and chapter 13 by Browning.

34. Mary Ann Glendon, *The Transformation of Family Law: State, Law, and Family in the United States and Western Europe* (Chicago: University of Chicago Press, 1989), 146.

35. See John Witte Jr., et al., eds., *Covenant Marriage in Comparative Perspective* (Grand Rapids: William B. Eerdmans, 2004).

36. Augustine, *On Original Sin*, chap. 39 [xxxiv], in *A Select Library of Nicene and Post-Nicene Fathers of the Christian Church*, 2nd series, reprinted edition, ed. Philip Schaff and Henry Wace (Grand Rapids: William B. Eerdmans, 1952), vol. 5, 251.

37. See John E. Coons, "The Religious Rights of Children," in *Religious Human Rights in Global Perspective: Religious Perspectives*, ed. John Witte Jr. and Johan van der Vyver (Boston: M. Nijhoff, 1996), 172: "In a faint echo of the divine, children are the most important Word most of us will utter."

Chapter 13
The World Situation of Families: Marriage Reformation as a Cultural Work

Don S. Browning

During the past several decades, a momentous debate has been sweeping across the world over the present health and future prospects of families. This debate has been especially intense in the United States, but during recent trips to Australia, South Korea, England, and South Africa, I learned that these countries have conflicts analogous to those in the United States.[1]

These debates are about real issues. There are powerful trends affecting both advanced and underdeveloped countries that are changing families and undermining their ability to perform customary tasks. These trends are often called the forces of modernization. Of course, theories of modernization are now being extended by theories of globalization. Yet however one refers to them—and they are distinguishable—these processes are having disruptive consequences on families in all corners of the earth. Older industrial countries have the wealth to cushion the blows of this disruption, but family upset throws economically fragile countries and their families deeper into poverty.

Of course, there are other sources of family disruption and poverty besides the forces of modernization and globalization. Wars, oppression, racial discrimination, and conflicts between cultures and religions are additional factors—the massive family disruptions in Bosnia and Afghanistan, and before that in Vietnam, Cambodia, and apartheid South Africa, are fresh on our minds. But I wish to address here mainly the disruptions to families stemming from modernization and globalization as such. Furthermore, we should not avoid observing that a significant subtext of the world struggle with the new terrorism is the perceived conflict between modernization and certain family patterns in Islam and other religions and cultures.

Most social scientists now acknowledge that modernization, independent of factors such as wars and famine, can by itself be disruptive to families in certain ways. But many distinguished sociologists believe there is little that can be done to allay these ambiguous consequences. The social forces producing them, they believe, are simply too deep and powerful to be stopped or changed. I do not share this view. I argue that much can be done, but only if we understand the task as a complex cultural work—one that is like weaving a richly designed tapestry containing many threads. The threads needed for this cultural task are religious, political, legal, economic, and psychological. No one perspective can accomplish alone what needs to be done. In addition, this cultural work must be worldwide in scope. Because there is an inevitable religious dimension to this cultural task, it should be viewed as a task of a practical philosophy of religion conceived as an international ecumenical endeavor.

Central to this practical philosophical task is the worldwide revival and reconstruction of marriage. Admittedly, this is a big idea. Some people will call it grandiose, perhaps hallucinatory. And, of course, I do not envision this renewal and reconstruction happening tomorrow. My point, rather, is this: The global disruption of families cannot be addressed solely with policies emphasizing jobs, education, and the economic liberation of women—the favorite strategies of the United Nations, the World Council of Churches, and other international agencies. I agree that such strategies are essential, but more is needed. Without this "more" that I have in mind, economic and development strategies can go awry. This additional emphasis should entail a culturally sensitive reconstruction of marriage and the roles males and females play in this institution. *I am calling for a new international practical-religious dialogue among the major world religions designed to place the matter of marriage before the world community.*

Modernization, Globalization, and the World Situation of Families

Of course, not all the changes wrought by modernity are negative for families. In fact, many of them are very positive. Higher incomes for large numbers of families must be seen as a plus. Better health and longer lives for millions are goods that are universally affirmed. But these positive consequences are unevenly distributed; at the same time that modernization pulls many into a better material life, others lose ground. The new educational and economic possibilities for women that accompany modernity are also promising, but they do not always convert into concrete benefits. Improvements for some women are frequently accompanied by negative consequences—such as the collapse of communal controls; the impoverishment of millions of mothers and their children due to abandonment, divorce, and nonmarital births; the increased violence of youth; new forms of coerced prostitution; and the growing absence of fathers from their children.[2]

I argue that the usual benefits of modernization in the form of better education and more jobs for both men and women must be supplemented by the worldwide revival and reconstruction of the institution of marriage. Notice that my argument does not pit modernization against marriage but endorses both modernization and marriage. Some people will accuse me of wanting it all. Many people say that we cannot have both; it must be one or the other. Marriage, they insist, belongs to a premodern age. To some extent, I agree with these criticisms. Modernization and marriage cannot coexist unless modernity is in some ways controlled and marriage is in many ways redefined.

The sociologists William Goode, David Popenoe, and Alan Wolfe have gained prominence by attempting to describe and assess the worldwide metamorphoses of family life. Although social scientists aspire to objectivity, these three scholars can be distinguished more by their philosophical and ethical assumptions than their empirical facts. In reviewing their work, we should not become preoccupied with overly refined distinctions between modernization and globalization. Modernization is generally defined, following Max Weber, as the spread of technical rationality into various domains of life.[3] Some theorists, including Weber, have seen this as a deterministic process that augurs well for the triumph of science, the narrow rationalization of all life (Weber's "iron cage"), and the final defeat of religion. The German social theorist Jürgen Habermas has complicated the theory of modernization; he argues that technical rationality can take the form of either market economics or bureaucratic control.[4] In either case, modernity is generally thought to flow from the West and the North to other countries of the world in the South and East.

There is much recent preoccupation in the press and among intellectuals with this first type of globalization—the spread of capitalism in the form of free trade among nations and the unrestricted flow of capital and labor across national boundaries. It is better, I contend, to conceive of capitalism, especially in the form of the fashionable neoliberal economics, as just one expression of technical rationality. Bureaucratic rationality, in the form of either welfare policies or harder kinds of socialism and Marxism, is also a form of modernization that can and has taken on global proportions, indeed global ambitions. These two kinds of modernization have technical rationality in common, that is, the belief that the efficient use of powerful technical means in the form of either business procedures or government bureaucracies can increase our individual and collective satisfactions.

But the inevitability of modernization as the triumph of technical rationality can be overstated. It is certainly not the only form of globalization. And modernization as technical rationality, although real, is not as inevitable and deterministic as some have thought. There is, as Arjun Appadurai has argued, another form of globalization that is both aided by but distinguishable from the worldwide spread of technical rationality.[5] This is the move of cultural influences across the world in all directions. Some of these cultural movements, although by no means all, are actually resisting technical rationality—even though, to a significant extent, they are communicated by it. Some see this resistance as a kind of "reflexive globalization" that is greatly aided by the rise of modern forms of electronic communication. But whether it is a form of resistance or a product of spontaneous cultural creativity, these currents are often thought to flow from the West through American movies, television, and news media. Increasingly, however, the cultural flow is also moving from the rest of the world back to the West in the form of art, music, fashions, immigration, trade, and even family patterns.

This form of globalization is a product of human imagination and practical reason (or *phronesis*) rather than the blind forces of technical rationality. And it is globalization driven by imagination and practical reason that would guide the kind of world reconstructive dialogue about marriage that I have in mind.

I am calling for the creation of new micro-narratives to counter modernity's dominant message about the inevitable decline of marriage. I am urging a new conversation between the various micro-narratives about marriage and family that can be found in the world's religions. These religions' stories about marriage have not been micro-narratives in the past, but they appear to many to be small and anemic at present. This is true because these narratives are not heard accurately either by their own adherents or the rest of the world. They are increasingly drowned out by the noisy narrative of technological expansion. But this situation can change.

William Goode: How Modernization Betrayed Families

William Goode is a leading figure in American sociology. In two massive books written thirty years apart, he fearlessly collected huge quantities of data and developed a theory to account for family change in places as diverse as Western Europe, the United States, Asia, and Sub-Saharan Africa. In both these books, he was using the concept of modernity in the first sense described above—modernization as technical reason with its offshoots in industrialization, urbanization, and the increased mobility of labor and capital. In 1963, he wrote *World Revolution and Family Patterns,* which demonstrated the global movement away from extended family patterns and toward the convenient fit between industrialization and what he called the "conjugal" or "companionate" family.[6]

Goode also shared a thesis developed even more powerfully by the historical sociologist Peter Laslett of Cambridge University. This thesis holds that in the nineteenth century, England and northern Europe exported to the world a modernizing trend that joined a conjugal family pattern to a wealth-producing industrialization process. In nearly every country he studied for his 1963 volume, Goode found the extended family on the defensive. He saw instead trends toward smaller families, more women working in the wage economy, more equality between husband and wife, more mobility, more education for both sexes (especially for women), and less control over the conjugal couple by the extended family. This conjugal family pattern, he believed, had helped both to create and then to serve the emerging industrial order.

Goode welcomed this new family form even though he acknowledged that there was no clear evidence that it would bring more happiness than older, extended, and patriarchal patterns. He celebrated this new, more individualized family pattern, not because it would bring more happiness but because it would bring more freedom and the "potentialities of greater fulfillment."[7]

Goode said all this in 1963. Three decades later, in 1994, when he published his massive *World Changes in Divorce Patterns,* his optimism about world trends toward the conjugal model had become tempered for all parts of the globe, including the areas of northern Europe that gave this pattern its birth. The comfortable fit between this family form and industrialization that he described in 1963 was perceived as breaking down in the 1990s. He now saw industrialization and modernization as playing dirty tricks on the conjugal family, even in the West, where their partnership once seemed to thrive. Modernity's speed of change, its capacity to subdue intimate relations to the dictates of rational production, the mobility that it induces, and its tendency to move labor and capital around the world without respect for enduring human relations—all had now made this old friend of the conjugal family pattern into a new enemy.

All Western and many non-Western societies are becoming what Goode calls "high-divorce societies."[8] Cohabitation and out-of-wedlock births have increased dramatically in Western societies and throughout the world. Hand-in-hand with these movements have come the growing poverty and declining well-being of significant percentages of women and children. This "feminization of poverty" has had negative social effects in wealthy countries, but it has had devastating consequences in poor ones. From one perspective, Friedrich Engels seemed correct in his prediction that modernization in the form of a market economy would destroy families.[9] Engels did not understand, some scholars are now adding, that modernization in the form of bureaucratization can have an equally devastating impact on families.

There are examples of stable high-divorce societies. Arabic countries, Goode claims, have historically been stable high-divorce and family-disruption societies because of the unilateral divorce privileges of males. This was also true, especially among newly wedded couples, in premodernizing Japan. In both societies, rejected women returned to the supports of extended family—

parents, brothers, uncles. And in most cases, these women remarried because of the high valuation of marriage in these societies.[10] Goode nominates Sweden as another kind of stable high-divorce and family-disruption society. Sweden's extensive system of social supports sustains divorced or never-married mothers, at least financially. It is clear that Goode would solve the emerging world family crisis by shipping something like the Swedish stable, high-family-disruption system to all countries of the world, be they rich or poor, East or West, North or South.

David Popenoe and Alan Wolfe

The American sociologists David Popenoe and Alan Wolfe have reviewed these same trends. They have analyzed the forces causing them in ways similar to Goode, but they propose vastly different solutions. Popenoe, in *Disturbing the Nest: Family Change and Decline in Modern Societies* (1988), measured family disruption in the United States and Sweden, with shorter forays into the low-divorce societies of New Zealand and Switzerland.[11] Alan Wolfe, in *Whose Keeper? Social Science and Moral Obligation* (1989), compared indices of family disruption in the United States and Sweden.[12]

Here are samples, and something of an update, of the kinds of statistics that worry Popenoe and Wolfe. Since the 1960s, the divorce rate has more than doubled in the United Kingdom, the United States, France, and Australia.[13] During this same period, nonmarital births increased from 5 to 33 percent in the United States, from 4 to 31 percent in Canada, from 5 to 38 percent in the United Kingdom, and from 6 to 36 percent in France.[14] In the United States since 1960, the rate of out-of-wedlock births has increased tenfold in the white community, to 25 percent, and threefold in the black community, from 22 to 70 percent of all births today.[15] The marriage rate in all advanced countries has declined significantly. In the United States, there has been a 30 percent decline in the marriage rate since 1960; overall, there has been an 11 percent decline in the number of people over age fifteen years that are married.[16] Much of this decline can be explained by later marriages and increased longevity. But some of it is due to increased lifelong singleness and cohabitation.

The number of couples cohabiting has increased eightfold since 1970 in the United States.[17] Cohabitation is almost a universal experience in most northern European countries. Studies in both the United States and Europe show, however, that cohabitation is much more unstable than marriage and correlates with higher divorce rates for couples that do go on to marry.[18] Recent research has shown that in the United States, a significant portion of births out of wedlock actually occur in cohabiting relationships; this suggests that the instability of cohabitation also contributes to the insecurity of the family environment for children.[19]

Increasingly, it appears that "responsible parenting" is becoming both the cultural norm and the core of government policy in European societies, with less and less interest in whether this parenthood takes place within or outside marriage. According to one news account, some British social scientists are predicting that "marriage is doomed and will be virtually extinct within 30 years." Duncan White, the head of Relate, an organization of 2,000 marriage counselors, believes that within thirty years, only one in five long-term couples will be married in the United Kingdom and that legal marriage will be rejected in favor of a "'constellation' of relationships where couples have a series of long-term relationships with children from each."[20] Although doubtless an exaggeration, such projections are being heard more frequently and should at least gain our attention.

In the face of such statistics and trends, the sociologist Linda Waite and the journalist Maggie Gallagher strike a very different tone. They conclude in their recent book *The Case for Marriage* (2000) that a couple's public and legal commitment to the formal institution of marriage appears in itself to contribute to the stability of the union.[21] This point seems, for the most part, to have been lost in public conversations about the significance of marriage, both in the United States and in Europe. Furthermore, these authors summarize and extend the mounting evidence indicating that the deinstitutionalization of the family and the decline of marriage have alarming negative consequences for the well-being of women, children, men, and society as a whole.

In the 1970s and early 1980s, American sociologists such as Jessie Bernard celebrated the new culture of divorce and nonmarriage as promising a future of creativity, experimentation, and freedom, especially for women.[22] But by the late 1980s, research by feminist legal scholars Lenore Weitzman and Mary Ann Mason on the negative economic consequences of divorce for women cooled this earlier optimism.[23] By the mid-1990s, reports by demographers such as Sara McLanahan and Gary Sandefur showed that children in the United States not living with both biological parents were on average two to three times more likely to have difficulties in school, in finding employment, and in successfully forming families themselves.[24] Income lessens these consequences, but only by 50 percent. Along the same line of the view of Waite and Gallagher on the importance of public commitments, recent research by the sociologist Steven Nock shows that couples choosing Louisiana's covenant marriage gain a stabilizing marital benefit simply from their multiple public commitments.[25] The apparent importance to marriage of publicly witnessed promises has been overlooked by those advocating the delegalization and privatization of marriage.

Although these are the kinds of facts that worry Popenoe and Wolfe, they advocate a different strategy than Goode. Popenoe accepts Goode's theory that modernization weakened first the extended family and then eventually the conjugal couple—the core of the family itself. But he also believes that cultural values such as expressive and utilitarian individualism, independent of the social processes of industrialization, are the main factors fueling family disruption.[26] This leads Popenoe to see the world cure for family disruption in a massive cultural conversion; he envisions the possibility of a worldwide renunciation of overdetermined, individualistic aspirations and the birth of a new familism. Handling family disruptions around the world by imitating Sweden's relatively stable high-divorce society, as Goode argues, is an option that Popenoe has considered but rejected as both economically unfeasible and culturally destructive. Evidence supporting his decision recently has been published in the British medical journal *The Lancet.*[27] In a study involving 1 million Swedish children, those from single-parent families were two to three times more likely to have psychiatric problems, be suicidal, and have problems with alcohol and drugs. The excellent financial supports of the Swedish welfare system seem unable to compensate for the country's high rates of family disruption.

Wolfe rejects the Swedish alternative as well. He joins Popenoe in seeing the Swedish strategy as culturally destructive; it undermines marriage and the family even as it attempts to save them. Wolfe uses the colonization theory of Habermas to show how different expressions of modernization, whether in its market or bureaucratic forms, are almost identical in their negative effects on families. Colonization theory teaches that technical rationality enters into daily life from two perspectives—the efficiency goals of the marketplace and the control goals of government bureaucracy. Both disrupt the face-to-face interactions of the "life world" and the intimate spheres of marriage and family. From the market comes the increasing absorption of both men and women into the wage economy and the subsequent erosion of the time for, and benefits from, parenthood and stable marital relations. From the state bureaucracy comes the control of the education of our children, the rise of the welfare state, its preemption of family functions, and its subtle encouragement of the transfer of dependencies from the family to the state. Wolfe argues that Sweden is the leading example of colonization of the life world from the perspective of government bureaucracy; the United States is the leading example of colonization from the perspective of market rationality.[28] In the end, the results for families of these two forms of colonization are approximately the same—more divorce, more out-of-wedlock births, and the declining well-being of children affected by these trends.

Wolfe joins Popenoe in distrusting Goode's great hope for a stable high-divorce and family-disruption society in the Swedish style for all parts of the world.[29] Popenoe and Wolfe have more faith in the prospects of cultural change and reconstruction as the way to address the family issue. On this note, they differ from many family sociologists in the United States—such as Larry Bumpass, Andrew Cherlin, and Frank Fuerstenberg—who acknowledge the sobering facts about family disruption but believe little can be done about them other than mitigating the pain of their consequences.[30] Indeed, Popenoe and Wolfe advocate a new moral conversation that would lead to a cultural rebirth of marital commitment, one tough and realistic enough to deal with the tensions of modernity.

The Neglect of Religion

Popenoe and Wolfe's views are close to my vision of the need for a new cultural work, initiated principally from the communities of civil society, that would attempt to revive and reconstruct the institution of marriage. Their vision, however, is not fully developed. It does not give voice to the various sectors or spheres of societies that need to be included in this cultural work. And they both neglect the category of religion. If the family issue is first of all a cultural issue, as Popenoe and Wolfe believe, then religion, as it did in the past, must play a decisive role even today in the reconstruction of marriage and family ideals.

Here are a few generalizations about the possible role of Christianity. I develop them at length in *Marriage and Modernization* (2003).[31] These generalizations show why Christianity, when rightly interpreted, is a major resource for the reconstruction of marriage and family theory for Western societies. It is not the only religious resource for the modern world. It is, however, a genuine resource. Parallel efforts to revive and reconstruct the marriage and family traditions of other religions are also possible; other religions can also contribute to this great cultural work.

Here is my sketch of the resources of Christianity. Early Christianity, especially pre-Pauline and Pauline Christianity, was a family revolution. It significantly qualified, although it did not completely dismantle, the honor and shame codes that dominated family and marriage in the Graeco-Roman world.[32] By honor and shame codes, I mean a family system in which free men gained honor by exhibiting qualities of dominance and agency and were shamed if they lost these perceived virtues, generally in conflict with other men. Women, in these societies, gained honor by restricting their lives primarily to the domestic sphere and submitting to male protection. They were shamed if they went beyond these boundaries or were violated by the intrusion into their private space of other males outside their family and clan. Christianity, we must remember, existed within a cultural context largely formed by Roman Hellenism that was itself saturated by these honor-shame codes.

Early Christianity never completely disconnected from these codes. Most students of early Christianity acknowledge their reemergence in the family hierarchies of the so-called pastoral epistles. But on the whole, the earlier Jesus movement and the authentic Pauline letters seriously challenged the honor-shame family patterns of antiquity. They did this by celebrating male servanthood rather than male dominance, by applying the golden rule and neighbor love to relationships between husband and wife, by requiring males to renounce their sexual privileges with female slaves and young boys, and by elevating the status of women.[33] As the American sociologist Rodney Stark has argued in *The Rise of Christianity* (1997), pagan women flocked to early Christianity because of its stand against infanticide, its restrictions on divorce (divorce in antiquity worked to the disadvantage of women), and its demand that men be responsible fathers and faithful husbands.[34] Jack Goody argues that it was not only the Protestant Reformation that gave birth to the modern conjugal and companionate family, as the historian Steven Ozment also has argued.[35] Goody believes that the seeds of the equal-regard marriage also go back to the value of the individual found in early Christianity and its emphasis on "inter-personal, rather than inter-group, bonds."[36]

This emphasis on the value of the individual, along with insights from Roman family law, led eleventh- and twelfth-century Roman Catholic canon law to make mutual consent between bride and groom the decisive factor defining marriage.[37] This move functioned to elevate the status of the conjugal couple over the power, prestige, and control of the extended family. This development limited the power of fathers arbitrarily to give their daughters in marriage for political and economic gain. According to the historian David Herlihy, this emphasis on the integrity and sanctity of the conjugal couple contributed to the downfall of polygyny and the elevation of monogamy wherever Christianity spread.[38] Although the Protestant reformers Martin Luther and John Calvin rejected the Roman Catholic idea of marriage as a sacrament of grace, they accepted most of the other accomplishments of Roman Catholic canon law on marriage, especially the emphasis on marriage as requiring mutual consent by bride and groom.

But Luther and Calvin added one important element that the societies influenced by the Protestant Reformation may be losing due to the increasing deinstitutionalization of marriage and family reflected in contemporary social and legal trends. Marriage, according to the reformers, was understood as both a public and private affair, a matter of both state and church. It was for them first of all a natural good and a contribution to secular society and the earthly kingdom. They thereby insisted that marriage be registered by the state and then blessed and sanctified by the church. Marriage for these reformers arose out of the love and consent of a couple, but it needed completion by both state and church.[39]

The Reformation move to make marriage a public institution requiring state registration gradually brought to an end the phenomenon of clandestine or secret marriages. Such marriages, although valid in the eyes of the Catholic Church, were not witnessed by family, priest, or civil magistrate. Their validity rested on their mutual consent—a consent, however, that one member of the couple could later deny without public contradiction. Ever since the Reformation, religion and state in most Western-oriented societies have cooperated to perform a great cultural work in bringing order and coherence to marriage by making it a public institution as well as a personal, consensual, and religious one.

Not only did the Protestant churches develop both an ecclesial and public theology governing marriage; they also contributed a rich and complex symbol system that applied to both tasks. The creation story of ancient Judaism is central to Christian marriage theology as well as foundational for much of the Western legal edifice covering marriage. The creation of Adam and Eve as male and female both carrying God's image (Gen. 1:27); their equal responsibility for procreation and "dominion" (Gen. 1:28); God's declaration that it is not good that Adam "should be alone" (Gen. 1:18); the statement that "a man leaves his father and mother and clings to his wife, and the two become one flesh" (Gen. 2:24); and the reaffirmation and recontextualization of these classic scriptures within the message of Jesus in Matthew 19:4–6—these are the scriptures that time and again were interpreted and appropriated by both Catholic and Protestant theologians and even by secular jurists up into the twentieth century.

It would be wrong to credit these scriptures, and the Christian interpretations of them, as the only source of the Western conjugal, public, and companionate marriage and family. To understand the complex synthesis of sources that went into a Christian theology of marriage makes it easier to dialogue with the marriage perspectives of other religious traditions. Christian marriage theology, like Christianity itself, is a complicated mixture of a variety of somewhat disparate elements. It included Aristotle's naturalistic view of family as well as elements of both Roman and Germanic law. Medieval Roman Catholic canon law and Saint Thomas Aquinas brought these sources together and bequeathed them to the Protestant Reformation, where they were reworked but largely retained.

This is a proud heritage that needs to be critically appreciated by Western societies today. It has often erroneously been understood in patriarchal ways that were oppressive to women and children. But when properly interpreted, the weight of this tradition gives rise to the idea of the equal-regard marriage that, in principle, shares the domestic responsibilities of child care and household duties as well as the public responsibilities of citizenship and economic pursuits. An ethic of equal regard, and the personal skills to enact this ethic, are the fundamental requirements for the reconstruction of marriage to meet and, to some extent, resist the demands of modernity. This view of marriage can be enriched by the resources of Christian history, but it should also be brought into critical conversation with the other marriage systems of the world. Properly interpreted, they may have contributions to make as well.

Notice that I have called "critical" both the task of properly interpreting Christianity and that of bringing Christianity into dialogue with the other religions. The two efforts of retrieval and dialogue are related dialectically. For Christianity to have a world conversation about marriage with other religious traditions, it must go through a critical hermeneutical retrieval of its own complex and multifaceted marriage traditions. With regard to the second task, the task of entering into a world conversation that is both comparative and critical, the goal is not to reduce other systems to distinctively Western and Christian models. The objective is to find points of analogy between diverse systems—points of analogy that can be tested, enhanced, and used to give orientation to an increasingly diverse cultural and religious environment developing in most modern societies.

I do believe that the Christian perspective on marriage contains the seeds of excellence. Empirically and historically, like everything else in this fallen world, it was often far from excellent in its actual implementation. But for it to resist the challenges of modernization discussed by Goode, Popenoe, and Wolfe, Christian theology should be a leader in a new multifaceted cultural effort designed to revive and reformulate marriage traditions throughout the world.

Conclusion

You may think this proposal to be far too ambitious and unrealistic. I want to conclude, however, by reminding you that several proposals for worldwide cultural and social change in our family and marriage traditions already exist. There is the little-known Howard Center's vision of averting the world collapse of marriage by a great refusal of the forces of modernization that threaten it. It would do this by reviving local agrarian communities throughout the world. The Howard Center insists that only the rhythms of farm life can make families integrated centers of mutual economic dependence of the kind that stable marriage requires.[40]

The Roman Catholic Church has taken a more lenient attitude toward the disruptions of modernization in the form of state bureaucracy and market efficiency. It does this in its teaching on subsidiarity. Subsidiarity theory contends that natural parents are more likely than other socializing agents to have the highest investment in raising their children. Hence, state and market should both contain and direct their interventions so that they always support married natural parents and do nothing to disrupt them or replace their proper functions.[41] At the same time, subsidiarity theory requires both state and market to take appropriate steps to assist needy and disrupted families that cannot support themselves without help from the wider society.

The United Nations and the World Council of Churches have taken a much more promodernization stance. They seek to stabilize families through the education of women and the increased use of technologies that control reproduction.[42] Neither has attended to increased worldwide father absence or the religio-cultural work of reconstructing marriage.

Then there is the strategy of the Religious Consultation on Population, Reproductive Health, and Ethics directed by the distinguished moral theologian Daniel Maguire. Somewhat in accord with my proposal, the consultation aspires to reconstruct the world's sexual ethics by engaging leading scholars of the world's major religions in a creative reinterpretation of these traditions. Although each great religion has undergone its distortions on family issues at the hands of political and cultural forces, the scholars contributing to the consultation believe that each still contains insights of great value. Most specifically, each contains deep ontologies about the goodness and sacrality of life. These are ontologies—views of life and being—that require us to treat life as an end in itself and a sacred gift.

These ontologies are the seedbeds of both gender equality and respect for nature. Christianity and Judaism express this ontology in their view of the goodness of all creation (Gen. 1:24) and the shared image of God in both male and female (Gen. 1:17). Islam does the same in its doctrine of creation and its belief that male and female are created "from a single being" (Qur'an 4:1). The authors of the consultation find analogous insights in Hinduism, Buddhism, and Confucianism, insights often ignored or distorted at certain points in the history of these traditions. These ontologies are the deepest sources for respect between the sexes and respect between humans and their environment. According to Maguire and his colleagues, these ontologies are the ultimate antidotes to modernity's drive to reduce both humans and the natural environment to the status of means toward the ends of satisfying our short-term desires.[43] According to their argument, it is precisely through the retrieval of our religious traditions that the utilitarian telos of modernity can be constrained and the fruits of modernity can be redirected.

The consultation, however, sadly neglects the task of reconstructing marriage. Furthermore, it does not attempt to show how religions relate to other parts of culture, such as government, law, the professions, or specific economies. Nonetheless, it points to at least part of the cultural work that I have proposed in this chapter. My goal has not been to illustrate the entire conversation among the religions that I think eventually is needed. My purpose instead has been to develop the thesis that such a conversation is both needed and possible. I have also sought to suggest what Christianity, with its foundations in Judaism, can offer to this great new cultural work of renewing and reconstructing the institution of marriage. Other religions will have their contributions to make as well.

Notes

1. This chapter expands on and combines themes from chapters 1, 3, and 9 of my recent *Marriage and Modernization: How Globalization Threatens Marriage and What to Do about It* (Grand Rapids: William B. Eerdmans, 2003).

2. For a discussion of Asian and American forms of coerced prostitution, see Rita Nakashima Brock and Susan Thistlethwaite, *Casting Stones: Prostitution and Liberation in Asia and the United States* (Minneapolis: Fortress Press, 1996).

3. Max Weber, *The Protestant Ethic and the Spirit of Capitalism* (New York: Charles Scribner's Sons, 1958), 181–83.

4. Jürgen Habermas, *Theory of Communicative Action*, 2 vols. (Boston: Beacon Press, 1984, 1987).

5. Arjun Appadurai, *Modernity at Large* (Minneapolis: University of Minnesota Press, 1996). Roland Robertson also has warned against equating globalization with capitalism; see his "Globalization and the Future of 'Traditional Religion,'" in *God and Globalization: Religion and the Powers of the Common Life*, vol. 1, ed. Max Stackhouse and Peter Paris (Harrisburg, Pa.: Trinity Press International, 2000), 53–68.

6. William Goode, *World Revolution and Family Patterns* (London: Free Press of Glencoe, 1964).

7. Ibid., 380.

8. William Goode, *World Changes in Divorce Patterns* (New Haven, Conn.: Yale University Press, 1994), 336.

9. Frederick Engels, *The Origin of the Family, Private Property, and the State* (New York: International Publications, 1972).

10. Goode, *World Changes*, 251–57.

11. David Popenoe, *Disturbing the Nest: Family Change and Decline in Modern Societies* (New York: Aldine de Gruyter, 1988).

12. Alan Wolfe, *Whose Keeper? Social Science and Moral Obligation* (Berkeley: University of California Press, 1989).

13. *Demographic Yearbook* (New York: United Nations, 1997).

14. Clarence Page, "When Marriage Goes Out of Style," *Chicago Tribune,* February 7, 2001, A17. Page is quoting statistics provided by Senator Daniel Moynihan in a September 2001 speech before the American Political Science Association.

15. Tom Smith, *The Emerging 21st Century American Family* (Chicago: National Opinion Research Center, University of Chicago, 1999), 3.

16. Barbara Dafoe Whitehead and David Popenoe, "Who Wants to Marry a Soulmate?" in *The State of Our Unions 2001* (Piscataway, N.J.: National Marriage Project, Rutgers University, 2001), 18. The marriage rate is measured by number of marriages per 1,000 of unmarried women age fifteen years and older.

17. Linda Waite, "The Negative Effects of Cohabitation," *The Responsive Community* 10 (winter 2000): 31. For a comprehensive summary of cohabitation trends in the United States, see R. Kelly Raley, "Recent Trends and Differential in Marriage and Cohabitation: The United States," in *The Ties That Bind: Perspectives on Marriage and Cohabitation,* ed. Linda Waite, Christine Bachrach, Michelle Hindin, Elizabeth Thomson, and Arland Thornton (New York: Aldine de Gruyter, 2000), 19–39.

18. David Popenoe and Barbara Dafoe Whitehead, "Should We Live Together? What Young Adults Need to Know about Cohabitation before Marriage," in *The State of Our Unions 1999,* ed. David Popenoe and Barbara Dafoe Whitehead (Piscataway, N.J.: National Marriage Project, Rutgers University, 1999); Popenoe, *Disturbing the Nest,* 173.

19. Pamela Smock, "Cohabitation in the United States: An Appraisal of Research Themes, Findings, and Implications," *Annual Review of Sociology* 21 (summer 2000): 1–20.

20. Sarah Harris, "Marriage 'Will Be Extinct in 30 Years,'" *Daily Mail,* April 20, 2002, 20.

21. Linda Waite and Maggie Gallagher, *The Case for Marriage* (New York: Doubleday, 2000), 18. Also see chapter 10 in this volume by Waite and Doherty.

22. Jessie Bernard, *The Future of Marriage* (New York: World Publishing, 1972).

23. Lenore Weitzman, *The Divorce Revolution* (New York: Free Press, 1985); Mary Ann Mason, *The Equality Trap* (New York: Simon & Schuster, 1988).

24. Sara McLanahan and Gary Sandefur, *Growing Up with a Single Parent* (Cambridge, Mass.: Harvard University Press, 1994).

25. Steven Nock, "Report on Covenant Marriage," lecture given at the Marriage, Democracy, and Families Conference, Hofstra Law School, Hempstead, N.Y., March 14–15, 2003.

26. David Popenoe, *Life without Father* (New York: Free Press, 1996), 46–48; Robert N. Bellah, Richard Madsen, William Sullivan, Ann Swidler, and Steven Tipton, *Habits of the Heart: Individualism and Commitment in American Life* (New York: Harper & Row, 1986), 32–35.

27. Gunilla Ringback Weitoft, Anders Hjern, Bengt Haglund, and Mans Rosen, "Mortality, Severe Morbidity, and Injury in Children Living with Single Parents in Sweden: A Population-Based Study," *The Lancet* 361 (January 25, 2003): 289–95.

28. Wolfe, *Whose Keeper,* 52–60, 133–42.

29. Popenoe, *Disturbing the Nest,* 243–49.

30. Larry Bumpass, "What Is Happening to the Family? Interaction between Demographics and Institutional Change," *Demography* 23 (November 1990): 486, 489, 493; Andrew Cherlin and Frank Fuerstenberg, *Divided Families* (Cambridge, Mass.: Harvard University Press, 1991).

31. Browning, *Marriage and Modernization.*

32. For review of the application of the insights of cultural anthropology on honor-shame societies to an understanding of the influence of early Christianity on families,

see Bruce Malina, *The New Testament World: Insights from Cultural Anthropology* (Louisville: Westminster John Knox Press, 1993); Carolyn Osiek and David Balch, *Families in the New Testament World* (Louisville: Westminster John Knox Press, 1997); and Don Browning, Bonnie Miller McLemore, Pamela Couture, Bernie Lyon, and Robert Franklin, *From Culture Wars to Common Ground: Religion and the American Family Debate* (Louisville: Westminster John Knox Press, 1997), 129–54.

33. For amplification of these points, see ibid., 129–56.

34. Rodney Stark, *The Rise of Christianity* (San Francisco: HarperCollins, 1997), 98–118.

35. Steven Ozment, *Protestants: The Birth of a Revolution* (New York: Doubleday, 1992), 151–69. Also see chapter 11 in this volume by Ozment.

36. Jack Goody, *The Development of the Family and Marriage in Europe* (Cambridge: Cambridge University Press, 1994), 23.

37. John Witte Jr., *From Sacrament to Contract: Marriage, Religion, and Law in the Western Tradition* (Louisville: Westminster John Knox Press, 1997). Also see chapter 12 in this volume by Witte.

38. David Herlihy, *Medieval Households* (Cambridge, Mass.: Harvard University Press, 1985), 61–62.

39. Witte, *From Sacrament to Contract*, 42–129; Witte, *Law and Protestantism: The Legal Teachings of the Lutheran Reformation* (Cambridge: Cambridge University Press, 2002), 199–256.

40. Allan Carlson, "Third Ways, Middle Ways and the Family Way: The Quest for the Virtuous Economy," an address given to the North American College, the Vatican, Rome, March 11, 1996. See also his "Why Things Went Wrong: The Decline of the Family," an address given before the bishops of North and Central America and the Caribbean, Dallas, January 31, 1994; Carlson's critique of socialist economies and their negative effects on families can be found in "Lessons from the Swedish Experiment," an address to the Civic Institute's Conference on Family Policy, Prague, January 21, 1995. Finally, see Carlson's numerous essays in his journal *The Family in America*, especially his recent "The Changing Face of the American Family," *Family in America* 15, no. 1 (January 2001): 1–7.

41. Pope Leo XIII, "Rerum Novarum," in *Proclaiming Justice and Peace: Papal Documents from Rerum Novarum through Centesimus Annus*, ed. Michael Walsh and Brian Davies (Mystic, Conn.: Twenty-Third Publications, n.d.), 20, 30, 34.

42. For relevant United Nations statements, see the Universal Declaration of Human Rights adopted by the United Nations on December 10, 1948; the European Convention of Human Rights (1950); the International Convention on the Elimination of All Forms of Racial Discrimination (1965); and, for our purposes, the Convention on Consent to Marriage, Minimum Age of Marriage and Registration of Marriage (1964). These can be found at the University of Minnesota Human Rights Library, http://www1.umn.edu/humanrts. For a complete copy of the *Convention on Rights of the Child* and detailed related information, see http://www.unicef.org/crc/crc.htm. For relevant positions of the World Council of Churches, see *Report of the International Conference on Population and Development* (New York: United Nations, 1994), 12; Birgitta Larson, "A Quest for Clarity: the World Council of Churches and Human Sexuality," *The Ecumenical Review* (http://www.findarticles.com/m2065nl_v50/20344100/p1/article.jhtml); and the report of the Berlin consultation, *Sexism in the 1970s: Discrimination against Women* (Geneva: World Council of Churches, 1975), 103.

43. For the principal publications of the consultation, see Howard Coward and Daniel Maguire, *Visions of a New Earth: Religious Perspectives on Population, Consumption, and Ecology* (Albany: State University of New York Press, 2000); John C. Raines and Daniel C. Maguire, *What Men Owe to Women: Men's Voices from World Religions* (Albany: State University of New York Press, 2001); Patricia Beattie Jung, Mary E. Hunt, and Radhika Balakrishnan, eds., *Good Sex: Feminist Perspectives from the World Religions* (New Brunswick, N.J.: Rutgers University Press, 2001); and Daniel Maguire, *Sacred Choices: The Right to Contraception and Abortion in Ten World Religions* (Minneapolis: Fortress Press, 2001).

Epilogue: It Takes a Society to Raise a Family

Robert N. Bellah

The Jewish and Christian scriptures begin the story of human life on this Earth with the family. Although it was a rather dysfunctional family, over the millennia its story has proved instructive. Here, as with so much in Genesis, the account cannot be taken literally, for human existence did not begin with the family but rather with society. Generations of Christian theologians have followed Genesis in holding otherwise. John Witte quotes a strong example from a book by the Lutheran theologian Justin Göbler published in 1550. Göbler wrote, "All orders of human society derive from the first estate, matrimony, which was instituted by God himself. On this origin and foundation, stand all other estates, communities, and associations of men. . . . From the administration of the household, which we call oeconomia, comes the administration of government, a state being nothing more than the proliferation of households."[1]

Witte summarizes a somewhat similar view in the seventeenth-century Anglican commonwealth model of the family. "The domestic commonwealth," he writes, "was the foundation of the English commonwealth. Its hierarchy of offices and duties was the model, even the source, of political authority and civic obligation. Its patriarchal construction was the foundation on which the monarchy and episcopacy of England was built."[2] This was, of course, the view of Sir Robert Filmer in his famous book *Patriarcha,* written about 1638 but published posthumously in 1680, later to be bitterly attacked by John Locke. But it was Filmer and not Locke whose position more closely resembled the traditional view.

It was my first hunch that the philosophical tradition as well as the theological tradition also began things with the family, and I half remembered Aristotle's *Politics* as the locus classicus for this view. But never count on your memory when it comes to Aristotle. Yes, at first glance, Aristotle does seem to begin with the family or, if not exactly the family, the household. In book one, chapter two, of the *Politics,* he speaks of two fundamental relationships, that between male and female and that between master and slave: "From these two partnerships, then, the household first arose, and Hesiod's verse is rightly spoken: 'first a house, and woman, and ox for ploughing'—for poor persons have an ox instead of a servant." Then, Aristotle says, there was a collection of households forming a village, and finally a collection of villages forming a city, a polis.

So was Filmer only echoing Aristotle? Not quite, for when we get to the polis, something remarkable happens. Not only does the polis differ from the village in that it is designed not just for living but for living well, but it is natural, not just an artificial assembly of more fundamental parts. "The city," says Aristotle, "belongs among the things that exist by nature, and man is by nature a political animal." We are, then, *homo politicus,* not *homo familiaris.* And so the priority gets reversed: "The city," says Aristotle, "is thus prior by nature to the household and to each of us. For the whole must of necessity be prior to the part." (It was not for nothing, then, that Émile Durkheim had his graduate students begin by reading Aristotle's *Politics!*)

So why is the polis prior by nature? Because, according to Aristotle, it is "complete," or "self-sufficient," whereas its constituent groups are not. "Polis" does not translate well into English because its meaning is broader than any one English word. So, although "city" is the usual translation, we can also translate it as "society," just insofar as it is complete or self-sufficient; it has not only political functions but economic, cultural, and other functions as well. But the real test of the priority by nature of the city lies in the fact that only in the city are human beings completed in one particular way. Aristotle writes, "Just as man is the best of the animals when completed, when separated from law and adjudication he is the worst of all." "Justice is a thing belonging to the city," he says, and without justice humans are the most savage of the animals and "the worst with regard to sex and food."[3] Without justice, which derives from the polis, the family, Aristotle implies, would be pitifully vulnerable.

I did not know that Aristotle was such a good evolutionary biologist until I looked closely at the text. The only shift we need to make in his argument is that society is prior to the family not only by nature but also chronologically. Let us consider human beings in relation to our nearest relatives, the chimpanzees and the bonobos. Both live in bands of fifty or more individuals. If we can speak of family at all among them, it is as an alliance of mothers and children, lasting longer perhaps among the bonobos than among the chimpanzees, but not including the male parent as either husband or father, a crucial difference from humans. Some solidarities exist between siblings, but they are not fundamental in either society. What is fundamental is a dominance hierarchy, based on alliances of males among chimpanzees and of females among bonobos. As Frans de Waal and others have shown, bonobos are far less aggressive than chimpanzees, but dominance is central in both groups, and dominance determines mating opportunities. The alpha male chimpanzee and his one or two closest allies do their best to monopolize the females, and lesser-status males succeed in mating furtively at best. Among the bonobos, the sons of the alpha female and her close allies do much better with females than do males of lower status. When a high-status female bonobo dies, her son loses status drastically and has much reduced mating chances.

For all that we have in common with the chimpanzees and the bonobos, our form of family is indeed different. De Waal has summarized succinctly the main differences: "Of three main characteristics of human society—male bonding, female bonding, and the nuclear family—we share the first with chimpanzees, the second with bonobos, and the third with neither. . . . Our species has been adapted for millions of years to a social order revolving around reproductive units—the proverbial cornerstone of society—for which no parallel exists in either *Pan* species."[4]

What accounts for the difference? The absence of a disposition for dominance? I do not think so. Rather, a different kind of society has made possible a different kind of family. Here I draw on the work of the anthropologist Christopher Boehm, particularly his book *Hierarchy in the Forest: The Evolution of Egalitarian Behavior.*[5] Boehm argues that we share with the chimpanzees and the bonobos a tendency toward despotism, that is, a disposition toward dominance. We also share with them two further dispositions: to submit when it looks like confrontation is likely to fail, and to resent domination once we have submitted.[6] But, Boehm asks, if we are a species with despotic tendencies, that is, a strong disposition to dominate whenever possible, how is it that the simplest known societies, namely, the nomadic hunter/gatherers, are uniformly egalitarian and probably have been so for thousands if not millions of years? His answer is not that hunter/gatherers lack dominance hierarchies but that they have what he calls "reverse dominance hierarchies," meaning that the adult males in the society form a general coalition to prevent any one of their number, alone or with a few allies, from dominating the others.[7] Male egalitarianism is not necessarily extended to females—the degree to which females are subject to male despotism varies, even among hunter/gatherers. But what the reverse dominance hierarchy prevents is the monopolization of females by dominant males, and what it therefore makes possible is the family as we know it, based on (relatively) stable cross-gender pair-bonding and the mutual nurturance of children by parents—precisely what is missing in our closest primate relatives.

Boehm insists that human egalitarianism does not come naturally, that it is not the absence of the disposition to dominate; rather, it requires hard, sometimes aggressive, work to keep potential upstarts from dominating the rest. Egalitarianism is a form of dominance, the dominance of what Rousseau would have called the general will over the will of each. The hunter/gatherer band is not, then, the family enlarged; it is the germ of the polis, the beginning of a society based on enforceable justice. Boehm summarizes: "There appear to be two components of this kind of egalitarian social control. One is the moral community incorporating strong forces for social conformity. . . . The other ingredient is the deliberate use of social sanctioning to enforce political equality among fully adult males."[8]

I would add a third component, related to the first, namely ritual, the common expression of the moral community without which the process of sanctioning would make no sense. Boehm is especially good on the way the sanctioning works. Potential upstarts are first ridiculed, then shunned; and if they persist, killed. Boehm describes in detail how this system of increasingly severe sanctions works, with examples from every continent. He is perhaps less good at what I think is equally necessary, that is, the strong pull of social solidarity, especially as expressed in ritual, which rewards the renunciation of dominance with a sense of full social acceptance.

Why the long history of egalitarianism based on the reverse dominance hierarchy comes to an end in prehistoric times with the rise of despotic chiefdoms and early states, and why despotism, though challenged, has continued to some degree ever since, is a story that would take us too far afield. Human history is peppered with successful upstarts; many—one thinks of Julius Caesar, Napoleon, Shaka Zulu, Mussolini—came to a bad end, though some died in bed. The tendency of upstarts to try to monopolize females and undermine the family is illustrated by the ancient Hebrew upstart David, who took Bathsheeba as his wife and had her husband killed, although Machiavelli warned potential upstarts not to fool with other men's wives because that can spark instant rebellion. Here I can only pause to point out that for an upstart to become a legitimate ruler requires the reformulation of the understanding of moral community and new ritual forms to express it, so that despotism becomes authority and therefore bearable by the resentful many who must submit.

I hope I have made my first major point, namely, that, contrary to a long line of thinkers, society is prior—both by nature and historically—to the family, and the family depends on society for its very survival. Without enforceable justice, the life of no man is safe and the chastity of no man's wife is safe, so the family could not survive. Nor is it only justice that makes society necessary for the family. The nuclear family is too fragile to survive in isolation. In all premodern societies, mortality rates are high, so it cannot be presumed that parents will survive until the maturity of the children. To paraphrase, it takes a whole hunter/gatherer band to raise a child. So, although marriage rituals exist in some hunter/gatherer societies, the family is not the primary focus of solidarity and ritual—the whole society is. I do not want to downplay the importance of the family—it is one of the defining features of our species, if not our genus—but it draws its life breath from the environing society. Society has never been an aggregation of preexisting families, attractive though that idea has been. It is their precondition.

In this epilogue, I certainly cannot give even an abbreviated theory of the origin of the state, a much-disputed topic in any case. I simply assume it, noting only that states, like pre-state societies, in spite of upstarts have done a reasonably good job of protecting and even nurturing families. But the religions of the Book, along with other religions of the axial age, move beyond both family and state and put both in an entirely new perspective. The powerful beings of the hunter/gatherers often represent the ancestors as an undifferentiated collectivity; the polytheistic deities of early state societies often represent the ancestors of royal or aristocratic lineages. But the biblical God, and thus the God of Judaism, Christianity, and Islam, is not fused with the social structure as in earlier societies. From the very beginning, even in the patriarchal narratives of Genesis, God speaks from beyond society and the family. The initiative that God took with respect to Adam and Eve, and Noah and his offspring, continues in the patriarchal narratives. God commands Abraham: "Go from your country and your kindred and your father's house to the land I will show you. And I will make of you a great nation, and I will bless you, and make your name great, so that you will be a blessing" (Gen. 12:1–2).

History of the Family

It is true that among God's plans for Abraham is his will to make Abraham's children as numerous as the sands of the sea. There is a greater emphasis on lineage and descent in Judaism than in Christianity and Islam, although the primacy of the will of God is never in question. Even so, the patriarchal narratives have been grist for the mill of the Filmers of this world, and the psychodramas of wifely jealousy and sibling rivalry recounted there are intelligible even in the context of our own understanding of family.

Yet it would be an enormous mistake to read our sense of the family into the patriarchal narratives or into any historic society, including our own, much before the nineteenth century. Abraham, Isaac, and Jacob did not have families as we understand the term; nor were they simply fathers as we think of fathers. What they had were vast households, consisting of thousands of livestock and hundreds of dependents, over whom they ruled. They were actually small-scale chieftains, capable of mounting effective military action against other similar groups, though no match for the great monarchies of Egypt or Mesopotamia. Genesis 14 tells us that when a group of kinglets made off with some of Abraham's property and some of his relatives, including his kinsman Lot, Abraham "led forth his trained men, born in his house, three hundred and eighteen of them, and went in pursuit as far as Dan" (Gen. 14:14), and brought them all back.

How many of us have 318 trained men born in our house? My point is that what we mean by family is not what family meant in Abraham's day. When we think of "family values" and the family as the basis of society, we are in fact thinking of a kind of family that is less than 200 years old and that never existed before the modern world. This is extremely hard for us to imagine, but its importance needs to be emphasized. Our whole understanding of the history of our species is severely distorted by the unique family form that we see as natural and universal.

Let me sketch, with great simplification, the history of the family in terms of what we need to understand the family and religion. The family begins with the reverse dominance hierarchies of the hunter/gatherers, whose egalitarian organization allows the existence of fragile nuclear families, deeply dependent on the environing society for their survival. The last thing they were was "isolated nuclear families," as ours have (not entirely incorrectly) been called. For the great majority of human beings, these fragile and socially dependent units were what families were throughout most of history. When I say fragile, I am talking above all about mortality. One in four children died before the age of one year, and half before the age of twenty. A child had a two-in-three chance that at least one parent would die before he or she reached marriageable age. Grandparents were more a fantasy than a reality. Serial marriages and blended families were as common as they are with us, but because of death not divorce. Most families in human history have lived in one-room huts, where cooking, eating, socializing, and sleeping all were done. No one had a bedroom and if, in case of unusual affluence, there was a bedroom, it would be only for the parents. Neighbors and even strangers entered unlocked doors unannounced—the family dwelling was as much public as private space.

But, with the rise of chiefdoms and the state no more than about 10,000 years ago, another kind of family appeared: the large households of ranked lineages, which included, as did Abraham's, not only relatives but many dependents and sometimes slaves. Thus these households were not simply families but political power centers as well. What is now clear is that the political nature of such families was not the result of the mere expansion of the kind of hunter/gatherer families that had existed for millennia, but that the political possibilities in agricultural and pastoral societies were the cause of this new kind of family. Such chiefly or aristocratic households were always a small minority of the population and were no more like our own than were peasant families. Even the Palladian villas that housed the Venetian aristocracy were full of dogs and chickens, with the stables near the living quarters and all manner of people running in and out.[9] The "family" almost never ate alone. The dining hall was full of retainers and visitors, or the family itself was on the road visiting other aristocratic households. Children were brought up by wet nurses and tutors or were sent away to school. The privacy and intimacy that we assume is essential to the family could be found at neither end of the status spectrum. And among low and high alike, social, religious, and ritual life did not celebrate the family as such but integrated it into the larger society, which was the real focus of life.

If in ancient Judaism, the will of God consistently overrode all familial, social, and political priorities—and this would be true of Islam as well—early Christianity had a suspicion of the family that was only rivaled by Buddhism. Far from glorifying the family, the Catholic Church came near to ignoring it for more than a thousand years. Family ties were respected but were long viewed as second best to virginity or monastic vows. Nor, when it came to family values, is the New Testament very supportive. The passages to the contrary are numerous and shocking, none more so than Luke 14:26, where Jesus says, "If any one comes to me and does not hate his own father and mother and wife and children and brothers and sisters, yes, and even his own life, he cannot be my disciple." Or Matthew 10:34–38: "Do not think that I have come to bring peace on earth; I have not come to bring peace, but a sword. For I have come to set a man against his father, and a daughter against her mother, and a daughter-in-law against her mother-in-law; and a man's foes will be those of his own household. He who loves father or mother more than me is not worthy of me; and he who loves son or daughter more than me is not worthy of me; and he who does not take his cross and follow me is not worthy of me."

Although Jesus does indeed say some moving words about marriage, and uses the idea of marriage to express spiritual truth, it is hard to avoid the degree to which the family is marginalized relative to the beloved community of his followers. Nowhere is this more starkly expressed than in Luke 8:20–21, where Jesus is told "Your mother and your brothers are standing outside, desiring to see you," and he replies, "My mother and my brothers are those who hear the word and do it." As far as the traditional obligations of the family are concerned, "let the dead bury the dead" seems to be Jesus' most common answer. I do not think I need to reiterate that Paul's teaching is no different.

I am not saying that early Christianity rejects the family—there are too many positive passages to say that—but that the New Testament makes the obligation to take up one's cross and follow Jesus far more central than the family. Any idea that "family values" are at the center of the Christian faith has to be a seriously distorted and modern reinterpretation of Christian scripture. We know that families were nurtured in the early church. We have examples of devoted spouses and children. But the life of the family was wholly encompassed by the life of the beloved community, which in every sense took priority over it. It would be many centuries before the family as a partially independent unit would get much attention.

A brief but immensely informative account of how marriage gradually became a central focus of Christian theological reflection is John Witte's extraordinary book *From Sacrament to Contract: Marriage, Religion, and Law in the Western Tradition*. Though Augustine used the word "sacrament" in connection with marriage, Witte makes it clear that it was not until the thirteenth century that a fully developed Catholic theology of marriage as sacrament was developed. It might surprise you to know that for over a thousand years, marriage was a private transaction; it did not take place inside the church. The couple had the option of meeting at the door of the church, but outside it, and receiving a blessing from the parish priest, but the binding contract of marriage depended on the exchange of promises between husband and wife, not any action of the priest. One cannot but think of the present custom in some communions of blessing gay unions but not performing a wedding ceremony. How traditional!

It was not until the Lateran Council of 1215 that the blessing of the priest at the church door became a mandatory religious duty, though the validity of the marriage did not depend on it. And it was not until the Council of Trent in 1563 that the Catholic Church required the celebration of the marriage by the parish priest as a condition of validity.[10]

As Witte has shown, the Protestant Reformation brought major changes in thinking about marriage and family and gave them a centrality they had not previously had (the ruling of the Council of Trent on marriage has to have been in part a response to these new developments within Protestantism). The key stimulus for the change was the Protestant renunciation of clerical celibacy and the strong encouragement of clerical marriage instead. Marriage was now to be celebrated within the church by a married priest, and the married state was to receive a new degree of honor and dignity.[11] I cannot summarize the rich details of Witte's treatment, but for my purposes what is significant is that although marriage and the family were given a new religious salience, they still took place very much within the encompassing community of the church (even where, as in Lutheranism, the law of marriage was given over to secular authorities to administer).

Even though, in premodern Christian societies as in premodern non-Christian ones, marriage was often based on utilitarian as much as or more than on emotional reasons, there was still a long tradition of encouragement of mutual respect and affection between spouses in the Catholic tradition, which the Reformation enhanced but did not invent. Nonetheless, before the nineteenth century in Catholic and Protestant lands alike, families tended to be either small, fragile peasant units or the great households of the landed aristocracy that I have described above, neither of which came close to what our modern idealized family has come to look like.[12]

The Victorian Family

It was only in the middle of the nineteenth century that the Victorian family, the first stage of the modern family—though the one we are most apt to think of as the "traditional family"—came into existence.[13] The Victorian family was the result of the spread of affluence, deriving from the new industrial society, to a much larger percentage of the population than ever before. The new middle class was able to create a form of family life that had some of the independence of the aristocratic family and much less of the vulnerability of the families of peasants and the urban poor. The development of urban transportation systems made possible the existence of suburbs, where the family could live in a semipastoral setting while the husband/father "breadwinner" could commute to his job in the city.

Before the Victorian age, Christians had lived in houses. Because they were only pilgrims on this earth, "home" was in heaven with the Heavenly Father. But now for the first time home was not in heaven but in the suburbs, and it was often described as a "paradise." Father returned from work each evening, through the gate in the picket fence and into the home where his loving wife and children awaited him. The fireplace had moved from the kitchen, first to the dining room and then to the living room, and the small family gathered around it to reaffirm their mutual affection before entering their individual bedrooms for the night.[14] Though in the case of the family, as in so many other realms of life, the rise of the bourgeoisie represented a generalization of aristocratic tastes to a much wider circle, there was a fundamental difference between the Victorian family and older aristocratic families. Aristocratic families were intensely public; the lord and lady of the manner were seldom alone, even when performing their most delicate functions.

The Victorian family, though its members continued to be engaged in many groups outside the home, was in an entirely new way private, and the privacy and intimacy of the family were seen as among its greatest virtues. Christopher Lasch took a phrase from the Victorian age to define this new kind of family: "a haven in a heartless world."[15] The wife/mother, and the children as long as possible, were to be protected from the harsh world of capitalist competition, whereas the husband/father was to leave it behind once he entered the sanctum of the home. Christians had always sought salvation from "the world," and the Victorian home offered a new form of that salvation. Because the family became, virtually for the first time, an end in itself and was no longer seen as part of a larger solidarity, it could now be called "the isolated nuclear family." Although, compared with earlier family forms, it was even more dependent economically on the rest of society, it was isolated in a new way: psychologically. The family was no longer a public place.

A massive shift in ritualization accompanied this new form of the family.[16] What we take for granted as major family holidays did not start out that way. Days of thanksgiving were decreed in the New England colonies to give thanks for divine favor, especially for the autumn harvest, but they were community festivals, not private ones. The first Thanksgiving in the Plymouth Colony famously included ninety Indians as participants in the collective celebration. But by the nineteenth century, Thanksgiving Day—only securely established at the national level by Abraham Lincoln—had become a family holiday. Well into the twentieth century, the Fourth of July was a community holiday, celebrating American Independence with parades and patriotic speeches, until it too became just an excuse for family picnics. But the greatest transformation of all was what happened to Christmas.[17]

In preindustrial society, Christmas was not a day but a season, and the whole community celebrated it. The effort to abolish all popular feast days among some early Protestant groups included Christmas as well. Unless it fell on a Sunday, it was not even considered a holiday. But Lutherans and Anglicans never went that far, and Christmas gradually reasserted itself even among more puritanical groups. In England as late as the eighteenth century, the Christmas season had a kind of carnival quality. Groups of young people, mummers, would go through the community, singing and begging for treats, sometimes cross-dressing and playing various stunts, something that was present in the American colonies as well. All doors were open to them. Gift giving was primarily from the lord of the manner to his dependents, or between groups, but not within families.

By the mid–nineteenth century, all that had dramatically changed. Gift giving to the poor continued, but it was now managed by impersonal charities rather than through personal contact. For the first time, gifts were given primarily within the family, especially for the children, and such gifts rapidly became the essence of Christmas. Though religious services were still held on Christmas Day, by the end of the nineteenth century, when Christmas became overwhelmingly a family festival, the main service was shifted to Christmas Eve, so as not to intrude on the privacy of the family celebration.

By the late twentieth century, Christmas had become such a bacchanalia of private consumerism that many businesses depended on it to be profitable for the year.[18] It was only in the second half of the nineteenth century that upper-middle-class employees were given summer holidays, though the custom gradually spread to all employees, and the summer vacation became a major family ritual. Poorer families saved for Christmas from summer until December and then started saving for the summer vacation, once Christmas was over.[19]

Conclusion

The isolated nuclear family that originated in Victorian times—of course only psychologically isolated because it always depended on the larger society for income and services—is in serious trouble today. Competitive capitalism, from which the family was designed to be a serene retreat, has opened the gate in the picket fence and walked in the front door. The father/husband is no longer the sole breadwinner. The wife/mother and the teenage children are also part of the labor force. The simple homemade gifts of the early family Christmases have been supplanted by the ever more expensive clothes and electronic gadgets that every child must have.[20]

In most households, the woman is still the homemaker, even though she has a job, doing "the second shift," as Arlie Hochschild put it in her book of that title.[21] But, increasingly fragmented and exhausted, she finds it ever more difficult to maintain the old ideal of the nuclear family alone. In her recently published book *The Commercialization of Intimate Life,* Hochschild shows how turning intimate functions over to bureaucracy and the market will only accelerate dysfunction because it provides only short-term solutions to what are at base deeply social communicative problems.[22]

Everything I have said suggests that an effort to resuscitate the traditional family—if that strange Victorian family, unprecedented in human history, is taken as what we mean by "traditional"—is bound to fail, to make our families worse, not better. Only a reintegration of the family into the larger community and society will make it viable. Cicero speaks of society as "an agreement with respect to justice and a partnership for the common good."[23] If justice is giving each his or her due, the family today is unable to enact justice to wife or husband, and especially to the children, who are supposed to be the primary end of the whole enterprise. Only a society that guarantees stability of employment, paid maternity and paternity leave, health insurance for all, and a decent education for every child can begin to again breathe life into embattled families. And only as families leave their television and computer screens at home to participate with their neighbors and friends in religious and civic life can they find the genuine meaning of family.

Churches are at present infirmaries for sick families, and they must continue to be so under present conditions. But if the illness is to be cured, they must bring the family back into the common life through activities and celebrations that join rather than isolate.[24] We enact the moral community and the justice it requires when we engage ourselves in solidarity with others to serve and to celebrate our humanity and our God.[25] Thus, if we really want to reappropriate the "traditional" family, it will not be the idealized Victorian house with Mom and Dad by the fireside but the much older idea of the family embedded in community.

Notes

1. John Witte Jr., *From Sacrament to Contract: Marriage, Religion, and Law in the Western Tradition* (Louisville: Westminster John Knox Press, 1997), 49.

2. Ibid., 175. In chapter 12 of this volume, Witte provides a concise overview of the several strands of religious and secular thought that lie behind our modern understanding of the family.

3. All the quotations in the preceding paragraphs are from book one, chapter two, of Aristotle's *Politics*.

4. Frans B. M. de Waal, "Apes from Venus: Bonobos and Human Evolution," in *Tree of Origin: What Primate Behavior Can Tell Us about Human Evolution,* ed. Frans B. M. de Waal (Cambridge, Mass.: Harvard University Press, 2002), 39–68, at 62. See also chapter 2 of this volume by Frans de Waal and Amy Pollick. In chapter 3 of this volume, Stephen Pope usefully relates the "laws of nature" that we learn from biology to the "natural law" that has developed through reflection on human moral life, and thus involves culture as well as biology.

5. Christopher Boehm, *Hierarchy in the Forest: The Evolution of Egalitarian Behavior* (Cambridge, Mass.: Harvard University Press, 1999).

6. Ibid., 147, 163.

7. Ibid., 10–11.

8. Ibid., 60.

9. James Fenton, "How Smelly Was the Palladian Villa?" (review of Witold Rybczynski, *The Perfect House: A Journey with the Renaissance Master Andrea Palladio*), *New York Review of Books,* October 24, 2002, 36–39. Fenton argues, in contrast to the book he is reviewing, that the Palladian villa was a working farm, not a quiet retreat. The word "villa" means a collection of buildings housing livestock, grain, and a multitude of dependents. Fenton believes the Palladian villa existed in unbroken continuity with the villas of antiquity and they were all the location of large households with many dependents, carrying on the various activities of a vigorous community.

10. "Marriage," *Encyclopedia Britannica* (Chicago: Encyclopedia Britannica, 1967), vol. 14, 927.

11. Witte discusses an early case of clerical marriage, that of Johann Apel, that illustrates Luther's condemnation of celibacy and monastic vows and his belief in the validity of clerical marriage. Witte, *From Sacrament to Contract,* 44–46.

12. In chapter 11 of this volume, Steven Ozment describes the kind of family that was probably the matrix for the development of the nineteenth-century pattern, i.e., the premodern urban commercial family. More prosperous premodern urban families were, however, often large households in which economic and family activities overlapped. Ozment

himself suggests that the Protestant Reformation provided a "new concept of marriage" in the increasingly prosperous period that began in the late fifteenth century. See Steven Ozment, *Ancestors: The Loving Family in Old Europe* (Cambridge, Mass.: Harvard University Press, 2001), 35. He also describes the new forms of family discipline and support provided by church and state in both Protestant and Catholic societies from the sixteenth century. See Ozment, *When Fathers Ruled: Family Life in Reformation Europe* (Cambridge, Mass.: Harvard University Press, 1983), 25–49.

13. On the Victorian family, see esp. John R. Gillis, *A World of Their Own Making: Myth, Ritual, and the Quest for Family Values* (New York: Basic Books, 1996), part II, 61–129.

14. Ibid., 61–80.

15. Christopher Lasch, *Haven in a Heartless World: The Family Besieged* (New York: Basic Books, 1977).

16. The relation between ritual and institutions, particularly the family, is the focus of my chapter 1 in this volume. In chapter 9 of this volume, Bradd Shore suggests why ritual is more than ever critical for the survival of contemporary families when other family supports have weakened. He also provides a valuable perspective on the privatization of ritual.

17. My description of the change from premodern Christmas celebrations to the Victorian Christmas draws from Gillis, *World of Their Own Making*, 98–104.

18. Richard Horsley and James Tracy, eds., *Christmas Unwrapped: Consumerism, Christ, and Culture* (Harrisburg, Pa.: Trinity Press International, 2001).

19. Gillis, *World of Their Own Making*, 104–8.

20. It should be clear that in this largely historical chapter the focus has been on the middle-class family, with "middle class" defined very much as in Shore's chapter 9 above. In chapter 6 of this volume, Claude Fischer and Michael Hout largely ignore the cultural problems of the middle-class family, so well described in chapter 10 of this volume by Jean Elshtain, while emphasizing the difficulties that poverty creates for a significant sector of the American population, something that Robert Wuthnow also treats in chapter 4 of this volume.

21. Arlie Russell Hochschild, *The Second Shift: Working Parents and the Revolution at Home* (New York: Viking Press, 1989).

22. Arlie Russell Hochschild, *The Commercialization of Intimate Life: Notes from Home and Work* (Berkeley: University of California Press, 2003).

23. Cicero, *De Republica*, I, xxv. Cicero clearly follows Aristotle here.

24. In this volume, chapter 4 by Robert Wuthnow and chapter 13 by Don Browning offer helpful analyses, and, even more important, practical suggestions as to how religious communities can more actively support the family in the contemporary world. Wuthnow, however, points out that social scientific studies of the relation of religion and the family are subject to multiple interpretations and must be used with caution, whereas Browning suggests that the cultural work that religious communities must undertake to meet the challenges that modernity poses to the family remains an unfinished project.

25. Albert Borgmann, in his recent book, argues eloquently for the recovery of public space by communities of celebration, and the common understandings that they can promote in even a pluralist society. See his *Power Failure* (Grand Rapids: Brazos Books, 2003).

Contributors

Robert N. Bellah is Elliott Professor of Sociology Emeritus, University of California at Berkeley.

Don S. Browning is Alexander Campbell Professor of Ethics and the Social Sciences Emeritus, University of Chicago Divinity School, and Robert W. Woodruff Visiting Professor of Interdisciplinary Religious Studies, Emory University.

William J. Doherty is professor of family social science and director of the Marriage and Family Therapy Program, University of Minnesota.

Jean Bethke Elshtain is Laura Spelman Rockefeller Professor of Social and Political Ethics, University of Chicago.

Claude S. Fischer is professor of sociology, University of California at Berkeley.

Michael Hout is professor of sociology, University of California at Berkeley.

Robert T. Michael is Eliakim Hastings Moore Distinguished Service Professor in the Irving B. Harris Graduate School of Public Policy Studies, University of Chicago.

Steven Ozment is McLean Professor of Ancient and Modern History, Harvard University.

Amy S. Pollick is a Ph.D. candidate in neuroscience and animal behavior, Department of Psychology, Emory University.

Stephen J. Pope is associate professor of theology and chair of the Theology Department, Boston College.

Bradd Shore is Distinguished Teaching Professor of Anthropology and director of the Center for Myth and Ritual in American Life, Emory University.

Steven M. Tipton is professor of the sociology of religion, Emory University.

Frans B. M. de Waal is Charles Howard Candler Professor of Primate Behavior and director of the Living Links Center at the Yerkes Regional Primate Research Center, Emory University.

Linda J. Waite is Lucy Flower Professor of Sociology and codirector of the Alfred P. Sloan Center on Parents, Children, and Work, University of Chicago.

Barbara Dafoe Whitehead is codirector of the National Marriage Project at Rutgers, the State University of New Jersey.

John Witte Jr. is Jonas Robitscher Professor of Law and director of the Center for the Study of Law and Religion, Emory University.

Robert Wuthnow is Gerhard R. Andlinger Professor of Sociology and director of the Center for the Study of Religion, Princeton University.

Index

Page numbers followed by f indicate figures; page numbers followed by t indicate tables.